The Complete Idiot's Reference Card

tear here

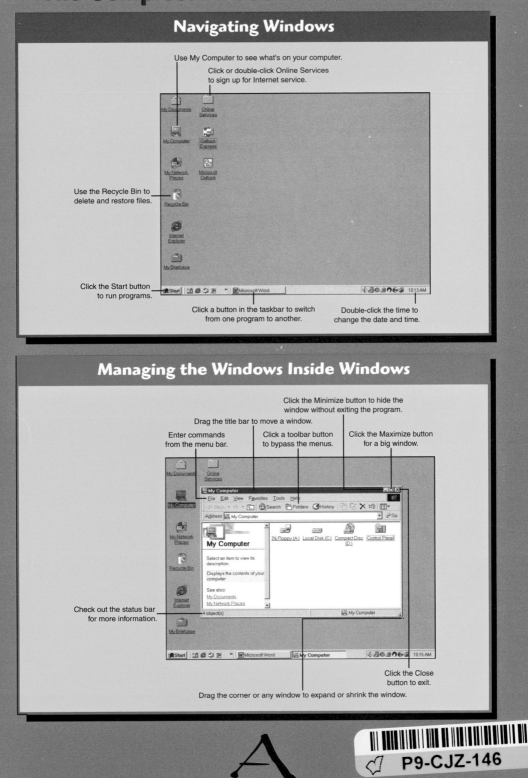

Navigating Windows

Use My Computer to see what's on your computer.

Click or double-click Online Services to sign up for Internet service.

Use the Recycle Bin to delete and restore files.

Click the Start button to run programs.

Click a button in the taskbar to switch from one program to another.

Double-click the time to change the date and time.

Managing the Windows Inside Windows

Click the Minimize button to hide the window without exiting the program.

Drag the title bar to move a window.

Enter commands from the menu bar.

Click a toolbar button to bypass the menus.

Click the Maximize button for a big window.

Check out the status bar for more information.

Click the Close button to exit.

Drag the corner or any window to expand or shrink the window.

ALPHA

P9-CJZ-146

Cutting Corners with Shortcut Keys

Press	To
Alt+F4	Exit the current program.
Alt+Tab	Cycle through the names of running programs. (Hold down the Alt key while pressing Tab repeatedly.)
Ctrl+A	Select all text or objects.
Ctrl+C	Copy the selected text, picture, or other object.
Ctrl+Esc	Open the Start menu.
Ctrl+P	Print a document.
Ctrl+S	Save a document.
Ctrl+V	Paste the cut or copied text or object.
Ctrl+Z	Undo the previous action.
Del	Delete the selected folder, file, or shortcut.
F1	Get Help.
F2	Rename the selected folder, file, or shortcut.
F3	Find files.
Shift+Delete	Permanently delete selected files.
Shift+F10	View a shortcut menu for the selected object.

⊞ Windows Key Shortcuts

Press	To
⊞	Open the Start menu.
⊞+Tab	Cycle through running programs.
⊞+F	Find a file.
Ctrl+⊞+F	Find a computer on a network.
⊞+F1	Display the Windows Help window.
⊞+R	Display the Run dialog box (for running programs).
⊞+Break	Display the System Properties dialog box.
⊞+E	Run Windows Explorer for managing folders and files.
⊞+D	Minimize or restore all program windows.
Shift+⊞+M	Undo minimize all program windows.

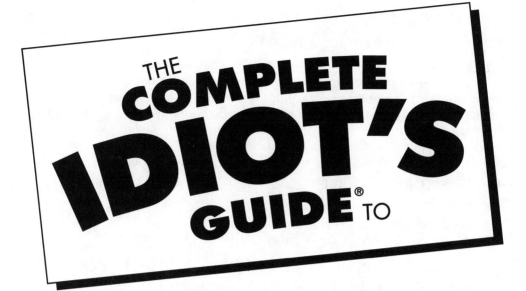

PCs

Eighth Edition

by Joe Kraynak

ALPHA

A Pearson Education Company

To Bob Dylan, for continually recharging my soul.

Copyright © 2002 by Joe Kraynak

THE COMPLETE IDIOT'S GUIDE TO and Design are registered trademarks of Pearson Education, Inc.

International Standard Book Number: 0-02-864275-9
Library of Congress Catalog Card Number: 2001093559

04   03   02   8   7   6   5   4

Interpretation of the printing code: The rightmost number of the first series of numbers is the year of the book's printing; the rightmost number of the second series of numbers is the number of the book's printing. For example, a printing code of 02-1 shows that the first printing occurred in 2002.

Printed in the United States of America

Note: This publication contains the opinions and ideas of its author. It is intended to provide helpful and informative material on the subject matter covered. It is sold with the understanding that the author and publisher are not engaged in rendering professional services in the book. If the reader requires personal assistance or advice, a competent professional should be consulted.

Publisher
Marie Butler-Knight

Product Manager
Phil Kitchel

Managing Editor
Jennifer Chisholm

Acquisitions Editor
Eric Heagy

Development Editor
Eric Heagy

Production Editor
Katherin Bidwell

Copy Editor
Rachel Lopez

Illustrator
Jody Schaeffer

Cover Designers
Mike Freeland
Kevin Spear

Book Designers
Scott Cook and Amy Adams of DesignLab

Indexer
Angie Bess

Layout/Proofreading
Steve Geiselman
Mary Hunt
Lizbeth Patterson

Contents at a Glance

Contents

Introduction: Keeping Up with the Jetsons

The computer revolution is in high gear. Almost all of us have a computer, and if we don't have one, we're figuring out a way to get one or get a better one. We want to save time. We want to waste time. We want to play games, make our own greeting cards, design our own homes, quickly balance our checkbooks, and fill out our own tax returns. We want to cruise the World Wide Web, send and receive e-mail, and hang out in Internet chat rooms. We want to understand all the inside computer jokes on Good Morning America!

To keep up in this fast-paced world of technology and communications, you had better get your own computer and learn how to use it. The trouble is that using a computer is not as simple as experienced users make it sound. It's not "just like flipping on a TV set" or "programming your VCR." Your TV set and VCR probably don't have a keyboard and mouse connected to them, they don't have software you must install and maintain, and they don't have files you have painstakingly created and can delete with a single click of a mouse button.

You need help, you need it fast, and you need it in a way that teaches you, in plain and simple terms, just what you need to know—no more, no less.

Welcome to *The Complete Idiot's Guide to PCs*

The Complete Idiot's Guide to PCs works on the premise that you don't need to be a computer technician to run a program. In this book, I won't pack your head with high-tech fluff. I'm not going to explain how a computer chip works, how a monitor displays pretty pictures, or how a printer prints. I promise.

Instead, you learn practical, hands-on stuff, such as …

- ➤ How to purchase a quality computer without maxing out your credit card.
- ➤ How to set up your computer when you get it home.
- ➤ How to kick-start your computer (and restart it when all else fails).
- ➤ How to move around in Microsoft Windows.
- ➤ How to install and uninstall programs.
- ➤ How to find, copy, delete, and undelete files.
- ➤ How to print your creations and what to do when your printer goes on strike.
- ➤ How to connect to the Internet, surf the World Wide Web, and send and receive e-mail.
- ➤ How to take advantage of the latest computer gadgets to manage your photos, edit home videos, and transform your computer into a custom jukebox.
- ➤ How to solve your own computer problems.

You'll be surprised at how little you need to know to use a computer and at how much you can know to use it more effectively.

How Do You Use This Book?

You don't have to read this book from cover to cover (although you might miss some savvy tidbits if you skip around). If you're going computer shopping, start with Chapter 1, "Savvy Consumer Guide to Buying a Computer." If you want a quick lesson on using Windows, skip to Chapter 5, "Windows Survival Guide." If you're already comfortable with the basics, go to Chapter 6, "Windows Tips, Tricks, and Traps," or Chapter 27, "Do-It-Yourself Computer Tune-Ups," to learn some slick, advanced moves. Each chapter is a self-contained unit that includes the information you need to survive one aspect of the computer world. To provide some structure for this hodge-podge of computer skills and techniques, I divided the book into the following six parts:

➤ **Part 1, "Basic Training,"** deals with the bare minimum: shopping for a computer, setting it up, turning it on, clicking, typing, working with disks and files, and finding your way around in Windows.

➤ **Part 2, "Get with the Program,"** focuses on applications (the programs you use to perform tasks, such as writing letters and creating graphs). Here you learn how to install and run programs, enter commands, save and open document files, and print your documents.

➤ **Part 3, "Get Organized! (Managing Disks, Folders, and Files),"** teaches you everything you need to know about disks, directories (folders), and files. Here you learn how to prepare disks for storing data, copy and delete files, organize files with directories, and find misplaced files.

➤ **Part 4, "Going Global with Modems, Online Services, and the Internet,"** launches you into the world of telecommunications. In this part, find out how to select and install a modem, connect to an online service, surf the Internet, send and receive e-mail, and much more.

➤ **Part 5, "Guerrilla Computing,"** shows you how to survive in the real world. In these chapters, you learn how to tune up your computer to enhance its performance, hit the road with a notebook computer, and enhance your life with some cool computer gadgets and gizmos.

➤ **Part 6, "Houston, We've Got a Problem,"** shows you how to prevent disasters and recover from the catastrophes you cannot avoid. Learn preventive maintenance, how to back up the files on your hard disk, how to fix common computer problems, and how to find professional help for the problems you can't fix yourself.

How We Do Things in This Part of the Country

I used several conventions in this book to make the book easier to use. For example, when you need to type something, here's how it will appear:

```
type this
```

Just type what it says. It's as simple as that.

Likewise, if I tell you to select or click a command, the command appears **bold**. This enables you to quickly scan a series of steps for the essential commands without having to read all the text.

If you want to understand more about the command you're typing, you can find some background information in boxes. Of course, you can skip over the information I put in the boxes to avoid the gory details, but then you might miss some important tidbits. These boxes are distinguished by special icons that appear next to them:

Techno Talk

In the computer industry, jargon and cryptic acronyms rule. When a computer term or concept baffles you or an acronym annoys you, check out the Techno Talk icon for a plain English explanation.

Inside Tip

When you've been in the computer business for as long as I have, you learn better ways to perform the same tasks and avoid common pitfalls. To share in my wealth of knowledge, check out my Inside Tips.

Whoa!

Before you click that button or press that key, check out the Whoa! icon for precautionary notes. Chances are I've made the same mistake myself. Let me tell you how to avoid the same blunder and recover from inevitable mistakes.

Notable Note

In these boxes, you find a hodgepodge of information, including background information and amusing anecdotes from yours truly.

Acknowledgments

Several people had to don hard hats and get their hands dirty to build a better book. I owe special thanks to Eric Heagy for choosing me to update this book, for his insightful additions to the outline, and for handling the assorted details to get this book in gear. Thanks to Bill Bruns for making sure the information in this book is accurate and timely. Kathy Bidwell deserves a free trip to the Bahamas for shepherding the manuscript (and art) through production. Special thanks also goes to Rachel Lopez for ferreting out all my typos and fine-tuning my sentences. The Alpha production team merits a round of applause for transforming my loose collection of electronic files and figures into such an attractively bound book.

Trademarks

All terms mentioned in this book that are known to be trademarks or service marks have been appropriately capitalized. Alpha Books and Pearson Education, Inc., cannot attest to the accuracy of this information. Use of a term in this book should not be regarded as affecting the validity of any trademark or service mark.

Part 1
Basic Training

This is war! From the time you press the power button on your computer to the time you beat it into submission, your computer is trying to defeat you. Its tactics are irrational and overwhelming. You enter a command and your computer emits an annoying, ambiguous beep. You click a button and the manuscript you've been working on for hours disappears in a flicker of light. You try to open a file you created and saved, only to find that it has apparently gone AWOL. With this constant barrage of illogical assaults, the computer hopes to wear you down, to force you into unconditional surrender.

To win the war (or at least put up a good fight), you need some basic training. You must learn how to purchase the right computer for your needs and within your budget, get it up and running, poke around with a mouse, identify the computer's disk drives, and navigate Microsoft Windows. This part runs you through the essential drills you need to survive your first encounter with the computer age.

Chapter 1

Savvy Consumer Guide to Buying a Computer

In This Chapter

➤ Buy a computer that won't be obsolete in a year

➤ Decide whether you really need a souped-up 1.5GHz processor

➤ Get a hard disk drive that's big enough—and fast enough

➤ Five important things to look for in a notebook computer

If you've already bought your dream computer, reading this chapter might be hazardous to your mental health. You might find out that the computer you have is already obsolete. Maybe you should have gotten 128 megabytes of RAM instead of 64. Maybe the mini-tower model wasn't the best choice and you really should have shelled out a couple hundred extra for AGP graphics (whatever that is). However, chasing the great American techno-dream can only make you bitter and broke, so skip ahead to the next chapter and retain your blissful ignorance.

For you chronic procrastinators who have put off buying a computer, read on. These pages show that although you might not be able to afford the ideal computer, you can make the right trade-offs to get the best computer for your budget.

Desktop or Notebook?

The decision of whether you should buy a notebook computer boils down to one main question: Is it worth double the money to be able to carry your computer on a plane or to your favorite cafe? That's at least how much extra a notebook computer costs over a comparably equipped desktop model. Here are some other drawbacks to notebook computers:

➤ The keyboard's dinky and if you spill something on it, you risk ruining the entire system.

➤ The screen is dinky (and if you want a bigger screen, it's going to cost big bucks).

➤ The CD-ROM drive is as fragile as a crystal wine glass.

➤ The speakers and microphone are lousy.

➤ The mouse is not included (although you can connect a mouse).

➤ It's tough to upgrade (on most notebooks, adding a hard drive or memory is a pain).

➤ They're hot (at least mine is). The Pentium 4 processor, which puts out a lot of heat, is right under the heel of my hand. That's what I get for not trying the system before buying it.

➤ They're really easy to steal (not that I've ever stolen one).

So, why would anyone even consider buying a notebook? Here are several good reasons:

➤ Because you have to. (If you need to work on the road, you don't have a choice.)

➤ Because you want to. (You can work and play anywhere.)

➤ You have lots of money and you want to look cool. You might even have enough money to buy a *docking station* so you can connect your notebook computer to a real monitor, keyboard, and speakers. (A docking station is a unit that contains receptacles for full-screen monitor, a printer, a keyboard, a mouse, additional drives, and other devices. You slide the notebook computer into the docking station to connect it to all the devices that are plugged into the docking station.)

➤ Your desk is already too cluttered.

➤ It's easy to add stuff. (Although adding a hard drive or memory is tough, PC card slots make it easy to add a modem, network card, or other peripherals.)

Techno Talk

Laptop computers got their name by being small enough to sit on your lap. Notebooks are small enough to fit in a briefcase (if you don't need to stick anything else in the briefcase) and weigh in at less than six pounds. Subnotebooks are even smaller and lighter. In this book, I use "laptop" and "notebook" interchangeably.

So, what have you decided? Notebook or desktop? Once you've made that decision, you've narrowed the field quite a bit. You're ready to move on to some real issues.

Computer Buyer's Checklists

After deciding whether to go with a notebook or desktop PC, the first thing you should do is go to your local computer store and check out what's available. Leave your credit card, cash, and checkbook at home so you won't buy something impulsively. Read the system descriptions next to each computer, play with the keyboard and mouse, open the CD-ROM drive, and so on. Pretend you're taking the computer for a test drive. Once you have done that, read some computer ads and reviews in magazines, such as PC Computing and Computer Shopper. This gives you some insight into prices, known problems with existing brands, and any late-breaking technologies you should be aware of.

To make sure you're considering the most important shopping issues, use the following buyer's guide checklists for desktop and notebook computers. Tables 1.1 and 1.2 list the most important considerations and favor power over price. If you're on a strict budget, you can make a few trade-offs. Don't let the techno-terms baffle you; just flip to the glossary at the back of this book.

Table 1.1   Desktop Computer Shopping List

Component	Minimum Requirements
RAM	64MB (or more) SDRAM or DDR. Make sure you can add another 64MB RAM without removing existing RAM chips.
Hard drive	10 gigabyte drive with access times ranging from 8–12ms (milliseconds); the lower the number the better.
USB ports	2 USB ports. You can plug in everything from a mouse to an extra hard drive in a USB port, so no system should be without USB.
IEEE1394 port	If you plan to connect a digital camcorder to your computer, make sure it has at least one of these ports, also called a FireWire port.
Monitor	SVGA, noninterlaced, 17-inch monitor with a dot pitch of .28 or less, 1024×768 resolution. The smaller the dot pitch, the greater the screen definition.
Display card	PCI or AGP graphics with 8MB RAM. AGP provides superior support for three-dimensional graphics and games, but PCI is sufficient.
Floppy drive	3 1/2" floppy disk drive.
CD-ROM/DVD	48X CD-ROM drive, or one of the new DVD drives (make sure it can play CDs). To record your own audio CDs or back up files to CDs, get a CD-RW (CD-ReWritable) drive.

Table 1.1   Desktop Computer Shopping List   (continued)

Component	Minimum Requirements
Backup drive	A CD-R drive or special tape backup drive. You can't back up your entire system to floppy disks.
Audio	32-bit wavetable sound card, speakers, and a good microphone. 64-bit sound cards are better. Don't settle for a 16-bit sound card; they're obsolete.
Game port	If your sound card does not have a game port, make sure the system has a separate game port or USB port.
Modem	56K data transfer, 14.4kbps fax transfer, plus voice support. If you want a faster connection, check into ISDN modems, cable modems, ADSL modems, or satellite PC support. If you decide to go with a cable connection, you'll also need a network card, commonly referred to as an "Ethernet card." Refer to Chapter 19, "First You Need a Modem," for details.

Techno Talk

Most ads list not only the amount of RAM but also the type, and you need to know the differences. *DRAM* stands for *dynamic random access memory.* Most types of PC memory are a variation of DRAM. *SDRAM* is *synchronous DRAM* and is the slowest DRAM within acceptable range. *DDR–SDRAM* (*double data rate SDRAM*) is twice as fast as standard SDRAM. *RDRAM* (*Rambus DRAM*) is six times faster than standard SDRAM and is commonly used on video adapters. *SLDRAM* (*SyncLink DRAM*) is currently being developed to compete with RDRAM.

Table 1.2   Notebook PC Buyer's Checklist

Feature	Minimum Requirements
Processor (CPU)	300MHz Celeron processor. If you're looking for desktop power, don't settle for less than a 650MHz Pentium III processor.

Feature	Minimum Requirements
RAM	64MB SDRAM. You can get by with 32MB, but not if you expect your notebook to hold its own against a desktop model. Find out how much memory you can add and the process for installing it.
Weight	4–8 pounds. Keep in mind that you'll be toting this thing around with you. In the notebook arena, the lightweights win.
Display	12.1-inch Active matrix TFT 800 X 600 resolution or better, 75 hertz or faster. Look at the display before you buy.
Hard drive	4GB or larger. Hard drives on notebook computers usually are smaller than those on desktops. If you plan on toting along a collection of your favorite digitized tunes, don't settle for less than 10GB.
Battery	Lithium-ion or better. A second battery bay is a real bonus. A battery bay that can accept either another battery or an additional hard drive is even better.
Swappable bays	Many notebooks now feature a combination hard drive/battery bay in which you can slip another hard drive or a second battery.
Keyboard	Roomy. Make sure the keys aren't too close together for your fingers.
Touchpad	Touchpads are not the best pointing devices around but they're the best you'll find on a notebook computer. Just make sure there's a free serial port for connecting a mouse.
Floppy drive	Yes. On many notebooks, you can plug the floppy drive into the parallel port, so you don't have to lug it around all the time.
CD-ROM/DVD	Yes. Most programs come on CDs. Don't settle for an external CD-ROM drive. Make sure it's built in and is at least 24X or faster. Also make sure you can upgrade to DVD later.
Audio	16-bit stereo or better. Make sure the notebook has input and output jacks for connecting a real pair of speakers and a high-quality microphone.
Game port	Most notebooks don't have a game port. If you want to use a joystick, find out what it takes to add a game port.
PCMCIA slots	Two PCMCIA slots. These slots enable you to insert credit card–sized expansion boards into the system to add devices, such as a fax/modem, CD-ROM drive connection, network card, game port, or even a hard disk drive. You simply pop one card out and another one in depending on what you want to do.

Table 1.2 Notebook PC Buyer's Checklist (continued)

Feature	Minimum Requirements
USB ports	Two USB ports. With USB, you have nearly unlimited expansion capabilities and installing add-ons is easy.
Infrared port	You might not use an infrared port to connect to a printer, but it's nice to have the option for network connections and for exchanging data between your notebook and palm computers.
Modem	33.6K or faster with fax. You'll need a modem to connect to the Internet even if you don't plan on traveling much.
Docking station	Available? You might not need one now, but if you decide to get one later, make sure you can. Docking stations typically are manufactured to work with only one type of notebook. You actually can damage your notebook by using a docking station that's not designed for it; if you do, your warranty won't cover the repair bills.

Planning for Future Expansion

When you're buying a computer for $2,000, the last thing you want to think about is shelling out more money for additional equipment. However, if you don't think about the future now, you won't be able to upgrade your computer later. Check for the following:

➤ **Open drive bays**   These enable you to add a hard disk, DVD, or backup drive to your computer later. The system unit should have at least two open (unoccupied) drive bays.

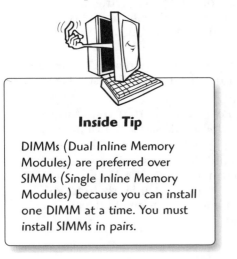

Inside Tip

DIMMs (Dual Inline Memory Modules) are preferred over SIMMs (Single Inline Memory Modules) because you can install one DIMM at a time. You must install SIMMs in pairs.

➤ **Expansion slots (three open PCI slots)**   These might become less important as the computer industry moves to USB; however for now, if you want to plug in extras (a sound card, external drive, scanner, or TV card) you'll need some open expansion slots. PCI expansion slots handle most newer expansion cards. ISA expansion slots are fast becoming obsolete.

➤ **Expandable Memory to 128MB or more**   Make sure you can add memory modules without removing the existing modules. If the computer comes installed with 32MB RAM, which occupy all of the RAM slots, you'll have to remove modules and pitch them or try to resell them.

Buying the Perfect Printer

I've made some mistakes in purchasing printers. First, I bought a black-and-white printer and had to listen to my kids complain about it for two years. Then, I bought a color printer with no scanner/fax/copy features because I really didn't need them at the time. Finally, I bought my dream printer: an all-in-one machine that prints in color, faxes, copies, and scans. To avoid the mistakes I've made and purchase a printer that you won't need to replace one year down the road, check out Table 1.3.

Table 1.3   Printer Purchase Checklist

Feature	What You Should Consider
Laser	Fast, but expensive. If you have the money, go with a laser printer.
Inkjet	Less expensive, but the print quality rivals that of a laser printer.
Color	Don't even consider buying a black-and-white printer. Even if you think you don't need color, you'll find that you can't live without color for occasional greeting cards, photos, and similar publications. Make sure the color and black ink cartridges are separate so you won't waste the color ink when you run out of black.
Quality	600 dpi (dots per inch) or higher. If you need near-photo-quality output, go with 1,200 dpi.
Speed	4–8 ppm (pages per minute) or faster for monochrome, 2–4 ppm for color. Otherwise, you'll be twiddling your thumbs waiting for the printer to spit out the last page.
Price	$200–$300 for a good inkjet. $400 or more for an entry-level laser. If you want a combination fax/copier/scanner/inkjet printer, expect to pay more than $500.
Consumables	Expect to pay 3–10 cents per page to print. How much do the print cartridges cost and how many pages can each one print? Do you need to print on special paper?
Envelope feed	The paper tray should have an easy way to feed business envelopes into the printer.
Fax	(Optional) 300 dpi, 14.4Kbps transmission, auto-redial, speed-dial numbers, page memory to store received faxes if the printer runs out of paper.
Scanner	(Optional) TWAIN-compatible color flatbed scanner that can handle 8.5×11-inch pages and scans at 600 dpi or better. 24-bit color, 8-bit grayscale. TWAIN enables you to quickly import scanned images into your documents.
Copier	(Optional) 600×300 dpi, multiple copies.

Scanners, Digital Cameras, TV Cards, and Other Toys

The PC has made great strides in restitching our social and economic fabric. We can chat with anyone in the world without leaving our homes, publish our own documents, avoid long-distance phone bills, do our own taxes, and even shop from our homes (or was that the Home Shopping Network that did that?). With the new toys available, PCs now are threatening the very existence of TVs, PhotoMarts, and video arcades. When you're out shopping for a computer, be sure to check out the latest gadgets:

➤ **TV tuners**   Many home PCs come with a TV tuner that enables your computer to double as a TV set. You plug in the cable or TV antenna, and you can pretend you're working as you watch the ball game.

➤ **Scanners**   When shopping for a scanner, consider quality first. If you want photo-quality scans, don't settle for less than 1,200 dpi color, although 600 dpi is sufficient for most general uses. Make sure the scanner is TWAIN compatible, so you can scan pictures into your documents, and that the scanner comes with good OCR (optical character recognition) software, so you can scan text. Before you buy, read some reviews.

➤ **Digital cameras**   The latest popular toy is the digital camera, which stores your pictures on floppy disks or special memory cards. Quality and price vary greatly. When you're out camera shopping, check the maximum resolution of the photos (don't settle for less than 1 megapixel, about 1,280×1,024) and the number of photos you can store on a disk or card. Find out how much additional disks or cards cost.

➤ **Video modems**   Are standard phone calls starting to bore you? If so, you can install a video modem, stick a digital video camera on your monitor, and talk face-to-face over the phone, assuming of course that the other person has a video modem.

➤ **Hand-held computers**   If a notebook PC is still too bulky, and you don't really need to type a lot on the road, consider a hand-held or pocket computer. Many of the new hand-held devices come with the Palm operating system or Windows CE (a scaled-down version of Windows), both of which make it easy to navigate the device. Weighing in at less than a pound, a hand-held computer has a miniature screen and just enough RAM to perform basic tasks (usually about 8MB). Don't set your expectations too high.

"Free" and Cheap PCs

In the good old days (1998–99), companies literally were giving away free PCs! If you were willing to disclose personal and financial information to one of these philanthropic organizations, agreed to use the computer at least 10 hours each month, and would put up with a steady stream of online advertisements, you could have qualified to receive a free PC. Not surprisingly, most of these companies went out of business, and the great computer giveaways dried up.

However, if you're on a tight budget, there are places where you can pick up a new PC dirt cheap. One company called eMachines offers some basic models at very reasonable prices. You might even be able to knock a few hundred dollars off the low prices by signing a multi-year contract with an online service, such as CompuServe. Most computer stores, including Best Buy and Circuit City, carry eMachine brand computers.

Another company called PeoplePC actually is an online service provider—a company that provides Internet service. You pick the computer you want and you get the computer, Internet service, and customer support for a monthly fee (starting as low as $24.95) for 48 months. If you don't mind being roped into a four-year contract, this deal gives you a fairly decent computer at a very affordable price.

Whoa!

Whenever you see an asterisk in an ad, chances are there is some fine print hiding somewhere on the page. Read it. The fine print usually indicates that there is an extended agreement you must sign or explains the finance charges.

Buyer Beware: Slick Sales Tricks

The computer market is very competitive, which makes computers much more affordable; however, it also forces manufacturers and dealers to cut corners. Their ads focus on all the positive aspects of their products but say nothing about how they are able to offer their computers to you for hundreds of dollars less than their competitors. Here are some of the shady practices you should watch out for:

➤ **Free software**   Don't buy a computer solely for the software that comes with it. Some manufacturers bundle lots of software with the computer to try to empty their stock of obsolete computers. Home PC buyers, dazzled by the long list of free games and programs, end up with anemic computers.

➤ **All RAM slots occupied**   Most computers have four slots for installing RAM chips. If you buy a computer with 64 megabytes of RAM and the manufacturer used four 16MB RAM modules, all the slots are occupied. Request that the dealer install two 32MB RAM modules or, better yet, one 64MB DIMM. That leaves you two or three open slots for future RAM upgrades.

➤ **All expansion slots occupied**   Although the computer has plenty of expansion slots, the manufacturer installed something in every slot, so there are none left to expand in the future.

➤ **EDO RAM**   Who cares what kind of RAM you get, as long as you get a lot of it, right? Wrong. Get SDRAM or better. EDO RAM can't keep up with your speedy processor.

➤ **Second-rate power supply**   The power supply feeds juice to all the computer components, including the motherboard and drives. Make sure the computer has at least a 300-watt power supply so it'll have enough juice for future upgrades.

➤ **Mini-tower case**   A mini-tower case sounds good if you have a small work area. However, mini-tower cases don't offer you the expansion options you will get in a full-size tower.

➤ **Old BIOS**   Manufacturers might try to cut corners by installing an outdated BIOS or going with the cheapest BIOS available.

➤ **Cheap video card**   You won't notice anything until your kid installs MDK2 and then hollers that there's something wrong with the computer.

➤ **Monitor sold separately**   This is the mother of all slick gimmicks. You're comparing prices between two systems and grab for the lowest price only to learn that you have to shell out another four hundred bucks for a monitor.

Inside Tip

Many of the companies listed here offer reconditioned computers at greatly reduced prices. If you simply can't afford a top-of-the-line PC, buy a used one. Of course, after drooling all over this chapter, a used PC probably is out of the question.

Shopping on the Internet

You can walk into Best Buy or CompUSA and purchase a pretty good computer for a pretty good price. However, you can usually get more power and higher quality for the same price by shopping through a mail-order company, such as Gateway 2000, Micron Electronics, or Dell. All these companies have Web sites where you can check out their current products without having to deal with a sales person, and if you have a credit card that isn't maxed out, you can even order your computer online. Or, if you like to talk to salespeople, you can call them using a toll-free number. The following is a list of popular mail-order companies, along with information on how to contact them:

➤ **Micron**   www.micronpc.com or 1-888-224-4247. Micron is good at offering its customers the latest technology although their computers cost a little more.

➤ **Dell**   www.dell.com or 1-800-915-3355. Great prices, a wide selection, and excellent customer support.

➤ **Gateway**   www.gateway.com or 1-800-846-4208. Gateway is one of the most popular online computer stores.

➤ **Compaq**   www.compaq.com or 1-800-888-0220. Compaq computers have the most innovative case designs on the market.

The Least You Need to Know

➤ Unless you absolutely need to travel with your PC, buy a desktop PC. You'll get a lot more computing power for the same price.

➤ Make sure the processor is powerful enough for your needs. Don't settle for a Celeron processor if you're going to be playing video games and working with complex graphics.

➤ Make sure the PC comes with 64MB or more of SDRAM (128 is better) and that you can add RAM without extracting existing RAM modules.

➤ When shopping for a printer, don't settle for less than 600 dpi, full-color printing. Look for a printer that uses separate cartridges for black-and-white and color printing and that you don't have to swap out cartridges.

➤ Don't buy a computer based on an ad alone. Check the fine print, and call the store to figure out if and where the dealer has skimped to reduce the price.

That's NOT what they mean...

Kick-Starting Your Computer

In This Chapter

➤ Set up your new computer

➤ Turn on your computer properly

➤ Restart your computer when it refuses to budge

➤ Turn off your computer without losing your work

Computers have come a long way. Back in the '80s you had to perform a little ceremony to start your computer: Insert a startup disk, search for hidden power switches, and even swap floppy disks in and out of your computer as you ran it. Now, turning on a computer is about as simple as turning on a television set (although the computer takes a little longer to warm up). You just press a couple buttons and watch your computer leap into action. In this chapter, you'll learn how to set up your computer, turn on all the computer parts in the proper order, and restart the beast when it refuses to budge.

Some Assembly Required

Chances are you didn't wait to read this book before you set up your computer. You probably ripped open the boxes and pieced the thing together on your own or with the assistance of a knowledgeable friend. However, if you just purchased your computer (or it just arrived at your front door), read the following cautions and tips before you do anything:

➤ Set all boxes on the floor in the room the computer will call "home" so nothing will fall and break.

➤ Don't cut into boxes with a knife. You might scratch something or hack through a cable.

➤ If your computer was delivered to you on a cold day, let it warm up to room temperature. Any condensation that forms inside the computer needs to dissipate before you turn on the power.

➤ Clear all drinks from the work area.

➤ Don't force anything. Plugs should slide easily into outlets. If you have to force something, the pins probably are not aligned with the holes.

➤ Pick a location next to a phone jack and a grounded outlet. If you're in an old house and you're not sure if the outlet is grounded, go to the hardware store and buy an outlet tester.

➤ Don't plug the computer into an outlet that's on the same circuit as an energy hog, such as a clothes dryer or air conditioner. Power fluctuations can hurt your computer and destroy files.

➤ Place your computer in an environment that is clean, dry, and cool. Don't place it near a radiator, next to a hot lamp, or in direct sunlight.

➤ Don't shove any part of the computer up against a wall, or stack books or other things on top, under, or around any part of the computer. The computer has fans and vents to keep it cool. If you block the vents, you'll end up with an expensive piece of toast.

➤ Keep the computer away from magnetic fields created by fans, radios, large speakers, air conditioners, microwave ovens, and other appliances.

➤ Don't turn on anything until everything is connected.

To determine where to plug things in, look for words or pictures on the back (and front) of the system unit, as shown in Figure 2.1. Most receptacles are marked and some newer systems even have color-coded cables. If you don't see any pictures next to the receptacles, try to match the plugs with their outlets. Look at the overall shape of the outlet, and look to see if it has pins or holes. Count the pins and holes and make sure there are at least as many holes as there are pins. As a last resort, read the documentation that came with the computer, and slog through the following sections.

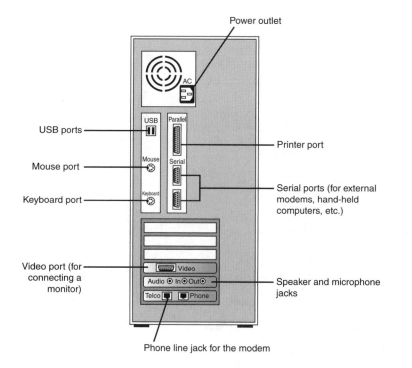

Figure 2.1

The back of the system unit usually shows where the plugs go.

Connecting the Monitor

Most monitors have two cables: a standard 15-pin VGA cable and a power cable. The 15-pin VGA connector has the shape of the letter D and plugs into a video port of the same shape, as shown in Figure 2.2. The connector fits only one way, so even if the video port is not marked, it's pretty easy to figure out. If the connector has screws on it, tighten the screws to secure the connector to the port. Don't worry about the power cable for now; we'll plug everything into power outlets later.

Connecting USB Devices

If your computer has at least one USB port and you have a USB device, such as a scanner, you can plug the device into the USB port or plug a multi-port hub into the USB port and then plug additional devices into the hub. Some devices, such as keyboards, printers, and monitors, have built-in hubs, enabling you to string several USB devices together in what is called a daisy-chain configuration, as shown in Figure 2.3. For instance, you can plug a keyboard into the USB port on the back of the computer and then plug a USB mouse into the keyboard.

17

Figure 2.2

Connect the monitor to the video port.

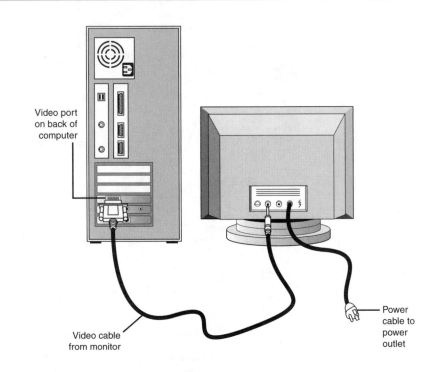

Video port on back of computer

Video cable from monitor

Power cable to power outlet

Connecting the Keyboard and Mouse

Connecting a keyboard and mouse was a much easier process a couple years ago. Older computers had a round PS/2-style keyboard port and an oblong, serial port for the mouse. Newer computers have two PS/2 style ports: one for the keyboard and one for the mouse. Even though these ports are still common today, you might have a USB-style keyboard or mouse instead of the standard fare. Following is a list of common connection types:

➤ **PS/2 style** Most mice use a PS/2 connector—a round, 6-pin connector that plugs into a PS/2 mouse port. A PS/2 connector typically has a line or arrow molded into the outside of the plug to indicate the top of the plug. Some mice come with a serial-to-PS/2 adapter that enables you to connect a PS/2 mouse to a serial port, in the rare case that your PC has no PS/2 port.

➤ **Serial** Older mice use a 9-hole, D-shaped, serial connector that plugs into a serial port of the same shape. The serial port might be marked COM1 or COM2 (*COM* is short for *communications*). Use the COM1 port for your mouse. Serial ports also might be labeled 1010, which indicates that the port is capable of sending a string of digital signals.

➤ **USB** If you have a USB keyboard and mouse, plug the mouse into the USB port on the keyboard and then plug the keyboard's USB connector into one of the USB ports on the front or back of the computer, as shown in Figure 2.3.

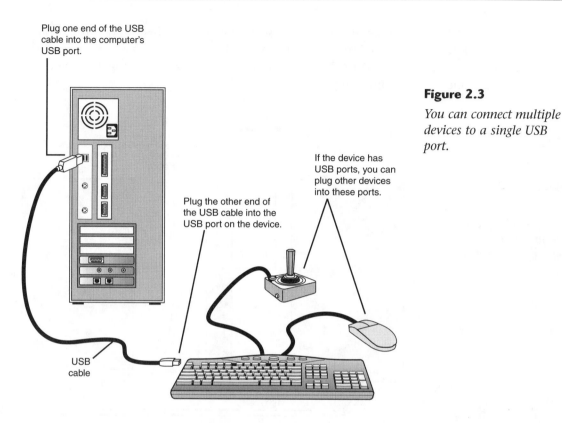

Plug one end of the USB cable into the computer's USB port.

Figure 2.3

You can connect multiple devices to a single USB port.

If the device has USB ports, you can plug other devices into these ports.

Plug the other end of the USB cable into the USB port on the device.

USB cable

➤ **Wireless**   Most wireless mice come with an infrared or RF (radio frequency) receiver that plugs into a PS/2 mouse or serial port. Plug the receiver into the port. If you have an infrared mouse, position the infrared receiver so that you can point your mouse directly at it. For best results, you should position the mouse 1–5 feet from the receiver.

➤ **Keyboard/mouse combination**   On some systems the mouse is attached to the keyboard, in which case you simply plug the keyboard into the PS/2 keyboard port or USB port.

Wiring Your Sound System

Nearly all new PCs have built-in audio support and come equipped with speakers and a microphone for inputting and outputting audio signals. The procedure for connecting the speakers and microphone is more similar to setting up a stereo system than it is to connecting other PC accessories. However, because of recent advances in PC audio technology, the procedures vary depending on the system. Follow one of these procedures depending on your system's configuration:

➤ **Standard two-speaker setup**   On most systems you connect only one of your two speakers to the computer. You plug the other speaker into a jack on the first speaker, as shown in Figure 2.4. If you have a microphone, plug it into the microphone in jack (commonly labeled *mic*).

Figure 2.4

On most systems you connect the left speaker to the audio out jack on the back of the computer.

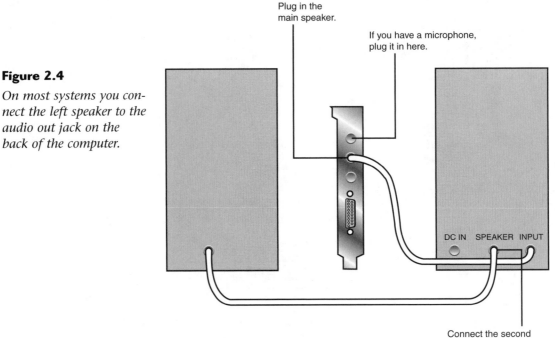

Plug in the
main speaker.

If you have a microphone,
plug it in here.

DC IN   SPEAKER   INPUT

Connect the second
speaker to the main
speaker.

➤ **Two speakers and a subwoofer**   A *subwoofer* is a speaker that increases the low-end bass output, which provides more realistic sounds for games, audio CD, and any DVD movies you play on your PC. Keep the subwoofer low to the ground and a couple feet from the monitor and any disks. In most configurations, you plug the subwoofer into the audio out jack on the back of the computer and then connect the main speaker to the subwoofer. Connect the secondary speaker to the main speaker and plug the microphone into the microphone in jack, as explained previously.

➤ **Speakers on the monitor**   If your monitor contains built-in speakers, the speaker connections might be built into the monitor cable, in which case you needn't connect the speakers separately. In other configurations, the speaker cables are separate or the main speaker cable splits off from the monitor cable; in either case, plug the main speaker cable into the audio out jack on the back of the computer.

Notable Note

To play sounds from an internal CD–ROM or DVD drive through your sound card, you needn't make any additional connections. A small cable inside the system unit connects the drive directly to the sound card. You can use the headphone jack on the front of the drive to listen to audio CDs, but you usually will experience greater sound quality by playing audio CDs through your sound card and speakers, especially if you have a subwoofer.

Connecting Your Printer

The printer connection should be the easiest of all your connections, assuming you received a printer cable with your printer. Many printers come without a cable, so you must purchase the cable separately. The type of cable you need depends on the printer type:

➤ **Standard printer**   You can use a standard Centronics printer cable or IEEE 1284 bi-directional printer cable. This standard cable has a 25-pin D-shaped connector to connect to the PC's parallel printer port and a Centronics 36 (flat) plug that connects to the printer.

➤ **Bi-directional printer**   You should use an IEEE 1284 bi-directional printer cable to avoid problems. The cable looks like a standard Centronics cable, but it supports bi-directional printing.

➤ **USB printer**   Newer printers might support USB, which allows for even faster printing than bi-directional printers. To connect a USB printer, you must have a USB cable.

To connect a standard (non-USB) printer, plug the 25-pin D connector into the 25-hole parallel port on the back of the system unit, as shown in Figure 2.5, and tighten any screws. Plug the Centronics 36 connector into the Centronics port on the printer and, if the Centronics 36 port has bail wires, push them in toward the plug till they snap in place.

Figure 2.5

Connect a standard printer to the 25-hole parallel port on the back of the computer.

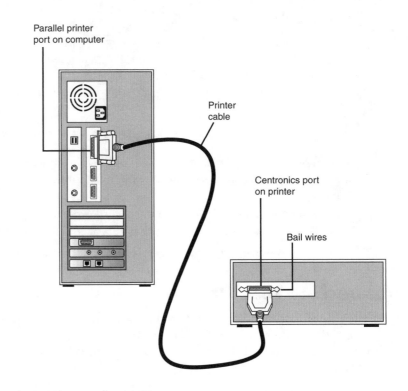

Connecting a Standard Modem

Connecting a standard internal modem to a phone jack is as easy as hooking up a telephone, but the modem has two jacks: line (or *Telco,* for telephone company) and phone (or Tel Set, for telephone set). Connect a standard telephone cable from the line jack to the jack on your wall, as shown in Figure 2.6. If desired, you can plug a phone into the phone jack so you can use your phone to place calls as you normally do.

An external modem requires three connections: to a phone jack (on the wall), to the serial port (on the back of the computer), and to a power supply. The phone jack connections are identical to those used for an internal modem. Once you've connected the phone lines, plug the modem's serial cable into the COM or serial port on the back of your computer.

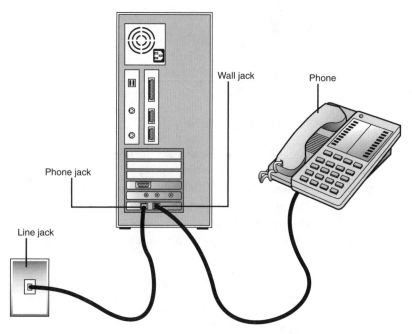

Figure 2.6
You can connect an internal modem to the phone line and to a standard phone.

Connecting Additional Peripherals

Your PC might have come with additional devices, such as a joystick or scanner, that you must connect to the system unit. To connect these accessories (peripheral devices), you follow the same steps you followed for connecting other devices: Match the plug to the outlet, plug in the device, and secure it to the system with the screws on the plug.

Connecting the Power Cables

Once you've connected all the accessories to your system unit, you can plug the system unit and accessories into a power outlet. Because you probably don't have enough outlets to plug in all your equipment, purchase a power strip, surge suppressor, or *uninterruptible power supply* (UPS). These devices have several outlets for plugging in additional equipment.

Plug the power strip, surge suppressor, or UPS into the outlet, and then plug your system unit and all external accessories into the power strip, surge suppressor, or UPS. If the power strip, surge suppressor, or UPS has a power switch, make sure it is turned on.

Whoa!

If you have a cable modem, don't try to plug it into a phone jack. A cable modem connects to your cable company's network using the same type of cable used for connecting your VCR or TV to cable service. You must also connect the cable modem to your computer's Ethernet (network) card using a special Ethernet cable.

Inside Tip

A simple power strip offers no protection against power surges and lightning bolts. Get a surge suppressor with a UL rating of 400 or less; the UL rating represents the maximum voltage that the surge suppressor will let pass through it. Make sure it has an *energy absorption rating* (which represents the amount of energy the suppressor can absorb before it's toasted) of 400 or more. A UPS has a built-in battery that supplies power to your computer for a short period of time during blackouts, giving you time to close documents and shut down your computer properly.

Software: Instructions on a Disk

Before your computer can do anything useful, it needs an education—some instructions that tell it what to do. In the computer world, these instructions are called *software*. I could bore you with a complete explanation of software, but all you need to know are the following facts:

➤ To start, computers need a special type of software called *operating system software*. Common operating systems are Windows 95, Windows 98, Windows Me, Windows NT, Windows 2000, and Windows XP (which was in development during the writing of this book. Chapters 5, "Windows Survival Guide" and 6, "Windows Tips, Tricks, and Traps" focus on Windows 98 and Windows Me (Millenium edition).

➤ If you just purchased a computer, it has the operating system software on its hard disk. When you turn on your computer, the operating system runs automatically.

➤ Once the computer starts, you can run other software called *applications* or *programs*. Applications include word processors, spreadsheets, games, backup programs, Web browsers (for the Internet), and any other program that lets you do something specific. Most computers come with several games and other applications preinstalled to give you immediate gratification without having to install a bunch of programs. See Part 2, "Get with the Program" to learn how to install and use applications.

Okay, Start 'Er Up

You've probably started your computer a hundred times already. You don't need a book to tell you how to do it, right? Well, maybe you're not turning it on properly. Run through the following procedure to make sure you're turning on all the parts in the right order:

1. Press the button on the monitor or flip its switch to turn it on. Computer manufacturers recommend that you turn on the monitor first. This allows you to see the startup messages and prevents the monitor's power surge from passing through the system unit's components. The monitor will remain blank until you turn on the system unit. (On many newer PCs, the monitor turns on automatically when you turn on the system unit.)

2. Turn on the printer if the printer has a power button or switch (many new printers have no power switch). Make sure the online light is lit (not blinking). If the light is blinking, make sure the printer has paper and then press the online button (if the printer has an online button).

3. If you have speakers or other devices connected to your computer, turn them on.

4. Make sure your floppy disk drive and CD-ROM drive are empty. If either drive has a diskette or CD in it, press the eject button on the drive and gently remove the diskette or CD. Otherwise, when you start your computer, it may look for the startup instructions on the diskette or CD, rather than looking on the hard drive, and display a startup error message.

5. Press the power button or flip the switch on the system unit. (On notebooks and some newer desktop models, you must hold the button for one or two seconds before releasing it.)

Inside Tip

As I was writing this book, Microsoft was busy working on a new version of Windows: *Windows XP*. (XP is short for *Experience*.) With Windows XP, Microsoft is combining the reliability of Windows 2000 with the multimedia and home-based features of Windows Me.

Ahhh, this is where the fun starts. Stuff appears onscreen; lights flash; disk drives grind. You hear beeps, burps, gurgles, and grunts. Eventually, your system settles down, and you see something useful on your screen.

If you hear some rude grinding and see a message onscreen telling you to insert a system disk in drive A or that you have an invalid system disk, don't worry. You (or someone else) might have left a disk in drive A (the computer's floppy disk drive) when you turned off the computer. The computer can't find the system information it needs to wake up. No biggy; remove the disk from the floppy drive and press Enter.

First Encounters of the Windows Kind

Before I can tell you what to do next, you have to figure out which operating system you have (if you don't know already). Most new computers are set up to run Windows automatically, in which case you should see a Start button in the lower-left corner of your screen. If you have an older system, you should see Windows 3.1 (which displays a bunch of tiny icons).

Telling the difference between Windows 3.1 and later versions of Windows is child's play; however, telling the difference between Windows 95, Windows 98, Windows Me, and later versions is tricky. The easiest way to figure out which version you have is to hold down the **Alt** key while double-clicking the **My Computer** icon (the small picture of a computer) in the upper-left corner of the opening screen. Windows displays the version number under **System**. Click the **X** in the upper-right corner of the window to close it. Figure 2.7 also can help you determine which version of Windows you have.

If you have Windows 95, 98, Me, XP, NT, or 2000, you're in luck; Chapters 5 and 6 provide a tour of the Windows opening screen and show you how to expertly navigate Windows.

Figure 2.7

Which operating system do you have?

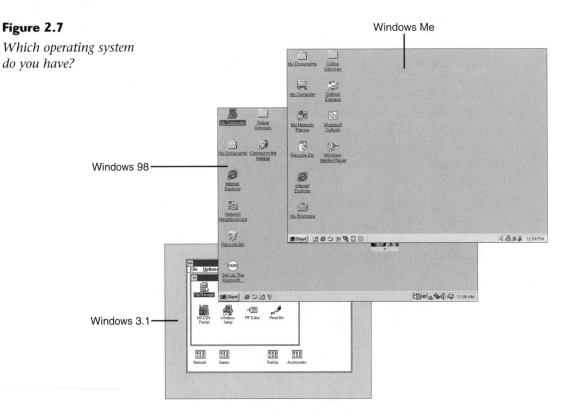

Restarting Your Computer When the Darn Thing Locks Up

At some point your computer might lock up, refusing to do any more work. You press the **Esc** key (typically used for escaping), click the mouse everywhere, press the **F1** key (usually used for getting help), and press all the other keys, and it gives you the same blank stare. When this happens, it's tempting to turn the computer off and then on or press the Power or Reset button. Resist the temptation.

Instead, try to *warm boot* the computer first. Warm booting forces the computer to reread its startup instructions without turning the power off and on. To warm boot the computer, hold down the **Ctrl** key and the **Alt** key while pressing the **Del** key. This key combination, **Ctrl+Alt+Del**, is commonly referred to as the "three-finger salute." Warm booting is preferred to cold booting because it doesn't jolt your computer with another startup surge.

If you try to warm boot from Windows you get a warning screen that explains the potential risks and your options. Read the entire screen before proceeding. In most cases, your computer is busy performing some task, or one of the applications you're running is conflicting with Windows. You can probably regain control without rebooting, simply by exiting the program that caused your computer to lock up. If you press **Ctrl+Alt+Del** and you see the Close Program dialog box, Windows might display [not responding] next to the name of the program that's causing problems. Click the program's name and click **End Task.** Repeat the steps to close any other programs that are causing problems.

If Ctrl+Alt+Del Doesn't Work ...

Sometimes, the **Ctrl+Alt+Del** key combination doesn't work; you press the combination and nothing happens. What next? If your computer has a Reset button, try pressing the **Reset** button to reboot your computer. Like Ctrl+Alt+Del, the Reset button

> ### Inside Tip
>
> If you recently purchased a new computer, you're lucky—it probably came with Windows Me or XP. If you have an old version of Windows 95, you can make it look like the new Windows by installing Internet Explorer 5.5. You can purchase it dirt cheap at most computer stores or get a free copy from Microsoft's Internet site (www.microsoft.com/windows/ie/). See Chapter 22, "Whipping Around the World Wide Web," to learn how to get a free copy of Internet Explorer from Microsoft's Internet site.

> ### Whoa!
>
> Reboot (warm or cold boot) your computer only as a last resort. If you are working on a project and you have to reboot, you might lose everything you did since the last time you saved your work.

reboots your computer without turning the power off and on. However, if you were working on a document and didn't save your work, you might lose the changes you made since the last time you saved the document.

The Cold Boot Restart: The Last Resort

If Ctrl+Alt+Del doesn't work and your computer doesn't have a Reset button, you will have to cold boot your computer. To cold boot your computer, start by flipping the system unit power switch to the off position. (Don't turn off the monitor or any other devices; only the system unit.)

Wait 30 to 60 seconds for the system to come to a complete rest and to allow the system to clear everything from memory. Listen to your computer carefully, and you should be able to hear it power down for a few seconds. You also might hear the hard disk drive spin to a stop. This is important, because if you flip the power back on before the hard disk drive stops spinning, the needle (read/write head) in the drive might crash down on the disk and destroy data stored on that part of the disk; this rarely happens on new PCs, but play it safe. After the sound of powering down ends, turn on the system unit.

Once you have rebooted, you should run a utility called ScanDisk to check your disk for any file fragments that might be causing your computer to crash and may continue to cause crashes. In most cases, Windows automatically runs ScanDisk when you start your computer after an improper shutdown. If Windows does not run ScanDisk on startup, refer to Chapter 27, "Do-It-Yourself Computer Tune-Ups," for instructions on running ScanDisk.

Turning Everything Off

Although your computer might look like nothing more than a fancy TV, you shouldn't just turn it off when you're finished working. Doing so could destroy data and foul up your programs. Here's the right way to turn off your computer:

1. Save any files you have open on a disk. When a file is open, your work is stored in RAM, which is like brain cells that require electricity to work. If you turn off the electricity without saving your work on a disk, your computer forgets your work—and you probably won't remember it either. See Chapter 10, "Making, Saving, and Naming Documents," for instructions on how to save your work.

2. Quit any programs you are currently using. When you close a program, it makes sure you've saved all your work to disk; then shuts down properly. To exit most programs, click the **Close** icon (the X in the upper-right corner of the program's window) or open the program's **File** menu and select **Exit**.

3. Click **Start** in the lower-left corner of the Windows screen and click **Shut Down**. A dialog box appears asking if you want to shut down the computer or restart it.

4. Open the **What Do You Want the Computer To Do?** list, click **Shut Down**, and then click the **OK** button.

5. Wait until Windows tells you that it is now safe to shut down your computer.

6. Put your floppy disks away. Floppy disks can become damaged if you leave them in the disk drives. First, make sure the floppy drive light goes off. Then, remove the floppy disk from the disk drive and put it away.

7. Make sure the hard disk drive light is off, then turn off the system unit.

8. Turn off the monitor and any other devices that are connected to the system unit. (On laptop computers and some newer desktop models, the system might shut down the monitor or place it in sleep mode automatically when you shut down Windows or turn off the system unit.)

Whoa!

If your screen goes blank and your computer stops making noise after you don't use it for several minutes, it probably is set up to go into Sleep or Hibernation mode. To bring the computer back to life, press the **Shift** key.

The Least You Need to Know

➤ Before you connect any devices, make sure they are turned off and unplugged.

➤ To determine where to plug in a device, match the plug on the device to the outlet on the computer, and make sure the pins on the plug are aligned properly with the holes in the outlet.

➤ When powering up your PC, turn on the monitor first, so you can see any startup messages it displays.

➤ If your PC is running Windows 95 or later, a Start button appears in the lower-left corner of the screen on startup.

➤ If your computer locks up in Windows 95 or later versions, press **Ctrl+Alt+Del** to view a list of programs that might be causing problems.

➤ Remember to save all your work before turning off the computer.

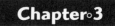

Chapter 3

Taking Control with Your Keyboard and Mouse

In This Chapter

➤ Ctrl, Alt, F1, and other funky keys

➤ Go beyond typing with a programmable keyboard

➤ Point, click, drag, and other manic mouse moves

➤ Alternative pointing devices for rodent phobes

If you believe all the techno-hype, in the not so-distant future we all will be wired to computers and have mini–hard drives implanted in our brains for enhanced memory. Instead of clicking little pictures, selecting options from onscreen menus, and typing commands, we'll be wrapped in virtual suits and work in three-dimensional programs—computing and getting a cardiovascular workout at the same time.

Until then, we have to communicate with our computers and programs using the standard low-tech tools—the mouse and keyboard. In this chapter, you'll learn how to use these standard tools along with a few other technologies to talk to your computer.

Pecking Away at the Keyboard

The keyboard and printer are pretty much all that's left of the old manual typewriter, and the keyboard hasn't changed much in its computer adaptation (see Figure 3.1). However, there have been a few key changes:

➤ **Function keys** The 10 or 12 F keys at the top or left side of the keyboard (F1, F2, F3, and so on) were frequently used in old DOS programs to quickly enter commands. F1 is still used to display help in Windows and most Windows programs, and you can assign function keys to perform specialized tasks in most programs.

➤ **Arrow keys, Page Up, Page Down, Home, and End**   Also known as cursor-movement keys, these keys move the cursor (the blinking line or box) around onscreen.

➤ **Numeric keypad**   A group of number keys positioned like the keys on an adding machine. You use these keys to type numbers or to move around onscreen. Press the **NumLock** key to use the keys for entering numbers. With NumLock off, the keys act as arrow or cursor-movement keys. Most computers turn on NumLock on startup.

➤ **Ctrl and Alt keys**   The Ctrl (Control) and Alt (Alternate) keys make the other keys on the keyboard act differently from the way they normally act. For example, in Windows, you can press Ctrl+A (hold down the Ctrl key while pressing A) to select all the text or objects displayed in the current window.

➤ **Esc key**   You can use the Esc (Escape) key in most programs to back out of or quit whatever you are currently doing.

➤ **Print Screen/SysRq**   This sends the screen image to the Windows Clipboard, a temporary storage area for data. To learn more about the Clipboard, see "Cutting, Copying, and Pasting Stuff" in Chapter 11, "Giving Your Documents the Editorial Eye."

➤ **Scroll Lock**   Another fairly useless key in some programs, Scroll Lock makes the arrow keys push text up and down on the screen one line at a time instead of moving the insertion point.

➤ **Pause/Break**   The king of all useless keys, Pause/Break is used to stop your computer from performing the same task over and over again—something that old programs seemed to enjoy doing.

Figure 3.1

A typical keyboard.

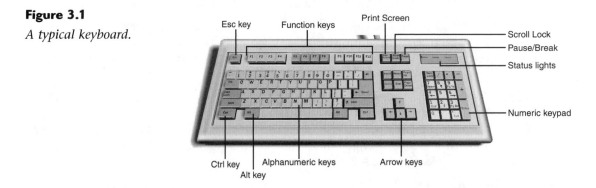

A Special Key, Just for Windows

Most keyboards manufactured after 1995 have an extra key that has the Windows logo on it. The key is typically located near the lower left corner of the keyboard—to the left of the spacebar. You can use this Windows key to quickly enter commands in Windows, as shown in Table 3.1.

Table 3.1   Windows Logo Key Shortcuts

Press	To
Windows	Open the Start menu.
Windows+Tab	Cycle through running programs in the taskbar.
Windows+F	Find a file.
Ctrl+Windows+F	Find a computer on a network.
Windows+F1	Display the Windows Help window.
Windows+R	Display the Run dialog box (for running programs).
Windows+Break	Display the System Properties dialog box.
Windows+E	Run Windows Explorer for managing folders and files.
Windows+D	Minimize or restore all program windows
Shift+Windows+M	Undo minimize all program windows.

Cramped Keys on Notebook PCs

Portable computers, including notebook and laptop PCs, typically don't have the space to lay out a full set of keys. To fit all the keys in this limited amount of space, many keys are assigned double duty. For example, some of the keys can be used to adjust the brightness and contrast of the display.

In most cases, the keyboard includes a key labeled Fn that is a different color (for instance, blue). Keys that perform double-duty have their primary functions displayed in black or white, and their secondary functions displayed in the same color used for the Fn key. To take advantage of the secondary function of the key, hold down the Fn key while pressing the key that is labeled with the desired secondary function.

Keyboards for the Rich and Famous (Programmable Keyboards)

Some clever inventors improved on the standard keyboard design by adding special buttons that enable you to quickly open your Internet home page, navigate the Internet, check e-mail, and put your computer in sleep mode. And, if you don't use a particular button for its designated function, you can reprogram it to perform some other time-saving shortcut. Figure 3.2 shows one of the more popular programmable keyboard models from Logitech.

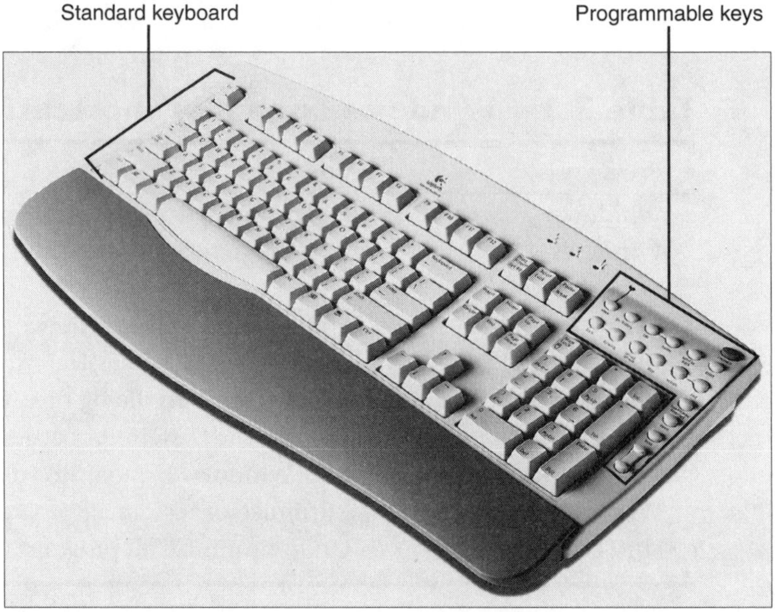

Figure 3.2

An Internet keyboard contains keys you can assign to your favorite Web pages and programs.

(Photo courtesy of Logitech, Inc.)

Standard keyboard   Programmable keys

Pointing, Clicking, and Dragging with Your Mouse

Unless you've been living in an abandoned mine shaft, you've seen the standard two-button computer mouse, as shown in the Figure 3.3. It fits in the palm of your hand and has a cable that attaches it to the system unit. You push the mouse around on your desk or on a designer mouse pad to move the onscreen pointer over the desired object. To use a mouse you must master the following basic moves:

➤ **Point**   Slide the mouse around till the tip of the onscreen arrow is over the item you want. Easy stuff.

➤ **Click**   Point to something (usually an icon or menu command); then press and release the left mouse button. When you click, be careful not to move the mouse when you click, or you might click the wrong thing or move an object unintentionally.

➤ **Right-click**   Same as click but use the right mouse button. A couple years ago, the right mouse button was pretty useless. Now it is used mainly to display context menus, which contain commands that apply only to the currently selected object.

➤ **Double-click**   Same as click but you press and release the mouse button twice real fast without moving the mouse. Mastering this move might take some practice.

➤ **Drag**   Point to an object and then hold down the left mouse button while moving the mouse. You typically drag to move an object, draw (in a drawing or paint program), or select text (in a word processing program). In some cases, you can drag with the right mouse button; when you release the mouse button, a context menu typically appears asking what you want to do.

Figure 3.3

A typical mouse.

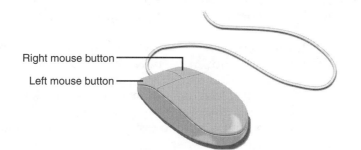

Right mouse button

Left mouse button

Building a Smarter Mouse (Microsoft's IntelliMouse)

Similar in shape to the standard two-button Microsoft mouse, the IntelliMouse has a small, gray wheel between the left and right buttons. Although it feels like a growth on an otherwise smooth mouse, the wheel gives you more control over scrolling and entering commands and is fairly easy to use.

The left and right mouse buttons work as they always have; however, in applications that support the IntelliMouse (including most new Microsoft applications), you can do two things with the wheel: spin it and click it. What spinning and clicking do depends on the application. For example, in Microsoft Word you can use the wheel to scroll more accurately, as described here:

➤ Rotate the wheel away from yourself to scroll text down; rotate toward yourself to scroll up.

➤ To pan up or down, click and hold the wheel while moving the mouse pointer

Whoa!

Most keyboards and mice have cables that attach them to the system unit. However, wireless versions are becoming more widely available. You now can purchase wireless mice and keyboards that connect to a special infrared port on the computer, sort of like a TV remote control, or send radio signals to a receiver attached to the computer. The radio-frequency adaptations work a little better because you don't have to point them directly at a receiver.

Techno Talk

A **driver** is special software that tells the computer how to use a particular device. Each device connected to your computer (the printer, monitor, mouse, sound card, joystick, and so on) requires its own driver. Windows includes many drivers for the most popular computer devices. In addition, each device typically comes with a CD or diskette that has a driver designed specifically for the device.

in the direction of the text you want to bring into view. (Panning is sort of like scrolling, but it's smoother.)

➤ To autoscroll up or down, click the wheel and then move the mouse pointer up (to scroll up) or down (to scroll down). Autoscrolling remains on until you click the wheel again.

➤ To zoom in or out, hold down the **Ctrl** key and rotate the wheel. Rotate away from yourself to zoom in or toward yourself to zoom out.

If you don't have an IntelliMouse, don't run out and buy one. It's not an essential toy. However, if you have some extra money lying around, it is kind of fun to play with. And don't rip one off from work unless you nab the *driver* for it, too. The driver comes on a floppy disk; you have to install it before you can take advantage of the wheel.

Other Devices for Poking Around on Your Computer

In search of the perfect pointing device, computer manufacturers have toyed with other ideas: trackballs, joysticks, touchpads, light-sensitive pens, and little gear shifts stuck in the middle of keyboards. I've even seen two-foot pedals set up to act like a mouse! The following list describes the more standard fare:

➤ **Trackball** A trackball basically is an upside-down mouse. Instead of sliding the mouse to roll the ball inside the mouse, you roll the ball yourself. The good thing about a trackball is that it doesn't require much desk space and it doesn't get gunked up from dust and hair on your desk. The bad thing about trackballs is that manufacturers haven't figured out a good place to put the buttons. You almost need two hands to drag with a trackball: one to hold down the button and the other to roll the ball. Stick with a mouse.

➤ **Touchpad** A touchpad is a pressure-sensitive square that you slide your finger across to move the pointer (very popular in the touchy-feely '90s). A typical touchpad has two buttons next to it that act like mouse buttons: You click or double-click the buttons or hold down a button to drag. With most touchpads you also can tap the touchpad itself to click or double-click. Touchpads are the pointing devices of choice on most notebook computers, but they can be a little temperamental, especially if you're fingers are a little sweaty.

➤ **TrackPoint or AccuPoint Pointers**   You've probably seen portable computers with a little red lever smack in the middle of the keyboard. The lever acts sort of like a joystick; you push the lever in the direction you want to move the mouse pointer. You use buttons next to the keyboard to click and drag.

➤ **Joystick**   A joystick is a must-have for most computer games. A standard joystick looks like a flight stick or one of those controls you've seen on video arcade games. It has a base with a lever sticking out of it, which you push or pull in the direction you want to move. The lever usually has a few buttons for blasting away at opponents and making a speedy getaway.

➤ **Voice activation**   For no-hands control over your computer, you can purchase voice activation software and bark commands into a microphone. With speech recognition software, such as IBM's Via Voice, you can even type without touching your keyboard. See "Can My Computer Take Dictation?" in Chapter 10, "Making, Saving, and Naming Documents" for details.

The Least You Need to Know

➤ The 12 function keys on your keyboard are positioned across the top or along one edge of your keyboard.

➤ The Ctrl and Alt keys augment the standard keyboard keys to provide extra functions.

➤ The cursor keys move the cursor or insertion point around onscreen.

➤ The five basic mouse moves are point, click, right-click, double-click, and drag.

➤ The center wheel on an IntelliMouse can be used to make scrolling through documents and Web pages easier.

➤ Other devices for poking around on your computer include a trackball, touchpad, trackpoint or Accupoint pointer, joystick, and voice recognition software.

Chapter 4

Playing Disk Jockey with Hard Disks, Floppy Disks, CDs, and DVDs

In This Chapter

➤ Point to your floppy disk drive

➤ Label your disk drives A, B, C, and D

➤ Touch a floppy disk without violating its integrity

➤ Insert a disk into a disk drive (and coax one out)

If you can stick a video tape in your VCR, you have all the technical expertise you need to insert floppy disks, CDs, and DVDs into your computer's disk drives. However, the computer complicates matters by assigning names to your drives that you might not recognize. For instance, instead of calling your floppy drive "Floppy," your computer refers to it as A or B. Your hard drive usually is C; however, it can be named anything from C to Z, and a single hard drive can be *partitioned* (divided) and assigned multiple letters. In addition, disk drives are not all created equal. You insert and remove disks into a floppy drive, whereas a hard disk is hermetically sealed inside the drive.

In this chapter, you'll learn everything you need to know about disks and drives, including how to insert and remove disks; recognize a drive by its letter; and keep your *disks,* CDs, and DVDs in good condition.

Techno Talk

A *disk* is a circular piece of plastic that's covered with microscopic magnetic particles. (A floppy disk is circular on the inside but is covered with a hard plastic case, so you never really see the disk part.) A disk drive inside the computer can "read" the charges of the magnetic particles on the disk and convert them to electrical charges that are stored in the computer's memory. The drive also can write information from memory (RAM) to the disk the same way a cassette recorder can record sounds on a tape. *Discs* (spelled with a c) are CDs or DVDs that store data using microscopic pits. The disc drive bounces laser light off the pits to read the stored data.

Disk Drives: Easy As A-B-C

Most computers have three disk drives, as shown in Figure 4.1. Your computer refers to the drives as A, C, and D. If you're wondering what happened to B, it's used only if the computer has a second floppy disk drive.

Figure 4.1

Your computer uses letters from the alphabet to name its disk drives.

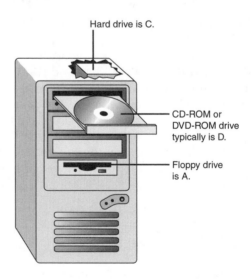

Hard drive is C.

CD-ROM or DVD-ROM drive typically is D.

Floppy drive is A.

The Floppy Disk Drives: A (and Sometimes B)

Your computer's system unit has one or more slots or openings on the front into which you can shove a floppy disk, a CD, or a tape depending on the type of drive it is. For now, look for a narrow slot that might be horizontal or vertical. This is your computer's floppy disk drive.

The Hard Disk Drive: C

The drive shown inside the computer in Figure 4.1, is the internal hard disk drive, usually called drive C. Some computers have an extra external hard drive that sits outside the computer and is connected to the system unit by a cable; the extra drive typically is assigned a letter that comes later in the alphabet, such as E or F. With hard drives you don't handle the disk; it's enclosed airtight inside the drive.

The CD or DVD Drive: D

A CD-ROM or DVD drive is standard equipment on every new computer. It typically is located right next to the floppy drive and rarely is vertical. The CD-ROM or DVD drive usually is drive D. Although most DVD drives can play standard CDs, CD-ROM drives cannot handle DVDs. If you have a newer computer, there's a good chance that it's equipped with a CD-R (CD-Recordable) drive. A CD-R drive reads CDs just like a CD-ROM drive, but it also has the capability to record data on special CD-R or CD-RW (CD-ReWritable) discs.

You might have seen people place the system unit on its side. Hey, it saves space and looks cool. However, if your system unit has a CD or DVD drive, you might have to sacrifice cool for functional. Although many CD drives can function if positioned vertically, some drives can't hold a disc when set on their sides. Make sure the drive has some way of securing discs in a vertical position before you flip your system unit on its side.

Techno Talk

A hard disk drive can be *partitioned* (or divided) into one or more drives, which the computer refers to as drive C, drive D, drive E, and so on. The actual hard disk drive is called the *physical drive;* each partition is called a *logical drive.* If you encounter a computer that displays letters for more than one hard drive, the computer might have multiple hard drives or a single drive partitioned into several logical drives.

What's on My Disks?

So, how can you figure out what's on a disk? You must use a file management utility to display the contents of the disk. Windows comes with two such utilities: My Computer and Windows Explorer. When you run My Computer, it displays icons for

41

every disk drive on your computer, as shown in Figure 4.2. Simply click the icon for the disk whose contents you want to view (or double-click if the icon names are not underlined). My Computer then displays the names of all the files and folders on the disk. See Chapter 5, "Windows Survival Guide," for details.

Figure 4.2

In Windows, My Computer displays an icon for each disk drive on your computer.

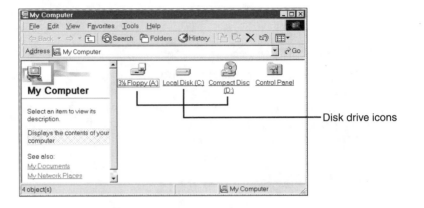

Disk drive icons

Serving Information to the Computer on Floppy Disks

Think of a floppy disk as a serving tray. To get information into the computer, you must deliver the information on a floppy disk. Likewise, if there is something in your computer that you want to store for safekeeping or share with another user, you can copy the information from the computer to a floppy disk.

Two characteristics describe floppy disks: *size* and *capacity*. You can measure size with a ruler. Although older computers used 5¼" disks, all new computers use 3½" disks. Capacity is the amount of information the disk can hold; it's sort of like pints, quarts, and gallons. A 3½" high-density disk (typically labeled HD) can store 1.44MB (megabytes). A 3½", double-density disk (typically labeled DD) can store 720KB (kilobytes).

Techno Talk

Capacity is measured in *kilobytes* and *megabytes* (MB). Each *byte* consists of eight bits and is used to store a single character—A, B, C, 1, 2, 3, and so on. (For example, 01000001 is a byte that represents an uppercase A; each 1 or 0 is a bit.) A *kilobyte* is 1,024 bytes (1,024 characters). A *megabyte* is a little more than a million bytes. A gigabyte is just more than 1,000 megabytes. *Grababyte* means to go get lunch.

Floppy Disk Handling DO's and DON'Ts

Every beginning computer book contains a list of precautions telling you what not to do to a disk. Don't touch it here, don't touch it there, don't get it near any magnets, blah blah blah …. Although these are good warnings, by the time you get done reading them, you're afraid to even pick up a disk.

My recommendation is to chill out when it comes to disks. They're pretty sturdy. Throw a disk across the room; it'll survive. Touch the exposed part (God forbid), and your data probably will remain intact. The best advice I can give you is to treat a disk as if it is your favorite CD or cassette tape. However, if you really want to ruin a disk, perform the following acts of destruction:

➤ Chew on it like a pen cap.

➤ Use a disk as a coaster to keep those ugly rings off your desk.

➤ Take a refrigerator magnet and rub it all over the disk in tiny circles. (Usually, if you just rest the magnet on the disk it won't do anything.)

➤ Press the eject button on the floppy disk drive when the light's still on. The disk drive will spit the disk out alright and nibble on it as you yank it out.

Sticking It In, Pulling It Out

A disk will fit into a floppy drive in any number of ways: upside down, sideways, even backward. But a disk drive is like one of those dollar changer machines: If you don't insert the disk the right way, the drive won't be able to read it. To insert the disk properly, take the following steps:

1. Hold the disk by its label with the label facing up. (If your drive is sideways [vertical]) the label should face away from the drive light and eject button.)

2. Insert the disk into the drive, as shown in Figure 4.3. (If the disk slot is vertical, hold the disk so the label faces away from the eject button.)

3. If the floppy drive has a lever or a door, close the door or flip the lever so it covers the slot.

Now that you have the disk in the drive, how do you get it out? Here's what you do:

1. Make sure the drive light is off.

2. Press the drive's **Eject** button.

3. Gently pull the disk from the drive.

4. Insert the disk into its pouch.

Figure 4.3

A disk drive cannot read a disk unless the disk is inserted properly.

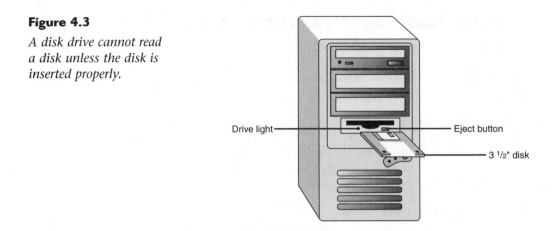

Drive light   Eject button

3 1/2" disk

Loading and Unloading CDs and DVDs

You can't just slide a CD into your computer like a quarter in a slot machine. You have to serve it to your computer on a tray just as if you were placing an audio CD into your CD player. Hold the CD or DVD only by its edges, so you don't get any gooey fingerprints on the surface that the drive reads.

Some CD-ROM drives come with a removable carriage. Remove the CD from its jewel case, place the CD into the carriage, and then insert the carriage into the drive. Other drives have a built-in carriage that's sort of like a dresser drawer: You press a button to open the drawer and then place the CD or DVD in the drawer and press the Load/Eject button.

If you ever have trouble playing a CD or DVD, it might be because the disc is dirty. To clean the disc, wipe it off with a soft, lint-free cloth from the center of the disc out to its edges. (Wipe the side without the picture or printing on it because this is the side that the drive reads.) If something sticky gets on the disc, dampen the cloth with a little distilled water and wipe. Let the disc dry thoroughly before inserting it into the drive.

Can I Play My Zeppelin CD?

CD-ROM drives can play audio CDs as well as computer CDs, so you can rock to your favorite tunes while balancing your budget. With Windows, you simply load the audio CD and Windows starts to play it. If your computer has a sound card, the audio will play through the speakers. If not, you must plug a set of headphones into the headphone jack on the CD-ROM drive.

If you can't hear your CD and you know that the speakers are turned on, chances are the volume is turned down. To crank up the volume, here's what you do:

1. Right-click the **Speaker** icon in the lower-right corner of your screen and click **Open Volume Controls.** Windows displays its volume controls, as shown in Figure 4.4.

2. Under Volume Control and CD Audio, make sure the Mute box is NOT checked (if it is checked, click the box to remove the check mark).

3. Hold down the mouse button and drag the **Play Control** or **Volume** slider (the little gray box) below the Volume Control and CD Audio Volume up. The volume control on your CD-ROM drive controls the volume for the headphones only.

4. If your sound card (where your speakers are plugged in) has a volume control on it, you also can adjust the volume using that control.

If you still don't get sound, see "I Can't Hear My Speakers!" in Chapter 32, "Do-It-Yourself Fixes for Common Ailments." To learn how to use Windows to record your favorite tracks, create custom playlists, and burn your own audio CDs (if you have a CD-R drive), see the section, "I Want My MP3: Digitizing Your Music Collection" in Chapter 29, "Now for the Fun Stuff! Computer Gadgets and Gizmos."

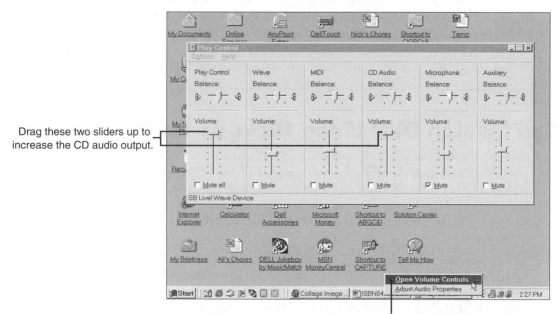

Drag these two sliders up to increase the CD audio output.

Right-click the Speaker icon and choose Open Volume Controls.

Figure 4.4

Windows provides several volume controls.

Your CD-ROM drive also can play *multimedia CDs* (CDs that contain text, pictures, video clips, and audio clips). The most common interactive multimedia CDs are encyclopedias. To play a multimedia CD, you must install it, as explained Chapter 7, "Do-It-Yourself Program Installation Guide." You then can play the CD as you would play any program; see Chapter 8, "Running and Juggling Programs," for details.

Whoa!

Windows should start to play the audio CD as soon as you insert it. If you're using Windows 98, Me, or XP and Windows does not start to play the CD, hold down the Alt key while double-clicking the **My Computer** icon and then click the **Device Manager** tab (Windows NT and 2000 do not display the Device Manager). Click the plus sign next to **CD-ROM,** and then double-click the name of your CD-ROM. Click the **Settings** tab and make sure there is a check mark in the **Auto Insert Notification** box. Click **OK** to save your changes and click **OK** again to close the System Settings dialog box. With Auto Insert Notification on, Windows should start playing your audio CD as soon as you insert it.

Can I Watch DVD Video Flicks on My PC?

The short answer is yes, if your PC has a DVD drive you can watch DVD videos on your PC. However, you probably won't want to watch DVD videos on your PC. I once watched Jaws on my 19-inch monitor and had a headache for two days. The picture was sharp and the sound was incredible—my computer has a better sound system than my TV—but the picture was so dinky I had to press my face to the screen to see anything.

At any rate, if your computer has a DVD drive, it probably has a DVD video player. Windows Me and later versions include a DVD player (on the Start, Programs, Accessories, Entertainment menu) but it might not appear unless you have a DVD decoder installed. As shown in Figure 4.5, the DVD player has its own onscreen controls for playing, stopping, pausing, fast-forwarding, and rewinding the video. You also can right-click the video as it is playing to access the video's built-in menu system.

Figure 4.5

The onscreen DVD player has controls comparable to a DVD player that's connected to a TV.

Inside the Belly of Your Computer: The Hard Disk

As I said earlier, floppy disks are bite-sized morsels—mere finger food for a computer. Any computer worth its salt can gobble up a handful of floppy disks and still grumble for more. To prevent the computer from always asking for more disks, computer engineers have given modern computers the equivalent of stomachs. The stomachs are called *hard disk drives* and can store lots of information.

The hard disk drive is like a big floppy disk drive complete with disk (you don't take the disk out; it stays in the drive forever). A small hard disk drive can store more than 2 gigabytes, the equivalent of about fifteen hundred 3½-inch, high-density floppy disks. Many new computers come with hard drives that can store more than 10 gigabytes! Sound excessive? When you consider that Microsoft Windows consumes about 200 megabytes and the latest version of Microsoft Office consumes nearly 300 megabytes, a gigabyte doesn't look all that big.

To get information to the hard disk, you copy information to it from floppy disks, CDs, or DVDs, or you save the files you create directly to the hard disk. The information stays on the hard disk until you erase the information. When the computer needs information, it goes directly to the hard disk, reads the information into memory, and continues working.

What About My Zip Drive?

If you purchased your computer in the last couple years, there's a good chance that it has a Zip drive. These drives use removable disks, like a floppy drive, but store gobs of data on a single disk like a hard drive. A single Zip disk can store up to 100MB; it acts just like a floppy drive and typically wears the letter D (or E, if your computer has a CD-ROM or DVD-ROM drive). This made Zip drives very popular for backing up files and storing huge data files, such as multimedia presentations. However, now that hard drives commonly store more than 10 gigabytes and CD-R (CD-Recordable) drives are so affordable, the Zip drive's popularity as a backup drive is waning.

Inside Tip

If you're in the market for a backup drive, get a drive that uses disks that are at least half the capacity of your hard drive. For example, if you have a 20–gigabyte hard drive, get a backup drive that uses 10-gigabyte disks. Most backup programs can cram 20-gigabytes of data on a 10-gigabyte disk by using file compression. You then can schedule backups to run automatically and you won't have to sit at the computer swapping disks into and out of the drive. Iomega, creator of the Zip drive, has a Peerless drive that stores 10 or 20 gigabytes per disk.

Going Diskless with Network Computers (Workstations)

If your computer is part of a network, it might not have a disk drive. If that's the case, forget all this babble about floppy disks and hard disks. Your network probably has a server with a disk drive as big as an elephant that stores all the information and programs you will ever need. A person called the *network administrator* acts as the zookeeper, feeding the server, making sure all the information you need is on hand, and keeping the server happy.

What's on a Disk? Files and Folders

Information doesn't just slosh around on a disk like slop in a bucket. Each packet of information is stored as a separate file that has its own name. Your computer uses two types of files: *data files* and *program files*. Data files are the files you create and save—your business letters, reports, the pictures you draw, the results of any games you save. Program files are the files you get when you purchase a program. These files contain the instructions that tell your computer how to perform a task. A program can consist of hundreds of interrelated files.

To manage all these files, you store the files in separate folders (also known as *directories*). Whenever you install a program, the installation utility (which places the program on your hard disk) automatically creates a folder for the program. To manage the files you create, you can make and name your own folders. See Chapter 17, "Copying, Moving, and Nuking Folders and Files," for more information.

The Least You Need to Know

➤ Your computer identifies your disk drives using letters: A and B for floppy drives; typically C for your hard drive; and D, E, F, and so on for additional drives, such as CD-ROM drives.

➤ Never expose a floppy disk to heat or magnets, and never bend or mangle them.

➤ When inserting floppy disks, CD-ROMs, and DVDs, never force the disk or disc into the drive. This can damage the disks and the drive heads.

➤ Current CD-ROM drives can play music CDs and other enhanced CDs with video or music clips.

➤ Using a special program called a DVD player, your DVD-ROM drives can play videodiscs.

➤ When you create and save a document, it is stored as a named file on your computer's hard disk.

➤ Folders hold a group of related files on a disk.

Chapter 5

Windows Survival Guide

In This Chapter

➤ Check out a few Windows programs

➤ Find out what's on your hard disk

➤ Dump stuff in the Recycle Bin and dig through your trash later

➤ Get instant help whenever you need it

If you're using a PC, chances are you're working with some version of Windows (Windows 95, 98, NT, 2000, Me, or XP). At this point, you should be face to face with the opening Windows screen, a Spartan screen with a lowly Start button that lets you run all of your programs. But how do you start? And how do you navigate this brave, new operating system? This chapter has the answers you need and specific instructions on how to perform the most basic Windows tasks.

We Now Have Control of Your TV

There's no starting Windows; there's no stopping it, either. Once it's installed, it comes up whenever you turn on your computer. After an interim screen welcomes you to Windows, you find yourself on the Windows desktop, as shown in Figure 5.1. The icons (little pictures) you see on your desktop might differ, depending on how you or the manufacturer installed Windows and whether you have additional programs.

If your icons are underlined, you have Windows 98 or Windows 95 with Internet Explorer. If the icon names are not underlined, you might have an earlier version of Windows or Web Style is turned off. (To learn more about Web Style, including how to activate it, see "Mastering the Active Desktop," in Chapter 6, "Windows Tips, Tricks, and Traps.") For now, just keep in mind that if the icon name is not underlined, click to select it and double-click to activate it; if the icon name is underlined, point to it to select it and click to activate it.

Figure 5.1

The infamous Windows desktop.

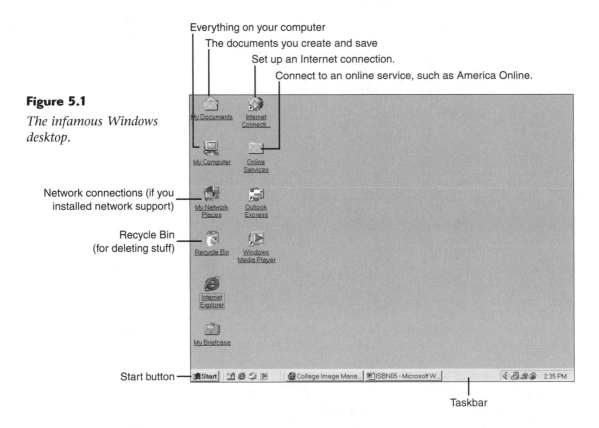

Windows might prompt you to log on at startup. You might need to log on to Windows or to your network if your computer is on a network. The logon dialog box prompts you to enter your name and password. If you work on a network, ask your company's network administrator for your password. If your computer is not on a network, you can type any password; if you leave the Password text box blank, Windows does not prompt you for a password next time. Click **OK**.

Taking Off with the Start Button

Granted, the Windows screen looks about as barren as the Bonneville Salt Flats. However, it does contain the one item you need to start working: a Start button. Click the big **Start** button; a menu with nine or more options appears, as shown in Figure 5.2. Slide the mouse pointer up to **Programs** (you don't have to click it), and another menu appears listing all the programs you can run. Move the mouse pointer so that it rests on the program you want to run and then click the icon to run the desired program.

Although the Start menu is designed to make your computer easier to use, it can be a bit difficult to navigate at first. Here are a few tips to help you through your first encounter:

➤ If you rest the mouse pointer on an option that's followed by a right arrow, a submenu appears listing additional options. You might have to go through several layers of submenus before you see the name of a program you want to run. (Programs commonly install themselves in separate program groups that appear as submenus on the Programs menu.)

➤ An option followed by three dots (…) opens a dialog box, which enables you to carry out an operation. For example, the Shut Down … option displays a dialog box that enables you to shut down or restart Windows.

➤ If you select an option that has no dots or arrows after it, you run a program. For example, if you open the Start menu and click **Help**, Windows opens the Help window offering a list of help topics.

➤ If your menu looks a little short and has a pair of arrows pointing down at the bottom of it, the menu is hiding some options. Click the double-headed down arrow to view the hidden submenus and programs. (Windows hides options to simplify menus, but this can cause some confusion when you're starting out.)

Whoa!

If you enter a password, write it down somewhere and hide it. If you forget your password, click **Cancel** when asked for your logon name. In My Computer, go to the Windows folder on drive C, find the file whose name matches your logon name and ends in .pwl, and delete it. Restart Windows and enter your logon name and a new password.

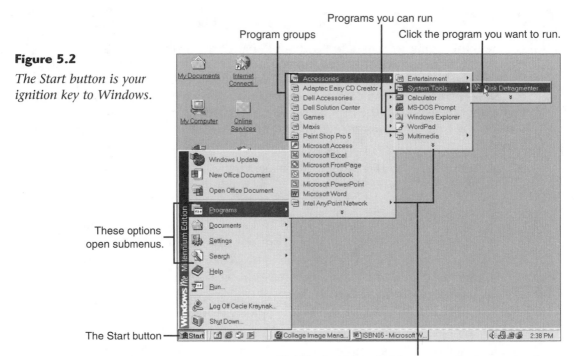

Figure 5.2

The Start button is your ignition key to Windows.

These options open submenus.

The Start button

Programs you can run

Program groups

Click the program you want to run.

Click the double-headed down arrows to view more options.

Using Windows Programs

Chances are your computer came loaded with all sorts of software. If you purchased a home PC, it probably came with Microsoft Works or some other program suite and a couple computer games. But even if your computer wasn't garnished with additional programs, Windows has several programs you can use to write letters, draw pictures, play games, and perform other tasks.

To run any of these programs, click **Start**, point to **Programs**, point to **Accessories**, and then click the program you want to run:

➤ **Games** is a group of simple computer games, including Solitaire. (You might find the Games submenu on the Programs menu rather than on the Accessories submenu.)

➤ **Entertainment** is a group of programs enabling you to play audio CDs and video clips and adjust the speaker volume.

➤ **System Tools** is a collection of programs that help you maintain your system. These tools include a backup program, a program for fixing your hard disk, and a hard disk *defragmenter,* which can increase the speed of your disk. See Chapter 27, "Do-It-Yourself Computer Tune-Ups," for details.

➤ 🖩 **Calculator** displays an onscreen calculator to perform addition, subtraction, division, and multiplication.

➤ 🖼 **Imaging** is a more advanced graphics program created in conjunction with Kodak. It enables you to view graphics saved in various file formats, scan images (if you have a scanner), resize, and enhance images.

➤ 🗒 **Notepad** is a text editing program useful for typing notes and other brief documents.

➤ 🎨 **Paint** is a graphics program for creating and printing pictures.

➤ 📞 **Phone Dialer** works with a modem and a phone to create a programmable phone. You can enter and store phone numbers in Phone Dialer and have Phone Dialer place calls for you.

➤ 📝 **WordPad** is a more advanced word processing program that enables you to create fancier, longer documents.

Dealing with Windows

Working in Windows is like being the dealer in a card game. Whenever you start a program or maximize an icon, a new window appears onscreen in front of the other windows, and a button for that program appears in the taskbar. If you open enough windows, pretty soon your screen looks like you've just dealt yourself a hand of 52-card pickup. To switch to a window or reorganize the windows on the desktop, use any of the following tricks:

➤ 🎴 Solitaire   To quickly change to a window, click its button in the taskbar (the bar at the bottom of the Windows desktop). See "Juggling Programs with the Taskbar" in Chapter 8, "Running and Jugling Programs," for details.

➤ In Windows 98 and later versions, clicking a program button in the taskbar when the program's window is in front minimizes the window. You can click the program's button again to redisplay the program window.

➤ If you can see any part of the window, click it to move it to the front of the stack.

➤ To quickly arrange the windows, right-click a blank area of the taskbar and from the shortcut menu that appears, choose one of the following options: **Tile Horizontally, Tile Vertically,** or **Cascade.** With Cascade you can see the title bar (at the top) of each window. Click inside a title bar to move the window to the front.

➤ 🗙 To close a window (and exit the program), click the Close button (the one with the **X** on it) located in the upper-right corner of the window (see Figure 5.3).

➤ ◻ 🗗 To make a window take up the whole screen, click the **Maximize** but ton (just to the left of the Close button). The Maximize button then turns into a Restore button. To return the window to its previous size and shape, click the **Restore** button.

➤ ➖ To shrink a window, click the **Minimize** button (two buttons to the left of the Close button). The minimized window appears as a button on the taskbar. Click the button on the taskbar to reopen the window.

➤ To resize or reshape a window, place your mouse pointer in the lower-right corner of the window, and when the pointer turns to a double-headed arrow, drag the corner of the window.

➤ To move a window, drag its title bar. (You can't move a maximized window because it takes up the whole screen.)

Figure 5.3

You can control each window individually.

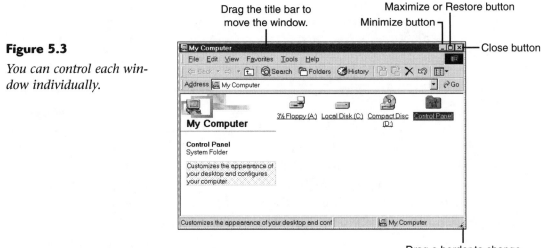

Drag the title bar to move the window.

Maximize or Restore button

Minimize button

Close button

Drag a border to change the window size and shape.

Seeing More with Scrollbars

If a window cannot display everything it contains, a scrollbar appears along the right side or bottom of the window. The scrollbar on the right enables you to scroll up and down; the scrollbar at the bottom lets you scroll left and right. You can use the scrollbar to bring the hidden contents of the window into view, as follows:

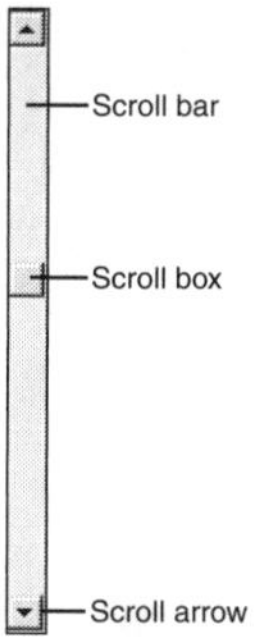

Scroll bar

Scroll box

Scroll arrow

➤ **Scrollbar**   Click once inside the scrollbar, on either side of the scroll box, to move the view one windowful at a time. For example, if you click once below the scroll box, you will see the next windowful of information.

➤ **Scroll box**   Move the mouse pointer over the scroll box, hold down the mouse button, and then drag the box to the area of the window you want to view. For example, to move to the middle of the window's contents, drag the scroll box to the middle of the bar.

➤ **Scroll arrow**   Click once on the scroll arrow at the top or bottom of the scrollbar to scroll incrementally (typically one line at a time) in the direction of the arrow. Hold down the mouse button to scroll continuously in that direction.

What's on My Computer?

Windows gives you two ways to poke around on your computer and find out what's on your disks. You can double-click the **My Computer** icon (located on the desktop) or use Windows Explorer. If you double-click My Computer, Windows displays icons for all the disk drives on your computer, plus an icon for the Control Panel (which enables you to change system settings), as shown in Figure 5.4.

Earlier versions of Windows (pre–Windows Me) commonly display other icons including Dial-Up Networking (for Internet connections) and Printers (for setting up and maintaining printers). In newer versions of Windows, you can find these icons in the Control Panel. To find out what's on a disk or in a folder, double-click its icon. (Remember, if your icons are underlined, click once; double-clicking these icons might perform the action twice.)

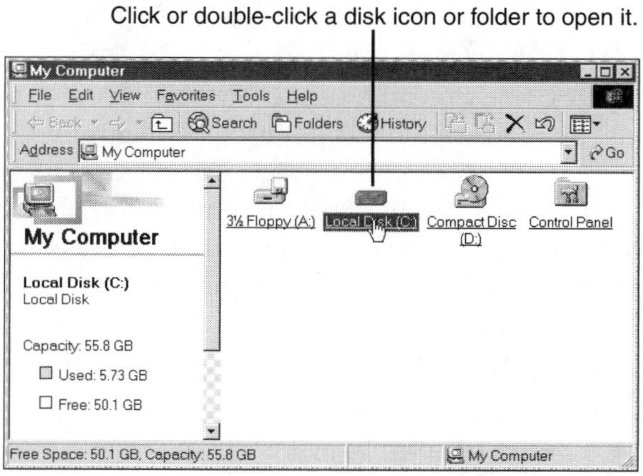

Click or double-click a disk icon or folder to open it.

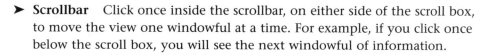

Figure 5.4

Use My Computer to browse the contents of a disk or folder.

57

Poking Around with Windows Explorer

Windows Explorer is My Computer's superior twin. It enables you to perform the same basic tasks as in My Computer but provides better tools for managing disks, folders, and files. To run Explorer, open the **Start** menu, point to **Programs**, and click **Windows Explorer** (or right-click **My Computer** and select **Explore**). You see a two-pane window, with a directory tree on the left and a file list on the right. This two-paned layout enables you to easily copy and move files and folders from one disk or folder to another by dragging them from one pane to the other. See Chapter 17, "Copying, Moving, and Nuking Folders and Files," for details.

Customizing My Computer and Windows Explorer

My Computer and Windows Explorer can seem a little unwieldy at times. The files might not be listed in the best order, the icons might seem too big or small, and there must be a faster way to enter commands. To take control of My Computer or Windows Explorer, try the following:

➤ To change the look of the icons in My Computer or Windows Explorer, open the **View** menu and click **Large Icons, Small Icons** (small icons with folders on the left), **List** (small icons with folders in the upper left), or **Details** (to display additional information, such as the date and time files were created).

➤ To rearrange the icons, open the **View** menu, point to **Arrange Icons**, and click **by Name** (list alphabetically by filename), **by Type** (list alphabetically by *file extension*), **by Size**, or **by Date.** You also can choose **View, Arrange Icons, Auto Arrange** to have the icons rearranged automatically whenever you drag an icon. (File extensions consist of three or fewer characters tacked on at the end of a filename. They indicate the file type; for example, .DOC for document. Windows might not display extensions for all files.)

➤ To display a toolbar enabling you to quickly enter commands, in either My Computer or Windows Explorer open the **View** menu and click **Toolbar.** Figure 5.5 shows how to use the toolbar to perform basic tasks. (Your toolbar might look much different, depending on the Windows version you are using.)

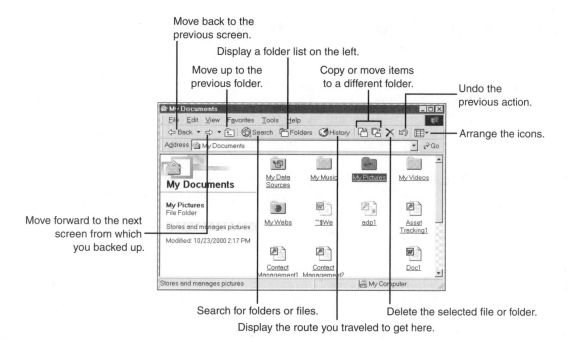

Figure 5.5

Turn on the toolbar for push-button commands.

Inside Tip

You can further customize My Computer or Windows Explorer by opening the **View** or **Tools** menu and choosing **Options** or **Folder Options** (depending on the Windows version you are using). In older versions of Windows, the Options command enables My Computer to display file name extensions (the last three letters following the period in a file's name) and enables you to keep a separate window open whenever you click a folder icon. In newer versions of Windows, the Folder Options command enables you to enter similar preferences, and to view your computer, disks, folders, and files as Web objects that you can single-click (see "Mastering the Active Desktop" in Chapter 6, for details).

Trashing Files in the Recycle Bin

Windows has an onscreen trash can into which you can dump the files and icons you no longer need. Simply drag an icon from the Windows desktop or from My Computer or Windows Explorer over the **Recycle Bin** icon and release the mouse button. The file is moved to the Recycle Bin. However, the file is not really deleted until you empty the Recycle Bin. You can still recover a file if you deleted it by mistake even if you have turned off the computer after deleting the file. There are other ways to send files to the Recycle Bin:

➤ Right-click a file or folder and select **Delete** from the context menu.

➤ Select the file or folder and click the **Delete** button in the toolbar (the button with the X on it).

➤ Select the file or folder, and then press the **Del** key on your keyboard.

Recovering Deleted Files

Pulling things out of the Recycle Bin is as easy as dragging them into it. Double-click the **Recycle Bin** icon to display its contents. Click the item you want to restore (**Ctrl**+click to select additional items); then perform one of the following steps:

➤ To restore the selected items to their original locations, open the **File** menu and select **Restore**.

➤ Drag the selected item onto the Windows desktop or into a folder displayed in My Computer or Windows Explorer.

➤ Right-click one of the selected files or folders and select **Restore**.

Notable Note

If you get an error message saying you are out of disk space, before you begin deleting programs and files you might need, check the Recycle Bin to make sure it's empty.

Emptying the Recycle Bin

The Recycle Bin can consume a good chunk of your hard disk space with the files you pitch in there. To reclaim this disk space you can empty the Recycle Bin; but be careful—you might not be able to recover the files after emptying the Bin. If you're sure the Recycle Bin does not contain any files you might need, take the following steps to empty it:

1. Double-click the **Recycle Bin** icon, located on the desktop. (Single-click if "Recycle Bin" is underlined.)

2. Make sure you will never ever need any of the files in the Recycle Bin. After emptying the Recycle Bin, retrieving files is nearly impossible.

3. Open the **File** menu, and click **Empty Recycle Bin.** Windows displays a dialog box asking you to confirm this action.

4. To proceed with the permanent deletion of the files in the Recycle Bin, click **Yes.** To cancel the operation, click **No.**

Help Is on the Way

If you get stuck in Windows, you don't have to flip through a book looking for help. Instead, open the **Start** menu and click **Help.** The Help window appears displaying links for the most common help topics. (Figure 5.6 shows the Windows Me Help window.) A link can be an icon, highlighted text, or a button that points to a corresponding document. Click the link for the desired help topic, and then follow the trail of links to find the information you need. If the trail of links leads to a dead end, click the **Back** button, as shown in Figure 5.6, to return to the previous screen, or click **Home** to return to the opening help screen.

Earlier versions of Windows display several tabs for navigating the help system. Click the **Contents** tab if you're searching for general information about how to perform a task or use Windows. Double-click a book icon to view additional subtopics and then double-click the desired topic. The help screen displays a description or instructions for the selected topic in a pane on the right.

For specific help you have two options: Enter a word or phrase in the Search box or use the index. To use the Search box, click the **Search** box, type one or two words to describe the topic you're looking for, and press **Enter.** This returns a list of links pertaining to your entry. Click the desired link. To search using the index, click **Index** to display an alphabetical listing of help topics that would make the most ambitious librarian cringe. Click the text box above the list and type the name of the feature, command, or procedure for which you need help. As you type, the list scrolls to show the name of the topic that matches your entry. Double-click the desired topic.

Inside Tip

To permanently delete a file or folder without sending it to the Recycle Bin, select the file or folder and press **Shift+Delete.** Be careful with this shortcut.

Notable Note

In Windows 95, display the Help screen, click **Contents,** and double-click **Tour: Ten Minutes to Using Windows.** In Windows 98, click the **Start** button, point to **Programs,** point to **Accessories** and then **System Tools,** and click **Welcome to Windows.** Click **Begin** to start the tour. In Windows Me, click **Tours & Tutorials** near the top of the screen, and then click the **Windows Millenium Edition Preview** link.

Type a topic here and press **Enter** to find specific help.
Click **Back** to return to the previous screen.
Click **Home** to return to the opening help screen.

Figure 5.6

*The Windows help system
teaches you the basics.*

Click the link for the
desired help topic.

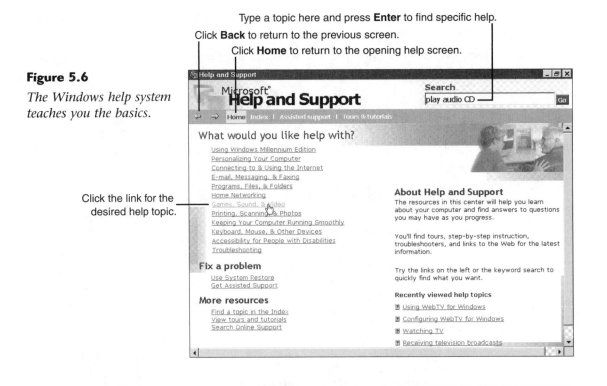

The Least You Need to Know

➤ If password protection is turned on in Windows, you must enter your name and password to log on.

➤ To run a program in Windows, click the **Start** button, point to **Programs,** and click the name of the desired program.

➤ You can find most of the programs included with Windows on the **Start, Programs, Accessories** menu or on one of its submenus.

➤ Click the **Maximize** button to make a window full-screen; the Minimize button to hide the window; or drag a corner or edge of the window to resize it.

➤ Use My Computer and Windows Explorer to check out what's on your computer.

➤ Use the Recycle Bin to delete files and folders and recover files you accidentally deleted.

➤ Use the Windows Help system if you can't find what you are looking for or need tips on using Windows.

Chapter 6

Windows Tips, Tricks, and Traps

In This Chapter

➤ Create your own shortcut icons

➤ Change the appearance of the Windows desktop

➤ Turn on a screen saver

➤ Make the Windows desktop look and act like a Web page

➤ Run programs automatically on startup

Once you've poked around on the Windows desktop, flipped through a few submenus on the Start menu, and played around with the taskbar, you know just about everything you need to know to use Windows. However, natural curiosity leads most users to experiment with Windows to customize its look, improve performance, and take advantage of some of the timesaving features built into Windows. This chapter gives you some hands-on training as you whip Windows into shape and learn to use it more efficiently.

Installing and Uninstalling Windows Components

The first step to taking control of Windows is figuring out which Windows components are installed on your computer. The Windows setup program performs a typical installation, meaning it installs the components it thinks you want. You can run the setup program again (assuming you have the Windows CD) to install additional components or remove components you don't use. To run Windows setup, take the following steps:

1. Insert the Windows CD into your CD-ROM drive.

2. Click the **Start** button, point to **Settings**, and click **Control Panel.** The Windows Control panel, which you'll meet again later in this chapter, appears.

3. Double-click the **Add/Remove Programs** icon. The Add/Remove Programs Properties dialog box appears.

4. Click the **Windows Setup** tab. Windows setup checks to determine which components are installed on your computer. The Components list displays groups of related components; for example, Accessories includes Paint and WordPad. The check boxes indicate the following (see Figure 6.1):

   ➤ **Clear box** (no gray, no check mark) indicates that none of the components in this group are installed.

   ➤ **Clear box with check** (check mark but no gray) indicates that all the components in this group are installed.

   ➤ **Gray box with check** (gray and check mark) indicates that some of the components in this group are installed.

No components are installed.

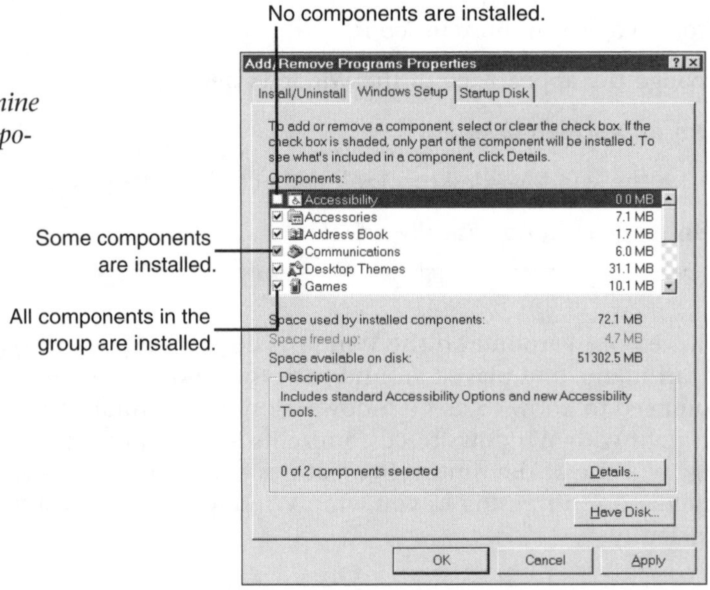

Figure 6.1

You can easily determine which Windows components are installed.

Some components are installed.

All components in the group are installed.

5. To view a list of components in a group, double-click the group's name or click the name and click the Details button. (Some groups might have only one component in which case no additional list is displayed.)

6. To install or remove a component, click its check box to add or remove a check mark. A check mark indicates that the component will be installed or is already installed.

7. Click **OK.** This returns you to the original list of component groups. Repeat steps 5 through 7 to add or remove other Windows components.

8. Click **OK.** Windows Setup copies the necessary files from the Windows CD or deletes files from your hard drive (hard disk) if you chose to remove a component. You might be prompted to restart your computer after Windows copies the necessary files. Follow the onscreen instructions.

Do-It-Yourself Shortcut Icons

If you look closely at the icons on your Windows desktop, you'll see that some icons have a tiny box with an arrow inside it. These are *shortcut icons;* they point to the original file on a disk or CD. You can place these cloned icons in any of several locations for convenient access to programs, folders, and files. For example, you can place a shortcut icon for a folder you commonly use right on the Windows desktop. That way, you don't have to run My Computer or Windows Explorer to open the folder.

Whoa!

In recent versions of Windows, Microsoft chose to hide most of the Control Panel icons. If you can count the number of Control Panel icons you have on both hands, you're missing some. Click **View All Control Panel Options** (on the left side of the Control Panel) to bring the hidden icons into view.

To create a shortcut icon for a file, folder, or program use the right mouse button to drag the folder, file, or program icon from My Computer or Windows Explorer over a blank area on the Windows desktop and release the mouse button, as shown in Figure 6.2. From the context menu that appears, choose **Create Shortcut(s) Here.** (To bypass the context menu, Ctrl+Shift+drag the icon with the left mouse button.)

After creating your first shortcut icon, check out these cool tricks:

➤ Drag an icon from the desktop, My Computer, or Windows Explorer over the **Start** button and release the mouse button. A shortcut is placed at the top of the Start menu.

➤ Right-click the Windows desktop, point to **New,** and choose **Folder.** Type a name for the folder and press **Enter.** Create shortcut icons for all the programs, folders, and files you commonly use and place them in this folder. You then can double-click the folder for quick access to the programs and files you use most often.

➤ If you have a folder in which you store all of the files you create, place a shortcut icon for that folder on the Windows desktop.

➤ You can create shortcut icons for your disk drives, too. Double-click My Computer, right-drag the disk icons to the Windows desktop, and choose **Create Shortcut(s) Here.**

Point to the program, folder, disk, or file icon and hold down the right mouse button.

Figure 6.2

Shortcuts easy as 1-2-3.

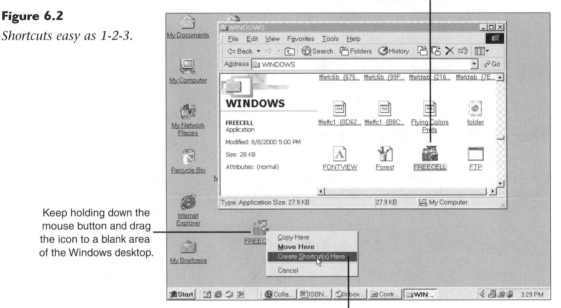

Keep holding down the mouse button and drag the icon to a blank area of the Windows desktop.

Release the mouse button and choose **Create Shortcut(s) Here.**

Giving Windows a Makeover

Your colleague down the hall has a screen with fish swimming across it; your neighbor's screen uses a baseball motif. Hey, you want to be cool, too. But where do you start? In the following sections you'll find tips and tricks for reinventing your Windows desktop.

Going Wild with Desktop Themes

Admit it: The Windows desktop is functional, but bland. Fortunately, Windows 95 with Plus! (a Windows add-on) or any more recent version of Windows (which have Plus! built-in) allows you to choose from a selection of desktop themes to breathe some life into Windows. Each desktop theme contains a graphical desktop background and specialized icons, mouse pointers, and sounds. For example, the Jungle theme places a jungle scene on the Windows background and plays animal sounds when certain events occur, such as Windows startup.

To use a desktop theme, first check the Windows Components list, as explained in "Installing and Uninstalling Windows Components" earlier in this chapter, to make sure the desktop themes are installed. If desktop themes are installed, take the following steps to pick the theme you want to use:

1. Click the **Start** button, point to **Settings**, and click **Control Panel.**

2. In the Control Panel, double-click the **Desktop Themes** icon. The Desktop Themes dialog box appears, as shown in Figure 6.3.

3. Open the **Theme** drop-down list and choose the desired desktop theme.

4. The selected theme appears in the preview area. To preview the screen saver, click the **Screen Saver** button. (See the following section for more information about screen savers.)

5. Windows plays the screen saver. Move the mouse pointer or press the **Shift** key to turn it off.

6. To preview mouse pointers, sounds, and icons click the **Pointers, Sounds, etc.** button.

7. The Preview window appears. Click the tab for the type of object you want to preview: **Pointers, Sounds,** or **Visuals.** Double-click an item in the list to display it in the preview area or play a sound. When you're done, click **Close.**

8. You can disable individual components of the desktop theme by clicking the name of each component to remove the check from its box. Click **OK** to save your settings.

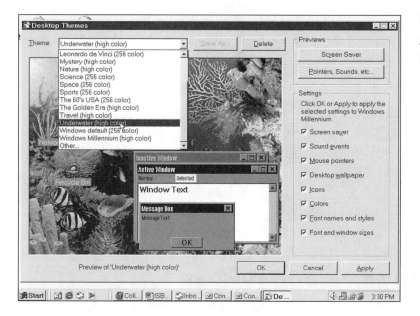

Figure 6.3

Select the desired desktop theme.

Turning on a Screen Saver

You've probably seen winged toasters flying across somebody's screen at work, or flying Windows, or maybe crawling cockroaches. These screen savers originally were developed to prevent stagnant images from being permanently burned into the screen. Newer monitors don't really benefit from screen savers anymore, but screen savers do prevent people from snooping at your screen when you're away from your desk.

To turn on a screen saver, right-click a blank area of the Windows desktop, and click **Properties.** In the Display Properties dialog box, click the **Screen Saver** tab, as shown in Figure 6.4. Open the **Screen Saver** drop-down list and click the desired screen saver.

Click the arrows to the right of the **Wait ___ minutes** spin box to specify how long your system must remain inactive (no typing, no mouse movement) before the screen saver kicks in. (You also can assign a password to the screen saver to prevent unauthorized access to your computer when you are away from your desk.) Click **OK.** When your computer remains inactive for the specified period of time, the screen saver kicks in. To turn off the screen saver, simply move your mouse or press the Shift key. (You can press any key on your keyboard to snap Windows out of screen saver mode, but pressing the **Shift** key is safest; Shift won't enter any inadvertent characters into your open documents.)

Figure 6.4

Turn on a screen saver.

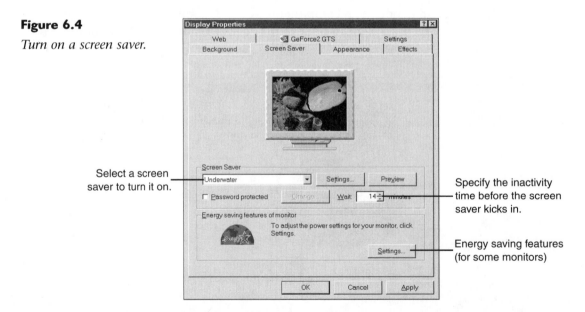

Select a screen saver to turn it on.

Specify the inactivity time before the screen saver kicks in.

Energy saving features (for some monitors)

Changing the Appearance of Windows

Computers are personal, and people enjoy customizing their displays by turning on background graphics, changing the screen colors, and changing other display properties to give their screens a unique look. To change the appearance of your Windows desktop, right-click a blank area of the desktop and click **Properties.** The Display Properties dialog box pops up on your screen. Now experiment with the following options (depending on the version of Windows you're running, your options might differ slightly):

➤ Click the **Background** tab and select an item from the **Pattern** or **Wallpaper** list to change the look of the Windows desktop.

➤ Click the **Appearance** tab and try selecting different color schemes from the **Scheme** drop-down list.

➤ If you don't like any of the color schemes, assign colors to various items on the desktop. Open the **Item** list and pick the item whose appearance you want to change. Use the **Size, Color,** and **Font** options to change the look of the selected item.

➤ Click the **Settings** tab. Make sure the **Color Palette** option is set to 256 or greater. You can drag the **Desktop Area** slider to the left to make items appear bigger onscreen or to the right to make them smaller (and fit more objects on the screen).

If you like the way your desktop looks in the preview area of the dialog box, click **OK.** If you really messed up the desktop, click **Cancel.**

Preventing Others from Messing with Your Desktop

If you share your computer with a colleague at work or with other family members at home, you don't want the other people reconfiguring Windows after you have painstakingly entered your preferences. To prevent others from messing up your desktop, you can set up Windows for multiple users. If you're using Windows NT or 2000, your computer is automatically configured for multiple users. If you're running Windows 95, 98, Me, or XP, you can configure Windows for multiple users by following these steps:

Inside Tip

In Part 4, "Going Global with Modems, Online Services, and the Internet," you will learn how to display Web pages and copy images from the Web. To use a Web page or image as your Windows wallpaper, first load the desired page or display the image in Internet Explorer. Right-click the page or image and click Set As Wallpaper.

Inside Tip

Check your Display Properties dialog box for a tab labeled Plus! or Effects. If you have a **Plus!** or **Effects** tab, click the tab to access additional options for changing the appearance of your desktop icons.

1. Click the **Start** button, point to **Settings**, and click **Control Panel.**

2. Double-click the **Passwords** icon.

3. Click the **User Profiles** tab.

4. Make sure **Users Can Customize Their Preferences and Desktop Settings** is selected.

5. Make sure both options under **User Profile Settings** are checked.

6. Click **OK.**

When you start Windows, a dialog box prompts you to enter your name and password. Instruct each person who uses your computer to enter a unique name and (optional) password when prompted to log on. Any preferences or desktop settings the user enters are then stored under that person's name, without affecting settings the other users enter.

When a user is done using the computer, he or she should log off. To log off, click the **Start** button and choose **Log Off [your name].** When the confirmation dialog box appears, click **Yes.** (In earlier versions of Windows, you must choose **Start, Shut Down** to display the option for logging off.) Windows restarts without restarting your computer and displays a dialog box prompting the next user for his or her name and password.

Using the Windows Control Panel

You can write a whole book on how to use the Windows Control Panel to customize Windows—but I won't do that to you. However, I will give you a quick way to open the Control Panel: Double-click **My Computer** and double-click **Control Panel.** Here's a list of the most commonly used icons to get you started (your Control Panel might be missing some of these icons or have additional icons, depending on which Windows components are installed):

➤ **Accessibility Options** If you have some hearing loss, vision impairment, or difficulty moving the mouse or using the keyboard, double-click this icon. Windows offers some helpful customization options.

➤ **Add New Hardware** If you connected a new device to your system, run the Add New Hardware Wizard. The Wizard leads you step by step through the process of setting up the new device. (When you connect a USB device, Windows runs the Add New Hardware Wizard automatically.)

➤ **Add/Remove Programs** Double-click this icon to install a new program. See Chapter 7, "Do-It-Yourself Program Installation Guide," for details.

➤ **Automatic Updates** Displays settings for receiving Windows updates automatically through an Internet connection. You can turn off Automatic updates if you prefer not to be reminded to download updates.

➤ 🗓 **Date/Time**   Double-click this icon to change the system date and time. (It's quicker to just double-click the time in the taskbar.)

➤ 🔤 **Fonts**   This icon opens a dialog box that enables you to add or remove fonts (type styles and sizes) from your computer. (Remove fonts only if your computer is running low on disk space.)

➤ 🎮 **Game Controllers or Gaming Options**   If you have a joystick connected to your computer, this icon lets you set up, configure, calibrate, and test the joystick. (This icon might appear as **Joystick** in your version of Windows.)

➤ 🌐 **Internet Options**   Prompts you to enter settings for connecting to the Internet. See Chapter 21, "Doing the Internet Shuffle," for details.

➤ ⌨ **Keyboard**   Double-click this icon to set the speed at which characters (or spaces) repeat when you hold down a key and the amount of time you must hold down a key before it starts repeating.

➤ 📟 **Modems**   If you have a modem you can double-click this icon to set it up and change any modem settings that might be giving you problems. See Chapter 19, "First You Need a Modem," for details.

➤ 🖱 **Mouse**   Change how fast or slow your mouse pointer travels across the screen and control how fast you must click twice for a double-click. You also can set up your mouse to swap the functions of the left and right mouse buttons and reprogram any additional buttons your mouse might have.

➤ 🔊 **Multimedia or Sounds and Multimedia**   This icon displays a dialog box that lets you enter settings for the audio, video, MIDI, and CD devices installed on your system. (A great way to crank up your speaker volume!)

➤ 🔑 **Passwords**   To change your password, click this icon and use the resulting dialog box to enter your new password.

➤ 🔋 **Power Management or Power Options**   Allows you to enter settings to conserve power on your computer. You can have Windows automatically shut down your monitor and disk drives if they have not been used for a specified amount of time. This is very useful for portable computers running on batteries.

➤ 🖨 **Printers**   Enables you to install a printer and enter preferences for installed printers. See Chapter 14, "Printing and Faxing Your Creations" for more information.

➤ 🌍 **Regional Settings**   Lets you control how numbers, currencies, dates, and times are displayed for your geographical region.

➤ 🔉 **Sounds or Sounds and Multimedia**   Lets you assign sounds to specific events in Windows.

➤ 🖥️ **System** This icon gives you a peek at what's on your system and enables you to change system settings. The dialog box that this icon calls up contains several settings for optimizing your computer. See Chapter 27, "Do-It-Yourself Computer Tune-Ups," for details.

➤ 📞 **Telephony** Enables you to enter dialing preferences for your modem. This is useful for setting up dialing preferences for a portable computer if you commonly travel outside your area code.

➤ 👥 **Users** Enables you to set up Windows for two or more users. Each user then can configure Windows according to his or her own needs without affecting settings entered by the other users.

When you double-click most of these icons you get a dialog box that lets you enter your preferences. Remember, if you don't understand an option in a dialog box, right-click the option and select **What's This?**

Mastering the Active Desktop

The Active Desktop, introduced in late versions of Windows 95, provides single-click access to disks, folders, programs, and files making your desktop act like a Web page. Skip ahead to Chapter 22, "Whipping Around the World Wide Web," to learn about clickable links on Web pages.

Before your Windows desktop can start acting like a Web page, you must turn on Web Style. Here's what you do:

1. Run **My Computer** and then open the **View** or **Tools** menu and click **Folder Options.**

2. Click Web Style or click **Enable Web Content on My Desktop** and **Enable Web Content in Folders;** then click **OK.**

3. If you choose Web Style and a particular folder does not appear in Web view (showing underlined icons), open the **View** menu and click **View As Web Page.** (Windows Me and later versions simplified the process of viewing folders as Web pages making this option obsolete.)

4. If the Windows desktop does not appear as a Web page, right-click a blank area of the desktop, point to **Active Desktop**, and click **View As Web Page** or **Show Web Content.**

With an Internet connection you can place components (called *active desktop components*) on the desktop that automatically download updated information from the Internet and display it right on the desktop. For example, you can place stock tickers, sports updates, and weather maps right on the Windows desktop!

If you don't have an Internet connection or you're not sure, read Part 4. You then can add active components to your desktop by taking the following steps:

1. Right-click a blank area of the Windows desktop, point to **Active Desktop**, and click **Customize My Desktop.** The Display Properties dialog box appears.

2. Click the **Web** tab. The Web options enable you to view the desktop as a Web page and add components.

3. Click **New.** The New Active Desktop Item dialog box appears asking if you want to go to the Active Desktop Gallery.

4. Click **Yes** or **Visit Gallery.** This runs Internet Explorer and connects you to the Internet if you are not already connected. Internet Explorer loads the Active Desktop Gallery Web page, as shown in Figure 6.5.

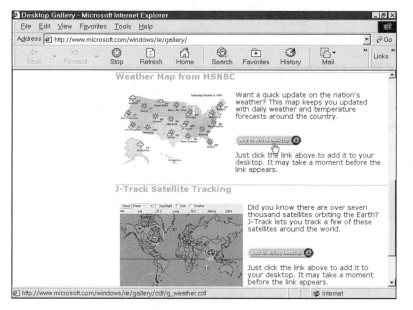

Figure 6.5

Active Desktop Components are readily available on the Web.

5. Follow the trail of links to the desktop component you want. A page appears describing the component and displaying a *link* or button for downloading it.

6. Click the link or button for the desired active desktop component to download it, and place it on your desktop. Internet Explorer displays a dialog box asking for your confirmation.

7. Click **Yes.**

8. A second dialog box appears indicating that you have chosen to download the selected active desktop component and display it on your Windows desktop. Click **OK.** Internet Explorer downloads the component and places it on the desktop.

Techno Talk

A **link** is an icon, graphic, or highlighted text that points to another Web page, file, or other object. Behind each link is the address of another page, image, or other object. When you rest your mouse pointer on a link, the mouse pointer transforms from an arrow into a pointing hand. When you click the link, your Web browser fetches the specified page or object and displays it (in the case of pages and graphics) or plays it (in the case of audio clips, video clips, and animations).

Ten Windows Productivity Tips

Everybody wants to be more productive; a computer can help you do just that. However, to become truly productive in Windows, you need a few professional tips. The following list reveals the top 10 secrets to becoming more productive in Windows:

1. **Make your own toolbar**   Drag a folder to any edge of the Windows desktop and release the mouse button to transform the folder into a toolbar. To nest the toolbar in the Windows taskbar, drag the folder over the taskbar and release the mouse button. (To turn off a toolbar, right-click it, point to **Toolbars,** and click the toolbar's name.)

2. **Quickly return to the Windows desktop**   If you have a bunch of windows open and need to get to the Windows desktop in a hurry, click the **Show Desktop** button in the Windows taskbar. Click the button again to return to your program windows.

3. **Open files quickly**   To quickly open a document file, double-click the file's icon in My Computer or Windows Explorer. When you install a program, Windows associates the program to types of files it can create. When you double-click a document file's name or icon, Windows runs the associated program, which then opens the file. A single click does the trick if Web Style is on and the icon's name appears underlined.

4. **Scrap it!**   Drag over text in a document or click a graphic image to select it. Drag the selection to the Windows desktop to create a scrap. You then can drag the scrap into another document to insert the text or graphic in that document.

5. **Alt+click an object to view its properties**   You can display the properties of a disk, folder, or file by right-clicking it and choosing **Properties.** A quicker way is to hold down the **Alt** key while clicking the icon.

6. **Bypass the Recycle Bin**   To permanently delete files without placing them in the Recycle Bin, hold down the **Shift** key while choosing the **Delete** command or pressing the **Delete** key. (This tip doesn't always work on the first try; you might have to repeat the step.)

7. **Ctrl+Esc to the Start menu**   This enables you to keep your fingers on the keyboard. Use the arrow keys to select the desired command or submenu and press **Enter.** If your keyboard has a Windows Logo key, you can press the **Windows Logo** key instead of pressing Ctrl+Esc.

8. **Drag-and-drop printing**   Open the **Start** button, point to **Settings,** and select **Printers. Ctrl+Shift**+drag the icon for your printer to a blank area of the Windows desktop to create a shortcut for it. To quickly print a document file, drag the file from My Computer or Windows Explorer over the printer icon and release the mouse button. See Chapter 14 for details on printing.

9. **Run programs on startup**   If you always use a program, you can have Windows run the program automatically when you start your computer. Simply create a shortcut for the program in the StartUp folder (C:_WINDOWS\Start Menu\Programs\StartUp). Alternatively, move the program's icon to the StartUp menu as explained in "Customizing Your Start Menu," in Chapter 8, "Running and Juggling Programs." (The location of the StartUp folder might differ on your computer.)

10. **Drag-and-Drop Start Menu**   In Windows 98 and more recent versions, you can rearrange the items on the Windows Start menu and its submenus simply by dragging them from one location to another. See "Customizing Your Start Menu," in Chapter 8 for more information on rearranging your Start menu.

The Least You Need to Know

➤ **Add/Remove Programs** in the Control Panel helps you determine which Windows components are installed on your computer.

➤ You can right–click the desktop to create a shortcut icon for a program, file, folder, or disk on your Windows desktop.

➤ You can customize your desktop with a Windows desktop theme if you have Windows 95 with Microsoft Plus! or a more recent version of Windows (98, Me, or XP).

➤ Right–click the Windows desktop and select Properties to display a dialog box for customizing the desktop's appearance, turning on a screen saver, and giving your desktop icons a makeover.

➤ In My Computer, choose **View Folder Options** or **Tools, Folder Options** to access the options for turning on Web style.

➤ To quickly open a document in Windows, click or double-click its icon in My Computer or Windows Explorer.

➤ To quickly print a document, drag its icon over the icon for your printer and release the mouse button.

Part 2

Get with the Program

You didn't buy a computer so you could watch the pretty pictures, drag icons across the screen, or play with the disk drives. You got a computer so you could do some work … and play a few games. Although this part can't possibly cover all the programs you can run on your computer, the chapters in this part teach you everything you need to know to survive in just about any program.

In this part, you learn how to install and run programs, quickly switch from one program to another in Windows, enter commands using menus and buttons, copy and paste data between documents, and print and fax the documents you create. In addition, you learn how to access online help in most programs so you won't have to forage through the documentation for specific instructions. By the end of this part, you'll know how to take any application out of its box and put it to work.

Chapter 7

Do-It-Yourself Program Installation Guide

In This Chapter

➤ Preinstallation: Can your computer run the program?

➤ Installing programs from CDs

➤ Installing programs from floppy disks

➤ Removing programs to reclaim valuable disk space

If you ran out and bought a computer without thinking much about what you were going to do with it, you probably are beginning to realize that your computer doesn't have all the programs you want to use. Maybe you need a financial management program or a game that's a little more animated than Solitaire. The problem is you don't really know where to start. In fact, you don't even know if your computer is equipped to run the program. This chapter can help; here you learn how to pick a program designed for your computer, check to make sure your computer has enough disk space and memory to run the program, and successfully install the program on your computer.

Does Your Computer Have What It Takes?

Before you buy any program, make sure your computer can run it. The minimum hardware and software requirements are printed on the outside of every software package. Here's what you need to know (later in this chapter we'll discuss how to gather this information):

➤ **Computer type** Typically, you can't run a Macintosh application on an IBM-compatible computer. If you have an IBM-compatible computer (commonly called a *PC*), make sure the application is for an IBM PC or compatible computer. (Some programs include both the Macintosh and PC versions on a single CD. Macintosh computers can run some PC programs, but PCs can't run Macintosh programs.)

➤ **Operating system** Try to find applications that are designed specifically for the operating system you use. Although Windows Me can run applications designed for Windows 98, Windows 98 might not be able to run some Windows Me programs very efficiently. If your computer's running Windows NT or 2000, it probably won't be able to run programs designed for Windows Me.

➤ **CPU requirements** CPU stands for *central processing unit,* which is the brain of the computer. If the application requires at least a Pentium III processor but you have a Pentium II processor, your computer won't be able to run the application effectively. The name or number of the chip inside your computer should appear on the front of your system unit, but if you purchased a used PC that the previous owner upgraded, the sticker might be wrong. Hold down **Alt** and double-click **My Computer** to display the System Properties dialog box, and look under Computer for the processor type.

➤ **Type of monitor** Here are the monitor types from best to worst:

  ➤ SVGA (Super VGA)

  ➤ VGA (Video Graphics Array)

  ➤ EGA (Enhanced Graphics Adapter), which is not even good enough to run Windows 95

If an application requires a VGA monitor and you have an SVGA, no problem. If the application requires an SVGA and you have VGA monitor, don't even think about purchasing the program.

➤ **Mouse** If you use Windows, you need a mouse (or some other pointing device). A standard, two-button Microsoft mouse is sufficient.

➤ **Joystick** Although most computer games allow you to use your keyboard, games usually are more fun if you have a joystick.

➤ **CD-ROM drive** If you have a CD-ROM drive, it usually pays to get the CD-ROM version of the application. This makes it easier to install and the CD-ROM version might come with a few extras. Also check for the required speed of the drive.

➤ **Sound card** Most new applications require sound cards. If you plan on running any cool games, using a multimedia encyclopedia, or even exploring the Internet, you'll need a sound card. Some applications can use the old 8-bit sound card; however, newer applications require a 16-bit or better sound card, which enables stereo output.

➤ **Amount of memory (RAM)**   If your computer does not have the required memory, it might not be able to run the application or the application might cause the computer to crash (freeze up).

➤ **Hard disk requirements**   Before using most applications, you must install (copy) the program files from the floppy disks or CD-ROM you bought to your hard disk. Make sure you have enough space on your hard disk to accommodate the new application. The next section shows you how to check disk space.

How Crowded Is Your Hard Disk?

A hard disk is like a refrigerator. You keep putting stuff in it until it's completely packed and you can't find anything. Before installing a program, you should make sure that you have enough free disk space for the program plus at least 30 megabytes for Windows to use as its workspace. To check disk space, simply right-click the icon for your hard disk drive in My Computer or Windows Explorer and click **Properties.** The Properties dialog box displays the total disk space, the amount in use, and the amount that's free, as shown in Figure 7.1.

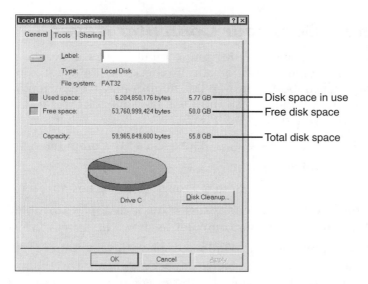

Figure 7.1

Windows displays the total disk space, free space, and space being used.

If your hard disk does not have sufficient free space for installing the program, you can free up some disk space by taking the following steps:

➤ Display the disk's Properties dialog box. Click the **General** tab, click the **Disk Cleanup** button (see the previous figure), and follow the onscreen instructions to clear unnecessary files from the disk. If you have an older version of Windows (Windows 3.1 or Windows 95 without the Internet Explorer upgrade), you don't have a Disk Cleanup button.

➤ If you don't have a Disk Cleanup button, skip to "Cleaning Your Hard Disk Without the Maintenance Wizard" in Chapter 27, "Do-It-Yourself Computer Tune-Ups," to learn how to manually remove unnecessary files from your hard disk.

➤ Uninstall any programs you no longer use. See "Uninstalling Programs You Don't Use" later in this chapter.

➤ Make sure the Recycle Bin does not contain any files you might need by double-clicking the **Recycle Bin** icon. To empty the Recycle Bin, open the **File** menu and click **Empty Recycle Bin.**

➤ Run Windows Setup again (as explained in Chapter 6 "Windows Tips, Tricks, and Traps") and remove any Windows components you no longer use.

➤ Convert your hard drive from the FAT to the FAT 32 file system, as explained in "Doubling Your Disk Space," in Chapter 27. The FAT 32 file system divides the disk into smaller storage units enabling the disk to store almost twice as much data. (If you have a newer computer, it's likely using FAT 32 or NTFS, the Windows NT file system, already.)

How Much Memory Does Your Computer Have?

If you're not sure how much memory (RAM) your computer has, you need to find out. When you start your computer, it automatically checks the RAM and displays the entire amount of installed RAM. However, this number may flash by too quickly for you to see it. Fortunately, Windows can show you how much RAM is installed on your system. Take the following steps:

1. In Windows 95 or more recent versions, double-click **My Computer.**

2. Double-click the **Control Panel** icon.

3. Double-click the **System** icon. The System Properties dialog box appears.

4. Click the **Performance** tab. The Performance status area displays the total physical memory (RAM) installed in your computer, as shown in Figure 7.2.

5. Click the **Virtual Memory** button. Windows displays the amount of disk space available for use as memory (don't change any settings here). This number should never be less than 30 megabytes. (Most programs specify the amount of physical memory that your system needs to run the program. *Virtual memory* helps when you are running several programs, but it is no replacement for *physical memory*, in the form of memory chips.)

6. Click Cancel to close the Virtual Memory dialog box, and click Close to close the System Properties dialog box.

Techno Talk

Most computers use three types of memory: *conventional, extended,* and *virtual.* Conventional and extended memory are types of physical memory, in the form of memory chips; that is, they store data electronically. Conventional memory is what most programs use; it is the first 640 kilobytes of memory. Extended memory consists of additional RAM beyond the first 640 kilobytes. (Windows NT, Windows 2000, and Windows XP treat conventional and extended memory the same.) Virtual memory is disk space that Windows can use as memory. However, because a disk drive transfers information more slowly than RAM transfers information, virtual memory is relatively slow.

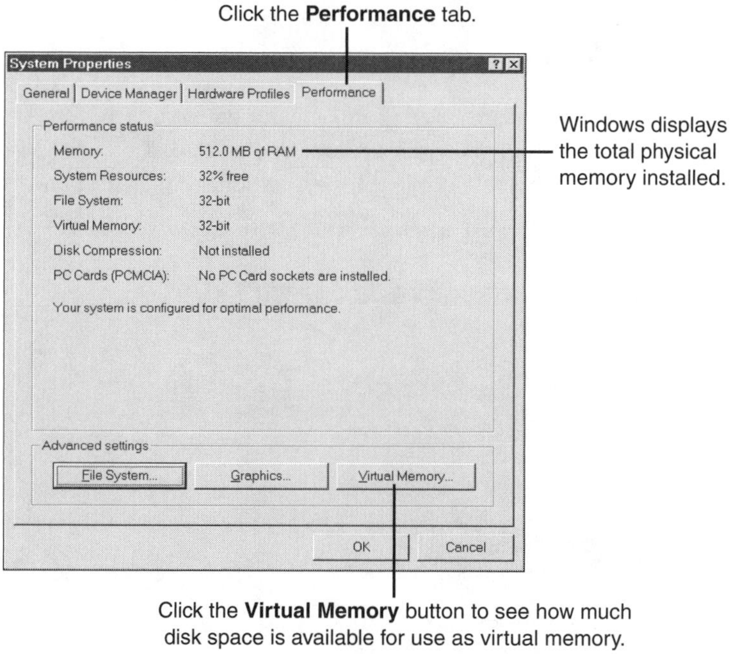

Click the **Performance** tab.

System Properties `? X`

General | Device Manager | Hardware Profiles | Performance |

Performance status

Memory:	512.0 MB of RAM
System Resources:	32% free
File System:	32-bit
Virtual Memory:	32-bit
Disk Compression:	Not installed
PC Cards (PCMCIA):	No PC Card sockets are installed.

Your system is configured for optimal performance.

Advanced settings

[File System...] [Graphics...] [Virtual Memory...]

[OK] [Cancel]

Windows displays the total physical memory installed.

Figure 7.2

Windows displays useful information about your system.

Click the **Virtual Memory** button to see how much disk space is available for use as virtual memory.

What Kind of Monitor Do You Have?

If your monitor was manufactured in 1995 or later, you can be pretty sure it's an SVGA monitor that supports at least 256 colors and a resolution of 800×600 dpi (*dots per inch*). To make sure, right-click a blank area of the Windows desktop and click

Properties. Click the **Settings** tab, as shown in the Figure 7.3. Open the **Colors** drop-down list and choose **256 Colors** or a higher color setting. If the available color settings go up to only 16 you have VGA; not SVGA.

Drag the slider under Screen Area to a 640×480 or 800×600 setting or higher. (Higher settings display smaller objects, fitting more of them on the screen.) If you can't change the setting to 640×480 or higher, you don't have SVGA. Click **OK** and restart your computer when prompted.

If you know that you have an SVGA monitor and display card, but you cannot enter the display settings recommended in the previous paragraph, you might not have the proper display driver installed in Windows. The display driver tells Windows how to control the image on your monitor. See "Finding Tech Support on the Web" in Chapter 33, "Help! Finding Tech Support," to learn how to obtain and install an updated driver.

Notable Note

Your monitor works along with the display card (video card) in your system unit to render images on the screen. The display settings rely as much on your display card as on your monitor. If you have a high-tech display card, you might have additional display options.

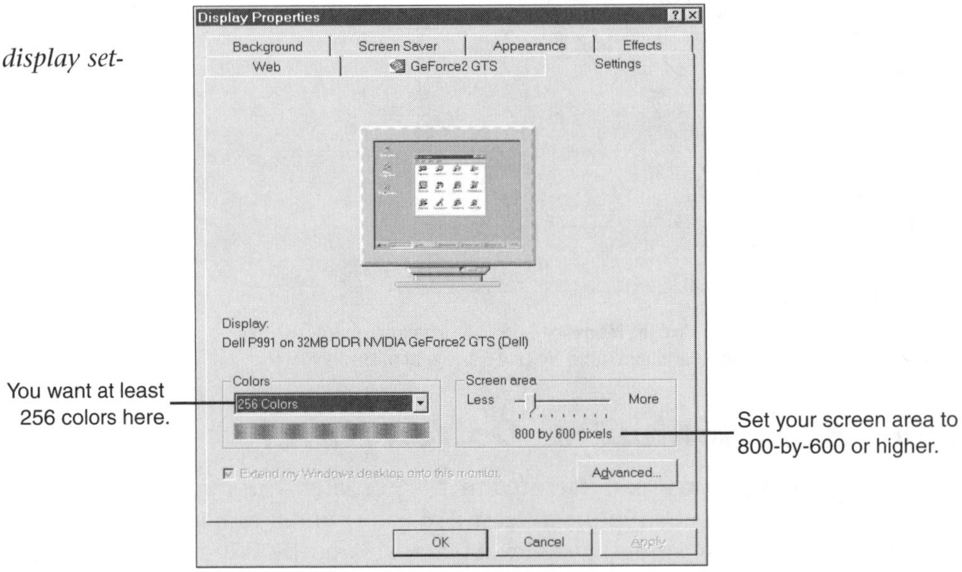

Figure 7.3

Check your display settings.

You want at least 256 colors here.

Set your screen area to 800-by-600 or higher.

Installing a Windows Program

Although "installing an application" sounds about as simple as installing central air conditioning, it's really more like installing a toaster. Most applications come with an installation program (called setup or install) that does everything for you. You just relax, eat donuts, swap disks in and out of a drive, and answer a few questions along the way.

Windows offers a convoluted procedure for installing programs that I suspect was designed for chimps. Because you're no chimp, I'll show you an easier way:

Inside Tip

If you are a chimp and you had trouble finding the Setup or Install file, here's how Microsoft wants you to install programs: Open the **Start** menu, point to **Settings,** and click **Control Panel.** Double-click the **Add/Remove Programs** icon. Click the **Install** button and follow the onscreen instructions.

1. Insert the program CD or first floppy disk into the disk drive. (Some CD-ROM programs automatically start the installation at this point; follow the onscreen instructions.)

2. Double-click **My Computer** on the Windows desktop.

3. Double-click the icon for your CD-ROM or floppy drive. This displays a list of files and folders on the disk or CD.

4. Double-click the file named **Setup, Install** or its equivalent (refer to the program's installation instructions if necessary). This starts the installation utility.

5. Follow the onscreen instructions to complete the installation.

No Install or Setup File?

Ninety-nine percent of the programs you encounter have an Install or Setup file, so you shouldn't have any problem. However, if the program does not have its own setup utility, installation still is typically easy. Just use My Computer or Windows Explorer to copy the files from the CD or floppy disk to a separate folder on your hard disk. See Chapter 17, "Copying, Moving, and Nuking Folders and Files," for details. To add the program to the Windows Start menu, see "Customizing Your Start Menu" in Chapter 8, "Running and Juggling Programs."

Special Considerations for Installing CD-ROM Programs

When you install a CD-ROM program, you might encounter a few variations on the installation process. First, many CDs are set up to play automatically when you load them into the CD-ROM drive. In such a case, the program will ask if you want to install it. Answer accordingly.

Whoa!

Some programs allow only a certain number of installations or require you to enter a password or registration number during installation. The installation utility then records this information on the floppy disk. In such cases, you might need to remove write–protection to proceed.

Second, the CD-ROM installation program might give you the option of installing the entire application or installing only the startup files. By installing only the startup files, you use little space on your hard disk (typically one to two megabytes), and the application runs from the CD-ROM (although more slowly). If you have a few spare megabytes, I recommend the full installation.

Does Anyone Use Floppy Disks Anymore?

Floppy disks are fast becoming extinct, but you might still receive small programs on floppy disks. Before installing a program from floppy disks, it's a good idea to write-protect the disks, if they are not already write-protected. If you hold the disk with the label facing up and away from you, the write-protect tab is in the upper-left corner of the disk. Slide the tab up so you can see through the hole in the disk.

Uninstalling Programs You Don't Use

If you are running low on disk space, it's tempting to just delete folders for programs you no longer use. That gets rid of the program, right? Not entirely, especially if the program you're trying to get rid of is a Windows program. When you install a Windows program, it commonly installs files not only to the program's folder but also to the \WINDOWS, WINDOWS\SYSTEM and other folders. It also edits a complicated system file called the Windows Registry; if you remove files without removing the lines in the Registry that refer to those files, you might encounter some serious problems.

To remove the program completely, you should use Windows's Add/Remove Programs utility:

1. Click the **Start** button, point to **Settings**, and click **Control Panel.**
2. Click the **Add/Remove Programs** icon. The Add/Remove Programs Properties dialog box appears.
3. Click the **Install/Uninstall** tab if it is not already selected. At the bottom of the screen is a list of programs you can have Windows uninstall, as shown in Figure 7.4.
4. Click the name of the program you want to remove.

5. Click the **Add/Remove** button.

6. One or more dialog boxes lead you through the uninstall process, asking for your confirmation. Follow the onscreen instructions to complete the process.

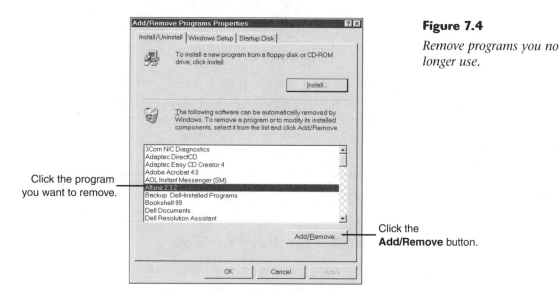

Click the program you want to remove.

Click the **Add/Remove** button.

Figure 7.4

Remove programs you no longer use.

If the name of the program you want to remove does not appear in the Add/Remove Programs list, you might be able to use the program's own setup utility to remove the program. Take one of the following steps:

➤ Click the **Start** button, point to **Programs**, and point to the program's menu name. Look on the submenu that appears for a Setup, Install, or Uninstall option. If the menu has such an option, select it and follow the onscreen instructions to remove the program.

➤ Use My Computer or Windows Explorer to display the contents of the folder for the program you want to remove. If you see a Setup or Install icon, double-click it and follow the onscreen instructions to remove the program.

In many cases, the program's setup utility enables you to remove the entire program or only selected components. If you use the program but do not use its advanced features, you can save disk space by removing only the components you do not use.

Inside Tip

If the program you removed has a shortcut icon on the desktop, you might have to delete this manually. Right–click the icon, click **Delete,** and click **Yes** to confirm the deletion.

Inside Tip

If you don't see a Setup or Install button, the best thing to do is to obtain a program that's designed especially to help you remove other programs from your hard drive. Remove-It and Clean Sweep are two of the more popular programs although they both require a good amount of technical expertise to avoid deleting the wrong files. Don't play with these programs unless you know what you're doing.

The Least You Need to Know

➤ Before you purchase any program, read the minimum system requirements on the box to determine whether your computer can run it.

➤ You should always determine how much free space is left on your hard disk before shopping for new programs.

➤ To make sure any program you buy will run smoothly, determine the amount of physical memory your computer has and the amount of disk space available for use as virtual memory. Alt+click My Computer to see how much memory is installed.

➤ Most programs come with a setup or install utility that leads you through the installation process. Run the Setup or Install file on the disk to initiate the utility.

➤ To conserve disk space, remove any Windows programs and components you no longer use.

Chapter 8

Running and Juggling Programs

> **In This Chapter**
>
> ➤ Order up programs from the Start menu
>
> ➤ Click a shortcut icon to quickly launch your favorite program
>
> ➤ Run a program without touching your mouse
>
> ➤ Jump from one program to another with the Windows taskbar
>
> ➤ Learn a few stupid taskbar tricks to dazzle your friends

Although Windows is not quite as user friendly as Microsoft claims it is, it has significantly improved the way programs run. You can run programs from the Start menu or the Windows desktop, flip from one program to another in the taskbar, and even open a document automatically in its program by double-clicking the document's icon. However, to take advantage of these modern conveniences you must learn how to run programs and switch from one program to another. This chapter provides all the basic instructions you need, plus a bushel of tips to make you work like a pro.

Five Ways to Fire Up a Windows Program

The only hard part about running a Windows program is deciding how you want to run it. The standard way to run a program is to open the **Start** menu, point to **Programs,** and then click the program's name. However, in some cases, you have to follow a trail of three or four submenus to hunt down the desired program.

Fortunately, Windows provides several alternative ways to run programs. You can launch programs from My Computer or Windows Explorer, create your own shortcuts on the Windows desktop, and even make your own toolbars to give your programs single-click access. The following sections explain your options.

Techno Talk

The file that runs a program is called an executable file; its name always ends in .EXE, .COM, or .BAT. However, Windows can be set up to hide the filename extensions. To display the extensions, open the **View** or **Tools** menu in My Computer and choose **Folder Options.** Click the **View** tab and remove the check mark from the **Hide File Extensions for Known File Types** box. Click **OK.**

1. Launch Programs from My Computer

You can launch programs from My Computer or Windows Explorer although the procedure is just as inefficient as using the Start menu. You simply change to the folder in which the program's files are stored (assuming you can find it) and then double-click the icon for running the program, as shown in Figure 8.1. You'll find most of your programs in a subfolder inside the Program Files folder.

The only trouble with this approach is that the folder that contains the program's files typically is packed with files that do not run the program. Look for the prettiest icon in the bunch; it's usually the icon for the *executable* file, which is the file that launches the program. If you view the folder in Web Style, the left pane displays the selected file's full name and indicates that it is an application file.

Sometimes it's easier to just double-click the name of a document file you created using the program. When you install most programs, the program sets up a *file association* that links the program to the document type you use the program to create. When you double-click a document file, Windows runs the associated program, which then opens the document.

Figure 8.1

You can run programs from My Computer or Windows Explorer.

Change to the folder that contains the program files.

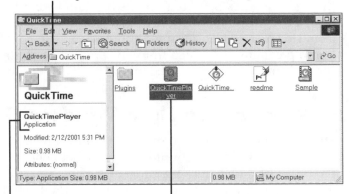

With Web Style on, Windows shows the name and type of the selected file here.

Click or double-click the pretty icon.

2. Make Your Own Program Shortcut

Are you fed up with the inefficiency of Windows? Here's what you do: Create a shortcut icon for every program you commonly use and place it on the Windows desktop. Then, instead of following a trail of menus or folders to find the program, you simply double-click its shortcut icon. To make a shortcut icon for a program, take the following steps:

1. Run My Computer or Windows Explorer and resize the window so you can see a blank spot on the Windows desktop.

2. Change to the folder that contains the icon for the program you want to run. The Windows/Start Menu/Programs folder and its subfolders contain icons for all the programs on the Start, Programs menu. (Look for additional programs in the C:\Program Files folder.)

3. Hold down the **Ctrl** and **Shift** keys while dragging the icon from My Computer or Windows Explorer to a blank area on the desktop.

4. Release the mouse button and the Ctrl and Shift keys. You now have a shortcut icon on the desktop.

5. To quickly arrange icons on the desktop, right-click a blank area of the desktop, point to **Arrange Icons,** and click **Auto Arrange.** (If you turn Auto Arrange off, you can drag icons anywhere on the desktop.)

Inside Tip

To create a desktop shortcut from a program listed on the Start menu or one of its submenus, here's what you do: Minimize or close all windows so you have a clear view of the desktop. Open the **Start** menu and follow the trail of submenus to bring the program's icon into view. Use the right mouse button to drag the icon to a blank area of the Windows desktop and release the mouse button. Click **Create Shortcut(s) Here.**

3. Assign a Shortcut Key Combination to Your Program

You can assign a key combination to program shortcut icons. Right-click the icon and choose **Properties.** Click the **Shortcut Key** text box and press the key that you want to use to run this program. You can use any key except Esc, Enter, Tab, Spacebar, Backspace, Print Screen, or any function key or key combination used by Windows.

If you press a function key (for example, F8), Windows inserts that key in the text box. (Don't use F1,because Windows uses that for Help.) If you press a number or character key, Windows automatically adds Ctrl+Alt+ to the key. For example, if you press A, you will use Ctrl+Alt+A to run the program. Click **OK**.

4. Do-It-Yourself Program Toolbar

If you have Windows 95 with Internet Explorer 4 or a more recent version of Windows, the taskbar at the bottom of your screen contains a toolbar called the Quick Launch toolbar (just to the right of the Start button). This toolbar contains four icons for running Internet Explorer, Outlook Express, Channels, or Windows Media Player; and for returning to the Windows desktop. To add your own toolbar to the taskbar, take the following steps:

Inside Tip

Many programs, such as Microsoft Word, have customiz-able button bars, giving you quick access to the commands you use most frequently. You can turn buttons on or off and even create your own buttons. Check the help systems in your pro-grams to learn about your cus-tomization options.

1. Right-click a blank area of the desktop, point to **New**, and click **Folder**. A new folder appears on the desktop.

2. Type a name for the folder and press **Enter**.

3. **Ctrl+Shift**+drag any program icons that you want to appear on the toolbar over the new folder icon and release the mouse button. This places a copy of each program icon in the folder.

4. Drag the folder icon over the taskbar or to any edge of the Windows desktop and release the mouse button. Windows transforms the folder into a toolbar and places its icons in the toolbar.

To remove the toolbar, right-click a blank area of the taskbar, point to **Toolbars**, and click the toolbar's name. (You also can drag a program or submenu from the Start, Programs menu or any of its submenus to an edge of the desktop or to a toolbar displayed on the taskbar.)

5. Launch a Document

When you install a program, the installation routine typically associates the program with a particular file type. For instance, if you install Microsoft Word, the installation routine associates Word with all files ending in .DOC. To run an application and open an associated document file with a single step, simply double-click the document file's icon in My Computer.

To view, delete, edit, or create new file associations, run **My Computer**, open the **View** or **Tools** menu, select **Folder Options**, and click the **File Types** tab. This displays a list of file types associated with programs and the options you need for creating and editing associations. Before you delete, edit, or create new file associations, read through the following two precautions:

➤ Don't try to create a file association for a file type that is already associated to another application. You must delete the existing file association before you can create a new one. Better yet, edit the existing file association instead of deleting it.

➤ Before deleting or editing a file association, write down all of its settings. If you mess up, you'll need the information to restore the file association.

Inside Tip

To quickly open a document you recently created, click the **Start** button, point to **Documents,** and click the document's name. The Documents menu stores the names of the 15 most recently opened documents.

Customizing Your Start Menu

Occasionally when you install a program it doesn't appear on the Start menu, or the program might appear on the third or fourth submenu down, making it difficult to access. Does that mean you have to live with it? Heck no—change it. First, click the **Start** button, point to **Settings**, and click **Taskbar** or **Taskbar and Start Menu.** This displays the Taskbar Properties or Taskbar and Start Menu Properties dialog box. Click the **Start Menu Programs** or the **Advanced** tab (in Windows Me or more recent versions of Windows). Now, do any of the following to customize your Start menu:

➤ To add a program to the Start menu or one of its submenus, click the **Add** button. This starts a wizard (a series of dialog boxes that leads you through the process). Follow the onscreen instructions to complete the operation.

➤ To remove a program from the **Start** menu, click the **Remove** button. This displays a list of all the Start menu items. To view the items on a submenu, click the plus sign next to the menu's name. Select the item you want to remove and click the **Remove** button.

➤ To rearrange items on the Start menu, click the **Advanced** button to display the contents of the Start menu in Windows Explorer, as shown in Figure 8.2. Again, you can click the plus sign next to a submenu name to view its contents. You can drag items up or down on the menu, drag programs to different submenus, and even delete items. (In recent versions of Windows, you can rearrange items on the Start menu by dragging them to the desired location on the menu.)

You can drag an icon to another folder to move it.

Figure 8.2

The Advanced option enables you to rearrange items on the Start menu.

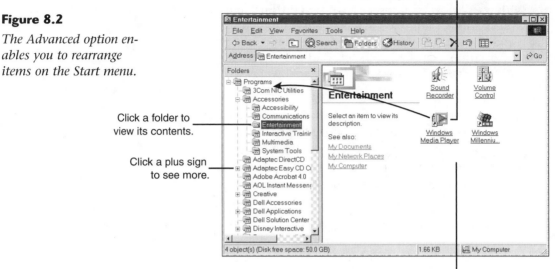

Click a folder to view its contents.

Click a plus sign to see more.

Contents of selected folder appear here.

Inside Tip

Try this: Get a few programs up and running. Now hold down the **Alt** key and don't let go till I tell you to. Press and release the **Tab** key once, twice, and a third time. A box showing icons for all your running programs appears in the middle of your screen. As you continue to hold the Alt key and press the Tab key, each open program is selected in succession. When you release the Alt key, Windows switches to the selected program. When the program you want to go to is highlighted, release the Alt key.

Juggling Programs with the Taskbar

Multitasking (working with several programs at once) used to be a Zen lesson in resignation: If you clicked the wrong spot, the window you were working in disappeared under an avalanche of other windows. If you were lucky, you might see an edge of the window that you could click to get it to jump in front of the other windows.

The latest versions of Windows have made it much easier to switch from one program to another. Windows displays a taskbar at the bottom of the screen giving you a button for each program that's running. If you happen to lose a window at the bottom of a stack, just click its button in the taskbar to get it back, as shown in Figure 8.3.

Keep in mind that each program you have open (the program button appears on the taskbar) uses part of your computer's memory. As you use more memory, the program you're using runs slower. If you're not using a program, exit it. To exit a program, click the **Close** button in the upper-right corner of the window, or open the program's **File** menu and choose **Exit.** You also can close a program by right-clicking its button in the taskbar and selecting Close.

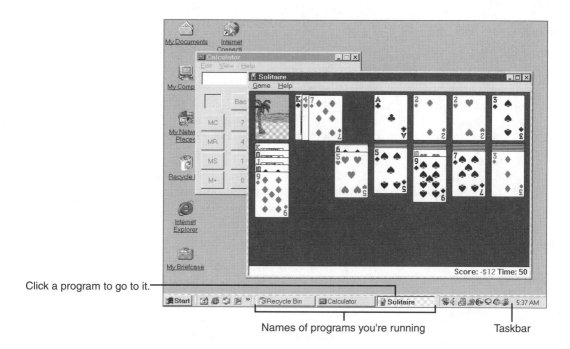

Click a program to go to it.

Names of programs you're running   Taskbar

Figure 8.3

Use the taskbar to quickly switch to a program.

Stupid Taskbar Tricks

Normally, the taskbar just lurks at the bottom of the screen until you need it. If you're bored, however, the taskbar offers some mild entertainment. Try the following:

➤ Drag the taskbar to the top of the screen or to the left or right side of the screen to move it. (Drag a blank, buttonless area of the taskbar.)

➤ Move the mouse pointer over one edge of the taskbar until the pointer turns into a double-headed arrow. Then, drag the edge up or down to resize the taskbar. You can make it really big so it displays more rows of buttons and toolbars.

➤ Double-click the time in the taskbar. This displays a dialog box that lets you set the time and date.

➤ Right-click a blank area of the taskbar and click **Properties.** A dialog box appears allowing you to change the way the taskbar behaves.

➤ To resize toolbars in the taskbar, drag the horizontal line that appears on the left or right edge of the toolbar.

Taskbar Woes

If your taskbar disappears, you might have turned on the Auto Hide option in the Taskbar Properties dialog box. If Auto Hide is on, you can bring the taskbar into view by resting the mouse pointer at the edge of the screen where the bar typically hangs out (the bottom of the screen, unless you moved the taskbar). The taskbar pops into view. To turn off Auto Hide, right-click a blank area of the taskbar, select **Properties**, click **Auto hide** (to remove the checkmark), and click **OK.**

The taskbar also might disappear if you shrink it. In this case, rest the mouse pointer at the edge of the screen where the taskbar usually appears; the mouse pointer turns into a double-headed arrow. Hold down the mouse button, and drag toward the center of the screen. This makes the taskbar bigger so you can see it.

The Least You Need to Know

➤ You usually can run a program by choosing it from the **Start, Programs** menu or one of its submenus.

➤ You can find programs on your hard disk using My Computer.

➤ To place a program in a convenient location, make a shortcut icon for running a program and place it on the Windows desktop.

➤ For ease of use, you can rearrange programs on the Start menu.

➤ You can easily switch from one running program to another using the taskbar.

Chapter 9

Barking Out Commands

In This Chapter

➤ Find out where a program hides its menus

➤ Bypass menus with toolbar buttons

➤ Bypass menus by pressing shortcut keys

➤ Display context menus with the right mouse button

Your computer essentially is an interactive television set. If you press **F1**, you get the Help channel. If you press **Alt+F4**, you exit your Windows program. There are even onscreen menus and buttons you can use to do everything from printing a file to zooming in on a page. The only thing you can't do is buzz in ahead of the other Jeopardy contestants. In this chapter, you learn how to take control of your television set (er ... computer) with your keyboard and mouse.

Ordering from a Menu

Menus are great! They provide a comprehensive list of available commands and options and make entering commands easier than ordering a burger at McDonald's assuming you can track down the menus and commands you need. To keep the screen free of clutter, Windows and most Windows programs keep the menus tucked away in the menu bar at the top or bottom of the screen. No matter where they hide, the following steps will help you flush out the menus and commands you need and make them do something useful:

Inside Tip

To quickly select a menu option in Windows, move the mouse pointer over the desired menu name. Hold down the mouse button while dragging the mouse pointer over the desired option on the menu. When you release the mouse button, Windows executes the highlighted command.

➤ Click a menu name. If you can't find the menus, they're probably hidden in the menu bar, as shown in Figure 9.1. Look around the top of the window for a horizontal bar that has names in it, such as File and Edit. To open one of these hidden menus, click its name. To select a menu item, click it or use the arrow keys to highlight the item; then press **Enter**.

➤ Hold down the **Alt** key while typing the underlined letter in the menu name. In most programs, the selection letter is underlined. In some programs, the selection letters appear highlighted only when you hold down the Alt key.

➤ Press **F10**. The F10 key typically activates the menu bar. Press the down arrow key to open the highlighted menu. Use the left and right arrow keys to move from one menu to the next or to the previous menu.

➤ Press **Esc** to close the open menu.

Figure 9.1

In Windows and most menu-driven programs, you can click a menu to open it.

Click a menu name.

Click the desired option.

As you flip through any menu system, you might notice that some of the menu options look a little strange. One option is pale. Another is followed by a series of dots. Still others have arrows next to them. Their appearance tells all:

Light gray options are unavailable for what you are currently doing. For example, if you want to copy a chunk of text and you have not yet selected the text, the Copy command is not available and appears light gray.

98

Clear ▶	An option with an arrow opens a submenu that requires you to select another suboption.
✔ Toolbar	An option with a check mark indicates that an option is currently active. To turn the option off, click it. This removes the check mark; however, you won't know it because selecting the option also closes the menu.
Find...	An option followed by ellipses (...) opens a dialog box that requests additional information. You will learn how to talk to dialog boxes later in this chapter.

Notable Note

The latest innovation in menu systems, the so-called *smart menu*, lists only the most frequently used commands, hiding commands you use less frequently. To view all available commands, double-click the menu's name, click the arrow at the bottom of the menu, or leave the menu open a few seconds. When you choose a command, the program moves the command up on the menu, theoretically making it easier to access. Personally, I hate smart menus because the commands are never where I expect them to be.

Button Bars, Toolbars, and Other Shortcuts

In an effort to give you even less room to do your work, software developers have added toolbars to the screen. Each toolbar contains a set of buttons you can click to bypass the menu system. The idea behind these time savers is that it's faster to click a button than to pull down a menu and select a command ... assuming, of course, you know what each button does.

Fortunately, programmers have figured out a way of telling you what these buttons are for. In most programs, if you rest the mouse pointer on the button in question, a tiny yellow box appears displaying the button's name or function, as shown in Figure 9.2. These little labels are fondly known as *ToolTips* (or *ScreenTips*). To see how they work, rest the mouse pointer on the time displayed on the right end of the Windows taskbar and see what happens. Once you get used to using toolbars, you will quickly wean yourself from the menu system.

Rest the mouse pointer on a
button to display a ScreenTip.

Figure 9.2

*Toolbar buttons enable
you to bypass the time-
consuming menu system.*

Toolbars

Copies the selection and puts it on the Clipboard

Quick Keyboard Commands

If your boss still thinks WordPerfect 5.1 is the best word processing program in the world (or is just too cheap to upgrade), you might find yourself having to memorize a long list of keyboard commands: **Shift+F7** to print, **F3** for help, and so on. Most of these keystrokes are not intuitive; you have to memorize the keystroke-command combination. Although difficult to learn at first, these shortcut keys can save you loads of time.

Like the Great White Whale and the Siberian tiger, function key commands are disappearing fast. Most programs now use **Ctrl+key** combinations that enable you to bypass their pull-down menus. For example, you might press **Ctrl+P** to print, **Ctrl+S** to save a file, and **Ctrl+C** to copy selected text. These Ctrl+key combinations are a bit easier to memorize, and most Windows programs display shortcut keys next to their corresponding commands on the pull-down menus.

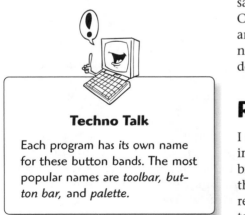

Techno Talk

Each program has *its* own name for these button bands. The most popular names are *toolbar, button bar,* and *palette.*

Right-Click Context Menus

I always thought the second mouse button was there in case the left one broke—sort of like an emergency brake. You never used it, but you were glad it was there. However, many programs have begun using the reserve button to do real work. If you right-click some text, a menu pops up that lets you copy, cut, or style the text. Right-click the window's title bar, and you get a menu that lets you print or save the file. Right-click the button bar, and you can turn it off (or turn a different one on).

As shown in Figure 9.3, context menus give you a quick look at what's available. Each pop-up menu contains only those options that pertain to the object you clicked, so you don't have to search the whole menu system to find your options. You can try this in Windows (95 or later) by clicking the right-mouse button in the following ways to display context menus for various objects:

➤ Right-click a blank area of the Windows desktop and click **Properties** to display options for configuring your work surface.

➤ Right-click the **My Computer** icon and click **Explore** to run Windows Explorer.

➤ Right-click the **Recycle Bin** icon and check out your options.

➤ Right-click the **Start** button and click **Explore** to display the items and folders on your Start menu.

➤ Right-click the **Speaker** icon on the right end of the taskbar and click **Open Volume Controls** to display the controls for adjusting the speaker volume on your computer.

Techno Talk

Programs that depend on special keystroke commands are called *command driven* as opposed to *menu driven*. However, menu-driven programs usually contain keyboard shortcuts that enable you to bypass the menu system.

Right-click an object to display its context menu.

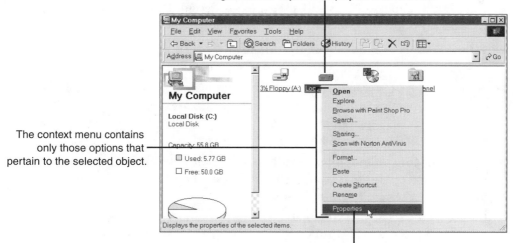

The context menu contains only those options that pertain to the selected object.

Click the desired option.

Figure 9.3

Use the right mouse button to display a context menu.

What Do You Say to a Dialog Box?

If you choose a menu command that's followed by a series of dots (…), the program displays a dialog box like the box shown in Figure 9.4. A dialog box essentially asks, "WHAT D'YA WANT?!" You click a few buttons, check a few boxes, or type specific settings and then click a command button to give your okay. The program then carries out the command according to the options and settings you entered.

Figure 9.4

A typical dialog box.

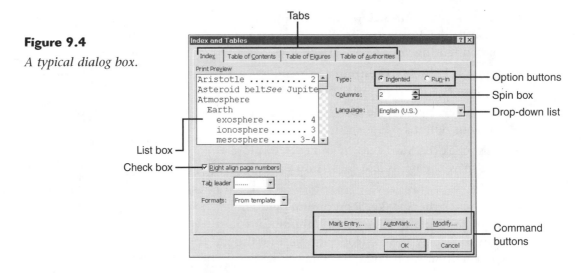

Trouble is, you rarely meet a typical dialog box. As developers search for the perfect box, they continue to add items and alter the box design. However, in any dialog box, you can expect to find one or more of the following items:

➤ **Tabs** Tabs allow a dialog box to contain two or more pages of options. To switch to a set of options, click its tab.

➤ **Text boxes** A text box stands for "fill in the blank"; it allows you to type text, such as the name of a file. To replace an entry in a text box, drag over the entry and then type its replacement. To edit an entry, click in the text box where you want to make your change and type your correction.

➤ **Option buttons** Option buttons (also known *as radio buttons*) allow you to select only one option in a group. Click the desired option to turn it on and turn off any other selected option in the group.

➤ **Check boxes** Check boxes enable you to turn an option on or off. Click inside a check box to turn it on if it's off, or off if it's on. You can select more than one check box in a group.

➤ **List box** A list box presents two or more options. Click the desired option. If the list is long, you'll see a scrollbar. Click the scrollbar arrows to move up or down in the list.

➤ **Drop-down list box** This list box has only one item in it; it hides the rest of the items. Click the arrow to the right of the box to display the rest of the list and click the desired item.

➤ **Spin box** A spin box is a text box with controls. You usually can type a setting in the text box or click the up or down arrow to change the setting in predetermined increments. For example, you might click the up arrow to increase a margin setting by 0.1 inch.

➤ **Slider** A slider is a control you can drag up, down, or from side to side to increase or decrease a setting. Sliders are commonly used to adjust speaker volume, hardware performance, and similar settings.

➤ **Command buttons** Most dialog boxes have at least three buttons: OK to confirm your selections, Cancel to quit, and Help to get help.

To get around in a dialog box, click items with the mouse, use the **Tab** key to move from item to item (**Shift+Tab** to move back), or hold down the **Alt** key while typing the underlined letter in the option's name. If you tab to a check box or option button, you typically press the spacebar to activate the option. If you tab to a command button, press **Enter** to choose the command.

Automated Computing with Macros

Unlike humans, computers can perform the same mundane tasks over and over without getting bored or acquiring carpal tunnel syndrome. Humans, on the other hand, detest repetition. That's why we need progressively better commercials to keep us interested in the Super Bowl. Whenever you notice yourself performing the same computer task over and over, it's a good sign that you need to delegate this task to your computer. You need a *macro*.

Most programs have a macro feature that can record your actions or keystrokes for you. You

Notable Note

In the upper-right corner of most dialog boxes is a button with a question mark on it. Click the button and a question mark attaches itself to the mouse pointer. Click an option in the dialog box to display information about it. You also can right-click the option and choose **What's This?**

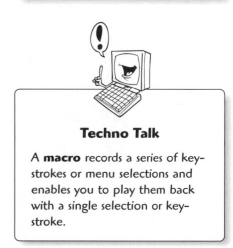

Techno Talk

A **macro** records a series of keystrokes or menu selections and enables you to play them back with a single selection or keystroke.

enter the command to record a macro and then perform the task as you normally would. When you finish, enter the command to stop recording. The program then asks you to name the macro and assign it to a keystroke. To play back the macro, you select it from a macro list or press the unique keystroke you assigned to it. Many programs even let you create buttons for your macros.

Of course, I can't tell you how to create macros here because the procedure differs from program to program. Use the index in your program's help system to find instructions for creating and playing macros. If your program has a Tools menu, you usually can find the macro commands on that menu.

The Least You Need to Know

➤ To enter a command in most programs, open the appropriate menu on the menu bar and click the desired command.

➤ From the mere appearance of a menu item, you often can predict what will happen before you select it.

➤ Once you locate the toolbar in your favorite program, you can display a ScreenTip for each button in the bar by pointing to it with the mouse.

➤ Most programs display shortcut key combinations for entering commands right next to the menu command. This is a great way to learn how to enter commands quickly.

➤ You can right-click different objects on the Windows desktop to view context menus.

➤ You can create a macro in most programs to activate a command you use often.

Chapter 10

Making, Saving, and Naming Documents

In This Chapter

➤ Make a successful transition from typewriter to word processor

➤ Skip around inside a document

➤ Give your document files meaningful names

➤ Open your document files later

➤ Find misplaced files in Windows

From the time you get your first box of Crayolas 'til you draw up your last will and testament, you're driven to create. Maybe this drive comes from some primitive need to further our species. Perhaps the hostile natural environment forces us to invent. Or maybe we're just trying to avoid boredom.

Computers further drive us to create. When you run a program, it presents you with a blank page daring you to make something. In this chapter, you will learn how to transform those blank pages into letters, ledgers, and other types of documents; save the documents you create; and open saved documents from your hard disk.

Inside Tip

Some programs come with a bunch of *templates*—starter documents that are already laid out for you. For example, spreadsheet programs usually come with a budget spreadsheet, and word processing programs come with templates for business letters and memos. You start with the template and then customize the document for your own use. To view templates in most programs, open the **File** menu and click **New.**

Techno Talk

A *field* is a fill-in-the-blank area on a database form. You type entries into the fields to create a *record.* Records make up the *database.* Think of a record as a single card in a Rolodex.

Type Away!

Most programs start you out with a blank "sheet of paper" or work area. The screen is about a third as long as a real sheet of paper, and the text usually is a little smaller or larger than it will appear in print, so you have to use your imagination. The program also displays a *cursor* or *insertion point;* anything you type will be inserted at this point. To try your hand at typing in WordPad; click the **Start** button, point to **Programs** and then **Accessories**, and click **WordPad.** Start typing and watch the characters spring into existence from the insertion point.

All Programs Differ

To type in a word processing program, you pretty much just do it. You type as you normally would, pressing the Enter key at the end of each paragraph. In other programs, typing is a little more complicated:

➤ In a spreadsheet, you tab to or click inside the *cell,* a rectangle formed by the intersection of a column and row (see Figure 10.1). When you type, your entry appears on an input line near the top of the spreadsheet and might appear in the cell itself. Type your entry and press **Enter.**

➤ In a database program, you type each entry into a field—in a box or on a line. You typically press the **Tab** key to move from one field to the next or click in the field with your mouse.

➤ In desktop publishing, graphics, and presentation programs, you must draw a text box before you can type anything. To draw a text box, click the text box button and then use the mouse to drag a text box onto your work area. Once an insertion point appears in the text box, you can start typing.

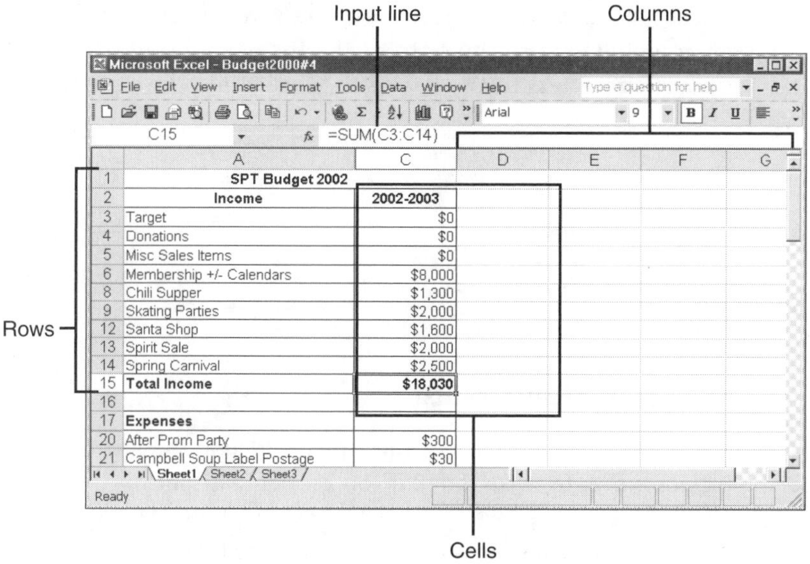

Input line   Columns

Figure 10.1

In a spreadsheet, you type entries in cells.

Rows

Cells

Easing the Transition

Moving from a typewriter to a keyboard can be a traumatic experience. I've known several people who developed nervous tics during the transition. To prevent you from going stark raving mad during your transitional phase, I'll give you some sage advice:

➤ In a word processing application, press **Enter** only to end a paragraph. The program automatically wraps text from one line to the next as you type.

➤ Don't move down until there is something to move down to. If you press the **down-arrow** key on a blank screen, the insertion point won't budge. To move the insertion point down on a blank screen press **Enter,** which starts a new paragraph.

➤ Text that floats off the top of the screen is not gone. If you type more than a screenful of text, any text that does not fit on the screen is scrolled off the top of the screen. You can see the text by pressing **PgUp** or using the **up-arrow** key to move the insertion point to the top of the document.

➤ Use the arrow keys or the mouse to move the insertion point. Many people try to move the insertion point down by pressing the **Enter** key. This frequently causes the word processor to create and print a blank page at the end of the document. Worse, some people try to move the insertion point left by pressing the **Backspace** key. Sure, this moves the insertion point, but it deletes any characters that get in its way. To move the insertion point safely, use the arrow keys.

107

➤ Delete to the right; Backspace to the left. To delete a character that the insertion point is on (or under) or a character to the right of the insertion point, press the **Del** (Delete) key. To delete characters to the left of the insertion point, press the **Backspace** key.

Notable Note

Most of the time you'll type in Insert mode; whatever you type is added at the insertion point, and surrounding text scoots over to make room. If you accidentally shift to Overstrike mode, whatever you type replaces existing text. In most programs, the status bar (at the bottom of the window) displays OVR when you are in Overstrike mode. Double-click OVR to switch back to Insert mode. If OVR is not displayed, try pressing the **INS** key to change modes or check the program's help system for instructions.

Zooming In and Zooming Out

Nothing is more annoying than text that's too small to read or so large that it runs off the right edge of the screen. Of course you could change the size of the text (as explained in Chapter 12, "Sprucing Up Your Documents with Formatting"), but that changes the size on the printed copy as well. The solution is to change the *display size*. Most programs offer controls that enable you to zoom in on a document so you can see what you're typing, or zoom out to get a bird's eye view. Check the menus and the button bar for zoom controls.

Skipping Around in a Document

Being in a document is like squeezing your way through a crowded city. You have all these characters onscreen elbowing each other for a peek at the parade. You are the insertion point, attempting to weave your way through the crowds. To move the insertion point, you have several options:

➤ **Mouse pointer** To move the insertion point with the mouse pointer, move the pointer to where you want the insertion point and then click the left mouse button.

➤ **Arrow keys** The arrow keys let you move the insertion point up, down, left, or right one character at a time.

➤ **Ctrl+Arrow keys**   To move faster (one word at a time), most programs let you use the **Ctrl** (Control) key along with the arrow keys. You hold down the Ctrl key while pressing the arrow key to leap from one word to the next.

➤ **PgUp and PgDn keys**   Use the **PgUp** key to move up one screen at a time, or use **PgDn** to move down one screen at a time. Remember, a screen is shorter than an actual page.

➤ **Home and End keys**   To move at warp speed, you can use the Home and End keys. The **Home** key usually moves the insertion point to the beginning of a line. **End** moves the insertion point to the end of a line.

Most programs also offer a scrollbar, as shown in Figure 10.2, that enables you to page up or down. However, scrolling does not move the insertion point. You must click the spot where you want the insertion point moved.

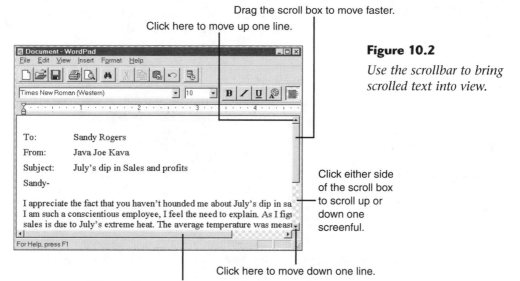

Drag the scroll box to move faster.

Click here to move up one line.

Figure 10.2

Use the scrollbar to bring scrolled text into view.

Click either side of the scroll box to scroll up or down one screenful.

Click here to move down one line.

This scrollbar lets you move left or right.

Can My Computer Take Dictation?

If your computer has a sound card and a decent microphone (a *close-talk microphone*, which is built into a headset), you might be able to use it to take dictation and carry out voice commands. Microsoft's latest edition of its Office Suite (Microsoft Office XP) has built-in voice recognition capabilities. If you don't have Office XP, you can purchase a separate voice recognition program, such as IBM ViaVoice or Dragon Software's NaturallySpeaking, and use it to add voice recognition to your other software.

Once you have the necessary equipment and the software installed, you must train the software to recognize your voice. Most of these programs run you through a 15–30 minute training program after the installation or the first time you run the program. As shown in Figure 10.3, the training session consists of you reading some sample text into your microphone. The program matches the sounds you make to specific words and sounds and creates a profile that it uses to interpret your speech.

Once you have trained the voice recognition software to recognize your voice, you simply strap on your microphone, turn on the software, and start talking. Some programs display a button or option you can click to change from dictation to voice command mode. In other programs you simply pause and then speak your menu command, such as "File, Save."

Whoa!

Voice recognition requires a fairly powerful system. If your system doesn't have at least 64 megabytes of RAM and a couple hundred megabytes of free disk space, forget it. Check the system requirements carefully before you purchase a voice recognition package.

Figure 10.3

Before you can use a voice recognition program, you must train it to recognize your voice.

Read the text aloud into the microphone.

Click **Record.**

> New User Wizard
> General Training – Calibration
> Read the following paragraph
>
> But now Texas was invisible, and even the United States was hard to see. Though the low-thrust plasma drive had long since been closed down, Discovery was still coasting with her slender arrowlike body pointed away from Earth, and all her high-powered optical gear was oriented toward the outer planets, where her destiny lay.
>
> Welcome
> Create user speech
> Adjust your microphe
> Train Dragon NaturallySpeaking
> Run Vocabulary Buil
> Setup complete
>
> Paragraph: 2 out of 16
> Record Pause   Back Up Skip Word
> Train   Cancel   Help

Saving Your Document for the First Time

As you smugly type away, your thoughts dancing across the screen, the computer stores your priceless creations in a very tentative area—RAM. If a squirrel fries himself on your power line, or someone trips the circuit breaker by running the toaster and microwave at the same time, your data is history. Why? Because RAM stores data electronically—no electricity, no data. That's why it's important to save your work to a disk, a permanent storage area.

The first time you save a *file,* your program asks for two things: the name you want to bestow upon the file and the name of the drive and folder where you want the file stored. Here's the standard operating procedure for saving files in most Windows programs:

1. Click the **Save** button (usually marked with a picture of a floppy disk) or open the **File** menu and click **Save.** A dialog box, usually called the Save As dialog box, appears asking you to name the file (see Figure 10.4).

2. Click the **File Name** text box and type a name for the file. In Windows 95 or later, the name can be up to 255 characters long and you can use spaces. In older versions of Windows, the name can be only 8 characters long with no spaces. See "File Name Rules and Regulations" later in this chapter for details.

3. (Optional) Following the name you typed, type a period followed by a three-character filename extension. An extension indicates the file type. For example, you might type .doc (word processor document file), or .xls (for an Excel spreadsheet).

4. If desired, select the drive and folder (*directory*) where you want the file saved. If you don't specify a folder, the program picks a folder for you. (See the following section, "Climbing Your Directory Tree," for details.)

5. Click the **OK** or **Save** button. The file is saved to the disk.

Techno Talk

A **file** is a collection of information stored as a single unit on a disk. Each file has a unique name that identifies it.

Whoa!

If you don't supply an extension, most programs add a period and the correct three letter extension to the file name automatically. For example, Word adds the extension .doc, and Excel adds the extension .xls. In some programs, if you type an extension the program adds another extension, which can get a little confusing.

111

Figure 10.4

The Save As dialog box asks you to name the file.

From now on, saving this file is easy; you don't have to name it or tell the program where to store it. The program saves your changes in the file you created and named. You should save your file every 5–10 minutes to avoid losing any work. In most programs, you can quickly save a file by pressing **Ctrl+S** or by clicking the **Save** button in the program's toolbar. (Some programs, including Microsoft Word, have an AutoSave feature that automatically saves your work at specified intervals.)

Climbing Your Directory Tree

Whenever you save a file for the first time or open a file you have saved, you must deal with a dialog box that's not very friendly. The following list takes you on a tour of these dialog boxes and explains how to change to a drive or folder (directory) and pick a file:

➤ The **Save In** or **Look In** drop-down list in the upper-left corner of the dialog box lets you select a drive or folder. When you select a drive or folder from the list, the dialog box displays the contents of the active folder, which might contain subfolders.

➤ To open a folder displayed in the main viewing area, double-click its icon.

➤ To move up a level in the folder hierarchy, click the **Up One Level** button, which is just to the right of the Save In or Open In list.

➤ At the bottom of the dialog box is a **Save As Type** or **Files of Type** drop-down list, which enables you to pick a file format for saving the file or specify the format of a file you want to open. In the Open dialog box, you can select a file type from this list to limit the number of filenames displayed; for example, if you pick something, such as Microsoft Word (.doc), the dialog box will display only those filenames that end in .doc.

➤ If you are saving a file, the dialog box might have a **New Folder** button. You can click this button to create a new folder inside the current folder. You then can name the folder, double-click its icon, and save the file in this new folder.

Techno Talk

Every file includes codes that work behind the scenes to control the appearance and layout of the data stored in the file. For example, if you center a title at the top of a document, the application inserts a code that centers the text. Each program uses a unique set of codes that control the file format of every document you save. Some programs can open files stored in other file formats; for example, Word can open files created in WordPerfect, Microsoft Works, Windows Write, and other applications. If you try to open a document that's saved as an incompatible file format, the application might display an error message refusing to open the document or display the document along with a confusing array of codes.

File Name Rules and Regulations

Windows 95 ushered in the era of long filenames. You now can give your files just about any name you can dream up: everything from LETTER.DOC to "Who came up with these numbers!" So, how long is long? 255 characters, including spaces, but not including any of the following taboo characters: \ / : * ? " < > or |. If you need to share a file with someone who is still running DOS or Windows 3.1, the rules are much more strict:

➤ A filename consists of a base name (up to eight characters) and an optional extension (up to three characters); for example, CHAPTER9.DOC.

➤ The base name and extension must be separated by a period.

➤ You cannot use any of the following characters:

" . / \ [ ] : * < > | + ; , ? space

(You can use the period to separate the base name and extension, but nowhere else.)

➤ Although you cannot use spaces, you can be tricky and use the underline character (_) to represent a space.

Inside Tip

When naming files, keep the filename short but descriptive. If you name all your reports Report01.doc, Report02.doc, and so on, you'll quickly forget which document file contains the report you're looking for. A better name might be InvestRptAug02.doc. This indicates that the report deals with investments in August, 2002. If you make the name too long (255 characters?!), the name takes up way too much space in My Computer and in the Open and Save dialog boxes.

What D'Ya Mean, Can't Save File?!

Occasionally, your program might refuse to save a file, rarely telling you what you're doing wrong. It could be something simple such as a mistyped filename, or maybe the disk is so full it can't store another file. Following is a list of cryptic error messages, what they mean, and possible remedies:

Notable Note

Look at the back of a 3$^1/_2$" disk (the side opposite the label), and hold it so that the metal cover is at the bottom. If you can see through a hole in the upper-left corner of the disk, the disk is *write-protected.* Slide the tab down to cover the hole and remove the write-protection.

Invalid filename Retype the filename following the file name rules given earlier.

Invalid drive or directory You probably tried to save the file to a drive or directory (folder) that does not exist. Save the file to an existing folder or create the folder before trying to save to it. If you are trying to save the file to a floppy disk, make sure a formatted disk is in the drive.

Disk full The file you're trying to save is too big for the free space that's available on the disk. Save the file to a different disk or delete some files from the disk you're using.

Error writing to device You tried to save the file to a drive that does not exist or to a floppy drive that has no disk in it. Make sure you typed the correct drive letter. If saving to a floppy disk, make sure there is a formatted disk in the drive and that the disk is not *write-protected.*

Closing Up Shop

When you're done with a file, close it. This takes it out of your computer's memory (RAM) making resources available for other files and programs. Before closing a file, save it one last time. To close a file in most programs, click the **Close** (X) button on the right end of the menu bar, or open the **File** menu and click **Close.**

Don't confuse the document window's Close button with the program window's Close button. Clicking on the document window's Close button closes the file. The program window's Close button (just above the document window's Close button) closes all document windows that might be open and exits the program.

Most programs have a safety net that prevents you from losing any changes you've made to a file. If you've made changes to a file and haven't saved your changes, and you choose to exit the program, it displays a dialog box asking if you want to save the changes before exiting. Once you give your okay (or choose not to save your changes), the program closes itself down.

Opening Saved Files

Saved files are essentially stapled to the disk. They stay there, waiting to be called into action. The quickest way to open a document is to double-click the document's icon in My Computer, Windows Explorer, or on the desktop. Windows launches the program used to create the document and the program opens the document automatically.

If the program is already running, you can use the standard File, Open command to open a document. The specific procedure might differ depending on the program. However, the following steps provide a general guide for opening files in a Windows program:

1. Run the program you used to create the file.

2. If the file is on a floppy disk or CD, insert the disk into the drive.

3. Open the **File** menu and select **Open.** A dialog box appears asking you to specify the name and location of the file you want to open.

Whoa!

The worst thing you can do to your data is to flip the power off before exiting your programs; doing this is a sure way to lose data. Before you turn off your computer, save any open documents and exit any active programs.

Inside Tip

Windows programs commonly add the names of the most recently opened files to the bottom of the program's **File** menu. To open one of these files, open the **File** menu and click the file's name.

4. Open the **Look in** drop-down list and select the drive letter.

5. In the folder list, double-click the desired folder.

6. To view the names of only those files that end with a specific extension, click the arrow to the right of the **Files of Type** list and click the desired file type. The program displays a list of files.

Notable Note

Most programs allow you to open files that were created using other programs. The program can convert the foreign file into a useable format. The Files of Type drop-down list typically displays the types of files that the current program can convert and use. However, don't expect a word processing program to be able to open a spreadsheet or graphics file; to share data between programs of different types, copy and paste the data from one program to the other.

7. Click the desired file in the **File Name** list.

8. Click the **Open** or **OK** button. The program opens the file and displays its contents onscreen.

Tracking Down Lost Files in Windows

When a program displays a dialog box asking where you want your file stored, it's tempting to just store it in the default folder. The trouble is that the default folder in one program might not be the same default folder in another program. You end up scattering your files like hayseed making it difficult to find them later. Fortunately, Windows can help you track down misplaced files.

If you recently worked on the file, the first place to look is the **Start, Documents** menu. This submenu lists the last 15 files you worked on. If you can't find the file there, try this:

1. Open the **Start** menu; point to **Find** or **Search**; and click **For Files or Folders** or just **Files or Folders**. The **Find** or **Search Results** dialog box appears asking what you're looking for as shown in Figure 10.5.

2. Open the **Look in** drop-down list, and click the drive or folder you want to search.

3. In the **Named** or **Search for Files or Folders Named** text box, type the file's name (or a portion of it). If you don't know the name, click the **Containing Text** text box and type some unique text that might be contained in the file.

4. Click the **Find Now** or **Search Now** button. Windows searches the specified disk drive and displays a list of files and folders that match the name or text string you typed.

If you can't recall the file's name, type a unique
text string that appears inside the document.

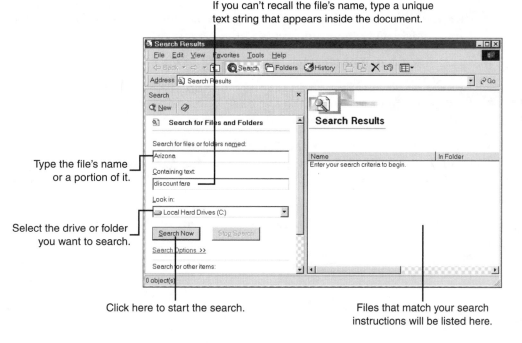

Type the file's name
or a portion of it.

Select the drive or folder
you want to search.

Click here to start the search.

Files that match your search
instructions will be listed here.

Figure 10.5

Windows can help you track down lost files.

Once Windows has found the file you want to work with, you can open the file by clicking or double-clicking its name in the search results list. You also can drag the file from the list into the program window, or if you're working in older versions of Windows, you might need to make a mental note of the file's location and then use the program's **File**, **Open** command to open the file.

The Least You Need to Know

➤ In your word processing program, press the Insert key to change from **Insert** to Overstrike mode or vice versa. In most word processing programs, click **OVR** in the status bar to change typing modes.

➤ To type entries in a spreadsheet, click the cell in which you want the entry to appear, type the entry, and press the **Enter** or **Tab** key.

➤ Press **Ctrl+S** to save a document in most programs.

➤ Give your documents brief, descriptive names, and don't worry about typing a filename extension; most programs add the extension for you.

➤ To open a file in most programs, press **Ctrl+O** or open the **File** menu and click **Open.**

➤ Most programs store a list of the last three or four documents you worked on at the bottom of the File menu.

➤ If you misplace a file, check the **Start, Documents** menu or use the Windows **Start, Find, Files and Folders** (or **Start, Search, For Files or Folders**) command to search for it.

➤ Before shutting down your computer, save any open documents (press **Ctrl+S**) and then exit the program (by choosing **File**, **Exit** or clicking the program's **Close** [**X**] button.)

Chapter 11

Giving Your Documents the Editorial Eye

In This Chapter

➤ Delete a few characters here and there

➤ Chop and move chunks of text

➤ Undo mistakes with the click of a button

➤ Share data between two documents

➤ Check your spelling and grammar

The cool thing about computerized documents is that you can fling text on a page like Jackson Pollock and then go back later and perfect it. You can delete a few characters or an entire paragraph, move a section somewhere else, and quickly replace one word with another throughout the document. In addition, most programs include editing tools to help you correct spelling and grammatical errors and fix your typos. Perhaps best of all, programs allow you to undo your changes when you goof! In this chapter, you learn about all this and more.

Making Minor Edits

You probably have figured out for yourself how to delete a character or word in a word processing program. You move the insertion point to the left of the character and then press the **Delete** key. Alternatively, you can move the insertion point to the right of the character or word and press the **Backspace** key.

However, if you are working in a different program, such as a spreadsheet or desktop publishing program, you might need to master a few additional techniques:

➤ In a spreadsheet program, you typically replace an entry in a cell by clicking the cell, typing the new entry, and then pressing **Enter.**

➤ To edit an entry in a spreadsheet cell instead of replacing it, double-click the cell. The insertion point appears in the input box near the top of the window (or inside the cell). Use the arrow keys to move the insertion point and then edit the text or value as you would in your word processor. Press **Enter.**

➤ If you need an extra cell, column, or row in a spreadsheet, open the **Insert** menu and choose the option for inserting **Cells**, **Rows**, or **Columns**. The program typically asks where you want the new cells, rows, or columns inserted or in which direction you want the surrounding cells shifted to make room for the new cells.

➤ In a desktop publishing program, text typically appears inside a text box. Click inside the text box to activate it and then edit the text just as you would in a word processor.

➤ In a database, you type each entry into a *field*, which essentially is a blank on a fill-in-the-blanks form. To replace an entry, double-click the field and type the new entry. To edit an existing entry, click the field, use the arrow keys to move the insertion point, and then use the **Delete** or **Backspace** key to delete individual characters.

➤ In some cases, you might want to replace a word or delete an entire sentence or paragraph. To do this, first select the text, as explained in the next section, "Cutting, Copying, and Pasting Stuff." Press the **Delete** key or just start typing; the selection is automatically deleted.

Cutting, Copying, and Pasting Stuff

Usually, revising a document is not a simple matter of changing a word here or there or correcting typos. You might need to delete an entire sentence or even rearrange the paragraphs to present your ideas in a more logical flow. To help you get it done, word processing programs offer cut, copy, and paste commands.

Before you can cut or copy text or change the text in any way (its type size, color, or position on the page), you must select it. Although each word processing program has its own techniques for selecting text, the following are fairly standard:

➤ Drag over text to select it.

➤ Double-click a word to select the entire word.

➤ Triple-click anywhere inside a paragraph to select the entire paragraph.

➤ Drag inside the selection area (the far-left margin) to select lines of text. (When you move the mouse pointer to the selection area, the pointer typically changes direction pointing to the right instead of to the left.)

➤ Hold down the **Shift** key while pressing the arrow keys to *stretch* (extend) the highlighting over text.

➤ Open the **Edit** menu and click **Select All** (or press **Ctrl+A**) to select the entire document.

To try out some of these selection moves, open WordPad (**Start, Programs, Accessories, Word-Pad**). Open a document or type something and then start dragging, double-clicking, and triple-clicking to get a feel for selecting text. Try double-clicking in the selection area to see what happens.

Once you have selected text, you can copy or cut the text. The Copy command leaves the selected text in your document and places a copy of it on the Windows Clipboard, as shown in Figure 11.1. The Cut command removes the text and places it on the Windows Clipboard. In either case, you can use the Paste command to insert the text from the Windows Clipboard into the same document, a different document in the same program, or a document created in another Windows program. To cut, copy, and paste text, follow these steps:

1. Select the text.

2. ✂ 📋 Open the **Edit** menu and click **Cut** or **Copy**, or click the **Cut** or **Copy** button in the program's toolbar. (Press **Ctrl+C** to copy or **Ctrl+X** to cut.)

3. Move the insertion point to where you want the cut or copied text placed. This can be in the same document, a different document, or a document created in another program.

4. 📋 Open the **Edit** menu and click **Paste** or click the **Paste** button in the program's toolbar. (Press **Ctrl+V** to paste.)

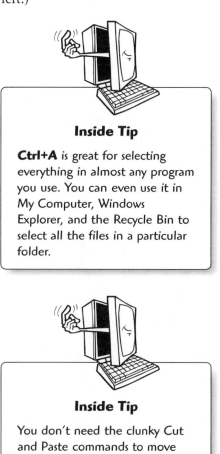

Inside Tip

Ctrl+A is great for selecting everything in almost any program you use. You can even use it in My Computer, Windows Explorer, and the Recycle Bin to select all the files in a particular folder.

Inside Tip

You don't need the clunky Cut and Paste commands to move text in a document. Select the text you want to move and then drag it to its new location. You can even drag data from one document to another assuming you can manage to display the source and destination documents side by side on your dinky monitor.

121

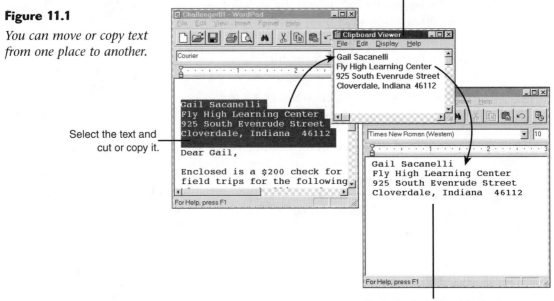

Figure 11.1

You can move or copy text from one place to another.

The cut or copied text is placed on the Clipboard.

Select the text and cut or copy it.

Paste the text where desired.

Edit/Undo: The Editor's Safety Net

If you enjoy the slash-and-burn, never-look-back approach to editing your documents, you might just decide to live with whatever changes you make. If you're a little more hesitant and you get that sinking feeling whenever you delete a sentence, you will feel safe knowing that most programs have an Undo feature. This feature allows you to take back any of the most recent edits you've made. To recover from the occasional boo-boo, use the undo and redo options as described in the following list:

➤ To undo the most recent action, open the **Edit** menu and choose **Undo**, or click the **Undo** button in the Standard toolbar, as shown in Figure 11.2. (In most programs, you can press **Ctrl+Z** to undo the most recent action.) You can continue to click the Undo button to undo additional actions. In fact, some Undo buttons double as menus. Click the arrow to the right of the Undo button to open the menu and display a list of actions you can undo. In most cases, if you select an action somewhere down the list, you undo that action and all actions above it.

➤ To recover from an accidental undo, use the Redo button (just to the right of Undo). It works just like the Undo button: Click the **Redo** button to restore the most recently undone action.

Undo button ─┐ ┌─ Redo button

Figure 11.2

If you act quickly after making a mistake, you usually can recover.

Finding and Replacing Text

Most word processing programs have a tool called Search and Replace that can sift through your document, find a specific word or phrase, and replace it with a different word or phrase. So, if you typed cog and you meant to type sprocket, Search and Replace can replace all occurrences of "cog" with "sprocket" for you. Here's what you do:

1. Open the **Edit** menu and click **Replace**.

2. Type the word or phrase you want to replace in the **Find What** text box and type the re-placement word or phrase in the **Replace With** box.

3. To start the search and replace, click the **Find Next** button. Search and Replace highlights the first occurrence of the text it finds and lets you replace the word or skip to the next occurrence (see Figure 11.3).

4. Click one of the following buttons to tell Search and Replace what you want to do:

Whoa!

Don't get too self-assured with the Undo feature. After you save a file and close it, your changes usually are final. If you reopen the document, you will find that the Undo list is empty.

➤ **Find Next** skips this text and moves to the next occurrence.

➤ **Replace** replaces this text and moves to the next occurrence.

➤ **Replace All** replaces all occurrences of the specified text with the replace-ment text—and does not ask for your okay.

➤ **Cancel** aborts the operation.

123

Whoa!

Search and Replace can be tricky. If you replace "play" with "performance" the program will replace all occurrences of "play" including its occurrences in other words like "play-ers," "playful," and "playwright." When replacing any string of characters that can be a part of other common words or phrases, click the Replace button instead of Replace All, so you can confirm each replacement individually.

Word highlights the text it is about to replace.

Figure 11.3

You can quickly replace all occurrences of a word or phrase with a different word or phrase.

Click **Replace All** for a global replacement.

Click **Replace** to replace only this occurrence.

Checking Your Spelling and Grammar

If spelling isn't your forte, your program's spelling checker might become your best friend. Word processing, spreadsheet, and most desktop publishing programs include a spelling checker that can check your document for spelling errors, typos, repeated words (such as "the the"), and incorrect capitalization (tHe).

The spelling checker typically hangs out on the Tools menu or in one of the program's toolbars. When you enter the command to check the spelling in the document, the spelling checker starts sniffing around in your document and then stops on the first questionable word it finds, as shown in Figure 11.4. You can skip the questionable word, replace it with a correction from the suggestion list, or type your own correction.

Some word processing programs also offer a tool that can check your document for grammatical errors, such as sentence fragments, subject/verb disagreement, passive voice, and run-on sentences. These grammar checkers work just like spelling checkers, stopping on questionable constructions and offering suggestions.

Word being questioned

List of suggested corrections

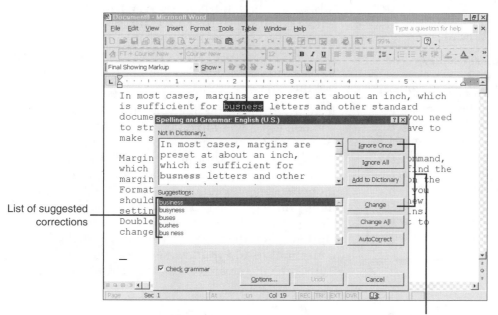

You can ignore the word or have the program correct it.

Figure 11.4

The spelling checker stops on questionable spellings and offers suggestions.

125

Redlining and AutoCorrect for Clean-As-You-Go Documents

The newest word processing programs automatically check your spelling on the go, giving you the feeling that your sixth grade English teacher is now living inside your computer. For example, Microsoft Word displays a squiggly red line under any words you type that do not match a word in Word's dictionary. You can right-click the word in question and choose a correct spelling from the context menu. If you have the grammar checker on, green squiggly lines mark common grammatical errors.

Whoa!

Although you should never send a document without running a spelling checker on it, don't think that a spelling checker or grammar checker will catch everything. If you typed to when you meant to type too, the spelling checker will not question you; "too" is spelled correctly; it's just the wrong word. The grammar checker might catch this, but you should proofread the document yourself.

Word also features AutoCorrect, which automatically corrects commonly mistyped and misspelled words and uppercases the first letter of the first word of a sentence. For example, if you type hte, AutoCorrect automatically changes it to "the." Sound great? Well, it is, assuming that when you type a string of characters, you agree with the correction. However, Auto-Correct also takes the initiative of replacing certain character strings with symbols, so if you mean to type :) and AutoCorrect inserts a happy face, you might not find it amusing.

If AutoCorrect is replacing your entry with a symbol you don't like, you can quickly press the **Backspace** key to retain your original entry. This undoes the AutoCorrect entry this time only; AutoCorrect will continue to "correct" your subsequent entries. For a more permanent solution or to add words you commonly mistype, you can configure AutoCorrect. Choose **Tools, AutoCorrect** (or **AutoCorrect Options**). You then can delete entries in the list of corrections or add your own entries. You can even use AutoCorrect to create your own electronic shorthand.

The Least You Need to Know

➤ You can use your **Delete** and **Backspace** keys to make minor edits.

➤ To select text in nearly any document, drag over the desired text to highlight it.

➤ To copy or cut text, highlight it and then choose the **Edit, Cut** command (to remove the highlighted text) or choose the **Edit, Copy** command (to retain the text and place a copy of it on the clipboard).

➤ To paste a selection you copied or pasted, move the insertion point to where you want it inserted and enter the **Edit, Paste** command.

➤ You can use the **Undo** or **Redo** commands to recover from accidental edits.

➤ You can use the **Edit, Find/Replace** function to make your word processing program replace one word or phrase with another word or phrase throughout your document.

➤ You can use a spelling checker, if your word processing program has one, to look for and correct most spelling errors.

Chapter 12

Sprucing Up Your Documents with Formatting

In This Chapter

➤ Widen your margins to fill the page length requirement for your next assignment

➤ Control the line spacing within and between paragraphs

➤ Make text big and bold like in newspaper headlines

➤ Make your word processor number the pages

➤ Use styles to quickly change the look of your text

Plain text just doesn't cut it anymore. People aren't satisfied with a typed page, no matter how ingenious its contents. If it doesn't look like the cover of *Rolling Stone*, your intended audience probably won't even pick it up. You need to add some character, some attitude. You need to format your text.

Messing with Margins

In most cases, margins are preset at about an inch, which is sufficient for business letters and other standard documents. However, if you're printing a poem or you need to stretch a four-page report to five pages, you need to make some adjustments. Margin settings often hide behind the Page Setup command, which typically is on the File menu. If you can't find the margin settings there, look for a similar command on the Format menu. When you find and select the command, you should get a dialog box like the one shown in Figure 12.1 that prompts you to enter new settings for the left, right, top, and bottom margins. Double-click in the text box whose setting you want to change and enter your change.

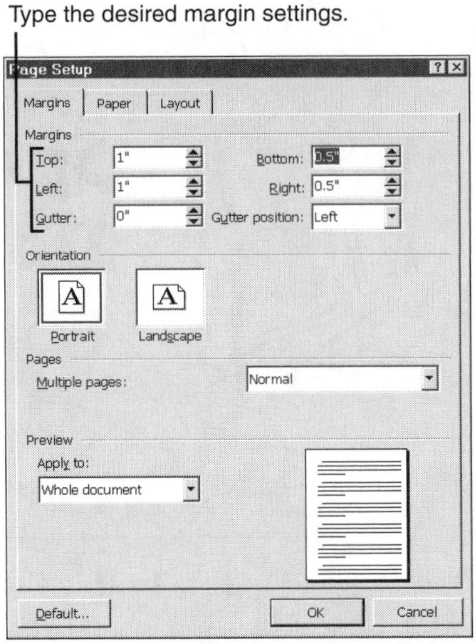

Type the desired margin settings.

Figure 12.1

The Page Setup dialog box typically contains the margin settings.

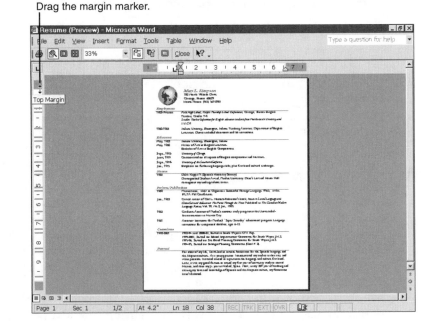

Another way to set margins is to choose the **Print Preview** command, available in most programs (try the File menu or the Standard toolbar; usually the topmost toolbar). This displays an aerial view of the page, as shown in Figure 12.2. Drag the margin markers to where you want the new margins placed.

Drag the margin marker.

Figure 12.2

Use Print Preview to set your margins.

Primping Your Paragraphs

It's tempting to do most of your paragraph formatting with the two universal formatting keys: the **spacebar** and the **Enter** key. Double space? No problem, just press **Enter** twice at the end of each line. Need to indent a paragraph? Just press the **spacebar** five times. The trouble with this approach is that it's sloppy, it makes it difficult to adjust text later, and formatting pros will snicker behind your back.

Word processors come with special paragraph formatting commands. To *format* an existing paragraph, click anywhere in the paragraph first; to format several paragraphs, select them (you need only select a portion of each paragraph you wish to format). In most programs, you go to **Format, Paragraph,** and you get a dialog box that enables you to enter all your preferences:

➤ **Line spacing**   You can single space, double space, or select a fraction; for example, 1.5 for a line and a half. In addition, you can specify the amount of space between this paragraph and the next one. For example, you can single space the lines within a paragraph and double space between paragraphs. That way, you don't have to press Enter twice to insert a blank line between two paragraphs.

➤ **Indents**   Normally, you indent the first line of each paragraph five spaces from the left margin. However, you also can indent the right side of a paragraph, or set off a long quote by indenting both sides. In addition, you can create a *hanging indent* for bulleted or numbered lists. (In a hanging indent, the first line appears without an indent, but all subsequent lines in the paragraph are indented.)

➤ **Alignment**   You can have text left-aligned (as normal), centered, right-aligned (pushed against the right margin), or fully justified (spread between margins as in newspaper columns).

Techno Talk

A document's **format** is its appearance as opposed to its content. When formatting a document, you change settings to improve its appearance. Formatting includes changing the margins and line spacing, changing text size and style, adding lines and shading, and numbering the pages.

Techno Talk

Some programs let you enter a setting for the *gutter margin*. The gutter margin adds space to the right side of left-hand pages and to the left side of right-hand pages, so you can bind the pages in a book.

➤ **Tab settings** Tab stops are typically set at every five spaces, so whenever you press the Tab key, the insertion point moves five spaces to the right. You can change both the tab stop position and its type. The tab stop type determines how the text is aligned on the tab stop, as shown in Figure 12.3.

Figure 12.3

The tab stop type controls how the text aligns itself on the tab stop.

| Left tab stop aligns the left side of each line on the tab stop. | Center tab stop centers the text under the tab stop. | Right tab stop moves the right side of each line against the tab stop. | Decimal tab stops are good for numbers: 12,345.89 198.67 2,198.90 |

Giving Your Characters More Character

To emphasize key words and phrases, you select from various *fonts* (also known as *typestyles*), sizes, and enhancements. In other words, you can make the letters look big and fancy like in a magazine. So, what's a font? A font is any set of characters that have the same design, such as Courier or Garamond. The font size is measured in *points*. (Just for reference, there are 72 points in an inch.) An enhancement is any variation that changes the appearance of the font. For example, boldface, italics, underlining, and color all are enhancements; the character's design and size stay the same, but an aspect of the type is changed.

Inside Tip

Most programs support the right mouse button. Drag over the text or cells you want to format and right-click the selection. If you get a pop-up menu, you're in business. Select the desired formatting option and enter your preferences.

To change fonts or typestyles, you select the text you want to change; then open the **Format** menu and choose **Font** or **Character.** This opens a dialog box, such as the one shown in Figure 12.4, that allows you to select the desired font, size, and enhancements. If you enter settings before you start typing, whatever you type appears as specified. (You can quickly change the font, size, or enhancements for selected words, phrases, or blocks of text by using buttons in the formatting toolbar. See "Quick Formatting with Rulers and Toolbars" later in this chapter.)

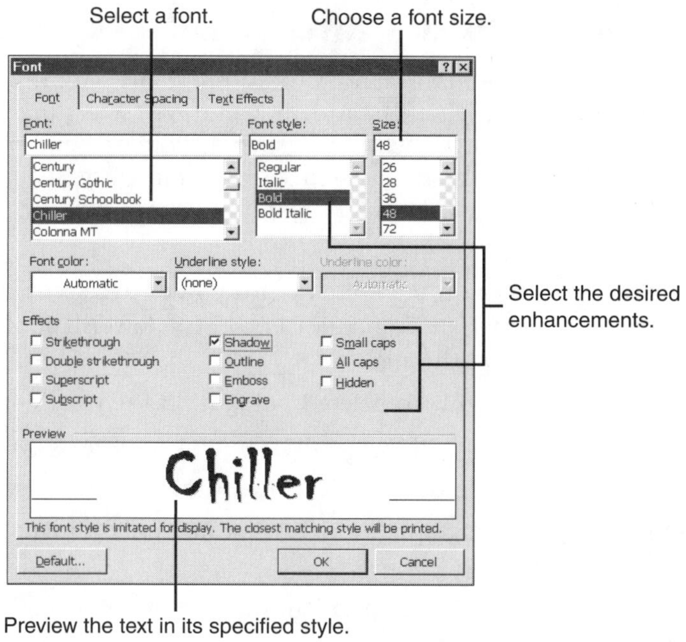

Select a font.   Choose a font size.

Figure 12.4

The Font dialog box gives you complete control over your text.

Select the desired enhancements.

Preview the text in its specified style.

Cell Formatting in Tables and Spreadsheets

Spreadsheets and tables have additional formatting needs. Not only can you change the fonts and text color for your entries; you also can add lines and shading to the cells and have values displayed as dollar amounts, percentages, or dates. In most programs, you get at these options by choosing **Format, Cell** or **Format, Borders and Shading**. The following list provides a rundown of the most common table and spreadsheet formatting options:

➤ **Alignment**   You usually want text aligned left within a cell. Dollar amounts typically are aligned along the decimal points.

➤ **Lines and shading**   You can add lines around the cells and shade cells to help mark rows and columns.

➤ **Column Width and Row Height**   If a column isn't wide enough for your entries, the spreadsheet might cut off the entry or display a value as a series of asterisks or number signs (#####). When this happens, you must widen the column. You usually can do this by dragging the right side of the column header (the box at the top of the column that contains the column's letter).

➤ **Value formatting**   When you type a number in a spreadsheet, it typically appears as a plain number (without a dollar sign or percent sign). To display these signs, select a value format.

133

Quick Formatting with Rulers and Toolbars

To give you quick access to commonly used formatting tools, programs typically provide a *formatting toolbar* near the top of the screen. To apply a format, select the text you want the format to affect and then click the button (such as Bold or Center) for the formatting you want to apply, or choose the desired setting from a list (such as the Font list). Onscreen rulers help you quickly indent text and change margins and tab stop settings (see Figure 12.5):

➤ To place a tab stop, click the button on the left end of the ruler to select the desired tab stop type (left, right, center, or decimal). Click in the lower half of the ruler where you want the tab stop positioned.

➤ To move a tab stop, drag it left or right. To delete it, drag it off the ruler.

➤ To indent the right side of a paragraph, drag the right indent marker to the left.

➤ To indent the left side of a paragraph, drag the left indent marker to the right.

➤ To indent only the first line of a paragraph, drag the first line indent marker to the right.

➤ To create a hanging indent, drag the hanging indent marker (or comparable control) to the right.

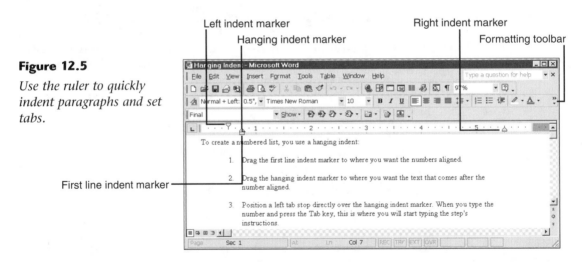

Figure 12.5

Use the ruler to quickly indent paragraphs and set tabs.

Left indent marker

Hanging indent marker

Right indent marker

Formatting toolbar

First line indent marker

Saving Time with Styles

Formatting probably is one of the most time-consuming and frustrating parts of making documents. You might spend hours tweaking your design before it looks just right. And when you're done, you don't want to put on a repeat performance. To help, many programs enable you to save your format settings and quickly apply them to other text in the same or other documents. You do this with *styles*.

Say you are creating a book, and each chapter title is to be set in 24-point New Century Schoolbook font, italic, and centered. Rather than change the font, style, point size, and indentation each time you type a chapter title, you can create a style called *Chapter Title*. This style would contain all the specified format settings. The next time you need to format a chapter title, you highlight the chapter title and choose the Chapter Title style. Check your application's online help system to learn how to access and make the best use of styles.

The biggest advantage of using styles is that you can quickly change the formatting of all the text formatted with a particular style. Suppose (in the preceding example) you decide the chapter title should be larger, say, 36-point type. Because you formatted all your chapter titles with the Chapter Title style, you can edit the style's definition changing the point size from 24 to 36. This changes all the chapter titles that were formatted with the Chapter Title style to 36-point type.

Inside Tip

Your word processor's formatting toolbar should have a drop-down list of styles you can use without having to create your own. For instance, Word's Style list includes styles for Heading 1, Heading 2, Heading 3, and Normal text. You can use these styles to quickly create an outline for a standard report. If you create a document using one of Word's templates, you get additional styles.

The Least You Need to Know

➤ To set the page margins, select **File, Page Setup** and enter your preferences.

➤ In most programs, you can center a paragraph by clicking anywhere in the paragraph and clicking the **Center** button in the Formatting toolbar.

➤ To change the line spacing and indents for a paragraph, open the **Format** menu, select **Paragraph**, and enter your preferences.

➤ To change the appearance of text in your documents, first select the text; then open the **Format** menu, choose **Font,** and enter your preferences.

➤ Highlight the text you want to format and right-click the selection to display a context menu featuring the most commonly used formatting options.

➤ Use the Formatting toolbar in most programs to quickly format your documents without having to wade through the Format menu commands.

Chapter 13

Picture This (Working with Graphics)

In This Chapter

➤ Add clip art to your letters, resumés, and spreadsheets

➤ Scan images and photos to paste in your documents

➤ Drag a picture to move or resize it

➤ Get text to wrap around a picture just like in a magazine

➤ Play graphic artist with Windows Paint

➤ Make your text look more graphical

In this age of information overload, most of us would rather look at a picture than wade through a sea of words. We don't want to read a newspaper column to find out how many trillions of dollars we owe as a nation. We want to glance at a graph that shows how much we owed in the year 2000 and how much we'll owe in the year 2010, or maybe a map that shows the percentage of families in the nation that could have built $100,000 homes given the amount of our debt. We want *USA Today*.

But what about your presentations and the documents you create? Are you as kind to your audience? Do you use pictures to present information more clearly and succinctly? Do you show as well as tell? After reading this chapter, you will know about several types of programs that will help you answer "yes" to these questions.

Clip Art for the Lazy and Untalented

Before we get into the nitty-gritty of graphics programs (drawing and painting programs), I should let you know that you might not need a graphics program. If you want to add pictures to your newsletters and other documents, you can buy collections of computerized clip art, sketches that some person born with artistic talent created using a graphics program.

Here's the scenario: You're creating a newsletter, and you want to spruce it up with some pictures. Nothing fancy; maybe a picture of a birthday cake for a company newsletter or a picture of a baseball player to mark upcoming games for the softball league. You create the newsletter and then enter a command telling the program to insert a piece of clip art. You select the piece you want, click **OK**, and voilá, instant illustration, no talent required!

Get It Where You Can: Sources of Clip Art

Some programs (desktop publishing, word processing, business presentation, and drawing programs) come with a collection of clip art on the installation disks or CDs. Some of this "free" clip art is very good—but some isn't fit for open house at the local preschool.

You also can purchase separate clip art libraries on disk just as you would purchase a program. These libraries typically include hundreds or even thousands of clip art images that are broken down into several categories: borders and backgrounds, computers, communications, people and places, animals, productivity and performance, time and money, travel and entertainment, words and symbols—you name it. Figure 13.1 shows a tiny sample of what one of the most popular clip art libraries, *MasterClips*, has to offer.

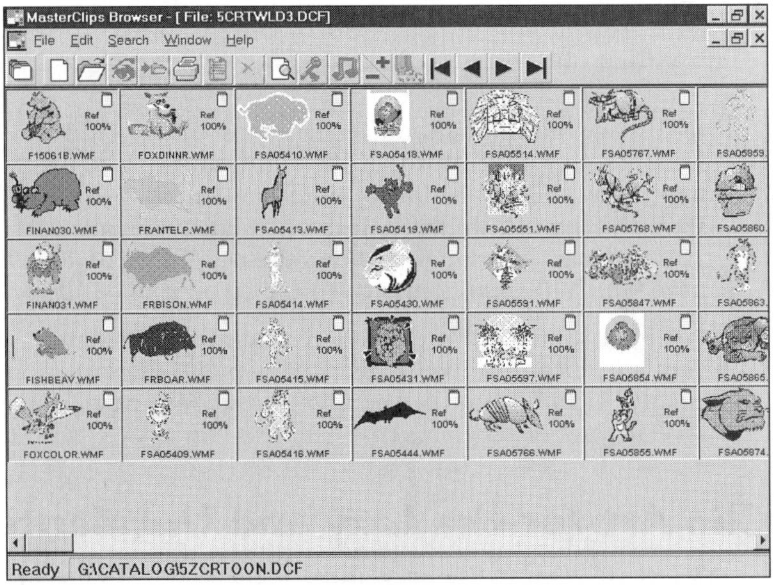

Figure 13.1

MasterClips *features a library consisting of hundreds of thousands of clip art images.*

You also can find gobs of graphics on the Internet, especially on the World Wide Web, as you'll see in Part 4, "Going Global with Modems, Online Services, and the Internet." You can use a Web search tool, as explained in Chapter 21, "Doing the Internet Shuffle," to find clip art libraries and samples. When you see an image you like, just right-click it and choose **Save Picture As.** (One warning, though: You shouldn't use a picture someone else created in your own publication without the artist's permission.)

Inside Tip

Before you plop down 50 bucks for a clip art library, make sure your word processing or desktop publishing program can handle the graphics format of the clip art. Most pictures are saved as .PCX, .BMP, .TIF, .JPG, or .GIF files, which most programs support. To determine which clip art formats your program supports, enter the Insert, Picture command (or its equivalent), and in the dialog box that appears, open the **Files of Type** drop-down list.

Pasting Clip Art on a Page

Now that you have a bushelful of clip art, how do you get it from the bushel into your documents? Well, that depends. Sometimes, you have to open the library, cut the picture you want, and paste it onto a page. Other times, you import or insert the image by specifying the name of the file in which the image is saved (it's sort of like opening a file). No matter how you do it, the program inserts the clip art in a box as shown in Figure 13.2. You then can use your mouse to shove the image around, stretch it, or squeeze it.

Hey, the Picture's Blocking My Text

When you lay a picture on top of text, the text typically moves to make room for the picture. In most programs, you can set text wrap options to control the way that text behaves around the picture. To set the text wrap options, click the picture and then enter the command for formatting the picture (for example, enter **Format, Picture**). The following list explains common text wrap options:

➤ **Square** Places the picture on an imaginary rectangle and wraps the text around the rectangle. For example, if you have a circular picture, you can set

139

text wrapping to square to prevent the text from following the curves of the circle.

➤ **Tight**   Makes the text follow the contour of the picture.

➤ **None**   Places the picture right on top of the text. Choose this only if you have a see-through picture that you want to use as a watermark. Otherwise, it will hide your text.

➤ **Top and Bottom**   Places text above and below the picture but does not wrap it around the sides.

➤ **Distance from Text**   Specifies how close the text can get to the image.

Figure 13.2

You can paste a piece of clip art onto a page.

Drag a corner of the object to resize it.

Drag the object itself to move it.

Scanning Photos, Drawings, and Illustrations

Another way that we, the artistically challenged, overcome our handicap is to scan photos and other images into the computer using a gadget cleverly called a *scanner*. A scanner is sort of like a copy machine, but instead of creating a paper copy of the original, it creates a digital copy that can be saved as a file. You can then print the image, fax it, or even insert it in a document.

Most scanners on the market are *flatbed* scanners. You lay the picture face down on the scanner's glass, and then run the scan program by pressing a button on the scanner or selecting the program from the Start, Programs menu. Another popular type of scanner is the *sheet fed*. With a sheet fed scanner, you load the original into a slot on the scanner, and the scanner pulls the original past its scanning mechanism to create the copy. The following steps run you through a typical scanning operation using a flatbed scanner:

1. Position the original image face down on the glass as specified in the scanner's documentation.

2. Press the button (on the scanner) to initiate the scanning program or click the scan program's name on the Windows desktop or the Start, Programs menu.

3. If necessary, select the command to start the scanning operation. This typically calls up a dialog box, like the one shown in Figure 13.3, that allows you to enter color settings, specify the resolution, and mark the area you want to scan.

4. If the dialog box has a button for previewing the image, click the button so you can mark the area you want to scan. Don't be shocked if the preview looks bad; the preview area typically shows a low-resolution version of the image.

5. Enter your preferences and click the Scan button (or its equivalent) to start scanning.

If you have an application that features TWAIN support, you can scan an image directly into a document. For example, in Microsoft Word, position the insertion point where you want the image inserted and choose **Insert, Picture, From Scanner or Camera.** Word runs your scanning program. Scan the image as you normally would. Open the scan program's **File** menu and choose the option to exit and return to your document. Word displays the image you just scanned.

Techno Talk

You can scan text documents as black-and-white images to file printed documents, such as contracts and bills, electronically. To edit the text on a scanned document, you first must convert the document to a text file using *OCR* (optical character recognition) software, which may or may not be included with your scanner. The OCR software converts the scanned text, which is in a bitmap format (each character made up of tiny dots) into text that you can edit in your word processor. The conversion is rarely completely accurate, so make sure you proofread the text carefully.

Figure 13.3

Before you scan an image, mark the area you want to scan and enter preferences for color and resolution.

Choose the desired color setting.

Select a resolution.

Mark the area you want to scan.

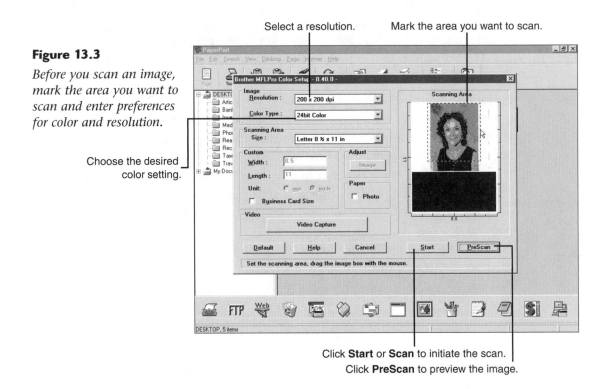

Click **Start** or **Scan** to initiate the scan.
Click **PreScan** to preview the image.

Watch the File Size!

When you first start playing with your scanner, the inclination is to crank up the resolution and color settings for the best possible scan. Don't. You'll end up packing your hard drive with 10-100MB files that are *too* good. Table 13.1 lists various resolutions and file sizes to help you gauge your scans.

Table 13.1   Increasing Resolution Increases File Size

Image size	Color depth	Resolution	File size
4×6 inch	24-bit	72dpi	360KB
4×6 inch	24-bit	300dpi	6.5MB
4×6 inch	24-bit	600dpi	26MB
8×10 inch	24-bit	600dpi	85MB

Tips for the Scan Master Wannabe

Anyone who can run a copy machine can scan an image—but only the master scanner knows how to do it right. Before you scan an image or document, you should check the scanner setup and options to make sure you obtain the optimum copy quality that requires the least amount of storage space for the intended use. Follow these guidelines to build a reputation as a master scanner:

➤ Don't overscan. If you're printing at 300dpi, scanning at 600dpi is a waste of time and disk space. In general, scan at 300dpi for outputting to most inkjet printers and 100dpi for Web pages and other electronic documents. Save the 1200dpi for high-end laser output or photo-quality output.

➤ Don't underscan. To scan large images (say 8×10 inches), scan at higher resolutions. If you're scanning small images (say 2.5×3 inches) and you plan on enlarging the image, scan at the maximum resolution so you don't lose details when you enlarge the image.

➤ Crop it. The larger the area you crop, the larger the file. Mark only the area you need to show before initiating the scan.

> **Notable Note**
>
> Many scan programs automatically save images in a special format that only the scan program recognizes. You might need to *export* the image to a different file format before you can paste it into your document. Check the scan program's File menu for an **Export** or **Save As** command. If you don't see such a command, check the program's documentation or help system.

➤ Use the right file type. BMP and TIFF are uncompressed file formats that produce the highest quality output. To save disk space, save scanned images in JPEG or GIF format. JPEG is referred to as a *lossy* format because it drops details from the image to reduce the size of the image file. JPEG graphics are commonly used on Web pages and sent by e-mail because they consume less space and travel faster across Internet connections.

Making Slide Shows and Overhead Transparencies

Even if you are not in sales or marketing, you probably have seen a business presentation sometime in your life—most likely on TV or in a movie. A sales or marketing representative stands up in front of the board of directors or some other group and shows a series of slides that pitch a new product or show how profitable the company is. How did that person create this presentation? Probably by using a presentation graphics program. Although this book doesn't provide the scope to describe the ins and outs of using every major presentation program, I can give you a pretty good idea of what they can do. Most presentation programs enable you to create the following:

➤ **Onscreen slide shows** You can create a slide show that plays on a computer screen. If you have the right equipment, you can project the onscreen slide show onto a projector screen or wall or play it on a TV. (This is the coolest way to go because you can include video clips, animation, music, and audio clips in your slide show.)

➤ **Web slide shows** You can create a slide show that other people can play on the Web. A user can open your Web slide show in his or her Web browser and click links or buttons to flip from one slide to the next. Of course, you need an Internet connection.

➤ **35mm slide shows** You can transform your presentation file into 35mm slides for viewing with a slide projector (great for encouraging unwelcome guests to leave early). If you don't have the required equipment to do this, you can send your presentation to a company that converts presentations into slides.

➤ **Overhead transparencies** Most printers will print your slide show on special transparency sheets instead of paper (or you can send them out to have them done). You then can display them with an overhead projector. (When printing transparencies, be sure to get transparency sheets that are specifically for printers; otherwise, you'll be sucking molten plastic out of your fancy laser printer!)

➤ **Audience handouts** Many business people use presentation graphics programs to create audience handouts, which can be used alone or in conjunction with slide shows.

If you're creating an onscreen slide show, you might be able to add some special effects:

➤ **Sounds** If your computer has a sound card (such as SoundBlaster), you can plug in a microphone and record your voice, music, or other sounds that will play when you move from one slide to the next.

➤ **Transitions** These are animated effects that control the movement from one slide to the next. For example, the current slide might transform into the next slide like vertical blinds.

➤ **Builds** This animation effect adds items to the slide while the audience looks on. For example, instead of displaying an entire bulleted list at once, a build would add one bullet at a time while you're giving your presentation.

All presentation programs are not alike. For information on how to work with a specific program, check your software documentation or pick up a book that's devoted to your presentation program.

Painting Your Own Picture

Remember the old Lite Brite toy? It consisted of a box with a light bulb in it, a pegboard, and a bunch of colored, translucent pegs. You stuck the pegs in the board in various patterns to create pictures. The light inside the box beamed through the holes in the pegboard, illuminating the lights. The same principle applies to paint programs. You turn on a bunch of onscreen dots to create a picture.

Windows comes with a paint program, called Paint, which you can find on the **Start, Programs, Accessories** menu. Run Paint to display the screen like the one shown in Figure 13.4.

Drawing and painting tools

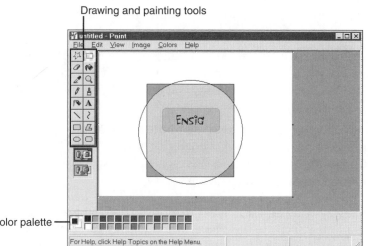

Color palette

Figure 13.4

Paint is a paint program that comes with Windows.

Once you have the Paint screen up, play around with some of the line, shape, and paint tools. The procedure is pretty basic: Click a line, shape, or paint tool (such as the Airbrush tool), choose a line thickness, and click a color. Then drag the mouse pointer over the "page." To create a filled shape, click the desired color for the inside of the shape, right-click the color for the outside of the shape and then drag your shape into existence.

Don't stop till you've tried out the paint can. Draw a closed shape on the screen (circle, square, whatever), and then click the paint can, click a color, and click anywhere inside the shape. I would tell you what to expect, but that would ruin the surprise. You can do much more in Paint, including adding text to your drawing, editing individual pixels (dots) on the screen, and using the color eraser to replace one color with another. Flip through the menus, and play around with the Zoom tool and other options.

Techno Talk

Your computer screen is essentially a canvas made up of hundreds of thousands of tiny lights called *pixels*. Whenever you type a character in a word processing program or draw a line with a paint or draw program, you activate a series of these pixels so that they form a recognizable shape onscreen.

145

Drawing Lines, Circles, and Other Shapes

You can purchase special drawing programs, such as Corel Draw, that allow you to create drawings by putting together a bunch of shapes. (The latest versions of word processors and desktop publishing programs include drawing tools that work much the same way.) For example, you might draw a cityscape by putting together a bunch of rectangles of various sizes and dimensions, or you might draw simple arrows, starbursts, or other objects right inside your documents. After working with Paint in the previous section, you might wonder how drawing tools differ from painting tools. Here are the main differences:

➤ In a drawing program, each shape is treated as a separate object. Think of each shape as being formed out of a pipe cleaner (you know, those fuzzy, flexible wire things). If you lay one shape on top of another, you can easily lift the shape off later without disturbing the other objects.

➤ In a paint program, think of each shape as being formed out of tiny beads. Each bead can be part of one shape, part of two overlapping shapes, or an individual speck in your painting. If the shapes share beads, you can't just lift one shape off the other without disturbing the other shape.

You draw a shape the same way you paint a shape: Click the shape you want to draw and then drag the mouse pointer to create the shape. You then can group shapes to move or resize them all at once, and you can shuffle the shapes to layer them on the page. If you have an advanced word processing or desktop publishing program, check its help system to see if it has a collection of drawing tools.

Moving and Resizing Your Graphics

Once you've drawn an object or inserted a piece of clip art or other picture in a document, handles appear around the object. You then can drag the object anywhere on-screen or change the object's shape, size, or orientation. To move an object, move the mouse pointer over the center or edge of the object (not on any of the handles). Hold down the mouse button and drag the object to the desired location.

To change an object's size or dimensions, move the mouse pointer over one of the handles and hold down the mouse button (this is commonly called *grabbing* a handle). Drag the handle toward the center of the object to make it smaller; drag the handle away from the center to make it larger. (You might need to hold down the **Shift** key while dragging a handle to ensure

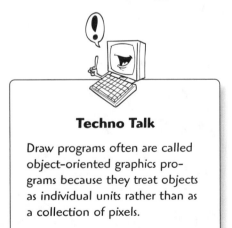

Techno Talk

Draw programs often are called object-oriented graphics programs because they treat objects as individual units rather than as a collection of pixels.

that the object's relative dimensions remain the same; otherwise, you might turn a tall skyscraper into a short, squat hut.)

The Painted Word: Text As Graphics

Although paint and draw programs are not designed to handle huge blocks of text, they do let you add labels and draw arrows to point out important areas of an illustration. Paint programs handle text as a series of pixels, making the text very difficult to edit. The process might require you to cut a portion of the text and paste in a revised portion. Aligning the revised text can be extremely difficult. Draw programs offer much more flexibility when dealing with text. The text is contained in a separate box and you can edit the text just as if you were using a word processing program.

Many desktop publishing and word processing programs also offer features that insert text as graphic objects. For example, Microsoft Word's WordArt feature enables you to create text objects that look like graphical banners. You can open the **Insert** menu, point to **Picture**, and click **WordArt**, and Word displays a selection of designs, as shown in Figure 13.5. After you choose the design you want and click OK, Word displays a dialog box that allows you to type your text.

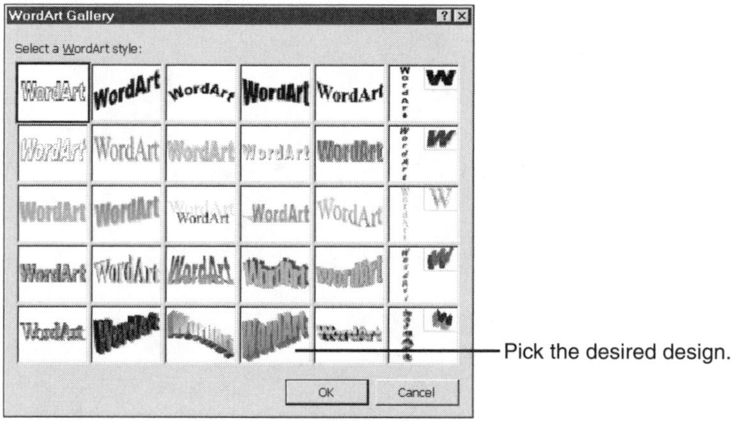

Figure 13.5

WordArt treats text as a graphic object.

Pick the desired design.

The Least You Need to Know

➤ You can insert clip art into a document you created in your word processing or desktop publishing program with the Insert command.

➤ To pull printed images or photos into your documents, you first must digitize them using a scanner.

➤ You can format a picture to control the way your program wraps text around it.

➤ You can paint your own picture using Windows Paint.

➤ Drawing programs enable you to create complex illustrations by assembling a collection of basic shapes.

➤ To resize a picture, drag one of its handles. To move a picture, drag it or drag one of its borders but not a handle.

Chapter 14

Printing and Faxing Your Creations

In This Chapter

➤ Install a printer in Windows

➤ Are you really ready to print?

➤ Check out your printing options

➤ Do other things while you print

➤ Faxing your documents without a fax machine

When printing goes as planned, nothing is simpler. You open the **File** menu, select **Print,** click the **OK** button, and then make yourself a pastrami sandwich while the printer spits out your document. However, rarely does a print job proceed without a glitch. You come back with your pastrami sandwich only to find a stack of papers covered with foreign symbols. Or you get an error message saying the printer's not ready. After hours of fiddling and mumbling, you find and correct the problem only to face a new problem: getting your printer back online.

In this chapter, you will learn all you need to know to print glitch free and recover from the occasional print failure. Additionally, if you need to fax your document, you learn how to transform your computer into a plain-paper fax machine and send faxes right from your applications.

Setting Up Your Printer in Windows

You can't just plug your printer into the printer port on your system unit and expect it to work. No, that would be far too easy. You also need to install a printer driver—instructions that tell your programs how to use your printer. (If you have a printer that supports plug-and-play, Windows leads you through the installation at startup.)

In Windows, you install one printer driver that tells Windows how to communicate with the printer. All your applications then communicate with the printer through Windows. When you set up a printer, Windows asks for the following information:

➤ **Printer make and model**   Windows comes with printer drivers for most common printers. In addition, your printer might have come with a disk containing an updated printer driver.

➤ **Printer port**   This is the connector at the back of the system unit into which you plug the printer. Most printers connect the LPT1 port, but many newer printers use the USB port. If you're not sure, but you know that the printer is plugged into the parallel printer port, try LPT1 (see Chapter 2, "Kick-Starting Your Computer" for information on identifying the ports).

Techno Talk

All printers are commonly categorized as either *parallel, serial,* or *USB.* Parallel printers connect to one of the system unit's parallel printer ports: LPT1 or LPT2. A serial printer connects to the system unit's serial port: COM1, COM2, or COM3. USB printers plug into one of the computer's USB ports. Most people use parallel or USB printers because they're faster; parallel and USB cables can transfer several instructions at once whereas a serial cable transfers them one at a time. However, serial communications are more reliable than parallel communications over long distances (16 feet or more).

When you installed Windows, the installation program asked you to select your printer from a list. If you did that, Windows is already set up to use your printer. If you're not sure, open the **Start** menu, point to **Settings,** and click **Printers.** If there's an icon for your printer, right-click it and make sure there's a check mark next to **Set As Default.** If there is no icon for your printer, take the following steps to install a printer driver for your printer:

1. If the Printers window is not displayed, click the **Start** button, point to **Settings,** and click **Printers.**

2. Double-click the **Add Printer** icon. The Add Printer Wizard appears.

3. Click the **Next** button. The next dialog box asks if you want to set up a network or local (desktop) printer.

4. Make sure **Local printer** is selected and click the **Next** button. A list of printer manufacturers and printer makes and models appears.

5. Take one of the following steps:

If your printer came with a disk or CD that has the printer driver for Windows, insert the disk, click the **Have Disk** button, and follow the onscreen instructions to select the printer driver. If you don't have a disk for the printer, you must use a printer driver that comes with Windows. Click the manufacturer of your printer in the **Manufacturers** list, click the specific printer model in the **Printers** list and then click the **Next** button (see Figure 14.1).

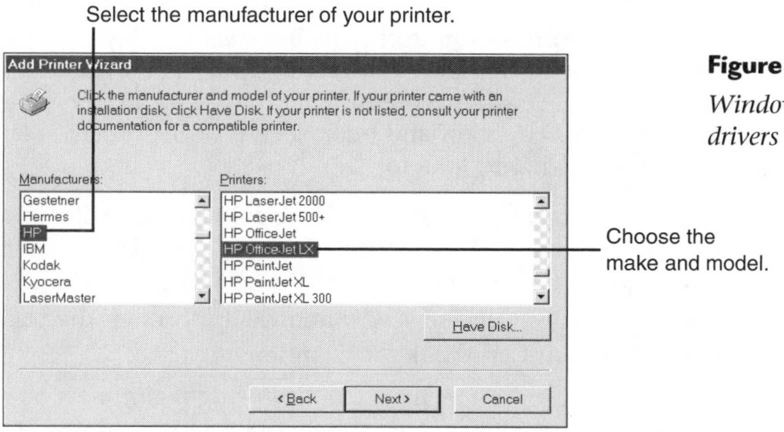

Select the manufacturer of your printer.

Figure 14.1

Windows includes printer drivers for most printers.

Choose the make and model.

6. Select the port into which you plugged your printer. This usually is LPT1 or USB. Click the **Next** button. You now are asked to type a name for the printer.

7. (Optional) Type a name for the printer. If you want to use this printer as the default printer, click **Yes**; then click the **Next** button. Windows asks if you want to print a test page.

8. Make sure your printer is on and has paper, click Yes, and click the **Finish** button. If you don't have a disk for the printer, a dialog box might appear telling you to insert the Windows CD.

151

9. If prompted to insert the Windows CD, insert the CD into your computer's CD-ROM drive and click **OK**. Windows copies the specified printer driver and prints a test page to make sure the printer is working properly.

If your printer did not appear on the list of printers and the printer did not come with its own Windows driver, you have several options:

➤ Select a printer that is like the one you have. For example, if an older model of your printer is listed, try selecting the older model.

➤ Select **Generic** in the Manufacturers list and click **Generic/Text Only** in the Printers list to print plain text. Do this only if you have a tight deadline and you need a printout of a text document really quick. Choosing a text only printer prevents you from printing any graphics or fancy fonts.

➤ Call the printer manufacturer and ask for an updated Windows driver for your printer. (If you have an Internet connection, usually you can copy the required driver from the printer manufacturer's Internet site. See Chapter 33, "Help! Finding Technical Support," for details.)

Preprint Checklist

Most programs display a print button in the toolbar that allows you to quickly send your document to the printer. It's tempting to click the button and see what happens. Resist the temptation. You can avoid nine out of ten printing problems by checking your document in Print Preview and making sure your printer is ready. The following checklist shows you what to look for:

➤ **Print Preview**   Most programs can display the document as it will appear in print. Open the **File** menu and choose **Print Preview** (or its equivalent command), or click the **Print Preview** button in the toolbar. Figure 14.2 shows a sample document in Word's Print Preview window. Flip through the pages to see how they will appear in print and look for the following:

   ➤ **Chopped text**   Many printers have a nonprinting region near the margins. If you set your margins so that the text falls in these areas, the text will be chopped off (not printed).

   ➤ **Strange page breaks**   If you want a paragraph or picture to appear on one page and it appears on the next or previous page, you might need to insert a page break manually.

   ➤ **Overall appearance**   Make sure your fonts look good next to one another, that text is aligned properly, and that no pictures are lying on top of text.

➤ **Does your printer have enough paper?**   If your printer runs out of paper, usually it will prompt you to load paper and then continue printing. However, sometimes this pause in the printing operation can cause problems.

➤ **Is the printer's On Line light lit?** When the online light is on, the printer has paper, is turned on, and is ready to print. If the printer is offline, Windows displays a message telling you so. You usually can put the printer back online by filling the printer with paper and then pressing the online button or its equivalent.

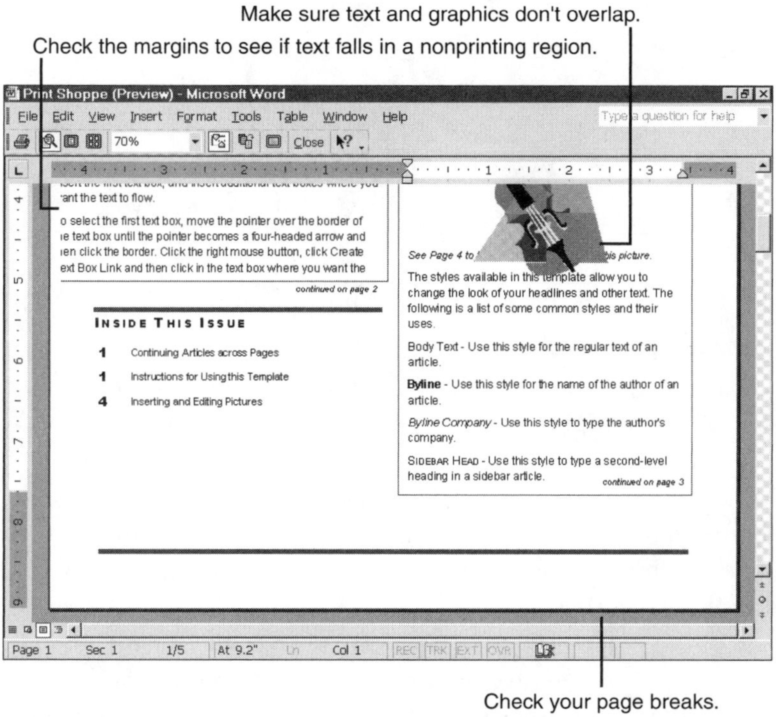

Make sure text and graphics don't overlap.
Check the margins to see if text falls in a nonprinting region.

Figure 14.2

Print Preview can reveal many problems you should correct before printing.

Check your page breaks.

Sending Documents to the Printer

Once your printer is installed and online, printing is a snap. Although the procedure for printing might vary, the following steps work in most Windows programs. If you just want to print one copy of your document, using the default settings click the **Print** button on the toolbar. If you need to customize a bit, follow these steps:

1. Open the document you want to print.

2. Open the **File** menu and click **Print.** The Print dialog box appears prompting you to enter instructions. Figure 14.3 shows a typical Print dialog box.

Figure 14.3

The Print dialog box lets you enter specific instructions.

[Print dialog box]
```
Print                                                    ? X
┌─ Printer ──────────────────────────────────────────────┐
│ Name:     Brother MFC-7000 Series        ▼    Properties │
│ Status:   Idle                                           │
│ Type:     Brother MFC-7000 Series                        │
│ Where:    \\Officepc\brother             ☐ Print to file │
│ Comment:                                 ☐ Manual duplex │
├─ Page range ─────────────┬─ Copies ────────────────────┤
│ ⦿ All                    │ Number of copies:  1      ▲▼ │
│ ○ Current page ○ Selection│                             │
│ ○ Pages:                 │   ┌─┐   ┌─┐    ☑ Collate     │
│ Enter page numbers and/or│   └─┘   └─┘                  │
│ page ranges separated by │                             │
│ commas. For example, 1,3,5–12                          │
├──────────────────────────┼─ Zoom ─────────────────────┤
│ Print what: Document showing markup ▼ │ Pages per sheet: 1 page ▼ │
│ Print: All pages in range ▼ │ Scale to paper size: No Scaling ▼ │
├──────────────────────────┴────────────────────────────┤
│ Options...                          OK        Cancel    │
└────────────────────────────────────────────────────────┘
```

3. In the **Print range** section, select one of the following options:

   ➤ **All** prints the entire document.

   ➤ **Selection** is available only if you highlighted text before choosing the Print command. Selection prints only the highlighted portion of the document.

   ➤ **Pages** prints only the specified pages. If you select this option, type entries in the **From** and **To** boxes to specify which pages you want to print. Some display a single text box into which you type the range of pages you want to print; for example, 3-10 or 3,5,7.

Inside Tip

To enter default settings for your printer (including the quality settings), click **Start, Settings, Printers**, right-click the icon for your printer, and click **Properties.** Enter your preferences and click **OK.** The default settings control the operation of the printer for all programs.

4. Click the arrow to the right of the **Print Quality** option (or click the **Options** or **Properties** button), and select the desired quality. (If you have a color printer, you might have the option of printing in grayscale or black and white.)

5. To print more than one copy of the document, type the desired number of copies in the **Copies** text box.

6. Click **OK.** The program starts printing the document. This could take a while depending on the print quality and on the document's length and complexity; documents that have lots of pictures take a long time.

7. Go make yourself a pastrami sandwich.

Whoa!

Did your printer spit out an extra blank page at the end of your document? If it did, you might have told it to by pressing the **Enter** key three or four times at the end of your document. That adds extra blank lines to your document, which can cause the program to insert a page break. If you see an extra page in Print Preview, delete everything after the last line of text in your document. Some programs also offer an option of spitting out a blank page to separate multiple documents. Check your printing options.

Managing Background Printing

Windows has a funny way of printing. Instead of printing directly to the printer, Windows sends all the information needed to print the document to your computer's hard disk. The printing information is stored in something called a *print queue* (a waiting line in which documents stand to be printed). Windows then feeds (*spools*) the printing information from the print queue to the printer as needed. This allows you to continue working in other programs while Windows prints your document.

If you ever need to stop, cancel, or resume printing, you must access the queue. Whenever you print a document in Windows, a picture of a printer appears next to the time in the taskbar. Double-click the printer icon to view the print queue, as shown in Figure 14.4. You then can perform the following steps to stop or resume printing:

➤ To pause all printing, open the **Printer** menu and select **Pause Printing.**

➤ To pause the printing of one or more documents, **Ctrl**+click each document in the queue, open the **Document** menu, and select **Pause Printing.**

Whoa!

If you choose to print only one copy of a document but your printer spits out several copies, this usually indicates that you printed the document more than once. When the printer doesn't start printing right away, many people lose patience and keep clicking the Print button. Each time you click the Print button, another copy of the document is sent to the queue, and your printer dutifully prints it.

➤ To resume printing, open the **Printer** or **Document** menu and click **Pause Printing**.

➤ To cancel all print jobs, open the **Printer** menu and select **Purge Print Jobs**.

➤ To cancel individual print jobs, **Ctrl+click** each print job you want to cancel, open the **Document** menu, and select **Cancel Printing**.

➤ To move a document in the print queue, drag it up or down.

If you choose to cancel printing, don't expect the printer to immediately cease and desist. Fancy printers have loads of memory and can store enough information to print several pages.

The Document menu controls printing for selected documents.

Figure 14.4

You can supervise and control printing using Print Manager.

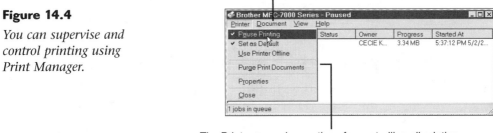

The Printer menu has options for controlling all printing.

Faxing Your Documents

Why spend extra money and further clutter your home or office with a separate fax machine when you can use your computer to send and receive faxes? That's right, with the right hardware and software, you can fax documents right from your applications or even fax printed documents. Here's a list of what you need to get started (you might already have some of this stuff):

➤ **Fax modem**   If your computer is less than five years old and has a modem, chances are that the modem is a fax modem. That is, it can send and receive faxes. It's likely that the modem came with its own fax software. Of course, you can't feed a paper document into the fax modem as you can with a standard fax machine, but you can fax the documents you type, and receive and print faxes.

➤ **Fax software**   To send and receive faxes, a fax modem needs special software, typically included with the modem. Check your Start, Programs menu and its submenus for program names that have "fax" in them.

➤ **Scanner**   To fax a paper document by fax modem, you need a device that can pull the image from the document and digitize it so your computer can use it. A scanner is just the tool you need. If you only want to receive faxes and fax documents you typed on your computer, you can skip the scanner.

Inside Tip

If you're in the market for a printer, get a multifunction printer and skip the fax modem, software, and scanner. Most multifunction printers can print, copy, scan, and fax. Some of these multifunction printers even have their own built-in fax modems, so you can use them just as you use a standard fax machine. Other multifunction devices use the computer's fax modem and special software to transmit faxes.

Faxing from Your Applications

You just finished typing a letter of praise to the service department at your local car dealership. You could print it and then run it down to the local print shop and have it faxed, but wouldn't it be cool if you could fax it as easily as you can print it? If you have a fax modem and your word processing application supports fax modems, you can fax your document right from the application.

First open the document you want to fax in the program you used to type it. Open the program's **File** menu and look for a **Send Fax** or **Send To** command (the Fax command might be hiding on a submenu). For example, in Microsoft Word, you choose **File, Send To, Fax Recipient.** Use the resulting dialog box, or series of dialog boxes to enter the recipient's name and fax number, choose a cover page, and initiate the fax operation. Word displays a series of dialog boxes, called the Fax Wizard, that lead you through the process (see Figure 14.5).

Faxing Paper Documents with a Scanner

With a scanner, a fax modem, and the proper software, you can scan pages and then fax them. It's likely that your fax modem or scanner came bundled with the software you need. One of the most popular scan programs bundled with scanners is Visioneer's PaperPort, so let's use it as an example. Here's what you would do to scan and fax a document using PaperPort:

Take one of the following steps:

➤ If you have a flatbed scanner, lay the document face down on the scanner's glass surface. (For multipage documents, start with the first page.)

➤ If you have a sheet-fed scanner, load the document into the feeder as instructed in your scanner's documentation.

157

Figure 14.5

Microsoft Word's Fax Wizard works along with your fax modem or multi-function printer to send a fax.

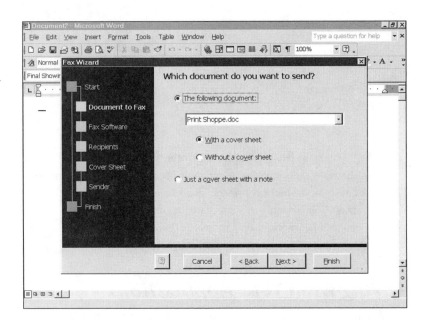

1. Scan the document as you normally would. (If you are prompted to choose a color setting, choose black and white or grayscale at 100 dpi.)

2. Repeat steps 1–3 to scan any additional pages of the document. The program displays a thumbnail image of each scanned page.

3. Select the pages you want to fax.

4. Enter the command to fax the document or drag one of the selected pages over the icon for your fax device and release the mouse button as shown in Figure 14.6.

5. Follow the onscreen instructions to enter the recipient's name and fax number, choose a cover page, and initiate the fax operation.

Receiving Faxes

Once you start sending faxes, you'll start receiving them, assuming, of course, that your computer is set up to receive faxes. If you have a multifunction machine with a built-in fax modem connected to a dedicated fax line, you don't have to do much to receive a fax. Just make sure your multifunction machine is connected to the phone line, is turned on, and has paper. The multifunction device will answer the phone when it rings, receive the incoming fax, and print it.

Select the pages you want to fax.

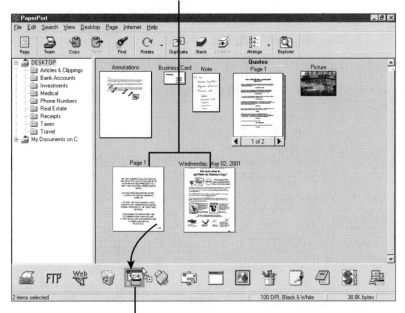

Drag one of the selected pages over the fax icon and release the mouse button.

Figure 14.6

With Visioneer's PaperPort software, you drag and drop your scanned document onto the fax icon.

If you plan to receive faxes through your computer's fax modem and software, make sure your computer is on and the fax software is running and is set up to receive faxes. You might need to enter special settings to specify how many times you want the phone to ring before the modem picks up. Some modem software is very advanced allowing you to set up the modem to answer the phone, play a recorded message, and store voice messages in addition to receiving faxes. Check the documentation to determine which settings you must enter.

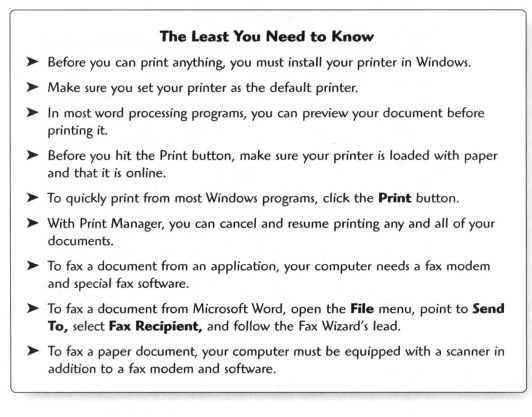

The Least You Need to Know

➤ Before you can print anything, you must install your printer in Windows.

➤ Make sure you set your printer as the default printer.

➤ In most word processing programs, you can preview your document before printing it.

➤ Before you hit the Print button, make sure your printer is loaded with paper and that it is online.

➤ To quickly print from most Windows programs, click the **Print** button.

➤ With Print Manager, you can cancel and resume printing any and all of your documents.

➤ To fax a document from an application, your computer needs a fax modem and special fax software.

➤ To fax a document from Microsoft Word, open the **File** menu, point to **Send To,** select **Fax Recipient,** and follow the Fax Wizard's lead.

➤ To fax a paper document, your computer must be equipped with a scanner in addition to a fax modem and software.

Surviving Without Documentation

Worst case scenario: You get a program, and there's no documentation. None of your friends know how to use the program, and the local bookstore doesn't have a book on the topic. What do you do? The following sections provide some tactics for dealing with such situations. Although they won't work for all programs, they will work for most.

Fake It with Online Help

Not so long ago, software developers gave you a book with your new program—some real documentation that told you how to enter commands and do something useful. Nowadays, you're lucky to get a pamphlet with installation instructions. In some cases, you get a CD and that's it—consider yourself lucky if you get a jewel case for it!

More and more software companies are cutting expenses by reducing or eliminating printed documentation. As a replacement, they provide the instructions through the program's help system or on special files that you'd never think of looking at. In most cases, you just open the **Help** menu, click **Contents** and **Index**, and then follow a trail of topics till you find the answer. The following sections show you how to navigate standard help systems.

Skipping Around with Hypertext Links

No matter how you get into a program's help system, you need some way to get around in the system once you're there. Most help systems contain *hypertext links,* as shown in Figure 15.1, that let you jump from one topic to another. The hypertext link is a highlighted word, phrase, or picture that, once selected, displays a definition of or additional information concerning that word or phrase. You usually have to click or double-click the hypertext link to display the additional information. Or you can tab to the link and press **Enter.**

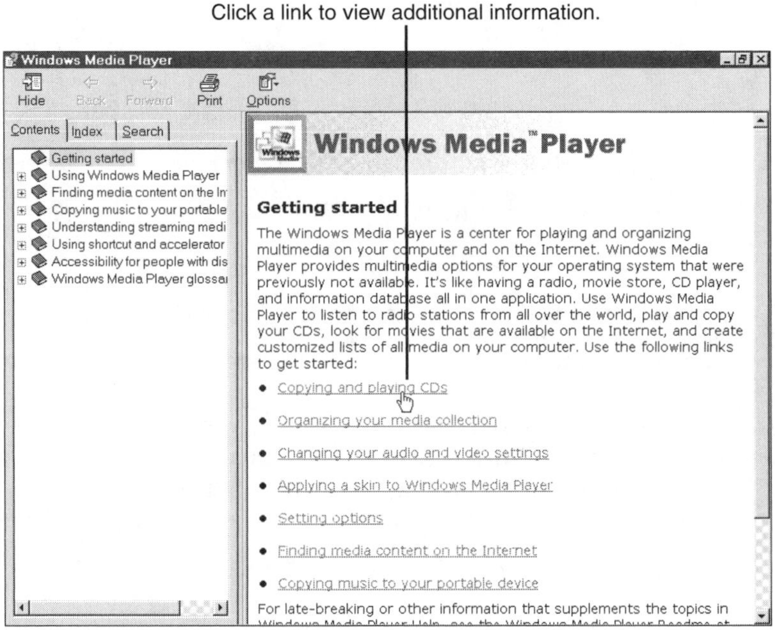

Click a link to view additional information.

Figure 15.1

Hypertext links let you jump from one topic to another.

Most help systems that allow you to jump from one topic to another also provide a way for jumping back. Look for the Back and History options. The **Back** option usually takes you back one topic at a time. The **History** option provides a list of topics you have looked at and allows you to select a topic from the list. These buttons vary from one help system to another, so be flexible.

Working with the Online Librarian

Advanced help systems usually provide a way for you to search for information on a specific topic or task. For example, you might want to search for information about setting margins or printing. Here's what you do:

1. Open the **Help** menu and click **Search,** or enter the **Search** command in the help system. (The Help window might have a **Find** button, tab, or some other way of searching.)

2. Start typing the name of the term or topic, as shown in Figure 15.2. As you type, a list of available topics that match what you type scrolls into view.

3. When you see the desired topic, double-click it, or highlight it and press **Enter.** A list of subtopics appears.

4. Double-click the desired subtopic. A Help window appears showing information that pertains to the selected subtopic.

Type here.

Double-click the desired topic.

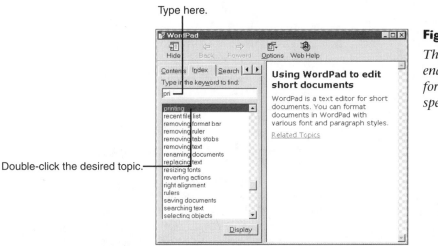

Figure 15.2

The Help System enables you to search for information on a specific topic.

What? No Help Menu?!

If you can't find a Help menu, don't give up. Some programs like to hide their help systems behind a keystroke. Try the following to call up the help system:

➤ Press the **F1** key. The F1 key is the 911 of the computer industry. Most programs use this key to call up the help system.

➤ Press the **F3** key. Some older programs prefer to use the F3 key for dialing help.

➤ Look for a Help button. Some programs display a Help button in a button bar or dialog box (it usually has a question mark on it). Click the **Help** button.

Inside Tip

One of the best ways to use a help system is to start performing the task and then press F1 when you get stuck. In most programs, this displays a *context-sensitive* help screen that provides the specific information you need to continue. However, some help systems aren't very perceptive when it comes to guessing what you're trying to do.

Inside Tip

The names of help files for Windows programs all end in .hlp. If you can't find the help file or you're just curious, click the **Start** button, point to **Find** or **Search,** and click **Files and Folders** or **For Files and Folders.** In the **Named** text box, type *.hlp. Open the **Look In** drop-down list and select the disk you want to search. Click the **Find Now** button to start the search.

If these techniques don't work, use My Computer or Windows Explorer to display the contents of the folder in which the program's files are stored. Look for a help icon, typically displayed as a book with a question mark on it. Double-click the **Help** icon. Windows opens the program's Help window.

A Built-In Tutor? You've Struck Gold

Some programs come with a tutorial that leads you through the process of using the program's major features. If you ran the Welcome to Windows tutorial, as explained in Chapter 5, you already have encountered an online tutor. In most Windows programs, you can get to the tutorial through the Help menu (assuming the help system features a tutorial). However, in some programs, you might have to run a separate program. In such cases, use My Computer or Windows Explorer to display the contents of the folder in which the program is stored, and look for a file with a name, such as TUTOR.EXE, TUTOR.COM, LEARN.EXE, or LEARN. COM. If you find such a file, double-click its name.

Getting Help in a Dialog Box

Some dialog boxes contain more than a hundred options spread out over a dozen or so tabs. Although the options are labeled, the labels might not tell you much. If you encounter a cryptic option in a dialog box, try the following to obtain additional information:

➤ **Press F1** If you're lucky, a context-sensitive help window appears displaying information about the dialog box and the options it contains.

➤ **Click the question mark button** If there's a question mark button in the upper-right corner of the dialog box, click the button and then click the option about which you want more information (see Figure 15.3). This typically displays a brief description of the option.

➤ **Right-click the option**   In many dialog boxes, right-clicking an option displays a menu containing a single option: What's This? Click **What's This?** to display a description of the option.

Notable Note

In an attempt to make your computer seem more personal, some programs, including Microsoft programs, offer animated characters that pop up on your screen whenever they think you need help. For example, if you start typing a letter in some versions of Microsoft Word, a cartoon character (an Office Assistant) might pop up and ask if you need help. Just click links as you would in a standard help system or click the **Close** button to tell him to go away.

Click this button and then click the desired option.

Figure 15.3

Context-sensitive help is available for most dialog box options.

Right-click the option and choose **What's This?**

Finding Answers in README.TXT

Most programs come with a help menu of some type, which is the most logical place to look for help. However, if you can't even get the program running (or running right), you won't be able to get into the help system. When that happens, the first thing you should do is look for a README file. A README file typically contains information about installing and running the program, details about how the program works, information about new features, and descriptions of known bugs.

Techno Talk

A *bug* is a problem in a program that causes it to behave erratically, lock up your system, and make you want to smash your computer with a baseball bat.

To view a README file, use My Computer or Windows Explorer to display the contents of the folder in which the program's files are stored or the contents of the program's installation disk or CD-ROM. Look for a file called README.TXT or README.DOC. If you have My Computer set up to hide filename extensions, you won't see the .TXT or .DOC. Instead, Windows indicates the file type graphically. A text (.TXT) file icon looks like a small spiral notebook; a document (.DOC) file icon appears with your word processor's logo on it (W, if you have Word). Double-click the file to open it in NotePad, WordPad, or in your word processor. Figure 15.4 shows the contents of a typical README.TXT file.

Figure 15.4

A typical README.TXT file displayed in Notepad.

```
README - Notepad                                              _ 8 X
File  Edit  Search  Help
README for SIMCITY 3000 UNLIMITED

For the latest up to date information on SimCity 3000 visit
http://www.simcity.com.


Table of Contents

SIMCITY 3000 UNLIMITED
        Performance Tips
        Troubleshooting
SIMCITY 3000 BUILDING ARCHITECT PLUS
        Performance Tips
        Custom Features
        Troubleshooting
SIMCITY 3000 SCENARIO CREATOR
        Performance Tips
        Troubleshooting
ONLINE REGISTRATION
GETTING SIMCITY UPDATES



SIMCITY 3000 UNLIMITED

Performance Tips
```

In rare cases, the README file is in the form of a program. If you find a file called README.BAT, README.COM, README.EXE, or a similar name with the extension .BAT, .COM, or .EXE, you can run the README file as you can run any program file: Just double-click its name.

The Least You Need to Know

➤ To get help in most Windows programs, check out the program's **Help** menu.

➤ Use the **Index** or **Search** features to find specific help on many topics.

➤ To obtain immediate help for a task you are currently trying to perform, try pressing the **F1** key.

➤ If you're having trouble in a dialog box, right-click an option and click **What's This?** to learn more about it. If there's a question mark button, click it and then click the desired option.

➤ Whenever you get a new program, locate its README.TXT file, open it in Wordpad or in your word processing program, and read through it to learn about bugs and other issues not addressed in the documentation.

Part 3

Get Organized! (Managing Disks, Folders, and Files)

You're a slave to your computer. You install programs where it tells you to install them. You save your document files to the default drive and folder. And when you stop using a program, you leave its files on your hard drive, afraid that any deletion will bring your system to a grinding halt.

In this part, you learn how to take control of your disks, folders, and files. You learn how to format floppy disks, create your own folders, rearrange files, and even remove some of the vagrant files that clutter your hard disk. And if you work on a network, you learn how to navigate its drives and resources.

Chapter 16

Formatting and Copying Floppy Disks and Recordable CDs

In This Chapter

➤ Format brand new floppy disks

➤ Reuse a floppy disk without formatting it

➤ Duplicate disks for fun and profit

➤ Preparing CD-R and CD-RW discs for data storage

In addition to acting as second-rate Frisbees and first-rate drink coasters, floppy disks and recordable CDs store files and enable you to transfer files from one computer to another. You simply copy the files from one computer to a floppy disk or CD and then insert the floppy disk or CD into the other computer and copy the files from it to the computer's hard drive. You can even send a floppy disk or CD in the mail to one of your friends or colleagues. However, before you can use them in this capacity, you need to know how to *format* the disks (prepare them to store data) and copy disks.

Making a Floppy Disk Useful

You get a brand-new box of disks. Can you use them to store information? Maybe. If the disks came preformatted, you can use them right out of the box. If they are not formatted, you must format them with a little help from Windows—but before you dive into this formatting thing, you should know that not all floppy disks are the same. Standard 3.5-inch disks come in two different capacities: 720KB (kilobytes) and

1.44MB (megabytes). Unless your computer is from the Stone Age, you have a 1.44MB drive, which can format and use 720KB or 1.44MB disks.

When formatting a disk, make sure you format to the *disk's* capacity not the *drive's* capacity; otherwise, you might lose data you try to store on the disk. (The disk's capacity should be marked on the disks or on the box that the disks came in; HD indicates "high density" or 1.44MB; DD indicates "double density" or 720KB.)

You can format disks using either My Computer or Windows Explorer. I prefer using My Computer because it's lying there right on my desktop. Just insert the unformatted disk and double-click its icon in My Computer or Windows Explorer; Windows displays a series of dialog boxes to lead you through the rest of the process, as shown in Figure 16.1. If My Computer displays the contents of the disk (or a blank window if the disk has no files on it), the disk is already formatted.

Techno Talk

Formatting divides a disk into small storage areas and creates a *file allocation table (FAT)* on the disk. Whenever you save a file to disk, the parts of the file are saved in one or more storage areas. The FAT functions as a classroom seating chart telling your computer the location of information on all of the disk's storage areas.

Figure 16.1

Enter your formatting preferences.

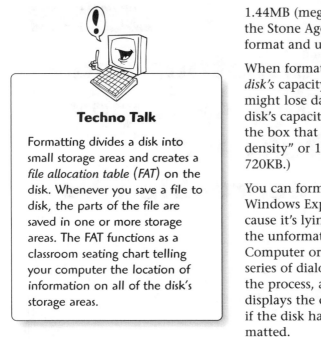

Specify the disk capacity.

Select **Quick** to reformat a disk or **Full** to format a new disk.

You can name the disk (its name or label will appear in My Computer).

Reusing Disks Without Losing Data

Once you've formatted a floppy disk, you shouldn't format it again because formatting erases any data stored on the disk. If you want to reuse the disk, make sure you no longer need the files it contains and then delete those files, as explained in Chapter 17, "Copying, Moving, and Nuking Folders and Files." If you start having problems with a disk, you might be able to fix it by *reformatting* the disk. However, I recommend you simply copy any salvageable files from the disk and then pitch the disk in the trash because it might have defective storage areas.

To reformat a disk, first copy any files you need from the disk to another floppy disk or to your hard disk. Insert the disk in the floppy disk drive, right-click the drive icon in My Computer, click **Format,** and follow the onscreen instructions.

Notable Note

Any of several factors can cause disk errors. The read/write head inside the disk drive might go out of alignment over years of use, storage areas on the disk might start to go bad, or the surface of the disk might be smudged or dirty. If you get disk errors with several floppy disks, have the disk drive cleaned, repaired, or replaced. If you're having trouble with a single disk, run ScanDisk on the disk as explained in "Refreshing and Repairing Disks with ScanDisk" in Chapter 27, "Do-It-Yourself Computer Tune-Ups." If ScanDisk makes the disk readable, copy files from the disk to a different disk or to your hard disk, and throw away the damaged disk.

Copying Disks for Friends and Colleagues

Although illegal, the main reason people copy floppy disks is to pirate software. For ten bucks, you can make Christmas presents for the entire family! I'm not going to lecture you on the evils of this practice. You know it's wrong, and if you thought there was any way you might get caught, you'd probably stop. However, I will say that the only reason you should copy floppy disks is so you can put your original program disks in a safe place, and use the copies for installing and using your program. Having done my duty for the software industry, let us proceed.

Get Some Blank Disks

To copy disks, obtain a set of blank disks that are the same size and density as the program disks you want to copy. You cannot copy low-density disks to high-density disks or vice versa. Don't worry about formatting the disks; your computer can format the disks during the copy operation. However, the copying will go faster if the disks are preformatted. While you're at it, write-protect the original disks (the ones you

173

want to copy; not the blank disks). This prevents you from accidentally copying a blank disk over an original disk and ruining it ... not that I've ever done that myself.

Copying Disks in Windows

You can copy disks using either My Computer or Windows Explorer. You simply right-click the icon for the diskette you want to copy, click the Copy command, and follow the onscreen instructions. The following is the step-by-step procedure as you would perform it in My Computer:

1. Insert the original disk you want to copy into one of the floppy disk drives.

2. Double-click **My Computer.**

3. Right-click the icon for the floppy disk drive and click **Copy Disk.** A dialog box appears, as shown in Figure 16.2, asking which drive you want to copy from and which drive you want to copy to.

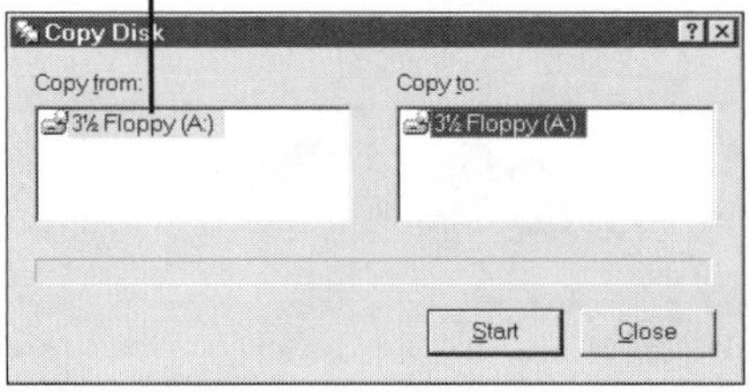

If you have only one floppy disk drive, you must use the same drive for the source and destination disks.

Figure 16.2

Windows asks which drives you want to use.

4. Click the same drive letter in the **Copy from** and **Copy to** lists.

5. Click the **Start** button.

6. Wait until a message appears telling you to insert the destination disk.

7. Remove the original disk and insert the destination disk.

8. Click **OK** and wait until the copying is complete.

Preparing Recordable CDs for Data Storage

If your computer has a *CD-R (CD-recordable)* or *CD-RW (CD-rewritable)* drive, you can use the drive to burn custom audio CDs and store data files on CDs. If you're planning to burn an audio CD, you don't need to format the CD. Just skip ahead to Chapter 29, "Now for the Fun Stuff! Computer Gadgets and Gizmos," to learn how to use an audio CD copy program to copy audio tracks from one or more CDs to a CD-R or CD-RW disc.

Before you can use a CD-R or CD-RW disc to store copies of files from your computer's hard drive (for backups or to transfer the files to another computer), you might need to format the disc. Windows Me and earlier versions of Windows have no built-in command for formatting recordable CDs, but your computer or CD-R/CD-RW drive should have come with its own program. (Windows XP includes a utility for formatting and copying CDs.)

The steps for formatting a CD vary depending on the formatting program you have, but you should be able to start your CD formatting program the same way you initiate a floppy disk format. Insert the CD-R or CD-RW disc in your CD drive, open **My Computer**, right-click the icon for your CD drive, and click **Format**. If the program prompts you to type a name or label for the disc, type a name (up to 11 characters in length) and click **OK**. If prompted to confirm the formatting, click **Yes** or **OK**, as shown in Figure 16.3. Once a CD-R or CD-RW disc is formatted, you can copy files to it using My Computer or Windows Explorer.

Whoa!

Formatting a CD-R or CD-RW disc to store data typically takes more than 25 minutes. When you're not busy working on your computer, format several discs, so you'll have them when you need them.

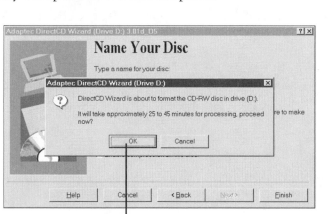

Click **OK** to initiate the formatting process.

Figure 16.3

You must format a CD-R or CD-RW disc before you can use it to store data files.

CD copying is fraught with errors. Frequently, the hard drive cannot feed information quickly enough to the CD-RW drive. This causes a buffer-underrun condition that can foul up the copy operation and even ruin the disc. To prevent buffer underruns, don't run any other programs during the copy operation, turn off any screen savers that might be turned on, scan and defragment your hard drive before you start (see Chapter 27), and (if possible) try performing the copy operation at a slower speed. If you still have problems, try a higher quality CD-R or CD-RW disc.

The Least You Need to Know

➤ You cannot save anything to a floppy disk unless the disk is formatted.

➤ You can reuse a disk without reformatting it by simply deleting the files stored on it.

➤ To clone a floppy disk, insert the disk you want to copy, right-click the icon for the floppy drive, click Copy Disk, and follow the onscreen instructions.

➤ To format a CD-R or CD-RW disc, insert the disk in your CD drive, right-click the CD's icon in My Computer, select **Format,** and follow the onscreen instructions.

Chapter 17

Copying, Moving, and Nuking Folders and Files

In This Chapter

➤ List the similarities between a landfill and a hard disk

➤ Jump from folder to folder in Windows

➤ Move files into a different folder

➤ Wipe out selected folders and files with a single click of the mouse

➤ Name a folder after your favorite actor

Right now, you might be thinking of your hard disk as an Information Age landfill. Each time you install a program, you can almost hear the dump truck beeping as it backs up to your disk, your hard disk groaning under the added burden. You wonder where future generations are going to dump their files.

Without *folders* (also called *directories*), this image might be accurate, but folders help organize the files into logical groups making them much easier to find and manage—assuming you know what you're doing. In this chapter, you learn how to take control of the files and folders on your disks by cleaning them up and making them more organized.

Climbing the Directory Tree

Before you lay your fingers on any folders or files, you should understand the basic structure of a directory tree. Shake that landfill analogy out of your mind and start thinking of your disk as a big, sterile filing cabinet stuffed with manila folders. Each folder represents a directory that stores files or additional folders.

The structure of a typical hard disk is shown in Figure 17.1. The monkey at the top of the tree, C:\, is the root directory; other directories branch off from the root. In the figure, the HOME folder branches off from the root directory (C:\) and includes four subfolders: MEGHAN, RYAN, MEDICAL, and TAXSTUFF. Each of these subfolders contains files. (Don't ask me why the root is at the top of the tree; that's just the way it is.)

Figure 17.1

A typical directory tree.

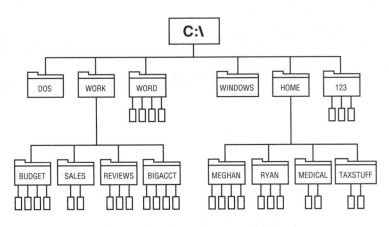

Techno Talk

A *path* is a map to the desired drive and folder. For example, in the figure, the path to the MEGHAN folder is C:\HOME\ MEGHAN. Backslashes are used to separate the folder names. When opening a file, you can type a path to its folder rather than double-clicking a series of folders and subfolders.

Selecting Folders and Files

If you're copying, deleting, or moving a single file or folder, selecting it is about as easy as picking a losing lottery number. If the file or folder name is underlined (Windows Web Style is on), simply rest the tip of the mouse pointer on the icon for the file or folder (in Windows Explorer, or My Computer). If the file or folder name is not underlined, click the file or folder. You would think that if you clicked another file or folder you'd select that one, too, but it doesn't work that way. Selecting another file deselects the first one. This can be maddening to anyone who doesn't know the tricks for selecting multiple files or folders; here's how you do it:

➤ To select neighboring (*contiguous*) files and folders, click the first file or folder and hold down the **Shift** key while pointing to or clicking the last one in the group (see Figure 17.2).

➤ To select nonneighboring (*noncontiguous*) items, hold down the **Ctrl** key while pointing to or clicking the name of each item.

➤ To deselect an item, hold down the **Ctrl** key while pointing to or clicking its name.

➤ You also can select a group of items by dragging a box around them. When you release the mouse button, all the items in the box are highlighted.

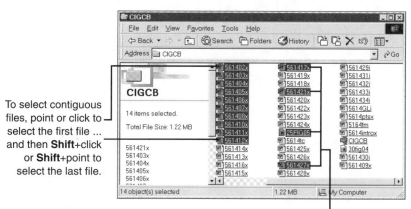

Figure 17.2

You can use the Shift and Control keys to select neighboring or nonneighboring files.

To select contiguous files, point or click to select the first file ... and then **Shift**+click or **Shift**+point to select the last file.

Ctrl+click or **Ctrl**+point to select noncontiguous files.

Keep in mind that if Web Style is on, you point to files or folders to select them and you click to open files or folders. With Web Style off, you click to select and double-click to open. To turn Web Style or single-click access on or off, open the **Tools** or **View** menu, click **Folder Options**, and enter your preferences.

If you're selecting groups of files, it often helps to change the way the files are sorted or arranged. Open the **View** menu and choose to sort files by name, by type (using their filename extensions), by size, or by date. For example, you can sort files by type to list all the document files that end in .DOC. You also can arrange the icons by opening the **View** menu and selecting one of the following options:

➤ **Large Icons**   Good if you want to select only a few files or folders.

Inside Tip

In Small Icons view, if you click an item in one column and **Shift**+click an item in another column, you select a rectangular block of items, just as if you had dragged a box around them. In List view, items snake up and down a page like newspaper columns. If you click an item in one column and **Shift**+click an item in another column, you select the two items you clicked and all the items in between.

179

➤ **Small Icons**   Displays tiny icons. Folders appear at the top, files at the bottom. In this display, you can drag a box around items down and to the right.

➤ **List**   Displays tiny icons (just like Small Icons view), but folders (directories) are listed on the left; files are listed on the right.

➤ **Details**   Displays additional information, such as the date and time at which files were created. (This view makes it tough to manage large numbers of files.)

Making Your Own Folders

You rarely need to create your own folders. When you install a program, it usually makes the folders it requires or uses existing folders. However, you need to make folders for your own data files so don't get mixed up with all your program files.

When creating folders, try to follow one rule: Keep the folder structure shallow. If you bury a file eight subfolders deep, you're going to have to do a lot of digging to get it out. On my drive, I have one folder for everything everyone in the family creates. It's called DATA. Under it, I have a subfolder for each book I write, a subfolder for my personal files, a subfolder for tax records, and a subfolder for the files that my kids and wife create. Most of the files are buried only two or three levels deep. This structure also makes it easy to back up only the data files we have created. I simply tell my backup program to back up the DATA folder and all its subfolders.

In Windows, you can create folders all over the place: in My Computer, Windows Explorer, or even on the Windows desktop. Give it a shot; try creating a new folder on drive C. You can always delete the folder later if you don't need it. Follow these steps:

Inside Tip

If the Windows desktop becomes too crowded with shortcuts and other icons, you can create folders to help organize the desktop. Right-click a blank area of the desktop, point to **New,** and click **Folder.**

1. Double-click the **My Computer** icon.

2. Double-click the icon for drive **C**. A window opens showing all the folders on drive C.

3. Right-click a blank area inside the window to display a shortcut menu.

4. Rest the mouse pointer on **New** and click **Folder,** as shown in Figure 17.3. Windows creates a folder on drive C, cleverly called New Folder.

5. Type a name for the folder (255 characters or fewer). As you start typing, the **New Folder** name is deleted and is replaced by what you type. You can use any character or number, but you cannot use any of the following characters: \ / : * ? " < > |.

6. Press **Enter.**

180

Click **Folder**.   Right-click a blank area in the window.

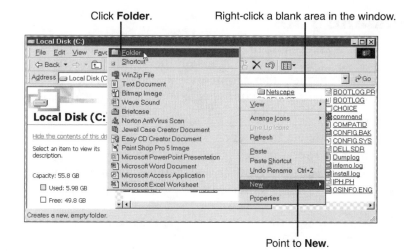

Point to **New**.

Figure 17.3

A new folder is a right-click away.

Long names (255 characters for folders and files) are great for programs that support them, but some older programs and DOS cannot display long names. In such cases, the program displays a portion of the name, such as letter~1.doc. This does not affect the contents of the file, and you can still open it.

Nuking Folders and Files

As you install programs and create your own document files, your computer's hard drive can become cluttered. You need some way to remove files you no longer use in order to free up some disk space. With Windows, you have all sorts of ways to delete folders and files. Take any of the following steps:

➤ Select the file or folder you want to delete and click the **Delete** button (the button with the big **X** on it) on the toolbar.

➤ Select the file or folder you want to delete and press the **Delete** key.

➤ Right-click a selected file or folder and click **Delete**.

➤ Resize the My Computer or Windows Explorer window so that you can see the Recycle Bin icon. Drag the selected file or folder over the **Recycle Bin** icon and release the mouse button.

When you delete one or more files or folders, Windows displays a dialog box or two asking you to confirm the deletion. When you respond accordingly, the selected items go away. If you accidentally delete a file or folder, you can drag it out of the Recycle Bin, as explained in Chapter 5, "Windows Survival Guide." Better yet, just right-click the file in the Recycle Bin window and click **Restore**. The Recycle Bin restores the file to its original location.

181

Renaming Folders and Files

Managing your folders and files is an exercise in on-the-job training. As you create and use folders, you find yourself slapping any old name on them. Later, you find that the name doesn't really indicate the folder's contents, the name is too long, or you are just plain sick of seeing it snake across your screen. Fortunately, renaming a folder or file is easy:

➤ If you click files and folders to select them, click the icon for the file or folder you want to rename. The name appears highlighted, as shown in Figure 17.4. Click the name of the file or folder and type the new name. Click a blank area of the screen to make the name change official.

When you choose to rename a file or folder, Windows highlights the current name.

Figure 17.4

You can easily rename files and folders.

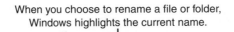

Type a new name and then press **Enter**.

Whoa!

My Computer and Windows Explorer both sport a toolbar that contains an Undo button. If you delete a file or folder by mistake, you can quickly get it back by clicking the **Undo** button or pressing **Ctrl+Z**.

➤ If you point to files and folders to select them, right-click the file or folder you want to rename and click **Rename**. Type the new name and press **Enter** or click a blank area in the window.

➤ Whether you point to or click files or folders to select them, highlight the file or folder name by pointing at it or clicking it, press the **F2** key, and type the new name. Press **Enter**.

In Windows 98 you might have trouble renaming files when View as Web Page is on. If Windows won't let you rename a file, open the **View** menu, click **View as Web Page**, and then rename the file.

Moving and Copying Folders and Files

You can quickly move files and folders to reorganize your hard disk. To move an item, simply drag it over the folder or disk icon to which you want to move it. When moving or copying files and folders, keep the following in mind:

Whoa!

Windows uses the names of program folders to find the program files it needs to run the programs. If you rename a program folder or file, Windows usually throws a fit and won't run the program for you.

➤ To copy or move multiple files or folders, select the items as explained earlier in this chapter. When you copy or move one of the selected items, all the other items follow it.

➤ If you drag a folder or file to a different disk (or a folder on a different disk), Windows assumes that you want to *copy* the item to that disk. To move the item, hold down the **Shift** key while dragging.

➤ If you drag a folder or file to a different folder on the same disk, Windows assumes that you want to *move* the item into the destination folder. To copy the item, hold down the **Ctrl** key while dragging.

➤ To move a file or folder to the Windows desktop, drag it from My Computer or Windows Explorer onto a blank area on the desktop and release the mouse button.

➤ If you're not sure what you want to do, drag the folder or file with the right mouse button. When you release the button, a context menu appears presenting options for moving or copying the item.

Sometimes the easiest way to move a file or folder is to cut and paste it. Right-click the icon for the item you want to move and click **Cut**. Now change to the disk or folder in which you want the cut item placed. Right-click the disk or folder icon (or right-click a blank area in its contents window), and click **Paste**. You also can copy and move items in Windows Explorer by dragging items from the Contents list (right pane) over a disk or folder icon displayed in the left pane, as shown in Figure 17.5. You also can drag items from one My Computer window to another.

Select the folder(s) or file(s) you want to move.

Figure 17.5

In Windows Explorer, you drag files or folders from the Contents list to a disk or folder icon.

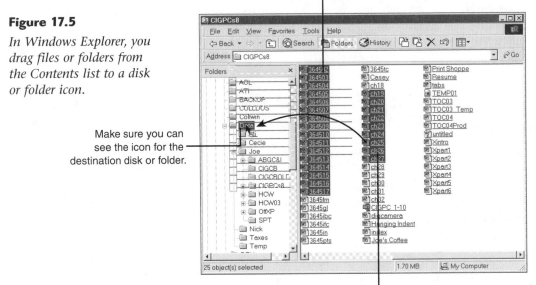

Make sure you can see the icon for the destination disk or folder.

Drag selected file(s) or folder(s) over the destination icon.

The Least You Need to Know

➤ **Shift+**click with your mouse to select neighboring files or folders in a list.

➤ **Ctrl+**click to select nonneighboring files or folders.

➤ To make your own folder, right-click a blank area, click **New, Folder,** and then type a name for the folder.

➤ Delete files or folders by dragging and dropping them into the **Recycle Bin.**

➤ Undelete files or folders by dragging them out of the **Recycle Bin.**

➤ Rename your files and folders.

➤ Move and copy files and folders using My Computer or Windows Explorer.

Chapter 18

Networking (for Those Corporate Types)

In This Chapter

➤ Learn enough about networking to fake your way through your next job interview

➤ Log on to a network so you can use stuff that's not on your computer

➤ Check out what's available on your network

➤ Make a folder on the network look like a folder on your computer

➤ Print a document from your computer to a printer that's not even connected to your computer

You have mastered the basics of using your computer. You can run programs; make documents; print, copy, and move files; and even dazzle colleagues with the Windows tricks you've learned. Now you find you need to deal with a network. Maybe your boss at work decided to install a network or you have two or more computers in your home, and you'd like to connect them to share a printer or an Internet connection or swap files and other resources between the computers. Whatever the case, you now face the challenge of navigating the network.

Perhaps you've heard about networks, and maybe you even have a general understanding of the concept behind them but you've never actually worked on a network, and you don't know what to expect. In this chapter, you will learn how to use several Windows features designed especially for networks so that you can get up to speed in a hurry.

Do I Need a Network?

When you think of networks, you usually think of large corporations. However, networks are popping up in churches, small businesses, home offices, and anywhere else two or more computers live. Why? Because when people have two or more computers, they find they need an easy way to exchange data among those computers and share expensive hardware.

For example, say you work out of your home and you have two kids, each of whom has his or her own computer. Without a network, you need three of everything: three modems, three color printers, and so on. With a network you can buy a top-of-the-line printer and the best modem on the market, connect the devices to any one of the computers on the network, and all of you can share those devices. In addition, you can quickly send each other messages and use a central calendar to keep everyone up to date. Of course, you have to shell out some money for the network cards and cables to connect the computers, but you still save money in the long run.

Inside Tip

I have networked the three computers in my home twice in the last five years. The first time, I bought the standard network cards and cables and struggled an entire weekend running network cable and getting the darn thing up and running. The second time, I purchased three Intel AnyPoint wireless USB devices, plugged one into each computer, installed the software that was included, and spent the weekend with my wife and kids. The installation took about an hour. (I had to add a USB port to the two older computers, but that was easier and cheaper than installing network cards.) If you're considering networking the computers in your home, I strongly recommend that you go wireless.

Client-Server Versus Peer-to-Peer Networks

The two basic types of networks are *client-server* and *peer-to-peer*. On a client-server network, all computers (the clients) are wired to a central computer (the network server), as shown in Figure 18.1. Whenever you need to access a network resource, you connect to the server, which then processes your commands and requests, links you to the other computers, and provides access to shared equipment and other resources. Although somewhat expensive and difficult to set up, a client-server network offers two big advantages: It is easy to maintain centrally through the network server, and it ensures reliable data transfers.

On a peer-to-peer network, computers are linked directly to each other without the use of a central computer, as shown in Figure 18.2. Each computer has a network card that is connected through a network cable to another computer or to a central hub (a connection box). Many small businesses use this peer-to-peer configuration because it doesn't require an expensive network server, and it is relatively easy to set up. However, a peer-to-peer network does have a few drawbacks: It is more difficult to manage, more susceptible to *packet collisions* (which occur when two computers request the same data at the same time) and is not very secure because no central computer is in charge of validating user identities.

Techno Talk

Client–server networks typically have a network administrator who is in charge of assigning access privileges to each computer on the network. For example, some users might only be able to open data files on the server and might not be able to run certain programs. The administrator assigns each user a user name and password. You then must enter your user name and password to log on to the network.

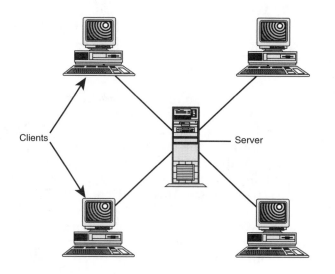

Figure 18.1

On a client-server network, clients are connected to a central server.

Figure 18.2

On a peer-to-peer network, each computer acts both as a client and a server.

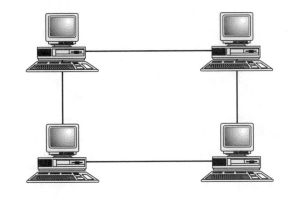

Logging On and Logging Off

To connect your computer to the network, you must log on with your username and password. This identifies you on the network and Windows establishes the connection between your computer and the other computers on the network, so you can access shared files and resources. If the network has an administrator, the administrator assigns the username and password. If you are on a small network, you and the other people on the network can discuss the usernames and passwords you want to use. The procedure for logging on is easy:

1. When you start your computer, Windows displays the Enter Network Password dialog box with your name in the User Name text box.

2. Type your password and click **OK**.

Techno Talk

An *intranet* is simply a network that is set up to look and act like the Internet, which you learn more about in Chapter 21, "Doing the Internet Shuffle." Corporations commonly set up their networks as intranets to make them easier to manage and use. Unlike the Internet, which encourages public access, most intranets are for internal use only.

If you are working on a client-server network, you should be aware that when you are using a program or file on the server, you can lose your work if the server is shut down for any reason. Often, the network administrator shuts down the server for maintenance. The administrator should notify all users in advance so that they can save their work and exit any programs before the shutdown. However, if the server crashes, you are automatically disconnected from the network and any changes you have made to a network file might be lost.

On a peer-to-peer network, you also can lose your connection with another computer on the network if that computer happens to lock up or its user decides to shut it down without asking for your okay.

Sharing Resources on Your Computer

Before you can access disks, folders, files, and printers on your network, the person whose resources you want to use must give you access to his or her computer. For example, a person might want everyone on the network to have access to a customer database but probably would not want to allow everyone on the network to modify that database.

The user or network administrator can assign various levels of access to specific users or resources to prevent unauthorized use of a particular resource on the server. In addition, before anyone else can access files or folders on your computer, you must enter settings that give that person access to your computer. To enable other users to access folders or files on your computer in Windows 95 or later versions, take the following steps:

1. Run My Computer or Windows Explorer.

2. Right-click the icon for the disk or folder you want to share and choose **Sharing.** The Properties dialog box for the selected disk or folder appears with the Sharing tab in front, as shown in Figure 18.3.

3. Click **Shared As.**

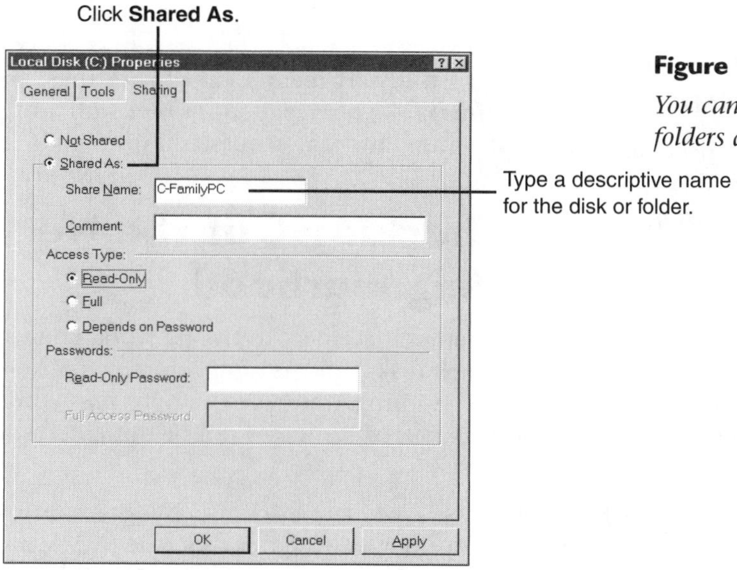

Click **Shared As.**

Figure 18.3

You can mark disks or folders as shared.

Type a descriptive name for the disk or folder.

4. The Share Name text box automatically displays the drive's letter or the folder's name as it will appear to users who access your computer. You can type a different entry in this text box if desired.

Inside Tip

To provide access to a disk or folder without prompting the person for a password, leave the Password text boxes blank. This saves time on a small network on which you fully trust the other users.

Notable Note

To terminate sharing, right-click the icon for the disk, folder, or printer and choose **Sharing**. Select **Not Shared** and click **OK**.

5. (Optional) Type any additional information in the **Comment** text box.

6. Under **Access Type**, choose the desired share option: **Read-Only** (to enable people to look at files on the disk or folder but not change them), **Full** (to authorize people to open and save files to the disk or folder), or **Depends on Password** (to use a different password for read-only or full access).

7. Under **Passwords**, type the password that people must enter to access the drive or folder. (If you chose Depends on Password in the previous step, enter a different password for read-only and full access.) Click **OK**.

8. If you entered a password, Windows prompts you to confirm it. Type the password again and click **OK**. You are returned to My Computer or Windows Explorer, and a hand appears below the icon for the shared disk or folder.

You also can enable other users to share your printer. Open the **Start** menu, point to **Settings**, and click **Printers**. Right-click your printer icon and choose **Sharing**. Enter the requested information and click **OK**.

Checking Out the Network Neighborhood

When you connect to the network, you can access any shared disks, folders, and printers on other computers that are connected to the network assuming you have the right password (if a password is required). However, locating shared resources can be difficult, especially on a large network.

Fortunately, Windows has tools to help you track down network resources and manage them. The most basic tool is the Network Neighborhood or My Network Places. When you click the **Network Neighborhood** icon or the **My Network Places** icon on the Windows desktop, a window displays icons for all the computers that are on the network. You then can browse the shared resources on that computer just as if they were on your computer. Figure 18.4 shows drive C on a network computer as viewed from another computer on the network.

A disk on the network computer
appears as a folder on your computer.

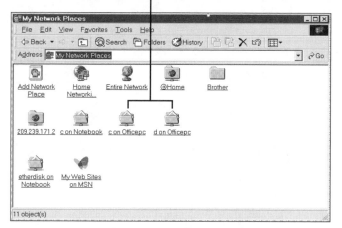

Figure 18.4
My Network Places displays icons for network resources.

Mapping a Network Drive to Your Computer

If you frequently access a particular disk or folder on the network, you can map the disk or folder to a drive on your computer or create an icon for it in My Network Places. Your computer then displays the disk or folder as a folder in My Computer and in the Save As or Open dialog box in any Windows program you use. This enables you to access the disk or folder just as easily as if it were on your computer.

The steps for mapping a network drive vary depending on the version of Windows you're using. If you're running Windows Me, take the following steps:

1. Click **My Network Places** on the Windows desktop.

2. Click or double-click the **Add Network Place** icon. The Add Network Place Wizard appears.

3. Click the **Browse** button. The Browse For Folder dialog box appears prompting you to select a computer, drive, and folder you want to add to your network places (see Figure 18.5).

Inside Tip

If the computer you want to access is not displayed in My Network Places, try clicking the workgroup icon. Sometimes the icon for a computer doesn't pop up in the first window. If the computer is still unavailable, it might be turned off or the network settings could be wrong. Open the **Start** menu, click **Help,** click the **Troubleshooting** link, choose the option for troubleshooting network connections, and follow the on-screen instructions.

4. Click the plus sign next to Entire Network, click the plus sign next to your workgroup name, click the plus sign next to the desired computer, and continue clicking plus signs until you see the disk or folder you want to add as a network place.

5. Click the icon for the disk or folder you want to add as a network place.

6. Click the **OK** button. You're returned to the wizard, where the path to the new network place is displayed.

7. Click **Next.** The wizard prompts you to type a more descriptive name for the drive or folder.

8. Type a brief but descriptive name of the drive or folder and click the **Finish** button.

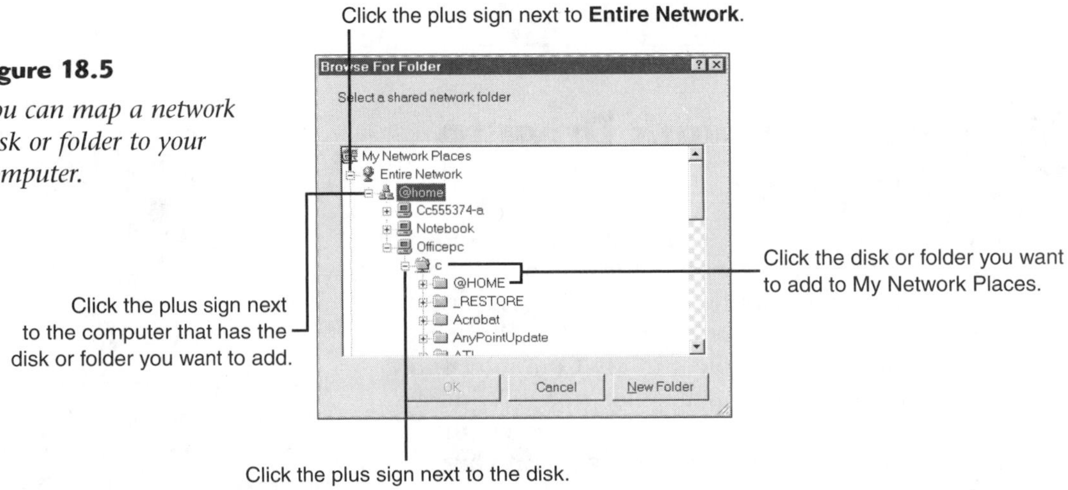

Click the plus sign next to **Entire Network**.

Figure 18.5

You can map a network disk or folder to your computer.

Click the plus sign next to the computer that has the disk or folder you want to add.

Click the disk or folder you want to add to My Network Places.

Click the plus sign next to the disk.

To map a disk or folder to your computer in Windows 98 or Windows 95, take the following steps:

1. In the Network Neighborhood, right-click the network disk or folder that you want to map to your computer and choose **Map Network Drive.** The Map Network Drive dialog box appears.

2. Open the **Drive** drop-down list and choose a drive letter to assign to the network disk or folder.

3. To have Windows automatically log on to this disk or folder on startup, click **Reconnect at logon** and click **OK**.

4. Switch back to the opening **My Computer** window. A new icon appears for the mapped disk or folder.

Using a Network Printer

To use a network printer, you must add the printer to your Printers folder. However, before you can add a network printer you must set printer sharing options on the computer that is connected to the printer, as explained earlier in this chapter. You then can run the Add Printer Wizard and select the network printer from a list of available printers. Take the following steps:

1. Click the **Start** button, point to **Settings,** and click **Printers.** The contents of the Printers folder appears.

2. Click **Add Printer.** The Add Printer Wizard appears.

3. Click **Next.** The Wizard asks if you want to install a local or network printer.

4. Click **Network Printer** and click **Next.** The Wizard prompts you to specify the path to the printer.

5. Click the **Browse** button. The Browse for Printer dialog box displays a list of all computers on the network.

6. Click the plus sign next to your workgroup's icon and click the plus sign next to the computer that is connected to the printer. The printer's icon appears, as shown in Figure 18.6.

7. Click the printer's icon and click **OK.** You are returned to the wizard where the path to the network printer is displayed.

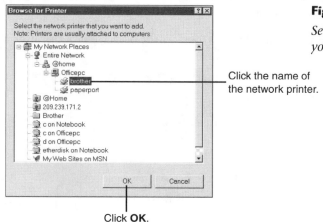

Figure 18.6

Select the network printer you want to use.

Click the name of the network printer.

Click **OK.**

8. Click **Next.** The wizard displays the name of the printer as it appears on the network computer. You can change the name if desired.

9. To use this printer as the default printer for all your Windows applications, click **Yes** and then click **Next.** The wizard asks if you want to print a test page.

193

10. Click **Yes** or **No**, and click **Finish.** If you chose to print a test page, the Wizard sends the page to the network printer. Windows copies the necessary printer files from the network computer to your computer and returns you to the Printers folder. An icon for the network printer appears.

After the network printer is set up, you can use it to print documents just as if the printer were connected to your computer. However, if you did not set up the network printer as your default printer, you must select the printer when you choose to print your document.

The Least You Need to Know

➤ A client-server network constitutes many client computers connected to a single server. Peer-to-peer networks link all computers directly together.

➤ To log on to a network, simply enter your username and password.

➤ Before you can access the contents of a disk on another computer on the network, the disk must be marked as shared.

➤ You can check out what's available on your network using the Network Neighborhood or My Network Places.

➤ You can map a network folder or disk to your computer to have it appear as a folder on your computer.

➤ You can use the Add Printer Wizard to set up a network printer on your computer.

Part 4

Going Global with Modems, Online Services, and the Internet

How would you like to get the latest news, weather, and sports without lifting your fingers from the keyboard? Connect to an online encyclopedia, complete with sounds and pictures? Order items from a computerized catalog? Send a postage-free letter and have it arrive at its destination in a matter of seconds? Mingle with others in online chat rooms? Or even transfer files from your computer to a colleague's computer anywhere in the world?

In this part, you learn how to do all this and more. You learn how to buy and install a modem that can keep up with traffic on the Internet; connect to America Online (the most popular online service in the world); tour the Internet; wander the Web; and chat and swap e-mail messages with your friends, relatives, and colleagues. With this section, a modem, and the right software, you're primed to master the information age.

Chapter 19

First You Need a Modem

In This Chapter

➤ List three available Internet connection types from slowest to fastest

➤ Read a modem ad and understand what it says

➤ Figure out which type of software you need to do what you want to do

➤ Hook up an internal or external modem

A modem is the single most liberating tool for your computer. With a modem and a computer, you can connect to other computers located down the block, across town, or anywhere in the world ... assuming the remote computer lets you in. Add an on-line Internet service and you can start cruising the Web; exchanging email; and chatting with friends, relatives, and complete strangers—but first you need a modem.

Smart Shopping for a Fast Connection

For your PC to access the Internet or establish a connection with a remote computer or network, it needs a device that can receive and send signals. For many years, standard modems have served this purpose. However, with the increasing popularity of the Web and the ever-increasing demands of media files, standard modems are becoming obsolete.

If you spend much time on the Internet, you want the fastest connection possible. How do you strike a balance between performance and cost? The following sections help you decide.

Chugging Along with Standard Modems

Short for modulator demodulator, a modem converts incoming analog signals traveling through phone lines into digital signals that the PC can process. To send a signal, a modem converts the digital signal (consisting of 1s and 0s) from your PC into an analog (wave) signal that can be transmitted over phone lines.

Modems transfer data at different speeds, commonly measured in bits per second (bps). The higher the number, the faster the modem can transfer data. Common rates include 28,800bps, 33,600bps, and 56,800bps. Because these modem speed numbers are becoming so long, manufacturers abbreviate them; you'll commonly see speeds listed as 33.6Kbps. When they start dropping the bps and list something like 56K, you know it's really fast. Although you pay more for a higher transfer rate, you save time and decrease your phone bill by purchasing a faster modem.

The bottom line is that if you're buying a standard modem, you should look for a 56Kbps modem; however, before you run out and buy one, you should know a few things:

➤ **56K limits**   56K pushes the limits of phone line communications. The phone company limits connection speeds to 53K, although there is some talk of raising the speed limit. You will rarely see data transfers at 56Kps. Expect a maximum speed of about 40–45Kbps, and that's only when your modem is receiving data. A 56K modem still sends data at 28.8–33.6Kbps because of other limitations, such as line noise.

➤ **x2 and 56Kflex and V.90**   x2 and 56KFlex are competing 56K standards. x2 was developed by U.S. Robotics (now 3COM), and 56KFlex was developed by Hayes, Lucent Technologies, Rockwell, and others. These proprietary standards were developed before *ITU* (the *International Telecommunication Union*) defined the standard for 56K modems as V.90. If you buy a 56K modem, make sure it supports the V.90 standard. Don't get stuck with an old x2 or 56KFlex modem.

➤ **ITU**   ITU is the international standard for 56K modems. If given the option of buying an x2, 56KFlex, or ITU, get the ITU. Because before the ITU standard was finalized, many modem manufacturers were making 56K modems following either the x2 or Flex standard; you can upgrade most x2 and 56KFlex modems to the ITU standard by running special software. Contact your modem manufacturer or visit its Web site to obtain the required update. To help you translate the various ITU standards you see in ads, Table 19.1 lists the standards and the corresponding modem speeds.

➤ **WinModem or Controllerless Modems**   To cut the cost of many newer modems, manufacturers designed the modems without their own controller chips. The modem uses the computer's central processor for its processing needs. These *controllerless* modems, also called *WinModems*, are relatively inexpensive but they can cause problems, especially on slower systems (266MHz or slower).

Table 19.1   ITU Modem Standards Translated into Speeds

ITU Standard	Modem Speed
V.32	4,800 to 9,600bps
V.32bis	14.4Kbps
V.34	28.8Kbps
V.42bis	33.6Kbps
V.90	56Kbps

When shopping for a standard modem, you also should consider the following optional features:

➤ **Fax support**   Like fully equipped fax machines, a fax/modem enables you to dial a number and transmit pages of text, graphics, and charts to a conventional fax machine or to another computer that has a fax/modem. You also can use the fax modem to receive incoming faxes and voice calls. Shop carefully. Some fax/modems are able to only send faxes not to receive them. If you want to receive faxes, make sure the fax/modem can handle incoming faxes. Also make sure your modem supports Class 1 and 2 Group III fax machines. Nearly 90 percent of faxes in use today are of the Group III variety.

➤ **Voice support**   If you plan to have your computer answer the phone and take messages, make sure the modem offers voice support. Without voice support, your modem can answer the phone, but it can only emit annoying screeching noises—which is useful for making telemarketers back off. Some modems also are designed to handle video calls sort of like on The Jetsons. However, if modems are too slow to handle simple file transfers, you can imagine how slow they are to transfer live video images.

➤ **Plug-and-play support**   Windows supports plug-and-play technology, which allows you to plug a device into your computer without having to worry about the device conflicting with other devices on your computer—you just connect the device. When you turn on your computer and Windows starts, Windows detects the device and installs the necessary driver for the device or prompts you to install the driver from the disk that came with the device. If you get a modem that does not support plug-and-play and it conflicts with another device, such as your mouse, you're going to face some complex troubleshooting steps to remedy the situation.

Standard modems offer three benefits: The modem itself is inexpensive and easy to install, the modem plugs into a standard phone jack, and online services offer modem connections at bargain rates. However, for speedy Internet connections, consider the options described in the following sections.

199

Speeding Up Your Connections with ISDN

Unlike standard modems that must perform analog-to-digital conversions, *ISDN* (*Integrated Services Digital Network*) deals only with digital signals supporting much higher data transfer rates: 128Kbps, more than twice as fast as 56K modems. ISDN modems use two separate 64Kbps channels, called B channels, which work together to achieve the 128Kbps transfer rates. This two-channel approach also allows you to talk on the phone while surfing the Web at 64Kbps; when you hang up, the modem can use both channels for PC communications. A third, slower channel (channel D) is used by the phone company to identify callers and do basic line checking.

Although ISDN might sound like the ideal solution for home and small business use, add up the costs before your decide. You can expect to pay about $150–$300 for the ISDN adapter and $100–$200 for the phone company's installation fee ($250–$500 total). In addition, expect monthly charges from both the phone company and your Internet service provider (ISP). Phone companies typically charge about $30–$50 per month, and most ISPs charge $20–$30 per channel (for a total of $70–$110 per month).

Shop for the ISDN service before you shop for an ISDN modem or adapter, and ask your phone company for recommendations. The performance of your ISDN connection relies on how well your ISDN adapter works with your phone company's connection. Many phone companies have a package deal that includes an ISDN. You also must choose the type of adapter you want:

Inside Tip

If you have a 28.8Kbps or 33.6Kbps modem and are thinking of moving up to a 56Kbps modem, test your phone line first. A 56Kbps modem needs a clean phone line to achieve 56K connections. You can download a free line test program at: http://modemupdate.usr.com/56k/need4_56k/linetest.html

➤ **External adapter** External ISDN adapters (sometimes called *ISDN modems*) grab the digital signals from your phone company and stuff them through the serial port. If you have an older PC, the serial port might follow the 16550 UART (Universal Asynchronous Receiver-Transmitter) standard, which supports speeds only up to 115Kbps (10 percent slower than the top modem speed). To determine whether your COM port supports UART 16650 or later, choose **Start, Settings, Control Panel**, and click or double-click the **Modems** icon. Click the **Diagnostics** tab, click the COM port you want to check, and click **More Info.** You might need to install a high-speed COM port or, better yet, install an ISDN adapter card instead.

➤ **Adapter card** An ISDN adapter card plugs into your PC's expansion slot, so it does not have the potential bottleneck you might experience with an ISDN modem.

➤ **Router**   A router enables you to connect several PCs to a single ISDN line. If you have a medium-size network, a router provides the perfect solution for multiple connections to an ISDN line. With smaller networks there are other solutions, including external adapters that have two or more serial ports.

Techno Talk

When you start talking high-speed communications, you need to know two terms: *bandwidth* and *broadband*. Bandwidth is the measure of the amount of data transmitted in a fixed period of time, such as kilobits per second. Think of a connection with high bandwidth as a big pipe that can carry lots of water. Broadband is a term that describes a connection that can carry multiple channels over a single medium, such as a wire or cable; for example, cable TV service provides a broadband connection. The original ISDN connections are not considered broadband because they use separate phone lines to carry the different channels. There is a type of ISDN, Broadband ISDN (or B-ISDN), which is a broadband connection, but it requires fiber-optic cables and is not readily available.

The New Kid on the Block: DSL Modems

Short for *digital subscriber line, DSL* promises to put a big dent in the ISDN market and challenge cable companies. Using standard phone lines, DSL can achieve data transfer rates of up to 1.5Mbps (9Mbps if you're within two miles of an ADSL connection center); this is about 25 times faster than a 56K modem connection. DSL achieves these rates over standard analog phone lines by using frequencies not used by voice signals. The only drawback is that DSL is a relatively new product (although the technology has been around awhile) and might not be available in your area or supported by your ISP.

As for costs, expect DSL to be slightly less expensive than ISDN, at least for now. The DSL modem and network card together run about $100–$200. Expect monthly service charges to range from $50–$70; this includes charges for the line itself and the Internet service. Your phone company also might charge $100–$200 for installation. Because there is no single DSL standard, don't purchase a modem without checking with your phone company. Most DSL providers market their services as a package deal and include a DSL modem that works with the service.

The Pros and Cons of Cable Modems

Like cable television connections, a cable Internet connection allows high-speed data transfers to your PC allowing you to cruise the Internet at the same speed you can flip channels. In addition to speed, cable modems are relatively inexpensive (starting at about $200) and are easy to install. You can expect to pay about $40–$60 per month for cable Internet access, which makes it competitive with DSL service and cheaper than ISDN. However, cable modems do have a few drawbacks:

➤ **Availability** Your cable company might not offer Internet cable service.

➤ **Variable connection speeds** Cable service is set up to serve a pool of users. The more users connected to one service station, the slower the connection. Although cable companies commonly advertise 8Mbps data transfer rates, the rate you'll experience likely will be around 1–2Mbps; this is about 30–50 times faster than a 56Kbps modem.

➤ **Upload problems** Cable was developed to bring signals into homes not carry them out. However, cable companies are developing two-way systems to eliminate this limitation. If your cable service handles only incoming signals, you'll need to install a standard modem, too.

When shopping for a cable connection, the primary consideration is how the cable service handles return signals. Most services use either telephone return or RF return. With RF return, the cable modem transmits signals along the cable. With telephone return, the modem sends signals along a standard modem connection. Before you purchase a modem, check with the cable service to determine the type of return system it uses.

High-Speed Satellite Connections

If you're tired of waiting for the standards battles to cool off and the cable and phone companies to lay new cables in your neighborhood, move up to a satellite connection, such as DirecPC from Hughes Network Systems (www.direcpc.com or 1-800-347-3272). DirecPC offers transfer rates of up to 400Kbps—three times faster than ISDN and seven times faster than 56K modems. And all you need to connect is the kit from Hughes Network Systems. However, as with all systems, DirecPC has its own shortcomings:

➤ **The kit is expensive** $300 for the satellite dish and adapter.

➤ **The service is expensive** $50 activation fee. Monthly rates vary: $30 per month for 25 hours (plus $2 for each additional hour) or $50 per month for unlimited connect time (If you already have an ISP, rates are slightly lower.)

➤ **Two-way service is extra** Satellite services originally were designed to send signals to the PC—not receive them from the PC—so you used to need a modem and a separate Internet account to handle upstream communications. Most satellite services now offer two-way communications, but it costs an additional $20 per month.

➤ **Clear line of site to satellite required**   If your house is nestled in a quaint wooded area or is surrounded by high rises, you might have trouble aiming the satellite dish at the communications satellite.

➤ **Complicated installation**   You can hire out the installation for $100–$200. Otherwise, you'll have to mount the dish to the side of your house (or the roof), run BNC cable from the dish to your PC, and figure out how to point the dish at a satellite floating somewhere near the equator. Once you get all that working properly, you might need to install a modem.

➤ **Fair weather friend**   Satellite communications are susceptible to rain, lightning, snow storms, sun spots, and other natural sources of interference. In addition, satellites sometimes wobble out of orbit and interrupt the transmissions, meaning you must readjust the dish to point it at a different satellite. However, for the most part, satellite communications are pretty reliable.

Despite these drawbacks, once you get your PC satellite dish up and running, you'll never want to go back to your 56K or ISDN connection again. Web pages pop right up on your screen without delay and large media files that used to take 15 minutes to download arrive in two minutes.

Inside Tip

Fixed wireless connections are becoming available in many areas where cable, ISDN, and DSL service are unavailable. With fixed wireless service, a connection is set up between your office or home and a tower via a wireless *microwave* connection. You mount a little receiver/transmitter modem on the outside of your house (typically up near the roof or on the roof) and run a cable from it to your computer. Fixed wireless service is an excellent option for high-speed Internet access in areas where cable and DSL service are unavailable, but this service is not available in all areas and has some of the same drawbacks as satellite service and cell phone connections.

Pre-Installation: Do You Need Another Phone Jack?

If you're going with a standard modem and you already have a phone jack near the computer but your phone is plugged into it, you don't need an additional jack. Most modems come with two phone jacks: one that connects the modem to the incoming phone line and another one into which you can plug your phone. When you are not using the modem, you use the phone as you normally would. If your modem doesn't have two phone jacks, you can purchase a split phone connector from an electronics store. The split phone connector enables you to plug both your phone and your modem into the same jack.

Installing Your Modem

Modem installation varies depending on whether you are installing an internal or external modem. With an internal modem, you must get under the hood of your PC, plug the modem into an open expansion slot, and plug the modem into the phone jack. Just about anyone can install an external modem. All you have to do is turn off the computer and make three connections:

➤ **Modem to serial port**   Connect the modem to the serial port (usually marked COM) on your computer using a serial cable.

➤ **Modem to power source**   Plug the modem's power cord into a receptacle on your wall or into your power strip or surge protector.

➤ **Modem to phone line**   Connect the modem to the phone jack. This is just like plugging a phone into a phone jack. (You also might want to connect your phone to the modem, as shown in Figure 19.1.)

Installing an internal modem is a bit more difficult. If you're a rank beginner, call one of your ambitious computer friends or relatives to lead you through the process … or at least read the documentation to you while you work. Just remember to turn off the power and unplug everything before removing the case from the system unit, and follow any safety precautions specified in the installation manual.

Whenever you install a new device, you also must install a driver that tells Windows how to use the device. If your modem is plug-and-play compatible, the Windows Add New Hardware Wizard runs when you start your computer and leads you through the necessary steps. If your modem is not plug-and-play compatible and the Add New Hardware Wizard does not start, open the Windows Control Panel (click **Start**, point to **Settings**, and click Control Panel) and double-click the **Add New Hardware** icon.

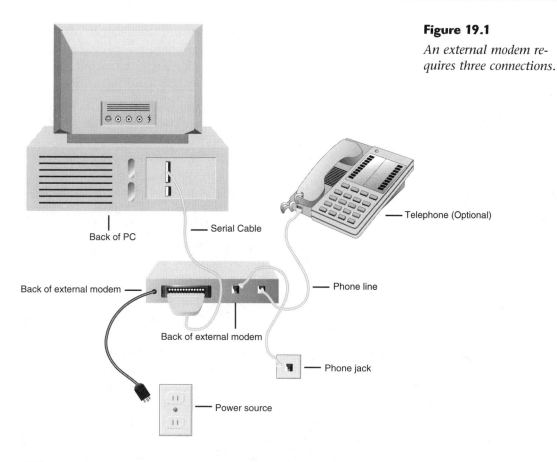

Figure 19.1

An external modem re-quires three connections.

Back of PC

Serial Cable

Telephone (Optional)

Back of external modem

Phone line

Back of external modem

Phone jack

Power source

Now, What Do You Want to Do with Your Modem?

Before you begin using your modem, you might need some additional software. To determine what software you need, ask yourself what you want to do with the modem. The following list describes some of the common uses for a modem and the type of program required for each use.

➤ **Online information services** If you want to connect to an online service (such as Prodigy or America Online), you must start an account and obtain a special program from the service. (Skip to the next chapter for details.)

➤ **Surf the Internet** This is sort of like connecting to an online service (in fact, you can connect to the Internet through an online service). You also can connect by using a local Internet service provider. The service provider usually equips you with the software and any other instructions you need to get started. (See Chapter 21, "Doing the Internet Shuffle.")

➤ **Games in two-player mode**   If you have a game that enables you to play games in two-player mode by using a modem, the program probably contains all the tools you need to play the game over the phone lines. Refer to the user manual that came with the game.

Inside Tip

To make sure your computer acknowledges having a modem, use your modem to make your next phone call (assuming you have a phone connected to your modem). Click **Start, Programs, Accessories, Communications, Phone Dialer.** Type the phone number you want to dial and click **Dial.** When someone answers, pick up the receiver on your phone and start talking.

➤ **Remote computing**   Say you have a computer at work and one at home. You can call your computer at work to get any files you might have forgotten to bring home or you can dial into your company's network. (See "Calling Your Desktop Computer or Network Through Your Modem" in Chapter 28, "Life on the Run: Notebook Computing," for details.) You also can obtain a special program, such as PC Anywhere, that enables you to use a remote computer just as if you were sitting at its keyboard.

➤ **"Free" long-distance calls**   You can't avoid long-distance charges to your pal across the country simply by placing the call with your modem. You and your pal both need an Internet connection and special software. (See Chapter 25, "Reaching Out with Chat and Instant Messaging," for details.)

All these tasks require different steps for dialing out and establishing a connection. Check the documentation that came with the telecommunications program or skip to the chapter referenced in the preceding list to determine the steps you need to take.

What Went Wrong?

Rarely do modem communications proceed error free the first time. Any minor problem or wrong setting can cause a major disruption in the communications between your computer and the remote computer. If you run into a glitch that prevents your modem from dialing, connecting, or communicating with a remote system, see "I Can't Get My Modem To Work" in Chapter 32, "Do-It-Yourself Fixes for Common Ailments," for possible fixes.

The Least You Need to Know

➤ If you're going the modem route, get a 56Kbps modem that features fax and voice support and supports the V.90 standard.

➤ For easy installation, get an external modem. To save desk space and reduce the number of cables, install an internal modem.

➤ ISDN modems are preferred over standard modems because ISDN deals with digital-to-digital signals, which support significantly higher data transfer rates than standard analog-to-digital modems.

➤ DSL modems offer faster connection rates than even ISDN and have the included advantage of being used over regular phone lines.

➤ Call your cable company to find out whether the company provides cable modem service for your area.

➤ You can use a modem to connect to the Internet or a commercial online service, play multiplayer games over the phone lines, connect to a desktop computer from a remote location, or place free long-distance phone calls over the Internet.

Chapter 20

Going Online with America Online and Other Services

In This Chapter

➤ Connect to one of the big four online services

➤ Pick a local access number (to avoid long-distance charges)

➤ Send and receive mail electronically

➤ Chat live with friends and strangers

➤ Access the Internet

One of the first things most people do with a modem is to connect to one of the big four online services—America Online, Microsoft Network, Prodigy, or CompuServe. When you subscribe to the service (usually for about 20 bucks a month), you get a program that enables you to connect locally to the service (assuming you live near a major town), and you get access to what the service offers. This includes electronic mail (e-mail), chat rooms (where you can hang out with other members), news, research tools, magazines, university courses, the Internet, and much, much more.

First Month's Free ...

What's the price you pay for all this? When you're shopping for an online service, compare subscription rates and consider the focus of each service. The following is a rundown of the four biggies (keep in mind, the prices quoted here are current as of this writing but are subject to change—check with the service for price specifics):

➤ **America Online** AOL offers several payment plans: $21.95 per month for un-limited use ($239.40 or $19.95 per month if you make a one-year commitment), $9.95 for five hours per month (plus $2.95 for each additional hour), or $4.95 per month for three hours (plus $2.50 for each additional hour). America Online is the most popular online service on the planet. It offers simple naviga-tional tools, great services, and a friendly, hip social scene. Call 1-800-827-6364 for a startup kit (complete with a free trial offer).

➤ **CompuServe** Charges $9.95 for 20 hours per month, plus $2.95 for each addi-tional hour; $19.95 for unlimited use or $199 per year for unlimited use (about seventeen bucks per month). Special services cost extra. CompuServe tradition-ally has been more technical and business oriented. Call 1-800-848-8990 for a startup kit (complete with a free trial offer).

➤ **Microsoft Network** MSN Internet Access essentially is an Internet service provider and offers little specialized content. The Unlimited plan costs $21.95 per month. If you have Windows 95 or later, you can double-click the Microsoft Network icon on the Windows desktop and sign up right now (you get one month free to try it out) or call 1-800-FREE-MSN (1-800-373-3676).

➤ **Prodigy Internet** Gives you unlimited access for $19.95 per month ($198 or $16.50 per month if you make a 1-year commitment). Prodigy also offers several other payment plans, including the Low Usage Plan ($9.95/month for 10 hours plus $1.50 for each additional hour). Call 1-800-PRODIGY (1-800-776-3449) for a startup kit. Prodigy Internet provides a connection to the Internet and enables you to navigate the Internet with Internet Explorer (see Chapter 22, "Whipping Around the World Wide Web," for details.)

Whoa!

Online services typically waive the first month's usage fee. If you choose to no longer use the service, be sure you cancel your membership before the next month's billing period begins. Check out the service's online help system.

Although all these online services offer different serv-ices and sport their own unique looks, they all are more like online service providers for the Internet. Every online service listed here can connect you to the Internet and all of them offer the programs you need to surf the Web, exchange e-mail messages, and perform other Internet-related tasks, as explained in later chapters.

When you first connect to any of the online services, keep tabs on your phone bill. If you use a modem to call long distance, your friendly neighborhood phone company charges you long-distance rates. However, most online services provide you with a local number for connecting to the service. You then can communi-cate with other people in different states by way of the local connection, thus avoiding long-distance charges.

Signing Up for an Online Account

Before you run to the phone and dial those numbers listed in the previous section, check your Windows desktop for an icon named MSN or Online Services. The MSN icon is for The Microsoft Network. The Online Services icon contains additional icons for America Online, EarthLink, Prodigy, and AT&T WorldNet. Click one of these icons and follow the onscreen instructions to install the online service's program from the windows CD, connect to the service, and sign up.

The installation program uses the modem to dial a toll-free number that lists local numbers. After you select a local number (and usually an alternate number, in case the first number is busy), the installation program disconnects from the toll-free connection and then reconnects you locally. Most services then ask you to supply the following information, as shown in Figure 20.1:

➤ Your modem's COM port. To determine the COM port, double-click the **Modems** icon in the Control Panel, click your modem's name, and click **Properties**.

Whoa!

If you live in a small town or in an area code that the online service doesn't serve, you could be in for a larger bill than expected. You either have to pay long-distance charges to connect to the nearest town or fork over additional money to get a special 800 number to dial. So much for the joys of living in the country!

Figure 20.1

Before you can use an online service, you must register.

Enter the requested information.

➤ Your modem's maximum speed. (Most services support up to 56K connections.)

➤ Any special dialing instructions, such as a number you must dial to connect to an outside line.

➤ Your name, address, and telephone number.

➤ A credit card number and expiration date. (Even if the service offers a free trial membership, you must enter a credit card number.)

➤ The name (screen name) and password you want to use to log on to the service. (Write down your screen name and password, in case you forget it. Without this information, you will not be able to connect.)

➤ An acceptance of the *terms of service* (*TOS*) or rules you must follow to continue to use the service. If you break the rules, the service might terminate your account. Read this so you know what you're getting into.

Connecting to Your Online Service

After you have a local number to dial, you can log on to the service at any time and start using it. Select the online service from the **Start**, **Programs** menu or double-click its icon on the Windows desktop. Enter your screen name (username) and password and click the **Dial**, **Connect**, or **Sign On** button (or its equivalent), as shown in Figure 20.2. The service dials the local access number, connects you, and displays an opening screen that enables you to start using the service.

Type your username.

Figure 20.2

*To log on to America Online, select your username, type your password, and click **Sign On**.*

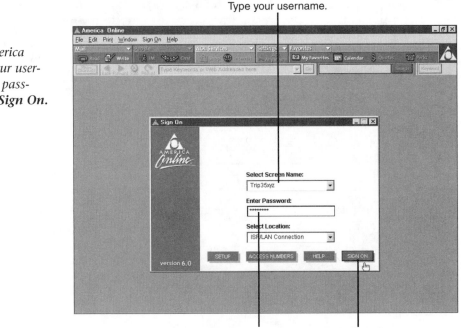

Type your password.   Click **Sign On**.

Although each online service offers different tools for moving around in the service, the tools are very similar. Most services display buttons and menus that enable you to use popular features, such as mail, news, and games. For example, the America Online program window (shown in Figure 20.3) contains buttons (and icons) for reading and writing e-mail, connecting to the Internet, checking stock prices and sports scores, reading the news headlines, and much more.

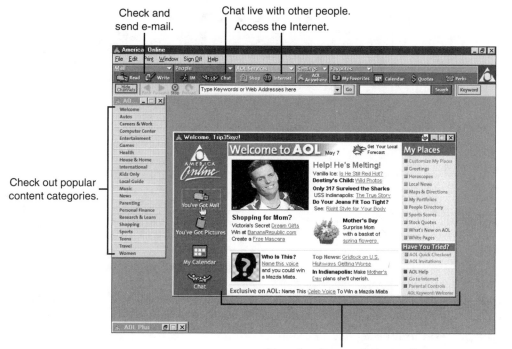

Figure 20.3

The Welcome screen enables you to quickly jump to various features of the service.

Keeping in Touch with E-Mail

How would you like to send a letter and have it reach its destination in less than a minute? With e-mail you can enjoy warp-speed delivery at a fraction of the cost. To send an e-mail letter, enter the **Compose Mail** command (or its equivalent). This opens a dialog box, like the one shown in Figure 20.4, that enables you to compose and address your correspondence.

Type the e-mail address of the person to whom you want to send the message (this usually is the person's screen name if she is a member of the same service). Click the

Description or **Subject** area, and type a brief description of your message. Finally, type your message in the **Message** area and click the **Send** button. In a matter of seconds, the message appears in your friend's mailbox. When your friend connects to the service, her screen will indicate that she has mail waiting for her.

Figure 20.4

Sending an e-mail message is a snap.

Type the person's e-mail address.

Use this toolbar to add fancy formatting, if desired.

Type a description of the message.

Type the message itself.

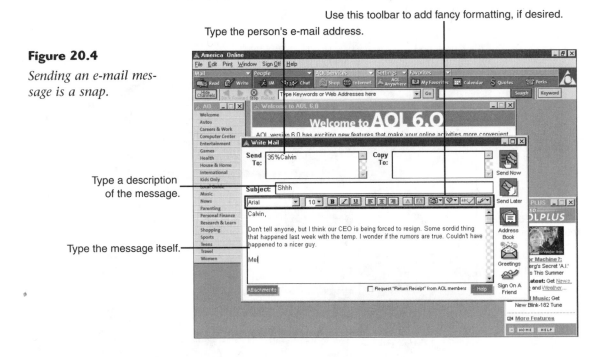

Everyone on your online service (including you) has an electronic mailbox. Whenever you sign on, the program indicates in some way whether you have mail waiting. To get your mail, you enter the **Get Mail** command or click the **Mail** button. This displays a list of waiting messages. Double-click the message you want to read. The message appears in its own window, which usually contains a Reply button, enabling you to respond immediately to the message.

Conversing in Chat Rooms

If you don't like waiting for mail, you can converse with your friends and colleagues in one of the many chat rooms the online service provides. You pick a room in which 20 or so people are hanging out and then start typing. Your messages appear on the screens of the other people in the room, and their messages appear on your screen. If you prefer to talk in private with one or more other users, you can create your own private room and invite other users to join you. To learn more about chatting, check out Chapter 25, "Reaching Out with Chat and Instant Messaging."

Sharing Common Interests

Online services started as digital community centers where people could share their ideas, problems, and solutions. This tradition is still alive in online forums and boards. You can find a *forum* or *message board* for almost any special interest category—from gardening and parenting to computers and automobiles. If you have a question, you simply post a message on the board. In a day or so, other members post answers in an attempt to help you out. You can get free legal advice, information on how to grow prize roses, and help finding long-lost relatives. Forums and message boards also are a great place to talk about your favorite books, movies, and TV shows although not all users will agree with your tastes.

On some online services, the forums are scattered throughout the service. For instance, on America Online, you can find places to read and post messages in Member Services, Gardening, and HouseNet. Just press **Ctrl+K**, type a couple words describing your interest, and click the **Go** button. You receive a list of places to go that might include links that take you to a message center on that topic. On the Internet forums and message boards are called *newsgroups*. To learn how to read and post messages in newsgroups, see Chapter 24, "Passing Notes in Newsgroups."

Whoa!

Although most chatters are harmless, you might bump into some less desirable types. Be careful about giving out sensitive information online, including your password, your last name, address, phone number, or anything else someone could use to track you down or use your account. If you have kids, use the software's parental controls to help block access to undesirable chat areas, and remember to check in on your kids every now and then.

Wandering Off to the Internet

You will learn all about the Internet in the next few chapters. However, before you leave you should know that most online services offer full access to the Internet. For example, on America Online, you can quickly access the Internet by opening the **AOL Services** menu, pointing to **Internet,** and clicking the desired Internet feature: **Go to the Web, Newsgroups,** or **FTP** (File Transfer Protocol).

If you choose Go to the Web, America Online runs its Web browser and displays its opening (home) page, as shown in Figure 20.5. To navigate the Web, click links just as you do for navigating America Online. The only difference is that the links might look a little different from what you are accustomed to seeing on America Online. Because you are wandering off the service to other services and sites, you don't get the consistent look and feel of America Online. To search for other sites and pages on the Web, click the **Search** button in the browser toolbar; a search form appears. Enter one or two words to describe what you're looking for and click the Search button. (For more information about navigating the Web, see Chapter 22.

When you are done, simply click the **Close** (**X**) button in the browser window. This returns you to the America Online service. To sign off, you can click the **Close** button in the upper-right corner of the America Online window or open the **Sign Off** menu and click **Sign Off.**

You can type a page address to open a specific page.

Figure 20.5

America Online has the tools you need to wander the Web.

Click links to go to other pages.

The America Online Web browser

The Least You Need to Know

➤ The four most popular online services are America Online, Microsoft Network, Prodigy, and Compuserve.

➤ Most online services offer free trial periods that can be accessed by using an icon on the Windows desktop.

➤ Many online services offer a toll-free or local connection number. Be sure to have all the connection and billing information handy when you order your service or dial up the first time.

➤ To send someone an e-mail message, look for the Compose Mail or Message command in your e-mail program.

➤ Commercial online services such as America Online have buttons that enable you to access the Web and other Internet features.

Chapter 21

Doing the Internet Shuffle

In This Chapter

➤ Describe the Internet in 25 words or less

➤ Name three ways you can connect to the Internet

➤ Use your modem to connect to the Internet

➤ Write a complete sentence using only Internet acronyms

Unless you've set up permanent residence in the New York tunnel, you've probably heard the terms "Internet" and "Information Superhighway." The Internet is a massive computer network connecting thousands of computers all over the world, including computers at universities, libraries, businesses, government agencies, and research facilities.

By connecting to the Internet you can tap many of the resources stored on these computers. You can copy (download) files from them, use their programs, send and e-mail, chat with other people by typing messages back and forth, get information about millions of topics, shop electronic malls, and even search for a job or a compatible mate.

What You Need to Get Started

Just because the Internet offers some pretty cool stuff does not mean that you're going to have to retool your computer. In fact, you probably already have everything you need to connect to the Internet now:

➤ **28.8Kbps (or faster) modem** Web pages contain graphics, video clips, and other media objects that take a long time to travel over phone lines. You should have a modem that can receive data at least at a rate of 56Kbps. For e-mail only, you can get by with a slower modem. (See Chapter 19, "First You Need a Modem," for details.)

➤ **SVGA monitor** The same graphics and video clips that take so long to download look fuzzy on anything less than an SVGA monitor. (See Chapter 1, "Savvy Consumer Guide to Buying a Computer.")

➤ **Speaker and sound card** If you want to listen to recordings or music clips on the Internet, you better have a sound card and speakers.

➤ **Internet service provider** The Internet service provider connects you to the Internet. Your modem dials the service provider's computer, which then establishes the required connection.

➤ **TCP/IP program** This program dials into your Internet service provider's computer using your modem and establishes the basic connection. You then can run specialized programs, such as a Web browser, e-mail program, and news reader to access specific Internet features. Fortunately, the TCP/IP program you need comes with Windows—it's called Dial-Up Networking.

➤ **Credit card** Perhaps the most important item, the credit card, enables you to start an account with an online service provider.

Whoa!

Most of the information in this chapter explains the procedure for establishing an Internet connection over the phone lines using a standard modem. If you connect using a cable or DSL modem, you have a permanent connection to the Internet just as if you were on a network—in fact, your computer is on a network. Once you set up your cable or DSL modem and install the software for your cable or DSL service, you are connected. You don't need to enter additional settings.

Finding an Entrance Ramp

Before you can navigate the Internet, you must find an entrance ramp—a way onto the Internet. You might choose a commercial online service, such as America Online, or go through your cable company or long-distance carrier for your Internet service. Before you start shopping, read through the following list to become more informed about your options:

➤ **Commercial online service**   The easiest way to connect to the Internet is to use a commercial online service. All the major online services (Prodigy, America Online, CompuServe, and The Microsoft Network) offer Internet access. However, usually you can get a better monthly service rate and better Internet service from a local Internet service provider.

➤ **Permanent connection**   If your company or university has a network that is part of the Internet and your computer is connected to the network, you have access to the Internet through the network. This is the least expensive (and fastest) way to go. Ask your network administrator if you're connected. If his eyes light up and he starts raving about a T1 line, you're connected—and you have a very fast connection.

➤ **Internet service provider (ISP)**   One of the least expensive ways to connect to the Internet is through a local service provider. Most local Internet service providers charge a monthly fee of $15 to $20 for unlimited connect time (or for a huge chunk of time, say 200 hours). You use your modem to connect to the service provider's computer, which is wired to the Internet. To find an ISP, ask at a computer store or users group in your area, or check the phone book.

To set up your account, you need information and settings that indicate to your computer how to connect to the service provider's computer. Obtain the following information:

➤ **Username**   This is the name that identifies you to the ISP's computer. It typically is an abbreviation of your first and last names. For example, Bill Fink might use bfink as his username. You can choose any name you like as long as it is not already being used by another user, and it conforms to the system's rules. Some providers have strict rules about the number of characters you can use and whether or not you can use special keystrokes, such as spaces, periods, or dashes.

➤ **Password**   The ISP might enable you to select your own password or may assign you a password. Be sure to write down the password in case you forget it. Without the right password,

Inside Tip

If your search for a service provider comes up short, use the Internet Connection Wizard (as explained later in this chapter) to set up your account. The Internet Connection Wizard can display a list of popular service providers in your calling area, and you can start your account simply by providing some billing information.

you are not able to connect to the service provider's computer. (And be sure you hide your password in a secure area away from your computer. If your computer is stolen, you don't want the thief to have access to your account.)

➤ **Connection type**   Most ISPs offer *PPP* (*Point-to-Point Protocol*). If your service provider offers only the older *SLIP* (*Serial Line Internet Protocol*), consider using a different service provider. Point-to-Point Protocol is easier to set up and provides faster data transfer, so most service providers don't offer SLIP.

➤ **Domain name server**   The domain name server is a computer that's set up to locate computers on the Internet. Each computer on the Internet has a unique number that identifies it, such as 197.72.34.74. Each computer also has a domain name, such as **www.whitehouse.gov**, which makes it easier for people to remember the computer's address. When you enter a domain name, the domain name server looks up the computer's number and locates it. Many services assign the domain name server *dynamically*—that is, when you initiate a connection. In such cases, the Domain Name Server option on your computer will be disabled.

➤ **Domain name**   This is the domain name of your service provider's computer, for example, internet.com. You use the domain name in conjunction with your username as your e-mail address, for example, **bfink@internet.com**.

➤ **News server**   The news server enables you to connect to any of thousands of newsgroups on the Internet to read and post messages. Newsgroups are electronic bulletin boards for special interest groups. The news server name typically starts with news and is followed by the service provider's domain name, for example, **news.internet.com**.

➤ **Mail server**   The mail server is in charge of electronic mail. You need to specify two mail servers: *POP* (*Post Office Protocol*) for incoming mail, and *SMTP* (*Simple Mail Transfer Protocol*) for mail you send. The POP server's name typically starts with POP and is followed by the service provider's domain name, for example, pop.internet.com. The SMTP server's name typically starts with SMTP or mail and is followed by the service provider's domain name, for example, **smtp. internet.com**. (See Chapter 23, "E-mail: Postage free, Same Day Delivery," for details.)

➤ **E-mail address**   If you plan to receive e-mail messages, you need an e-mail address. Your address typically begins with your username followed by an at sign (@) and the domain name of your service provider—for example, **bfink @internet.com**.

Signing On with the Internet Connection Wizard

Once you have all the information you need, you can run the Internet Connection Wizard and enter the connection settings. The wizard displays a series of screens prompting you to enter each piece of information. The wizard then creates a Dial-Up Networking icon that you can click to establish your connection.

Although I really would like to give you step-by-step instructions for using the Internet Connection Wizard, the steps vary depending on which Internet Connection Wizard you are using, how you plan to connect to the Internet (by modem or a network connection), and whether you have an ISP or need to shop for one. The wizard that's included with Internet Explorer 4 is vastly different from the one included with Internet Explorer 5; however, I can tell you how to start the wizard and tell you what to watch out for. Keep the following in mind:

➤ To start the Internet Connection Wizard, click **The Internet**, **Internet Explorer**, **Connect to the Internet** or **Internet Connection Wizard** icon on your Windows desktop.

➤ If the previous step doesn't work, the Connection Wizard might be hiding on your system. Check the **Start, Programs, Accessories, Internet Tools** or **Communications** menu for an option named **Get on the Internet** or **Internet Connection Wizard**, or check the **Start, Programs, Internet Explorer** menu for an option called **Connection Wizard** or **Internet Connection Wizard.**

➤ After the wizard starts, follow the onscreen instructions to set up your Internet account. The second screen (Setup Options) is the most important screen. If you already have an ISP, choose the option for using your existing ISP; otherwise, choose the option for locating a new ISP and setting up an account.

➤ If you need to find an ISP, the wizard asks for your area code and the first three digits of your phone number; it then downloads a list of ISPs available in your area, as shown in Figure 21.1. You need to register with the service and provide a credit card number. The wizard downloads the required connection settings for you, so you won't have to enter them manually.

Whoa!

To connect to the Internet using a standard modem, a Windows component called Dial-Up Networking must be installed. If it is not available (in either My Computer or the Control Panel), see "Installing and Uninstalling Windows Components" in Chapter 6, "Windows Tips, Tricks, and Traps," to install Dial-Up Networking. You will find it listed in the Communications category.

Select an Internet service provider.

Figure 21.1

The Internet Connection Wizard can help you locate an ISP in your area.

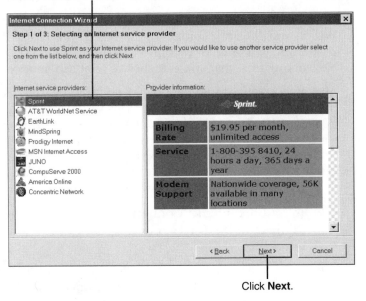

Click **Next**.

➤ If you have already set up an account with a service provider in your area, you must manually enter the connection settings. This is no biggie; the wizard steps you through it. However, when asked whether you want to view the Advanced settings, click **Yes** so that you can check the settings.

➤ If asked to specify a logon procedure, leave **I Don't Need to Type Anything When Logging On** selected even though your ISP requires you to enter a name and password. This option is for services that require you to manually log on using a terminal window or logon script. Most ISPs do not require this.

➤ Most ISPs automatically assign an IP (Internet Protocol) address to you when you log on, so don't choose to use a specific IP address unless your ISP gave you one.

➤ If your ISP gave you a specific DNS address, choose **Always Use the Following** and enter the DNS address in the **DNS Server** text box. If your ISP offers a secondary DNS, enter it so you can still navigate if the first DNS is busy.

➤ Refer to Chapters 23 and 24 for information about entering settings for your ISP's e-mail and news servers.

After running the Internet Connection Wizard, run **My Computer** and double-click the **Dial-Up Networking icon**; if the Dial-Up Networking icon is not shown, double-click the **Control Panel** icon and double-click the **Dial-Up Networking icon**. The Dial-Up Networking folder contains icons for any ISPs that you have set up. Drag the icon for your ISP to a blank area of the Windows desktop to place it in a more convenient location.

Connecting for the First Time

After you have an icon for connecting to your ISP, you can double-click it to connect to the Internet. When you double-click the icon a dialog box appears, as shown in Figure 21.2, prompting you to type your username and password (supplied by your service provider).

Whoa!

If you don't have the Save Password option, Client for Microsoft Networks is not installed. In the Control Panel, double-click the **Network** icon, click the **Add** button, and double-click **Client.** Click **Microsoft** and then double-click **Client for Microsoft Networks.** Make sure **Client for Microsoft Networks** is selected as the **Primary Network Logon** and click **OK.** If prompted to restart your computer, shut down any programs that are running, and click **Yes** or **OK** to restart.

Figure 21.2

When you double-click the icon you just created, this dialog box appears.

— Enter your user name.

— Type your password.

Click the **Connect** button.

Type your username and password. If desired, check the **Save Password** check box. This saves your username and password so you won't have to type it again the next time you log on. If you share your computer with someone else and you do not want that person using your Internet connection, leave the check box blank. Click the **Connect** button.

After you click the Connect button, Dial-Up Networking dials into your service provider's computer and displays messages indicating the progress, Dialing... Checking username and password ..., and Connecting .... Assuming that Dial-Up Networking could establish a connection, a dialog box appears indicating that you are now connected. You now can run Internet programs (explained in later chapters) to navigate the World Wide Web, send and receive e-mail, and so on.

What Went Wrong?

If your connection proceeds smoothly the first time, lucky you. Most first attempts fail for some reason or another (these are computers, after all). Sometimes, your ISP's computer is too busy to take your call, the computer cannot match the name or password you entered, or the phone line is a little fuzzy. If the connection fails, check the following:

➤ Did you type your username and password correctly? (If you mistyped this information or if your service provider entered it incorrectly on the system, Dial-Up Networking typically displays a message indicating that the system did not accept your password.) Retype your username and password and try connecting again. (Passwords typically are case sensitive so type the password exactly as your service provider specifies.)

➤ Was the line busy? Again, Dial-Up Networking typically displays a message indicating that the line was busy. If several people are connected to the service, you might need to wait until someone signs off. Keep trying to connect.

➤ Did your modem even dial? Go to the Windows Control Panel and check your modem setup. Make sure that you've selected the correct modem and COM port.

Whoa!

If your modem does not respond, see "My Modem Doesn't Work," in Chapter 32, "Do-It-Yourself Fixes for Common Ailments," for additional troubleshooting tips.

➤ Do you have reliable phone lines? Unplug your modem from the phone jack and plug a phone into the jack. Do you get a dial tone? Does the line sound fuzzy? If you don't hear a dial tone, the jack is not working. If the line is fuzzy when you make a voice call, it has line noise, which might be enough to disconnect you.

➤ Are your Dial-Up Adapter settings correct? Display the Windows **Control Panel** and double-click the **Network** icon. Click **Dial-Up Adapter** and click the **Properties** button. Click the **Bindings** tab and make sure there is a check mark next to **TCP/IP>Dial-Up Adapter.** (If NetBEUI or IPX/SPX are listed, make sure they are not checked.)

➤ Have you selected the correct server type? In the **Control Panel**, double-click the **Dial-Up Networking** icon. Right-click the icon for connecting to your ISP, and select **Properties**. Click the **Server Type** tab. Open the **Type of Dial-Up Server** drop-down list, as shown in Figure 21.3, and choose the correct server type (specified by your service provider)—PPP or SLIP.

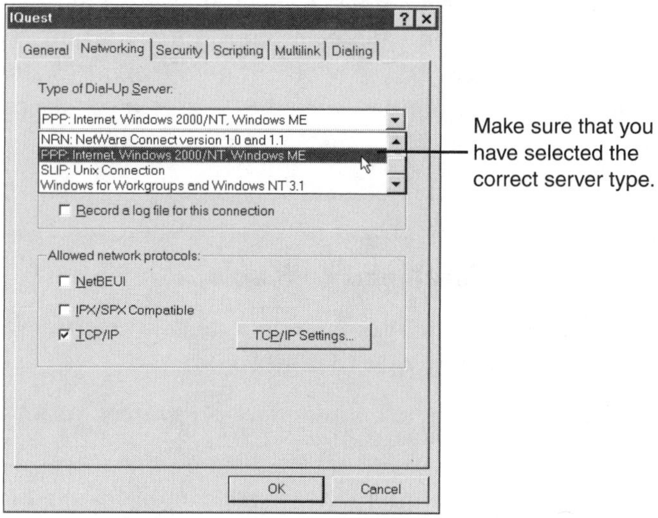

Figure 21.3

Check the settings for your dial-up connection.

Speeding Up Your Internet Connection

When Dial-Up Networking establishes a connection, it displays the speed at which data is being transferred. Expect the speed to be slightly less than your actual modem speed. For example, if you have a 28.8Kbps modem, expect an actual speed of 24 to 26Kbps. If you're using a 56K modem, expect speeds in the range of 40 to 45Kbps. These speed dips might be the result of line noise or problems with your service provider.

If Dial-Up Networking shows that the speed is half of what your modem is capable of, you should be concerned. For example, if your 28.8Kbps modem is chugging along at 14,400bps, you should check the following:

➤ The trouble could be line noise. If you typically connect at a higher speed, you may have a bad connection. Try disconnecting and reconnecting. If the connection is always slow, check the phone lines in your house and call your local phone company to report line noise.

➤ Check your modem setup. In the **Control Panel**, double-click the **Modems** icon. Click the name of your modem and click the **Properties** button. Under **Maximum Speed**, open the drop-down list and choose a speed that is higher than your modem's speed. Try the highest setting. Disconnect and reconnect to see if your connection speed has increased.

➤ Be sure your service provider supports your modem speed. Some service providers support only up to 33.6Kbps modems. If you have a 56Kbps modem, it only transfers data at the rate that the service provider's modem is operating.

➤ Check and see if your service provider knows that you're using a high-speed modem. In many cases, the service provider gives you a different phone number to use to connect at a specific speed. You may be set up to dial into a slower modem than what the service provider has available. Call your service provider for more information.

The Least You Need to Know

➤ Don't even think of trying to surf the Internet with a modem that's slower than 28.8Kbps—Web access is slow even at that speed.

➤ Before you start, obtain all the connection information you need to set up your account from your ISP.

➤ When you're first starting out on the Internet, test drive a full-featured commercial online service, such as America Online.

➤ When you have a little experience under your belt, try a local Internet Service Provider (ISP). Local ISPs often offer more reliable, faster Internet-only service.

➤ To set up your Internet connection in Windows, run the Internet Connection Wizard and use it to enter the required connection settings.

➤ If you have trouble connecting to your ISP's computer, retype your username and password and try again to connect.

➤ If you still have trouble connecting to your ISP's computer, or you have a consistently slow connection, make sure your modem speed setting matches the modem speed setting required by your ISP.

➤ A connection that is occasionally slow is normal. If your connection is always slow, your phone lines might have noise or you might need to contact your ISP to verify your connection settings.

Chapter 22

Whipping Around the World Wide Web

In This Chapter

➤ Visit Web sites advertised on TV

➤ Pull up pages full of text, pictures, sounds, and video clips

➤ Skip from one Web page to another and hop back

➤ Find information and people with Web search tools

➤ Mark your favorite Web pages for quick return trips

The single most exciting part of the Internet is the World Wide Web (or Web for short). With an Internet connection and a Web browser you have access to billions of electronic pages stored on computers all over the world. Whatever your interest—music, movies, finance, science, literature, travel, astrology, body piercing—you can find hundreds of pages to explore.

What Exactly Is the Web?

The Web is a collection of documents stored on computers (called *Web servers*) all over the world. What makes these documents unique is that each contains a link to other documents contained on the same Web server or on a different Web server (down the block, across the country, or even overseas). You can hop around from document to document, from Web server to Web server, and from continent to continent by clicking these links.

These documents are not some dusty old text documents like you'd find in the university library. Web documents contain pictures, sounds, video clips, animations, and even interactive programs. When you click a multimedia link, your modem pulls the file into your computer where the Web browser or another program plays the file. All you have to do is tilt your chair back, nibble on popcorn, and watch the show.

First You Need a Web Browser

To do the Web, you need a special program called a *Web browser,* which works through your service provider to pull up documents on your screen. You can choose from any of several Web browsers, including the two most popular browsers, Netscape Navigator and Internet Explorer. In addition to opening Web pages, these browsers contain advanced tools for navigating the Web, finding pages that interest you, and marking the pages you might want to revisit.

Windows comes with Internet Explorer, which already should be installed on your computer. Internet Explorer also includes several additional Internet programs, including Outlook Express (for e-mail and newsgroups), NetMeeting (for Internet phone calls), and FrontPage Express (for creating Web pages).

Inside Tip

You can use your existing Web browser to download a different browser or an updated version of your current browser. Go to **www.netscape.com** to download Netscape Navigator (Netscape's Web browser) or Netscape Communicator (a suite of Internet applications that includes Navigator and an e-mail program). You can pick up the latest version of Internet Explorer at **http://www.microsoft.com/windows/ie/default.htm**. See "Hitting Specific Sites with Addresses" and "Copying (Downloading) Files from the Internet" later in this chapter for details on going to specific Web sites and copying files. If you like to buck trends, try Opera, billed as "the fastest browser on earth," at **www.opera.com**.

Navigating the Web

If you're using Internet Explorer as your Web browser, click the icon named **The Internet** or **Internet Explorer** on the Windows desktop, or choose **Internet Explorer** from the **Start, Programs** menu or the **Start, Programs, Internet Explorer** menu. To run Netscape, click the **Netscape Communicator** or **Netscape Navigator** icon on the Windows desktop.

If your computer is not connected to your service provider, the Connect To dialog box appears. Type your username and password, as explained in the previous chapter, and click the **Connect** button. After Dial-Up Networking establishes your Internet connection, your browser loads its *home page* (whatever page it is set to load on startup). Figure 22.1 shows Internet Explorer in action.

Click the **Back** button to display the previous page.

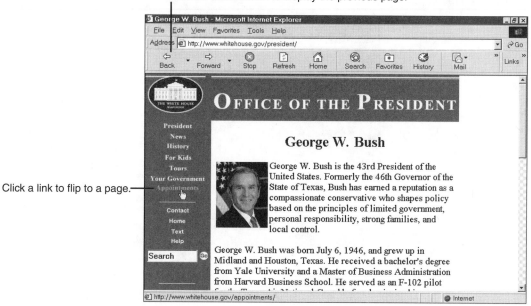

Click a link to flip to a page.

Figure 22.1

Internet Explorer makes it easy to navigate the Web.

You can wander the Web by simply clicking *links* (typically blue underlined text, buttons, or graphic site maps). Click the **Back** button to flip to a previous page, or click **Forward** to skip ahead to a page that you've visited but backed up from.

Hitting Specific Sites with Addresses

You've seen them on TV, in magazines, maybe even in your daily newspaper: bits of odd-looking text, such as **www.whitehouse.gov** or **www.nfl.com**. What are these things? They're addresses of specific Web pages, called *URLs* (*Uniform Resource Locators*). You enter the address in your Web browser, usually in a text box called **Go to** or **Address** near the top of the window, and your Web browser pulls up the page (see Figure 22.2).

All you really have to know about a URL is that if you want to use one, type the URL exactly as you see it. Type the periods as shown, use forward slashes, and follow the capitalization of the URL. If you make any typos, a message appears indicating that the page doesn't exist or that the browser will load the wrong page.

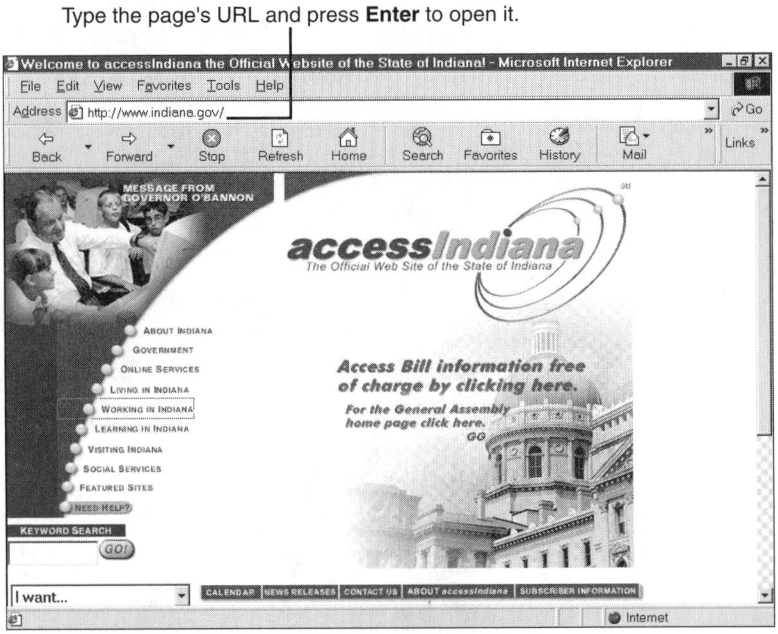

Type the page's URL and press **Enter** to open it.

Figure 22.2

If you know the address of a page, you can go directly to it.

Techno Talk

All Web page addresses start with http://. Newsgroup sites start with news://. FTP sites (where you can get files) start with ftp:// ... you get the idea. HTTP (short for HyperText Transfer Protocol) is the language used to transfer pages over the Internet. The rest of the address reads from right to left (from general to specific). For example, in the URL http://www.mitsubishi.co.jp, jp stands for Japan, co stands for corporation (a company in Japan), mitsubishi stands for Mitsubishi (a specific company), and www stands for World Wide Web (or Mitsubishi's Web server, as opposed to its FTP server or mail server). Addresses that end in .edu are for servers at educational institutions. Addresses that end in .com are for commercial institutions. You can omit the http:// when entering Web page addresses.

If a URL ends in .com, you might be able to omit the www at the beginning of the URL and the .com from the end. For example, instead of typing www.yahoo.com, simply type yahoo and press **Enter.** Some browsers automatically complete the entry for you; others, such as Internet Explorer 5, send you to a search page that helps you track down the site.

Using Internet Search Tools

How do you find information on the Web? Many Web sites have search tools that filter through an index of Internet resources to help you find what you're looking for. You simply connect to a site that has a search tool, type a couple words that specify what you're looking for, and click the **Search** button. The following are the addresses of some popular search tools on the Web:

➤ www.google.com

➤ www.yahoo.com

➤ www.lycos.com

➤ www.go.com

➤ www.altavista.com

➤ www.webcrawler.com

Most Web browsers have a Search button that connects you to the browser's search tool of choice or displays a list of search sites. For example, if you click **Search** in Internet Explorer, you connect to MSN's search page, which lets you search for Web sites, a person's mailing address, a person's e-mail address, a business, or a map. The cool thing about the Search button is that it opens a separate pane that displays the search results. You then can click links in the left pane to open pages in the right pane without having to click the **Back** button to return to the search results, as shown in Figure 22.3.

You also can use special search tools to find long-lost relatives and friends on the Internet. These search tools are like electronic telephone directories that can help you find mailing addresses, phone numbers, and even e-mail addresses. To search for people, check out the following sites:

➤ people.yahoo.com

➤ www.bigfoot.com

➤ www.whowhere.lycos.com

➤ www.switchboard.com

➤ www.anywho.com

Figure 22.3

The Search pane provides an easy way to flip through a list of discovered sites.

The Search pane displays a list of sites that match your search phrase.

Click a site's name in the **Search** pane.

Click the **Search** button to display the Search pane.

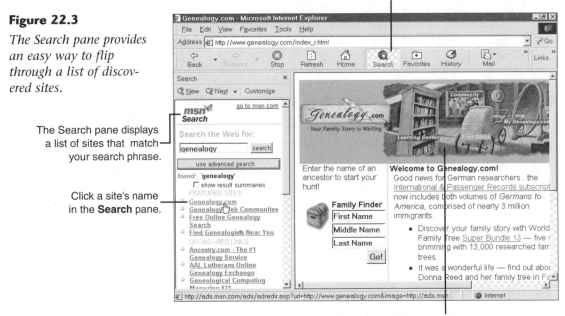

The selected site's opening page appears here.

Tagging and Flagging Your Favorite Pages

As you wander the Web, you stumble upon pages that you want to revisit—maybe the home page of your favorite actress or a Web site that lists updated prices for your mutual funds. In such cases, you can mark these pages and add them to a menu—typically called a *Bookmark* or *Favorites* menu. The next time you want to pull up the page, you simply select it from your customized menu. You can mark pages several ways, depending on the Web browser you are using. In Netscape and Internet Explorer, the easiest methods are as follows:

➤ In Navigator, drag the little icon that's next to the **Location** text box over the **Bookmarks** icon and release the mouse button. This places the page name on the Bookmarks menu. You also can drag links over the **Bookmarks** icon.

➤ In either browser, right-click a blank area on the current page, or right-click a link and choose **Add Bookmark** or **Add to Favorites.**

➤ In Internet Explorer, open the **Favorites** menu and click **Add to Favorites** to add the page's name to the Favorites menu. The Add Favorite dialog box appears, as shown in Figure 22.4. Enter your preferences and click **OK.**

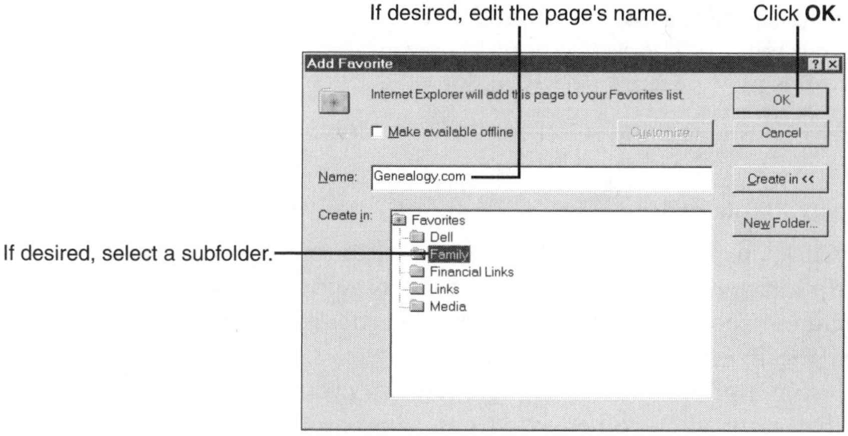

If desired, edit the page's name.   Click **OK**.

If desired, select a subfolder.

Figure 22.4

Use the Add Favorite dialog box to add a page's name to the Favorites menu.

Saving Pages to Read at Your Leisure

If your online service agreement charges you by the hour, you live in the boonies and face long-distance charges every time you dial your connection, or you share a single phone line between your phone and your computer, you want to spend as little time as possible on the Internet. Your objective is to hit the Internet, get what you want, and hang up. Fortunately, most Web browsers have an option for saving pages to the hard drive and viewing those pages offline.

You have two options: You can save the pages to disk and open them later or you can set up *site subscriptions*. With a site subscription, your browser connects automatically at a specified time (say three o'clock in the morning when Internet traffic is light), downloads the pages you specify, saves them to disk, and then disconnects.

The steps for saving a page to disk are fairly basic: Choose the **File, Save** command, enter your options, pick the desired drive and folder, and click the **Save** button. The browser typically offers you the option of saving a text version of the page (no graphics) or saving a complete version (with both text and graphics).

After you have saved all the pages you want to view offline, open the browser's **File** menu and select the **Go Offline** or **Work Offline** command (or its equivalent). If the browser does not automatically disconnect you from your ISP, right-click the Dial-Up Networking icon (on the right end of the Windows taskbar) and click **Disconnect.** You then can use the browser's **File, Open** command to open and view the Web pages you saved to disk. To go back online, you must reconnect to your ISP and then select the **File, Work Offline** command to turn off the Work Offline option.

235

Site subscriptions automate the download procedure for your favorite Web content. In Internet Explorer, you can choose to set up a site subscription when you add a page to your Favorites menu. Here's what you do:

1. Open the **Favorites** menu and select **Add to Favorites.** The Add Favorite dialog box appears.

2. Click **Make available offline.**

3. (Optional) Click **Customize** and follow the onscreen instructions to specify your subscription preferences. You can have the subscriptions delivered only when you choose Tools, Synchronize or have Internet Explorer download the pages automatically on specified days and at specified times. (If you do not customize your subscription, Internet Explorer assumes you want to download subscribed content only when you choose Tools, Synchronize.)

4. Click **OK.**

In Netscape Navigator, you can set up a site subscription by changing the properties of a bookmark. Open the **Bookmarks** menu and select **Manage Bookmarks.** Open the folder that has the bookmark for the page to which you want to subscribe. Right-click the bookmark and select **Properties.** Click the **Schedule** tab, enter your preferences, as shown in Figure 22.5, and click **OK.**

Figure 22.5

In Netscape Navigator, you can enter subscription preferences for bookmarks.

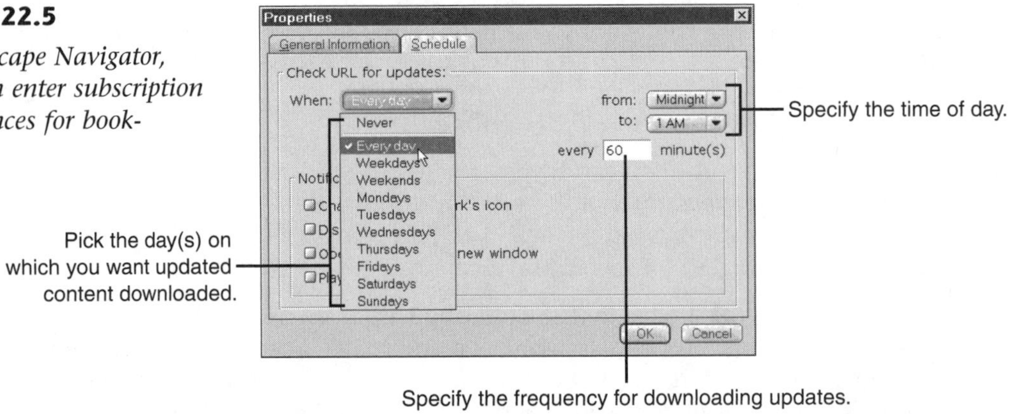

Pick the day(s) on which you want updated content downloaded.

Specify the time of day.

Specify the frequency for downloading updates.

Copying (Downloading) Files from the Internet

The Internet is chock-full of files that you can *download* (copy to your computer) and use. You can download pictures, sounds, video clips, shareware (play before you pay) programs, software updates, and other free stuff. In the past, you needed a special program to connect to *FTP (File Transfer Protocol)* sites and download files. Although you still can use these specialized programs, it's much easier to download files with your Web browser by taking the following steps:

➤ In Internet Explorer, right-click a link for the file you want to download and click **Save Target As** or **Save Picture As.** Use the Save As dialog box to name the file and select a folder in which you want to save it.

➤ In Netscape Navigator, right-click a link for the file and click **Save Link As, Save Page As,** or **Save Image As.** Again, use the Save As dialog box to name the file and select a folder in which to store it.

As your Web browser downloads the file, it displays a dialog box showing the progress. The time it takes to download the file depends on the file's size, the speed of your connection, and how busy the site is.

Accessorizing Your Browser

Web browsers are designed to open and display Web pages. Most browsers also are capable of displaying common graphic files (pictures) and playing some sounds. To play file types, the browser cannot handle—some graphic file types, audio clips, and video clips, for instance—Web browsers need the help of specialized applications. Internet Explorer mainly uses ActiveX controls, which add capability to the browser itself. Netscape Navigator primarily uses plug-ins, which Navigator automatically calls into action when needed.

Obtaining Popular Helper Plug-Ins and ActiveX Controls

Fortunately, your Web browser can help you find the most popular plug-ins and ActiveX controls on the Internet. In most cases, you can carelessly click links. Whenever you click a link for a file that the browser cannot play, the browser checks to see if it has the plug-in or ActiveX control it needs. If the plug-in or control is not available, the browser prompts you to download and install it or displays a page with links to various add-ons that can do

Inside Tip

You can get fancy with Favorites and Bookmarks by creating submenus. In Navigator, open the **Bookmarks** menu and select **Manage Bookmarks.** In Internet Explorer, open the **Favorites** menu and select **Organize Favorites.** In either program, you get a window that enables you to rearrange your bookmarks or favorites, create submenus (folders), and perform other feats of magic.

Notable Note

Most sites store *compressed* files, so they take up less disk space and travel across the Internet faster. If you are lucky, you get self-extracting compressed files— you double-click the file and it decompresses itself. In other cases, you need a special decompression program, such as WinZip, which can extract the files for you. You can get WinZip at **www.winzip.com.** It extracts files that have the ZIP extension.

the job. You simply follow the onscreen instructions to download and install the plug-in or ActiveX control.

Locating Popular Plug-Ins and ActiveX Controls

If the browser doesn't know what to do (sometimes it can't figure out which file type you are trying to play), it displays a dialog box asking you either to pick the program you want to use to open the file or to save the file to your hard disk, so you can play it later. For now, save the file to your hard disk so you can go in search of the program you need to play it.

Various sites on the Internet serve as repositories of plug-ins and ActiveX controls along with various product reviews. When you need to find a plug-in or ActiveX control, try the following sites:

➤ **Stroud's Consummate Winsock Applications List**   cws.internet.com

➤ **TUCOWS**   www.tucows.com

➤ **CNET Downloads**   download.cnet.com

➤ **ZDNet**   www.zdnet.com (click on the **Free Downloads** link and register)

Most of these sites provide a description of each add-on program and indicate whether it is an ActiveX control (for Internet Explorer) or plug-in (for Navigator). Make sure you get the version of the add-on designed for your browser. The reviews of these add-on programs typically contain links to the developer's home page, where you can obtain additional information.

Making Your Own Web Page

After you've pulled up a few Web pages, you might feel the urge to make your presence known on the Web. You can do this by creating and publishing your own Web page. When you're just starting out, keep it simple. With Yahoo! GeoCities, you can create a single Web page right on the Web. You don't need to learn a whole new program or even worry about transferring your page from your computer to a Web server. You make your page on the Web, and your site can be up and running in less than a half hour. So let's get on with it and publish a simple Web page at Yahoo! GeoCities:

1. Run your Web browser and go to **geocities.yahoo.com**.

2. Unless you have registered with Yahoo! earlier, follow the series of links required to register as a new user. (Because Web sites are notorious for changing steps and commands, specific instructions would only confuse you. You have to wing it—trust me.)

3. Fill out the required form, read the legal agreements, and jump through whatever hoops you need to jump through to get your free membership. This gives you an ID (member name) and password so you can sign in.

4. Use your ID and password to sign in to Yahoo! GeoCities. Your browser loads the Yahoo! GeoCities welcome page.

5. Click the **Yahoo! PageWizards** link. Yahoo! GeoCities displays a list of pre-designed Web page templates you can use to get started.

6. Click one of the Page Wizard designs. Yahoo! GeoCities displays a brief introduction to the wizard.

7. Click **Launch Yahoo! PageWizard** to start the wizard with the selected design, or click one of the alternative color schemes or designs near the bottom of the page. The first Page Wizard dialog box appears, as shown in Figure 22.6, welcoming you to the wizard.

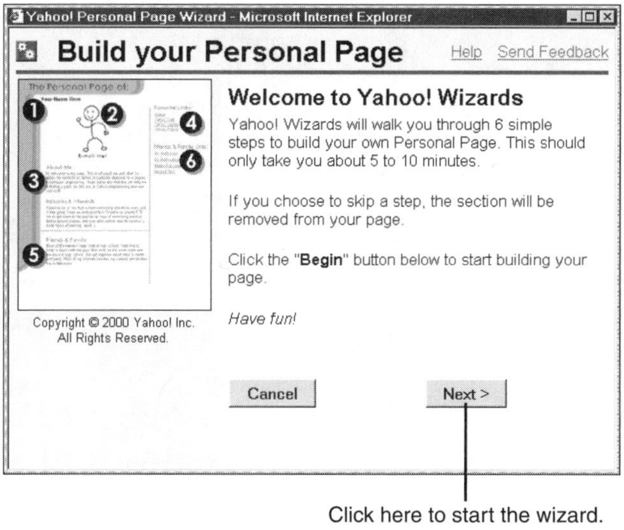

Click here to start the wizard.

Figure 22.6

Yahoo! GeoCities provides a brief introduction to the selected wizard.

8. Click the **Begin** or **Next** button. The wizard prompts you to select a color scheme.

9. Click the desired color scheme and click **Next >.** The wizard prompts you to enter your name and e-mail address.

10. Follow the wizard's instructions to complete your Web page and save it to the Yahoo! GeoCities Web server. (The steps vary, depending on which wizard you're running.)

You can change your page at any time. Just go to Yahoo! GeoCities at geocities. yahoo.com, sign in, and run the Page Wizard. When the Page Wizard appears this time, it displays an option for editing an existing page. Click **Edit Existing Page**, open the drop-down menu, and click the name of the page you want to edit. Click **Next >** and follow the onscreen instructions to enter your changes.

Whoa!

To delete a Web page, whether you created it with a wizard or with PageBuilder, you must use PageBuilder. Run PageBuilder, open the **File** menu, and click **File Manager.** Click the check box next to the file you want to delete, and then click the **Delete** button.

For more options and control over your Web page design and layout, use Yahoo! PageBuilder. This is a full-featured Web page creation and editing tool. To run PageBuilder, simply open the Yahoo! GeoCities home page and click **Yahoo! PageBuilder.** This displays an introduction to PageBuilder. Click the **Launch PageBuilder** link to run the program.

Of course, there are standalone programs you can use to create fancier Web pages and manage complex sites. Microsoft's FrontPage, included with most versions of Microsoft Office, is a full-featured Web site management tool that provides powerful tools for laying out Web pages and keeping Web sites running smoothly. You also can download a 30-day shareware version of one of the most popular Web page editors, HotDog, at www.sausage.com. or visit Internet Software Technologies at www.ist.ca to download an evaluation copy of HTMLed Pro. These programs are commonly called *HTML editors*.

Inside Tip

Most standalone Web page editors let you view the HTML codes that control the appearance of a Web page. In FrontPage, open the Web page whose codes you want to view, and then open the **View** menu and select **Reveal Codes.** In Word, open the **View** menu and select **HTML Source.** Most Web page editors even offer a button to toggle between the Page Display mode and HTML Code mode.

The Least You Need to Know

➤ Run your Web browser by clicking its icon on the Windows desktop, in the Quick Launch toolbar, or on the Programs menu.

➤ Navigate the Web with links and the **Back** and **Forward** buttons.

➤ To open a specific Web page, enter its address in the URL box at the top of the browser.

➤ Use an Internet search tool to help you find information; products to purchase; and the names, addresses, and e-mail addresses of your friends and family members.

➤ Use the **Favorites** or **Bookmarks** menu to flag pages you might wish to revisit. The next time you wish to visit that page, simply open the **Favorites** or **Bookmarks** menu and click the link.

➤ To get help creating your first Web page and placing it on the Web, go to **geocities.yahoo.com.**

Chapter 23

E-Mail: Postage Free, Same Day Delivery

In This Chapter

➤ Send e-mail messages to your friends and relatives

➤ Read and reply to incoming e-mail messages

➤ Attach files to outgoing messages

➤ Place your e-mail address on an organization's listserv mailing list

---

Over the last 10 years, the United States Postal Service has taken some lumps. Criticized for slow delivery and high rates, the postal service has lost ground to competitors, such as UPS and Federal Express. It has tried to become more competitive by offering new services and marketing its services a little more creatively.

However, the postal service cannot battle its fiercest and most silent competitor: e-mail. E-mail enables anyone with an Internet connection to send a message anywhere in the world and have it reach its destination in a matter of seconds or minutes instead of days. Sure, you still need the postal service to haul your other parcels, but for typed messages and computer files, e-mail can run circles around any postal service on the planet. It's a lot cheaper, too. In this chapter, you will learn how to use an e-mail program to quickly send, receive, and read e-mail messages.

Ugh! Setting Up Your E-Mail Program

The hardest part about e-mail is getting your e-mail program to connect to your Internet service provider's e-mail server, which acts as an electronic post office. If you are using one of the major commercial online services, such as America Online or Microsoft Network, you can relax; the installation program took care of all the details for you. You simply click the e-mail button and start using it.

Inside Tip

You don't need a special e-mail program to send and receive e-mail. You can set up a free e-mail account at any of several sites, the most popular of which is Hotmail at **www.hotmail. com.**

Inside Tip

This chapter focuses on Outlook Express, the e-mail program included with Internet Explorer. If you are using a different e-mail program, some of the options described in this chapter might differ; however, the steps for sending and receiving e-mail are similar for most e-mail programs.

However, if you have a local service provider and are using a dedicated e-mail program, such as Microsoft's Outlook Express, first you must enter information telling your e-mail program how to connect to the mail server. Make sure you have the following information from your service provider:

➤ **E-mail address**   Your e-mail address usually is all lowercase and starts with your first initial and last name (for example, jsmith@iway.com). However, if your name is John Smith (or Jill Smith), you might have to use something more unique, such as JohnHubertSmith@iway.com.

➤ **Outgoing mail (SMTP)**   Short for Simple Mail Transfer Protocol, the SMTP server is the mailbox into which you drop your outgoing messages. It's actually your Internet service provider's computer. The address usually starts with *mail* or *smtp* (for example, mail.iway.com or smtp.iway.com).

➤ **Incoming mail (POP3)**   Short for Post Office Protocol 3, the POP server is like your neighborhood post office. It receives incoming messages and places them in your personal mailbox. The address usually starts with *pop* (for example, pop.iway.com).

➤ **Account**   This one is tricky; it could be your username—the name you use to log into your service provider (for example, jsmith)—or something entirely different, depending on your service provider.

➤ **Password**   Typically, you use the same password for logging on and for checking e-mail. I can't help you here; you picked the password.

After you have the information, you must start your e-mail program and then enter the information to set up a new account. If you're using Outlook Express, click the **Outlook Express** icon on the Windows desktop or in the Quick Launch toolbar, or run the program from the **Start**, **Programs** menu or **Start**, **Programs**, **Internet Explorer** menu.

When you first run your e-mail program, it should step you through the process of entering the required information. Just follow the onscreen instructions. If the Internet Connection Wizard does not start or you need to enter information for a different e-mail account, enter the command for creating a new e-mail account (for example, in Outlook Express, you open the **Tools** menu, select **Accounts**, click the **Add** button, and choose **Mail**). Enter the requested account information as shown in Figure 23.1.

> **Whoa!**
>
> If you have a unique name, such as Kryzminski, you might want to use a more cryptic e-mail address to deter people from tracking you down.

Figure 23.1

Before you can send or receive e-mail you must enter connection settings.

Sending Mail Without Licking Stamps

The procedure for sending messages over the Internet varies, depending on the e-mail program or online service you're using. In most cases, you first enter a command for composing a new message. For example, in Outlook Express, you click the **New Mail** or **New Message** button. A dialog box or window appears, prompting you to compose your message. If you're using Web-based e-mail, such as Hotmail, you click a link for composing a new message and then type the recipient's e-mail address and your message in text boxes on a Web page.

Notable Note

On many Web pages, the creator might place a link at the bottom of the page that enables you to quickly send the person an e-mail message. If you click such a link in Internet Explorer, the e-mail program starts automatically and displays the window for composing a message. It even inserts the person's e-mail address for you.

You type the person's e-mail address, a brief description of the message, and the contents of the message in the appropriate text boxes, as shown in Figure 23.2. You then can click the **Send** button. Some e-mail programs immediately send the message. Other programs place the messages you send in a temporary outbox; then you must enter another **Send** command to actually send the messages. For example, in Outlook Express, you click the **Send and Receive** button. Outlook Express then sends all messages from the Outbox and checks for incoming messages.

Figure 23.2

Sending mail with a typical Internet e-mail program (Outlook Express).

Type the person's e-mail address here.

Click here to send the message.

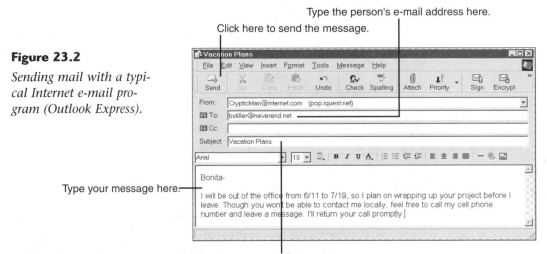

Type your message here.

Type a brief description of the message here.

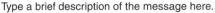

Advanced Message Formatting

Although you rarely need to adorn your messages with fancy text or pictures, e-mail programs enable you to use special type styles and sizes, add backgrounds, insert pictures, and embellish your messages with other formatting options. You can even add links to Web pages! In other words, the e-mail program enables you to create and send the equivalent of a Web page. The only trouble is you have to make sure the recipient's e-mail program is capable of displaying the formats you add; otherwise, the person might receive a message packed with funky codes.

Outlook Express offers a toolbar that contains buttons for the most common enhancements. In Outlook Express, as shown in the following figure, you can use the toolbar to make text bold or italic; add bulleted and numbered lists; and insert pictures, horizontal lines, links, and other objects. (If the toolbar does not appear, check the **Format** menu for an **HTML** option. HTML stands for HyperText Markup Language, the coding system used to format Web pages.)

Inside Tip

Most e-mail programs, including Outlook Express, include e-mail address books. Instead of typing the person's e-mail address you simply select it from a list. To quickly display the address book, press **Ctrl+Shift+B** in Outlook Express.

Create a bulleted or numbered list.

Align text left, right, or center.

Insert an image.

Make text bold, italic, or underlined.

Indent text.

Insert a link.

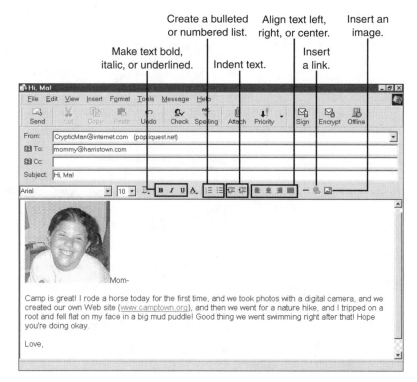

Figure 23.3

Many e-mail programs take you far beyond plain text messages.

You might have used similar formatting tools in Chapter 12, "Sprucing Up Your Documents with Formatting." The only new thing here is the button for inserting links. To insert a link that points to a Web page, you drag over the text that you want to appear as the link. You then click the button for inserting the link, type the address of the Web page to which you want it to point, and click **OK**. You also can drag links from a Web page into the message area and plop them right down in the message area.

Checking Your Inbox

Whenever someone sends you an e-mail message, it doesn't just pop up on your screen. The message sits on your service provider's mail server until you connect and retrieve your messages. There's no trick to connecting to the mail server as long as you entered the connection information correctly. Most programs check for messages automatically on startup or display a button you can click to fetch your mail. The program retrieves your mail and displays a list of message descriptions. To read a message, click its description, as shown in Figure 23.4. In most programs, you can double-click a message description to view the message in its own window.

Click the message description.

Figure 23.4

You can quickly display the contents of messages you receive.

Double-click the message description to view the message in its own window.

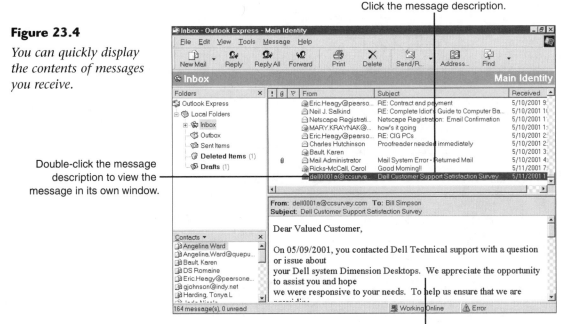

The message contents appear in the preview pane.

To reply to a message in most e-mail programs, click the **Reply** or **Respond To** button. This opens a window that automatically inserts the person's e-mail address and a description of the message. Many e-mail programs also quote the contents of the previous message, so the recipient can easily follow the conversation. To indicate that text has been quoted, e-mail programs typically add a right angle bracket > at the beginning of each quoted line. To respond, type your message in the message area and click the **Send** button.

Exchanging Files Using E-Mail

Most e-mail messages are nothing more than three or four lines of text saying very little. People shoot these terse missives back and forth like volleys of buckshot. However, sometimes you want to send something more substantial perhaps an outline for a book, a graphic image of yourself, or a copy of an article you found on the Web.

Whatever the case, you can send files along with your messages by creating *attachments*. The process is fairly simple, but the steps vary depending on which e-mail program you use. In most e-mail programs, you perform the same steps you take for composing and addressing the message. You then click a button (for example, **Attach** or **Insert File**). This displays a dialog box that enables you to select the file that you want to send. The dialog box looks just like the dialog box you use to open files. Change to the folder that contains the file you want to send and double-click the file's name. (In most programs, you can attach more than one file to a message.) When you are ready to send the message, along with the attachment, simply click the **Send** button.

If you receive a message that contains an attached file, your e-mail program usually displays some indication that a file is attached. For example, Outlook Express displays a paperclip icon, as shown in Figure 23.5. If you double-click the message (to display it in its own window), an icon appears at the bottom of the window or the file's name appears in the Attach text box. You can double-click the icon to open the file, or right-click and choose **Save** to save the file to a separate folder on your hard drive.

Whoa!

If you receive a program file or document from someone you don't know, be careful about running the program or opening the document; it might contain a virus. If you want to use the file, be sure to check it first with an antivirus program (see Chapter 26, "Online Security Issues," for details).

Click the paperclip to display
a menu for the attachment(s).

Figure 23.5

If you receive an attachment, Outlook Express displays a paperclip icon next to the message.

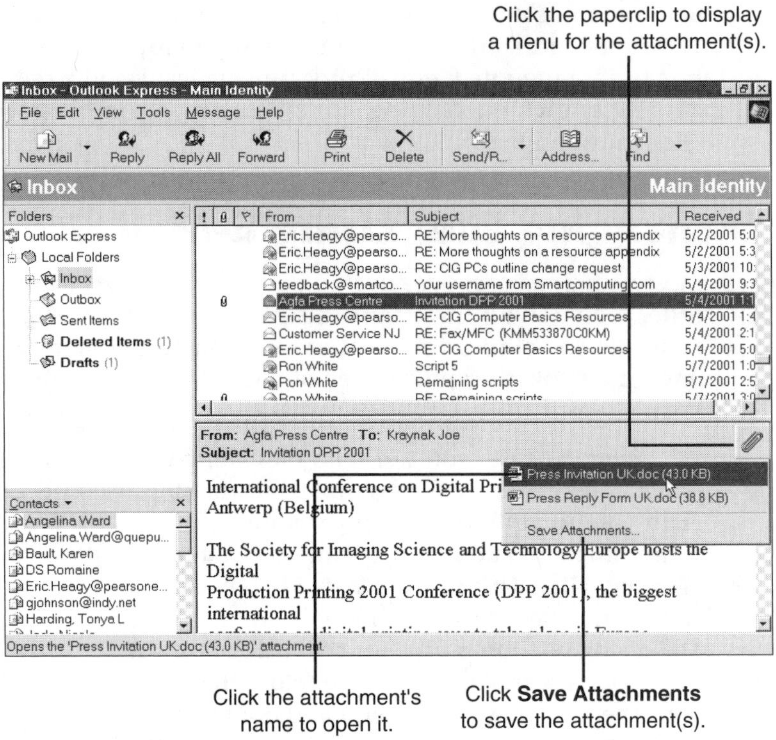

Click the attachment's
name to open it.

Click **Save Attachments**
to save the attachment(s).

Putting Your Name on a Listserv Mailing List

Many professional organizations, clubs, and special interest groups communicate using automated mailing lists generically referred to as *listservs*. (Listserv is a commercial e-mail list server product, but the term "listserv" is commonly used to refer to any automated e-mail list server, including Listserv, Majordomo, and many others.) On a listserv, a member sends an e-mail message to the listserv, which automatically compiles all the messages it receives and then distributes the compilation to all members of the listserv. (The listserv can be moderated to screen out some messages making it less automated.)

To find a listserv that interests you, fire up your Web browser and open a Web search tool (for example, **www.lycos.com**). Type a word or two that describes your interest and then tack on "listserv," "mailing list," or "mail." For example, you might type **dog listserv.** Click the **Search** or **Find** button. The results should provide plenty of links to appropriate listservs.

Many listservs have their own special instructions for subscribing and unsubscribing. If you have the instructions, read and follow them. You also should write them down, print them, or save them to your disk, so you know how to unsubscribe later. If you don't have instructions, usually you can perform the following steps to subscribe to an automated listserv:

1. Compose a new e-mail message addressed to the listserv. (Most listservs have a subscription address and a posting address. Be sure to use the subscription address.)

2. Leave the **Subject** or message description text box blank.

3. Type `subscribe [listname] [yourname]` in the message area (of course, replace `[listname]` with the name of the mailing list and `[yourname]` with your name, no brackets). If the listserv has only one mailing list, you might be able to omit the listname.

4. Send the message.

You receive mailing lists just as you receive e-mail messages, although the message contents typically are much longer. A popular mailing list can contain hundreds of postings. In many cases the mailing list itself includes instructions at the top or bottom on how to post messages and unsubscribe from the list.

The Least You Need to Know

➤ Before you can send and receive e-mail using a special e-mail program, you must enter connection settings for your e-mail program.

➤ Before you can send or receive e-mail, you must enter settings that tell the e-mail program how to connect to your ISP's mail server.

➤ To create a new e-mail message, click the **Compose** or **New Message** button or its equivalent in your e-mail program.

➤ Incoming e-mail messages often are stored in the Inbox. Simply click the **Inbox** folder and then click the desired message to display its contents.

➤ The **Reply** buttons enable you to quickly reply to a message you received.

➤ Outlook Express has a paperclip icon on the toolbar to enable you to attach a file to an outgoing message.

➤ If you receive a message that has a file attached to it, right-click the file's name and click the **Save** command.

Chapter 24

Passing Notes in Newsgroups

You would think that a newsgroup would consist of a bunch of guys with typewriters sitting around smoking cigars and typing news stories. Well, newsgroups aren't quite like that. A newsgroup is more like a bulletin board where people can share ideas, post questions and answers, and support one another. They're more like discussion groups, and people are beginning to call them that.

The Internet has thousands of these newsgroups covering topics that range from computer programming to cooking, from horses to cars, from politics to tattoos. With your Internet connection and a newsreader, you have access to newsgroups 24 hours a day, seven days a week. In this chapter, you will learn how to connect to these newsgroups, subscribe to newsgroups that interest you, and read and post newsgroup messages.

Setting Up Your Newsreader

The best way to access newsgroups is to use a specialized program called a *newsreader,* whose sole purpose is to connect to newsgroups and display messages. This chapter focuses on Outlook Express, the e-mail/newsreader program included with Internet Explorer. If you are using a different newsreader, some of the options described in this chapter might differ.

To access newsgroups, you must set up your newsreader to connect to your service provider's *news server.* This consists of entering the news server's address (for instance, news.internet.net). The first time you run your newsreader it should lead you through the process of setting up a news server account. You can check your settings or create a new account in Outlook Express by performing the following steps:

Techno Talk

If you've ever heard the term *USENET* bandied about and were curious, it's the formal name of the network used to exchange messages in newsgroups. USENET is short for *user's network.*

Inside Tip

If you don't know your news server's address, stick "**news**" at the beginning of your service provider's domain name. For example, if your service provider's domain name is internet.com, the news server address likely would be news.internet.com.

1. Open the **Tools** menu and select **Accounts.** The Internet Accounts dialog box appears.

2. Click the **News** tab. Assuming you have not set up a newsgroup account, the News list should be blank.

3. Click the **Add** button and click **News.** The Internet Connection Wizard appears prompting you to type your name.

4. Type your name as you want it to appear in messages that you post to newsgroups, and then click **Next.**

5. Type your e-mail address and click **Next.** Sometimes, instead of or in addition to posting a reply in a newsgroup, a person will reply to your post through e-mail.

6. Type your news server's address, as shown in Figure 24.1.

7. If the news server requires you to log on to use it, click the check box next to **My News Server Requires Me to Log On,** and then click the **Next** button.

8. If in Step 7 you indicated that you are required to log on, enter your username and password in the appropriate text boxes, and click **Next.** Otherwise, skip to Step 9.

9. Click **Finish.** Outlook Express creates a new newsgroup account for you and displays its name in the News list.

10. Click the **Close** button.

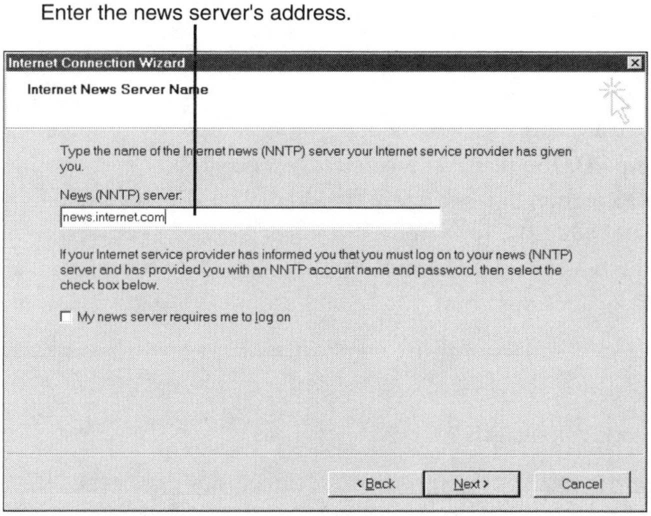

Enter the news server's address.

Figure 24.1

To connect to a news server you must enter its address.

Subscribing to Newsgroups (It's Free!)

Before you can start reading messages about do-it-yourself body piercing or other topics of interest, you must download a list of the newsgroups that are available on your news server and subscribe to the newsgroups that interest you. Your newsreader might automatically download the list the first time you connect. Be patient; even over a fairly quick modem connection, it might take several minutes to download this very long list. You then can subscribe to newsgroups to create a list of newsgroups that interest you.

Although the steps you take to subscribe to newsgroups vary depending on the newsreader you're using, the procedure is fairly easy in any newsreader. Let's take a look at just how easy it is by following the procedure in Outlook Express:

1. Click the Outlook Express icon on the Windows desktop or on the Quick Launch toolbar.

2. At the bottom of the folder list (left pane), click the name of your news server.

3. Click the **Newsgroups** button in the toolbar. The Newsgroups dialog box appears, as shown in Figure 24.2, displaying a list of available newsgroups. (You can update the list at any time by clicking the Reset List button.)

Techno Talk

You usually can determine a newsgroup's focus by looking at its address. Most addresses are made up of two or three parts. The first part indicates the newsgroup's overall subject area; for example, **rec** is for recreation and **alt** stands for alternative. The second part of the address specifically indicates what the newsgroup offers. For example, **rec.arts** is about the arts. If the address has a third part (most do), it focuses even further. For example, **rec.arts.bodyart** discusses the art of tattoos and other body decorations.

Figure 24.2

Outlook Express displays a list of newsgroups.

Type a topic that interests you to narrow the list.

This icon indicates that you are subscribed to the newsgroup.

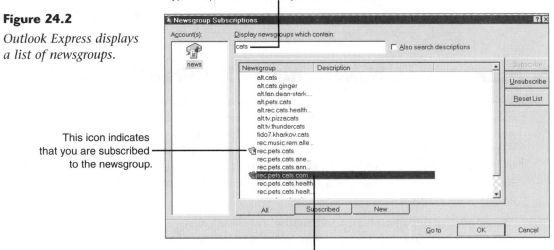

Double-click a newsgroup name to subscribe or unsubscribe.

4. In the **Display Newsgroups Which Contain** text box, type a topic (for example, type **cats**). This filters the list to show only those newsgroups that have "cats" in their name.

5. Double-click the name of the newsgroup to which you want to subscribe. A newspaper icon appears next to the name. (You can unsubscribe by double-clicking the newsgroup's name again.)

6. Repeat steps 3 and 4 to subscribe to additional newsgroups and then click the **OK** button.

7. In the folder list (left pane), click the plus sign next to your news server to display a list of subscribed newsgroups.

8. Click the newsgroup's name to display a list of posted messages in the upper-right pane.

Reading and Responding to Posted Messages

Although the names of newsgroups can provide hours of entertainment by themselves, you didn't connect to a news server just to chuckle at the weirdoes (well, maybe you did). You connected to read what people have to say and to post your own messages. If you used Outlook Express to read e-mail messages in the previous chapter, you find that the steps for reading newsgroup postings are similar:

1. Click the plus sign next to your news server's name to display a list of subscribed newsgroups.

2. Click or double-click the name of the desired newsgroup. Descriptions of posted messages appear.

3. Click a description to display the message contents in the message pane, as shown in Figure 24.3, or double-click the message to display it in its own window.

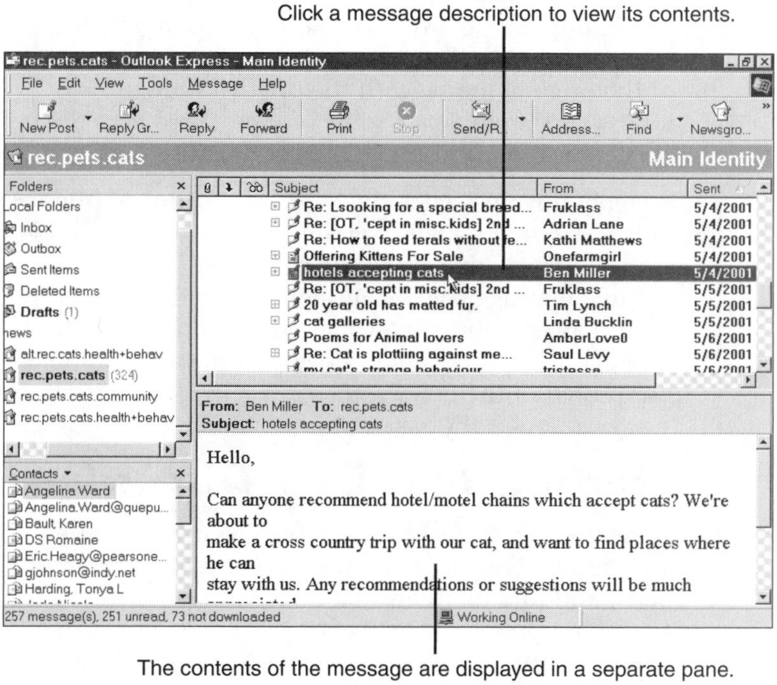

Click a message description to view its contents.

Figure 24.3

Outlook Express displays a list of messages in the selected newsgroup.

The contents of the message are displayed in a separate pane.

Whoa!

Before you post a message in a newsgroup, get a feel for its culture and history as if you were visiting a foreign country. See if the newsgroup has a FAQ (frequently asked questions list) to determine if the question you wish to ask or the issue that you want to address has already been addressed. And don't pick a fight unless, of course, that's what the newsgroup is all about.

Notable Note

Most newsreaders enable you to attach files to your messages. Although most messages consist of simple text, people post graphics in some newsgroups, such as hk.binaries.portrait. photography. (For details on how to work with file attachments, refer to Chapter 23, "E-Mail: Postage Free, Same Day Delivery.")

Following a Meandering Discussion

As people post messages and replies, they end up creating *discussions*. Most newsreaders are capable of displaying related messages as *threads,* so you can follow the discussion from its beginning to its end. If you see a message that has a plus sign next to it, you can click the plus sign to view a list of replies to the original message. You then can click the descriptions of the replies to view the contents of the replies.

Replying Publicly and Privately

When you read a message that inspires you to write a reply, you have two choices: You can reply to the group by posting your reply in the newsgroup or reply to the individual through e-mail. Some people request that you reply through e-mail for privacy or just because they're too lazy to check for replies in the newsgroup itself.

In Outlook Express, you can reply to the group by clicking the **Reply to Group** button. This displays a window that addresses the message to the current newsgroup and to any other newsgroups in which the original message was posted. It also quotes the contents of the original message. (If the original message was long, you should delete some of the quoted material.) Type your reply and click the **Post Message** button.

To reply privately, click the **Reply to Author** button. This starts your e-mail program, which displays a message window addressed to the person who posted the original message. Type your reply and click the **Send** button as you normally would do to send an e-mail message. The reply is sent directly to the author and is not posted in the newsgroup.

Starting Your Own Discussions

Newsgroups are great for expressing your own ideas and insights, having your questions answered by experts, and finding items that might not be readily available in the mass market (for example, books that are no longer in publication, parts for your '57 Chevy, and so on). When you need help or you just feel the overwhelming urge to express yourself, you can start your own discussion by posting a message.

258

Posting a message is fairly easy: First you connect to the newsgroup in which you want the message posted. Click the **New Message** button (or select the command for posting the new message). Your newsreader automatically addresses the message to the current newsgroup, as shown in Figure 24.4. (You also can add newsgroup addresses to post the message in other newsgroups.) Type a brief but descriptive title for your message, type the contents of your message, and click the **Post** button. Your message is posted in the newsgroup, where anyone can read it. It might take awhile for people to reply, so check back every couple days for responses. (Sometimes nobody responds, so don't expect too much.)

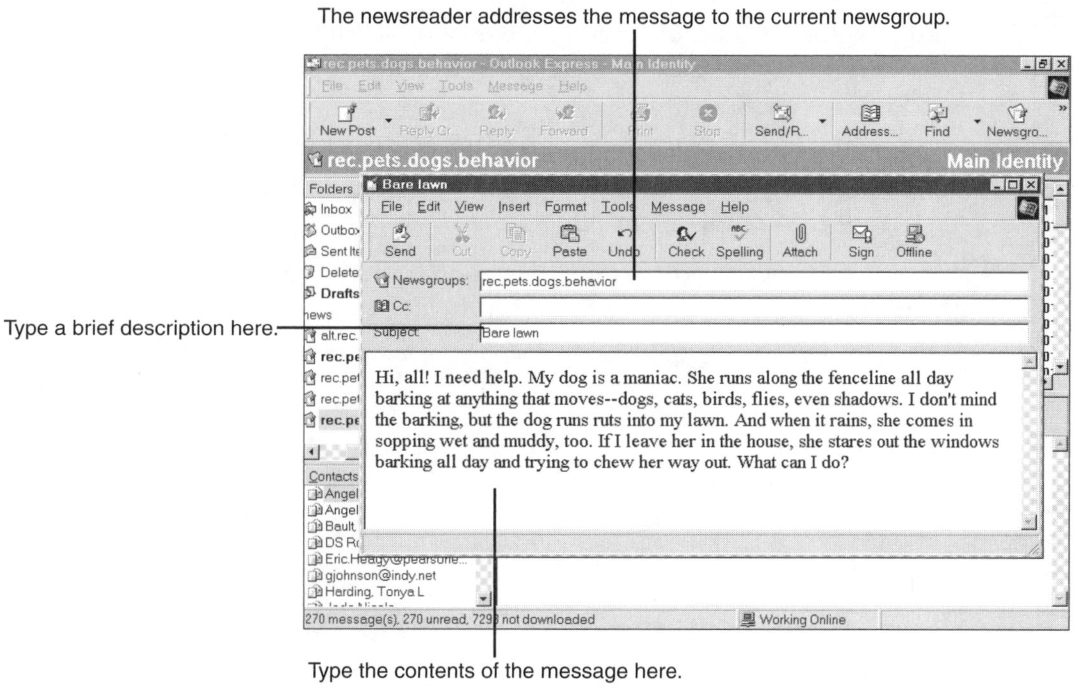

The newsreader addresses the message to the current newsgroup.

Type a brief description here.

Type the contents of the message here.

Figure 24.4

You can start a discussion by posting your own message.

The Least You Need to Know

➤ To connect to your ISP's news server you must specify the news server's address in your newsreader. In Outlook Express, choose **Tools, Accounts.**

➤ When you first connect to a news server, your newsreader downloads a list of available newsgroups.

➤ To give yourself convenient access to your favorite newsgroups, subscribe to those newsgroups.

➤ To display the contents of a newsgroup message, click the description of the message. Double-click the description to display the message in its own window.

➤ To post a reply to the newsgroup, enter the **Reply to Group** command. To reply privately by e-mail to the person who posted the message, enter the **Reply to Author** command.

➤ You can start your own newsgroup discussion by posting a new message to the newsgroup.

Chapter 25

Reaching Out with Chat and Instant Messaging

In This Chapter

➤ Type messages back and forth with people you've never met

➤ Prowl cyber rooms when you can't sleep

➤ Chat on the Web

➤ Chat privately with friends, relatives, and others using instant messages

➤ Phone a friend anywhere in the country free

The Internet has revolutionized the way we communicate. We correspond with e-mail, post messages in newsgroups, and read magazines on the Web. But that's just the standard fare. The Internet also offers more dynamic and immediate forms of communication through online chat, instant messaging, and Internet phone. This chapter provides a tour of these innovative tools and shows you how to use them.

Chatting on the Web

Many companies on the Internet have realized that chat sells. If you set up a wide selection of dynamic chat rooms, people gather to hang out and jabber. After they get hooked on chat, they are more likely to visit other areas of the Web site, where they learn more about the company's products and services and possibly buy something. These companies focus on building a community first and marketing to that community later.

Chatting It Up at Yahoo!

Yahoo! has always been considered a premier Internet search site. Now, Yahoo! has injected its power and simplicity into Internet chat. All you need to access Yahoo! Chat is a Web browser that supports *Java* or ActiveX (most Web browsers do).

To sign up for Yahoo! Chat, use your browser to pull up Yahoo!'s Chat Page at **chat.yahoo.com**, and then click the **Sign Up for Yahoo! Chat!** link. Onscreen instruc-

tions walk you through the process of registering and entering a chat room. Once you're registered, you can chat at any time by going to **chat.yahoo.com** and entering your member name and password.

After you are in a chat room you can start chatting, as shown in Figure 25.1. The ongoing discussion is displayed in the large frame in the upper left. To send a message to the other chatters, click the **Chat** text box just below the ongoing discussion, type your message, and press **Enter**. When you tire of this simple banter, try the following:

Techno Talk

Java is a programming language that makes it possible for Web developers to create programs that run on Web pages. What has made Java so popular is that the same Java program runs on any computer (for instance, a PC or a Macintosh). All the computer needs is a Java–enabled Web browser to interpret the programming code.

➤ Click the **Emotions** button and double-click an emotion (bow, agree, smile, or some other gesture) to send a text description of it.

➤ Right-click the name of someone in the room. This displays a dialog box, which enables you to find out more about the person, send the person a private message or a file, add the person to a list of friends, or ignore the person (prevent the person's messages from appearing on your screen).

Inside Tip

If you hit it off with someone online or just want to chat with a friend or relative in private, you can create a private room whose name does not appear in the Yahoo! rooms list. To enter the room, someone who knows your chat name has to follow you into the room. If you are invited to a private room, here's what you do to go there: Type \goto roomname in the text box where you type messages and press **Enter**. A room ceases to exist as soon as everyone leaves—no post-party cleanup!

➤ In the lower-left corner of the window is a list of tools. Click a tool to change to a different chat room, find out who's online, create your own room (public or private), edit your identity, get help, or exit. (You can edit your identity to provide additional information about yourself. Other chatters then see this information if they check your profile.)

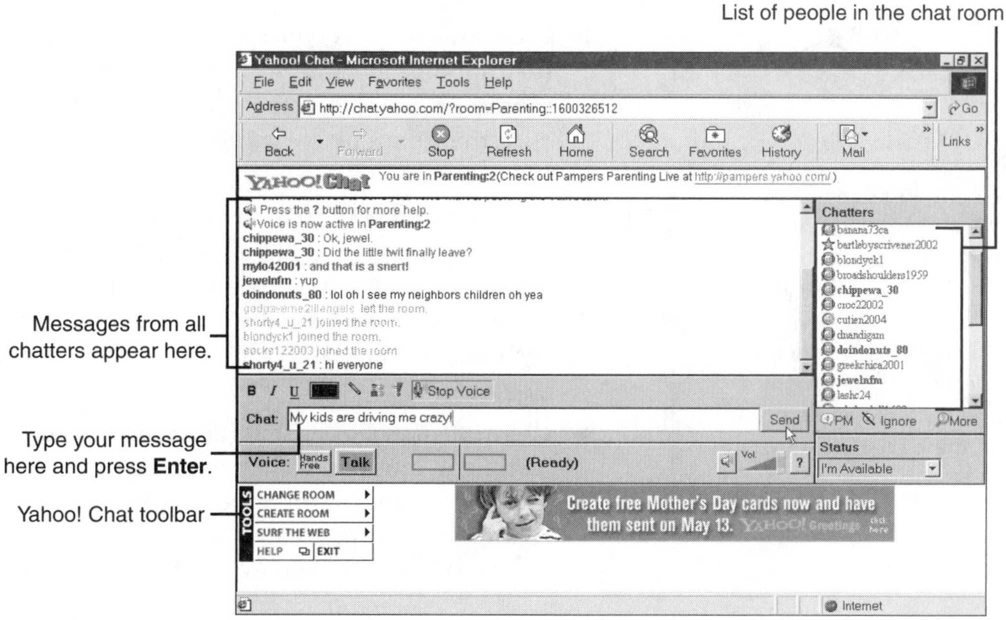

List of people in the chat room

Figure 25.1

Yahoo! Chat brings chat to the Web.

Other Web Chat Areas

Although Yahoo! is on the cutting edge of Web chat, there are some other Web chat services that you can try out. Most of these services offer access through Java, an ActiveX control, or a plug-in. The following list provides an overview of some of these chat areas along with a page address showing where to go for additional information:

➤ MSN Chat (**chat.msn.com**) is a little flashier than Yahoo! Chat and features some very well-populated chat rooms. When you connect to MSN Chat, you will be prompted to download and install the chat add-on. Click **Yes** to get the software and proceed to the chat rooms.

➤ Web Net (**www.webchat.org**) is similar to Yahoo! Chat in that it uses a Java applet for its chat interface, but it's not quite as sleek and graphic as Yahoo!. If you run out of people to chat with at Yahoo! or you want to dabble in the world of IRC chat without having to download and install an IRC program, check out one of Web Net's many rooms.

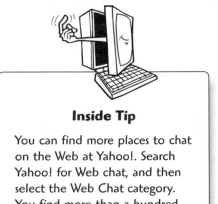

Inside Tip

You can find more places to chat on the Web at Yahoo!. Search Yahoo! for Web chat, and then select the Web Chat category. You find more than a hundred chat offerings each offering a wide selection of chat rooms. However, the chat applets that some of these chat areas use are not the best.

➤ Talk City (**talkcity.com**) is a virtual community where anyone can hang out and chat in a wide variety of rooms.

➤ Lycos (**www.lycos.com**) is a Web search site (like Yahoo!) that also features its own chat rooms. After opening the Lycos home page, click the Chat link to register and roam the Lycos chat circuit.

➤ Spinchat (**www.spinchat.com**) has its own chat program that pops up in a separate window. When you arrive at Spinchat's opening page, enter a nickname to use in the chat room, pick the desired room, and start chatting. It's as easy as that.

➤ CleverMedia's CleverChat (**clevermedia.com**) features a Shockwave chat application in which you choose an icon to represent you in the chat room. The chat program is very innovative and cool, but the chat rooms are sparsely populated.

Using Special Chat Programs

Although Web chat is becoming more popular, you can find more people chatting with specialized chat programs to access IRC (Internet Relay Chat). The following is a list of some of the better chat programs and information on where you can get them:

➤ **mIRC** One of the most popular shareware IRC programs around because it is so easy to use. It even comes with its own IRC primer to help new users get up to speed in a hurry. You can visit the mIRC home page at **www.geocities.com/ SiliconValley/Park/6000/index.html**, where you find a link for downloading it. (The file is self extracting, so just double-click its icon after downloading it.)

➤ **Orbit IRC** This is one of the most intuitive IRC programs I have had the pleasure of using. The program's window is tab based, so most IRC features are readily available at all times. You simply click a server, click the Connect button, pick a chat type (private or public), pick the desired room, and start chatting. You can download a 90-day trial version of Orbit IRC at **www.orbitirc.com.**

➤ **PIRCH**   Although not quite as popular as mIRC, PIRCH is a solid chat program with a relatively easy-to-use interface, a useful help system, and plenty of online support (through the Web). You can pick up a copy of PIRCH at **www.pirchat. com**.

➤ After you install a chat program, establish your Internet connection and then run the chat program. You then must use the program to connect to a chat server and pick the desired chat room. The following sections show you what to expect.

Connecting to a Chat Server

Before you can start chatting, you must connect to a *chat server* (a computer on the Internet specialized for handling IRC). The chat server to which you connect is connected to other chat servers to make a network (such as EFnet or Undernet). The chat rooms on a particular network are available to everyone who is connected to that network even if they are connected to different servers.

Most IRC programs prompt you to select a server on startup. A dialog box appears typically offering a list or drop-down list of available servers, as shown in Figure 25.2. You select the desired server from the list; enter your name, e-mail address, and other information; and then click the **OK** or **Connect** button to connect to the server. If the IRC program does not prompt you to choose an IRC server, scan the button bar or the menu system for the required command. If you can't connect to a server, try a different one.

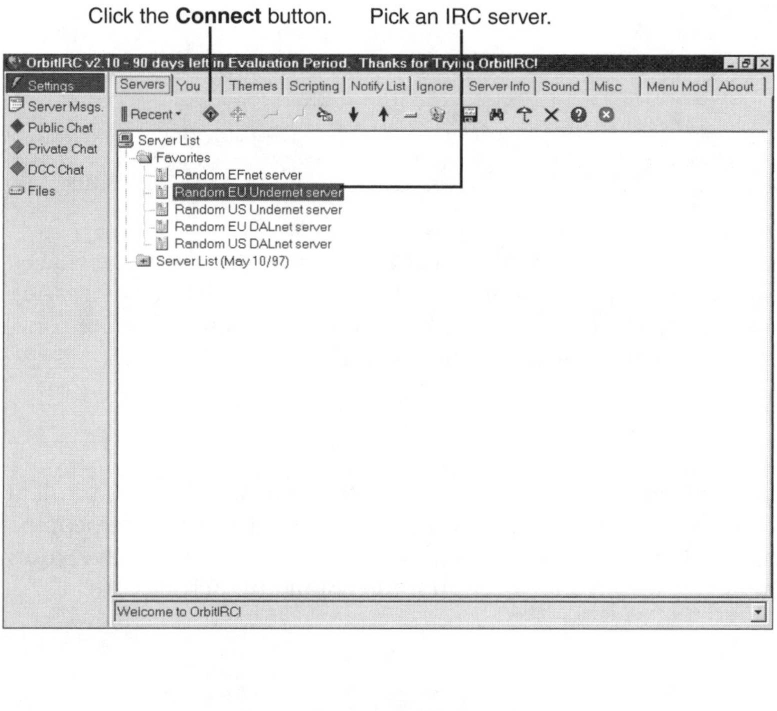

Click the **Connect** button.   Pick an IRC server.

Figure 25.2

Most IRC programs prompt you to select a server at startup.

Entering and Leaving Chat Rooms

As soon as you connect to a chat server, your chat program downloads a list of the available *chat rooms* (sometimes called *channels*) and prompts you to pick one. If the list doesn't pop up on your screen, check the button bar or menu system for the command to display the list of available rooms.

In most cases, the list displays the room name and the number of people in that room, as shown in Figure 25.3, to give you some idea of how popular it is. The list also might include a description of each room if the person who created the room added a description. Simply double-click the desired room name or click the name and click the button for entering or joining the room.

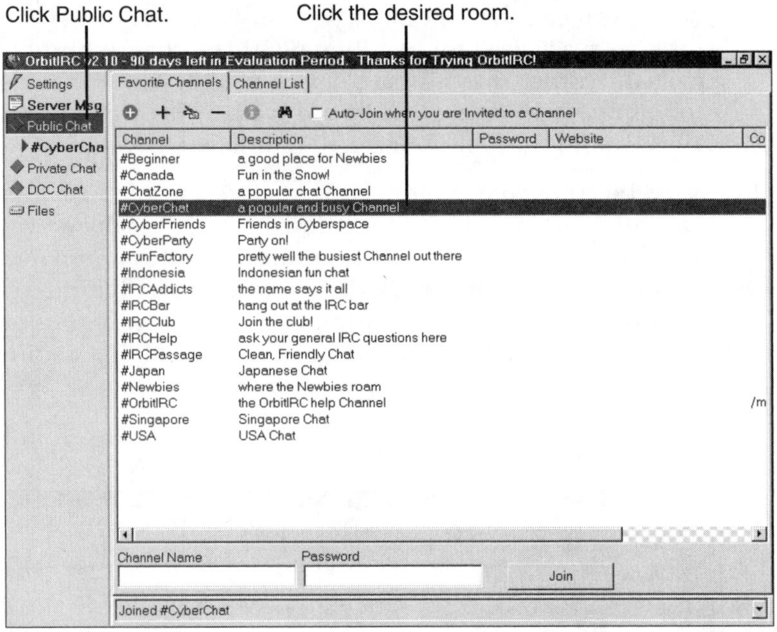

Click Public Chat.   Click the desired room.

Figure 25.3

The IRC program displays a list of available chat rooms or channels.

If you find that the current discussion doesn't appeal to you, you can leave the chat room. Check the toolbar or menu system for an **Exit Room** or comparable command or click the chat window's **Close (X)** button. To enter a different room, enter the command to display the list of available rooms and then select the desired room.

Chatting Away!

Now the fun starts. In a room that's populated with talkative typists, messages scroll at a frenetic pace. The room can take on a party atmosphere, where two or three people in the room are carrying on their own conversation, completely oblivious to everyone else in the room. Just hang out for awhile and watch the comments scroll past.

When you get a feel for the room, look for a text box for sending your own messages, as shown in Figure 25.4. The box typically is right below the area where the running discussion is displayed. Type your message and click the **Send** button or press **Enter.** Your message appears on your screen and on the screens of all the other people in the room.

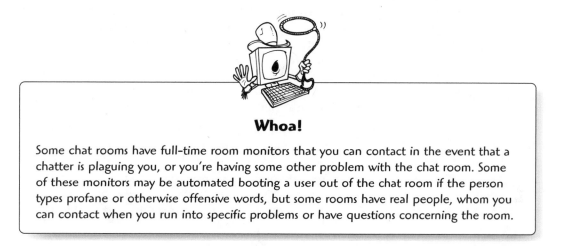

Whoa!

Some chat rooms have full-time room monitors that you can contact in the event that a chatter is plaguing you, or you're having some other problem with the chat room. Some of these monitors may be automated booting a user out of the chat room if the person types profane or otherwise offensive words, but some rooms have real people, whom you can contact when you run into specific problems or have questions concerning the room.

The chat window displays a list of people currently in the chat room. In most cases, you can view information about the person, send the person a private message or a file, or choose to ignore the person. Try right-clicking the person's name to view a context menu with the available options. If that doesn't work, try double-clicking the person's name. In most cases, double-clicking displays a dialog box for sending the person a private message.

Names of the
other chatters

The running discussion

Type your message and press **Enter.**

Figure 25.4

Start chatting.

Keeping in Touch with Online Pals Using Instant Messaging

Hanging out with strangers can be interesting, but if you'd like to chat with friends and relatives, spotting them in crowded chat rooms can be a bit difficult. To help you track down individuals on the Internet, you can use an *Instant Message* program. You simply add the names and tracking information (typically an e-mail address) of each person you might want to contact, and the program lets you know when the person is online. Assuming your friends and relatives run the same program (and are online), a dialog box pops up on your screen indicating that the person is available. You then can start your own private chat with that person.

Where do you get such a program? You can pick up America Online's Instant Messenger at **www.aol.com**, grab a copy of Yahoo!'s Messenger (formerly known as Yahoo! Pager) at **messenger.yahoo.com,** or snatch MSN Messenger Service from Microsoft at **messenger.msn.com.** If you and your pal have audio connected to your computers, you can even engage in a little voice chat and avoid long-distance charges. The following sections show you how to get started with AOL's Instant Messenger.

Downloading and Installing Instant Messenger

If you try only one instant messaging program, make sure it's AOL Instant Messenger. This is one of the easiest full-featured instant messaging programs around, and because it is so popular, it's the instant messaging program that your friends and relatives most likely will be using. To download and install AOL Instant Messenger, connect to AOL's home page at **www.aol.com** and click the **AOL Instant Messenger** link. Scroll down the page and click the **Get It Now** link. Complete the registration form and click **Continue.** Follow the onscreen instructions to download and install Instant Messenger.

Running AOL Instant Messenger

If you want people to be able to track you down, you must be connected to the Internet and Instant Messenger must be running. (You're not going to get any phone calls if your phone isn't plugged in.) Your name then will show up on the *buddy list* of anyone who added you to his or her buddy list. Your "buddy" will then know that you're online and ready to receive messages.

To run AOL Instant Messenger, double-click the **AOL Instant Messenger (SM)** short-cut on the desktop. Enter the screen name and password you entered when you registered for Instant Messenger. Click **Save Password** to have Instant Messenger remember your login information. Click the **Sign On** button.

Making a Buddy List

The most useful feature of Instant Messenger is that it notifies you when friends and relatives are online. It does this by using a *buddy list*. You enter a person's screen name to your buddy list and when the person connects to the Internet, the person's screen name pops up in your copy of Instant Messenger to let you know your pal is online. To add a person's name to your buddy list, take the following steps:

1. Click the **List Setup** tab, as shown in Figure 25.5.
2. Click the folder in which you want to insert the person's name.
3. Click the **Add a Buddy** button.
4. Type the person's screen name and press **Enter**.

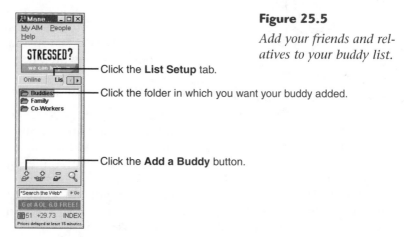

Figure 25.5

Add your friends and relatives to your buddy list.

Click the **List Setup** tab.

Click the folder in which you want your buddy added.

Click the **Add a Buddy** button.

Sending an Instant Message

Whenever someone on your buddy list connects to the Internet, the person's screen name appears on Instant Messenger's Online tab. You then can choose the person's name and send a message. Just click the person's screen name, click the **Send Instant Message** button, type your message, and click **Send**, as shown in Figure 25.6.

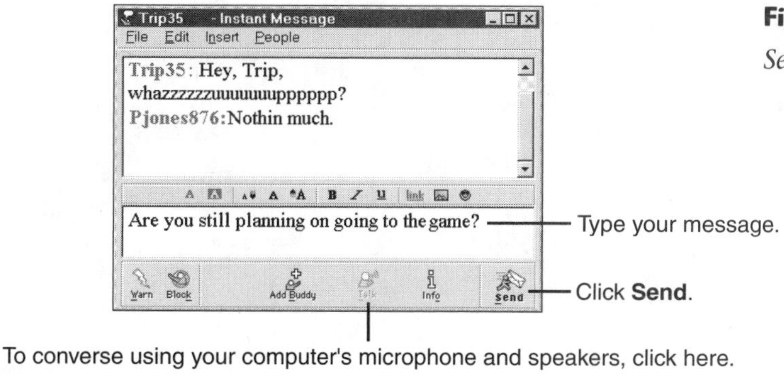

Figure 25.6

Send an instant message.

Trip35 : Hey, Trip, whazzzzzzuuuuuuuuppppppp?
Pjones876:Nothin much.

Are you still planning on going to the game? —— Type your message.

Warn Block   Add Buddy Talk   Info Send —— Click **Send**.

To converse using your computer's microphone and speakers, click here.

Free Long-Distance Calls with Internet Phone

The phone company has been overcharging us for years, but they're running scared. With your Internet connection and one of the new Internet phone programs, you can place a long distance call to anywhere in the United States free of charge and anywhere in the world for a lot less than a dime a minute. What's the catch?

Well, you can't just plug your phone into your modem and dial the number; you must have a special Internet phone program. You also need a sound card, speakers, and a microphone. Another drawback is that the audio quality suffers a bit when calls are placed over the Internet. Expect to experience a slight pause between the time when someone speaks and the person at the other end hears the words.

With Net2Phone, you can place free PC-to-PC calls over the Internet to any PC, anywhere in the world. Within the United States you can even place free PC-to-phone calls; however, these calls typically are limited to 5 minutes or less. Net2Phone also offers inexpensive rates for international PC-to-phone calls.

To get a trial copy of Net2Phone, go to **www.net2phone.com** and follow the trail of download links to download the program. After you have downloaded the installation file, double-click its name and follow the onscreen instructions to install, run, and register the program. Once you have registered, placing a call is as simple as dialing the number using an onscreen keypad (see Figure 25.7). As soon as the person you called answers (or the answering machine picks up), you can start talking just as if you had called the person using your phone.

Inside Tip

If you and your buddy both have speakers and a microphone attached to your computers, you can carry on a "phone" conversation. To talk to your pal, click the **Talk** button at the bottom of the window. Assuming your friend answers your call, you can carry on a conversation over the Internet toll free!

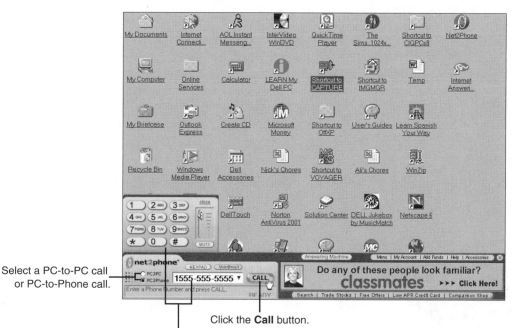

Select a PC-to-PC call or PC-to-Phone call.

Dial the number or type it here.

Click the **Call** button.

Figure 25.7

Use Net2Phone to place toll free calls from your computer to any phone in the United States.

The Least You Need to Know

➤ By connecting to Yahoo! Chat through the Internet, you can start chatting without installing any additional programs.

➤ To find other places to chat on the Web, use your favorite search tool to search for Web chat.

➤ IRC provides access to the largest population of chatters. However, it also can be the most difficult way to chat on the Internet.

➤ Use an instant message program to notify you when your friends and relatives are online and to immediately strike up a conversation with them.

➤ To use AOL Instant Messenger, the two people who want to converse must be connected to the Internet and must have AOL Instant Messenger installed and running on their computers.

➤ Use Net2Phone to place free PC-to-PC or PC-to-phone calls anywhere in the United States.

Chapter 26

Online Security Issues

In This Chapter

➤ Safely place a credit card order on the Web

➤ Prevent destructive computer code from entering your system

➤ Block access to the Playboy channel

➤ Don't worry so much about Internet security

The Internet is no place for the paranoid. Files that you download and run could infect your system with a virus. Information you enter on a form could be intercepted and read by some whiz kid computer hacker who might decide to make your life miserable. Your kids could just happen upon the Porn Central Web site.

Yes, all that is possible, but if you worry about all the things that could possibly go wrong, you will never experience anything. The trick is to proceed with caution. In this chapter, you will learn how to enable a few safeguards to protect your data, your system, and your kids on the Internet so that you can experience the Internet completely without worrying too much.

Safely Exchanging Information on the Web

Forms, such as the search forms used in Yahoo! or other search programs, enable you enter information and receive feedback, order products, register your software, join clubs, and even play interactive games. The problem with entering any personal information (including credit card numbers) on a form is that the information is not sent directly to the server where that information is used. Instead, the information bounces from one server to the next until it finds its destination. At any point in this little adventure, someone with the proper know-how can read the information. How often this happens, no one really knows—but it can happen, and that's the concern.

Most Web browsers, including Internet Explorer and Netscape Navigator, have warning messages that pop up whenever you are about to submit information using an insecure form, so you can cancel the operation before sending sensitive information. If you're only submitting a search phrase, you can cancel the warning and go ahead with the operation.

If you tire of these warning messages popping up on your screen and you don't enter any sensitive information, you can deactivate the warnings. In most browsers, the warning dialog box contains an option for preventing the warning from appearing again. Even if you deactivate the warning messages, you can determine whether you are using a secure form by doing the following:

➤ If the Web page address starts with **https** instead of **http**, the site is secure.

➤ In Internet Explorer, look at the right end of the status bar at the bottom of the window. If you see a padlock icon, the site is secure (see Figure 26.1).

➤ In Netscape Navigator, look at the lower-right corner of the window for a lock icon. An open lock on a dark background indicates that the site is not secure. A closed lock on a bright background indicates the site is secure.

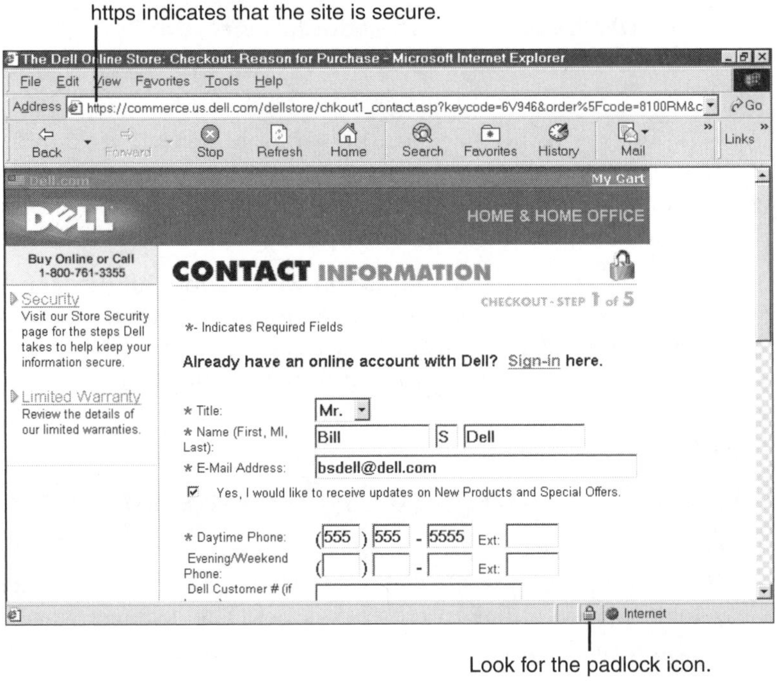

Figure 26.1

Even with the warnings turned off, Internet Explorer shows you when a site is secure.

https indicates that the site is secure.

Look for the padlock icon.

Whoa!

A savvy criminal can steal your credit card number more easily by rummaging through your trash or looking over your shoulder when you're in the checkout lane than by lifting it from a secure form on the Web. Use common sense. Place credit card orders only at well-established sites that you trust. Just because a site has a Visa or Mastercard icon on it doesn't mean the site is legitimate. If you have any concerns, ask your friends for references, research the company online, and check with your local consumer protection agency or the Better Business Bureau.

Preventing Viruses from Entering Your System

Picking up a virus on the Internet is like coming home from vacation and finding that someone has broken into your house and trashed it. You were having so much fun; how could this happen? And how can you prevent it from happening again? First, follow a few simple rules:

➤ Download programs only from reputable and known sites. If you know the company that created the program, go to its Web page or FTP server and download the file from there. Most reputable sites regularly scan their systems to detect and eliminate viruses.

➤ Don't accept copies of a program from another person (for example, by e-mail). Although the program might not have contained a virus when the other person downloaded it, the other person's computer could have a virus that infected the program. Ask the person where he or she got the file, and then download the file from its original location yourself.

➤ Use your Web browser's security features, as explained in the following sections. Your Web browser can warn you if you are about to receive a component that could contain a virus.

➤ Run an antivirus program on a regular basis. By identifying and eliminating a virus early, you prevent it from causing additional damage. Two of the best antivirus programs on the market are McAfee VirusScan and Symantec's Norton AntiVirus. You can download a trial version of McAfee VirusScan at **www.nai. com**. Go to **www.symantec.com** for details about Norton AntiVirus.

Running an infected program or opening an infected document is the most common way you can introduce a virus into your system; however, the Internet poses some additional threats through programmed objects, such as Java applets and ActiveX components. Java is a more secure programming language than ActiveX because it has built-in security features that prevent Java applets from performing destructive acts, such as deleting system files and reformatting your hard drive; however, clever hackers have proven that Java is not completely safe.

Whoa!

If you receive e-mail, you'll eventually receive virus warnings indicating that a nasty new virus is infecting thousands of computers all over the world and wiping out hard drives. Most of these warnings are hoaxes, and you should not forward the message as it instructs you to do. Check the source of the hoax first. If the message says that IBM just discovered the virus, check out IBM's Web site. Another good place to verify the integrity of a virus warning is McAfee's Virus Hoax list at **vil.mcafee.com/ hoax.asp.**

ActiveX is less secure because it places the security burden on you and relies on a system of certificates to help you determine whether the ActiveX component is safe. ActiveX components have no built-in security features that prevent the component from performing destructive acts. This makes ActiveX components powerful but poses greater risks. Before downloading and installing an ActiveX component, your Web browser displays a dialog box indicating whether the component has been certified or not. If the component has not been certified, it's up to you to cancel the download.

Zoning in on Security In Internet Explorer

As you send data and receive active content on the Web, Internet Explorer supervises both your actions and the actions of the remote server and warns you of any risky activity. You can control these warnings by using Internet Explorer's security zones. Each zone has different security settings enabling you to relax the security settings for sites that you trust and tighten security settings for untested sites or those that you don't trust. Internet Explorer offers the following four security zones:

➤ *Internet* enables you to specify security settings for untested sites. When you wander off to sites that you do not frequent, you might want to tighten security. All sites that are not in one of the other zones in this list fall into the Internet zone.

➤ *Local Intranet* enables you to relax security for sites on your company's intranet or network, so you can freely access those sites without being bombarded with warnings. By default, the security level for local intranet sites is set at low.

➤ *Trusted sites* enables you to deactivate the security warnings for sites you trust. This prevents you from being inundated with warning messages at the sites you visit most frequently.

➤ *Restricted sites* enables you to create a list of sites that you do not trust and tighten security for those sites. For example, you might want to prevent a particular site from automatically installing and running programs on your computer.

You can add sites to the Trusted and Restricted sites zones. To add a site to a zone, open the **View** or **Tools** menu, select **Internet Options**, and click the **Security** tab. Click the desired zone at the top of the dialog box, as shown in Figure 26.2, or open the **Zone** drop-down list and choose the desired zone. Click the **Add Sites** or **Sites** button and enter the desired addresses. Click **OK** as needed to save your changes and close the dialog boxes.

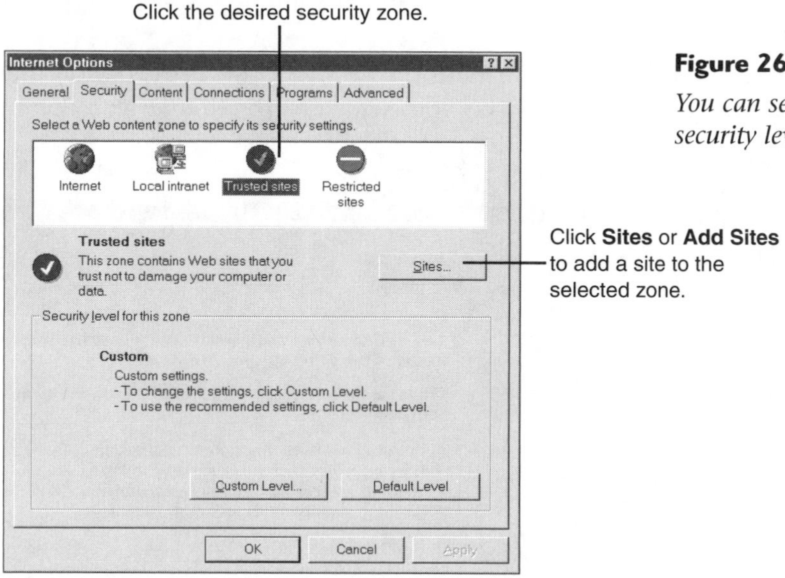

Click the desired security zone.

Figure 26.2

You can select a different security level for each zone.

Click **Sites** or **Add Sites** to add a site to the selected zone.

To specify a security level for a zone, open the **View** menu, select **Internet Options**, and click the **Security** tab. Click the desired zone at the top of the dialog box or open the **Zone** drop-down list and select the zone whose security level you want to change. Select the desired security level. The levels range from **high**, which allows you to do very little at a site (good for restricted sites), to **low**, which disables all prompts (good for trusted sites). In Internet Explorer 5 and later, drag the slider to set the desired level; in Internet Explorer 4 and earlier versions, click the **Option** button and enter your preferences.

Configuring Security Settings in Netscape Navigator

Navigator (Netscape Communicator's Web browser) stores its security settings in two places. To enter security settings for submitting information securely on the Web, open the **Tasks** menu, point to **Privacy and Security**, and select **Security Manager**.

Click the **Applications** tab. You then can select any of the following options to activate or deactivate them, as shown in Figure 26.3:

➤ **Entering a Site That Supports Encryption**   Displays a warning whenever you view a Web page that complies with the latest security standards. Personally, I prefer to have this option turned off. Look to the padlock icon to determine whether you are at a secure site.

➤ **Leaving a Site That Supports Encryption**   This is another warning you can deactivate. If you're leaving, why do you care whether it's secure?

➤ **Viewing a Page with an Encrypted/Unencrypted Mix**   If part of the page is secure and another part isn't, you want to know about it. Make sure this option is on.

➤ **Sending Unencrypted Information to a Site**   This is the option that makes the security warning pop up on your screen all the time. If you don't trust yourself, leave it activated.

Figure 26.3

You can activate or deactivate the security warnings.

Security warning options ——

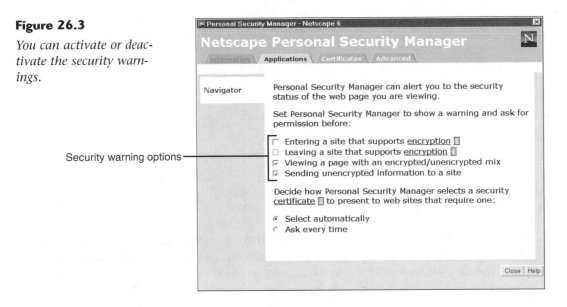

If desired, you can also disable Java. Open the **Edit** menu, choose **Preferences**, and click **Advanced** (at the bottom of the left column). You then can uncheck any of the options on the list to disable Java applets or JavaScript.

Notable Note

Cookies are like ID badges that a Web page pins on your browser when you connect to the page or enter information. They stay with your browser enabling the Web server to identify you or track items you have ordered. You can disable cookies or have your Web browser display a warning whenever a site tries to send you a cookie. Most cookies are designed to make your Web browsing experience more productive and enjoyable. Although cookies typically do not store your name and e-mail address, they can track you by using your computer's IP address assigned by your service provider. If you are concerned about this, disable cookies. For additional details about cookies, search your browser's help system for "cookie" and check out **www.cookiecentral.com**.

Enhancing Security with Antivirus Software

In most browsers, Internet security consists of displaying warning messages when you are about to perform an action or receive a file that potentially poses a risk. Most sites you visit are safe, and 99.9 percent of the files you download are virus free, so the warnings eventually become nothing more than a nuisance. Most users eventually turn off the warnings.

To obtain some real Internet security, you should install an antivirus program on your computer. Pick up a copy of McAfee VirusScan or Symantec's Symantec's Norton AntiVirus, and install it on your computer. After you install the program, it runs automatically on startup and scans your startup files for viruses. It also runs in the background, scanning any files you download and any files you open. If it detects a virus, the antivirus program notifies you and leads you through the process of eliminating the virus from your system.

Keeping Hackers at Bay with a Firewall

Whenever you are connected to the Internet, you run the risk of having a mischievous hacker break into your system, steal information, and even damage some files. Hackers rarely break into home PCs that are connected to the Internet by modem but if you have a DSL or cable modem connection, you should consider installing a *firewall* to prevent unauthorized access to your system.

A *firewall* typically functions in one of two ways: It filters incoming and outgoing data to block anything that seems suspicious or it uses a *proxy server* between you and your Internet service provider to hide your computer making it much more difficult for a hacker to find it.

If you connect to the Internet through your company's network, chances are the network administrator set up a firewall to protect the network. If you connect to the Internet at home using a DSL or cable modem, you should consider installing your own firewall. You can download shareware versions of firewall software at any of the popular Internet add-on sites, such as **cws.internet.com**, **www.tucows.com**, or **download.cnet.com**.

Censoring Naughty Net Sites

The Internet is a virtual world, providing access to the best that our society has to offer: literature, music, creative arts, museums, movies, and medicine. However, like the rest of the world, the Internet has its share of pornography, obscenity, and violence—not to mention rude and obnoxious behavior.

Over the years, people have debated the issue of whether the government should censor the Internet. As society wrestles with this issue, offensive material remains readily available. In the following sections, you learn what you can do on your end to prevent this material from reaching you or your children.

Enabling and Disabling Internet Explorer's Censor

Before you can censor sites with Internet Explorer, you must activate the Ratings feature. Open the **View** or **Tools** menu, click **Internet Options**, and click the **Content** tab. Under Ratings or Content Advisor, click the **Enable** button and click **OK**. The Create Supervisor Password dialog box appears. In both text boxes, type a password that you'll remember but that your kids will have a tough time guessing. Keep clicking **OK** to save your changes and close the dialog boxes.

Now, don't set the kiddies in front of the screen just yet. Test your setup first. Try going to **www.playboy.com**. If you see some scantily clad maidens, Ratings isn't on. Close Internet Explorer, run it again, and then try going to the nudie page. You should see the Content Advisor dialog box, as shown in Figure 26.4, indicating that the site is not rated or displaying a list of reasons you have been denied access to this site (as if you didn't know). Click **OK**.

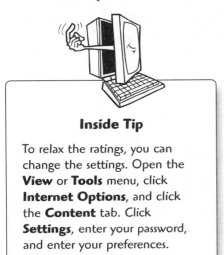

Inside Tip

To relax the ratings, you can change the settings. Open the **View** or **Tools** menu, click **Internet Options**, and click the **Content** tab. Click **Settings**, enter your password, and enter your preferences.

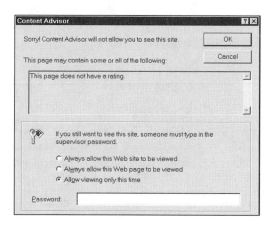

Figure 26.4

The Content Advisor blocks access to sites that might contain objectionable material and to unrated sites.

Censoring the Web in Navigator

Netscape Navigator does not have any built-in features to censor the Internet. However, several specialized programs are available that can work along with Navigator to block access to objectionable Web pages and Internet newsgroups. The following is a list of some of the better censoring programs along with addresses for the Web pages where you can find out more about them and download shareware versions:

➤ **Cyber Patrol (www.cyberpatrol.com)**   The most popular censoring program. It enables you to set security levels, prevent Internet access during certain hours, and prevent access to specific sites. Passwords enable you to set access levels for different users.

➤ **CYBERsitter (www.solidoak.com)**   Another fine censoring program. Although a little less strict than Cyber Patrol, CYBERsitter is easier to use and configure. CYBERsitter has a unique filtering system that judges words in context, so it won't block access to inoffensive sites, such as the Anne Sexton home page.

➤ **Net Nanny (www.netnanny.com)**   This is unique in that it can punish the user for typing URLs of offensive sites or for typing any word on the no-no list. If a user types a prohibited word or URL, Net Nanny can shut down the application and record the offense forcing your student or child to come up with an excuse. However, to make the most of Net Nanny, you'll have to spend a bit of time configuring it.

The Least You Need to Know

➤ To determine whether a form you are filling out is secure, make sure its address starts with **https://** and check your Web browser's status bar for a locked padlock icon.

➤ To protect your system and files against computer viruses, download files only from reliable sites; don't run program files attached to e-mail messages from unknown users and scan any files you receive with a good antivirus program before running or opening them.

➤ To control the frequency of security warnings in Internet Explorer, configure the security zones.

➤ If you use Internet Explorer, you can censor Web content by enabling the Content Advisor. However, when you choose to block access to unrated sites, your Web browsing is extremely limited.

➤ The best way to censor Internet content without completely blocking access to wholesome sites is to use an add-on program, such as CyberPatrol or CYBERsitter.

Part 5

Guerrilla Computing

You know the basics. You can survive any program, rearrange your files, and even surf the Internet. You can use your computer to perform specific tasks and have some fun.

However, if your computer is running out of memory and disk space, do you know what to do? Can you tune up your computer to make it run at optimum speed? Can you fix a floppy disk that your computer refuses to read? Do you know how to use the portable computing features in Windows? Do you know how to take advantage of the latest computer gadgets and gizmos to download music from the Internet, burn custom CDs, send and receive photos through e-mail, and edit your home videos?

In this part, you will learn how to survive in the trenches—how to tune up your own computer with a few savvy techniques, clear useless files from your hard disk, repair diskettes, take your work on the road with a notebook computer or hand-held PC, and have fun with some high-tech computer gear.

Chapter 27

Do-It-Yourself Computer Tune-Ups

In This Chapter

➤ Run the Windows Maintenance Wizard

➤ Streamline the Windows startup

➤ Clear useless files from your hard disk

➤ Repair hard disk storage problems with ScanDisk

➤ Double your disk space without installing a new drive

Your computer is like a car: You might be able to use it without ever tuning it up or changing the oil, but it probably won't last as long or run as well. In this chapter, you will learn some basic computer maintenance that helps keep your computer running trouble free and at peak performance.

Tuning Up Windows with the Maintenance Wizard

As you install programs, wander the Web, and create documents, your system becomes slower and less efficient. If a program's installation utility automatically adds the program to the StartUp menu, Windows starts more slowly. When you wander the Web, your Web browser saves files to your hard disk without asking you, cutting down on available space. When you create and edit documents, programs often place temporary files on your disk that remain there until you delete them. And files on your hard disk become increasingly fragmented as parts of files are stored on separate areas of the disk.

The Windows Maintenance Wizard (included with Windows 98 and newer versions) can help you keep your computer in tip-top condition. It automatically performs a series of tests and corrections at a scheduled time to check for problems on your hard disk, defragment files, delete temporary files, remove programs from the StartUp menu, and optimize your hard disk. With the Windows Maintenance Wizard, you rarely have to go behind the scenes with Windows to perform these tasks manually. (If you don't have Windows 98 or a more recent version, later sections in this chapter show you how to use Windows 95 tools to optimize your system.)

To run the wizard, follow these steps:

1. Click the **Start** button, point to **Programs, Accessories, System Tools**, and click **Maintenance Wizard**. The Maintenance Wizard dialog box appears.

2. Click **Express** and click **Next**. Express tells the wizard to delete temporary files and Web files from your hard disk, optimize your hard disk, and check it for errors; however, Express does not tell the wizard to remove programs from the StartUp menu. The Wizard prompts you to select a time of day for performing its maintenance tasks, as shown in Figure 27.1.

3. Click the desired time (when you normally have your computer on but are not using it) and click **Next**.

4. The Wizard displays a list of optimization activities it performs at the scheduled time. To have the Wizard perform these activities now, choose **When I Click Finish Perform Each Scheduled Task for the First Time**.

5. Click the **Finish** button. Be sure to leave your computer on at the scheduled time so that Windows can perform the optimization activities at the scheduled times.

Figure 27.1

The Windows Maintenance Wizard optimizes your system on schedule.

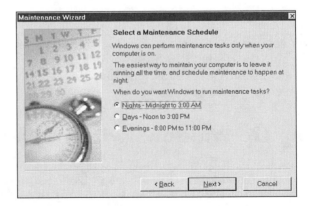

Making Windows Start Faster

Windows is a slow starter even on a quick machine. If you have some power saving features on your computer you can make Windows start a lot faster. Instead of turning your PC off and on, use the Power Management or Power Options icon in the

Control Panel to have Windows put your PC in standby mode when you're not using it. You can quickly restart by pressing the **Shift** key or rolling the mouse around. When the computer wakes up it displays any Windows that were open before it entered standby mode, so you can immediately resume working. To check and adjust the Windows power management settings, take the following steps:

1. Open the **Start** menu, point to **Settings**, and click **Control Panel.**

2. Click or double-click the **Power Management** or **Power Options** icon. The Power Options Properties dialog box appears, as shown in Figure 27.2. (Your Power Options Properties dialog box might differ, depending on the Windows version you're running and on the power management features your computer supports.)

3. Under Power Schemes, open the drop-down list and click **Home/Office Desk** or **Portable Laptop.**

4. Open the **Turn Off Monitor** list and select the desired length of time you want your computer to be inactive before Windows automatically shuts down the monitor.

5. Open the **Turn Off Hard Disks** list and select the desired length of time you want your computer to be inactive before Windows automatically shuts down the hard drives. (If your computer is on a network, you might not want to turn off the hard disks; it can prevent other users from accessing your hard disks or using any equipment that's connected to this computer.)

6. If you have a **System Standby** list, open it and select the desired length of time you want your computer to be inactive before Windows automatically puts your system in standby mode. (In Standby mode, Windows turns off the monitor, disk drives, and fan and places other components in a low-power state.)

7. If you have a **System Hibernates** list, open it and select the desired length of time you want your computer to be inactive before Windows automatically puts your system in hibernation mode. (In Hibernation mode, Windows takes a snapshot of your desktop and saves it to disk. Windows then completely shuts down your computer. When you power up your computer, the system returns to the state it was in before entering hibernation mode.)

8. Click **OK.**

Although you can have Windows place your computer in standby or hibernation mode automatically after your computer remains inactive for a specified period of time, you might prefer to place your computer in standby or hibernation mode yourself. Click the **Start button**, click **Shut Down**, and then open the **What Do You Want the Computer To Do** drop-down list and click **Stand By or Hibernate.** Click OK.

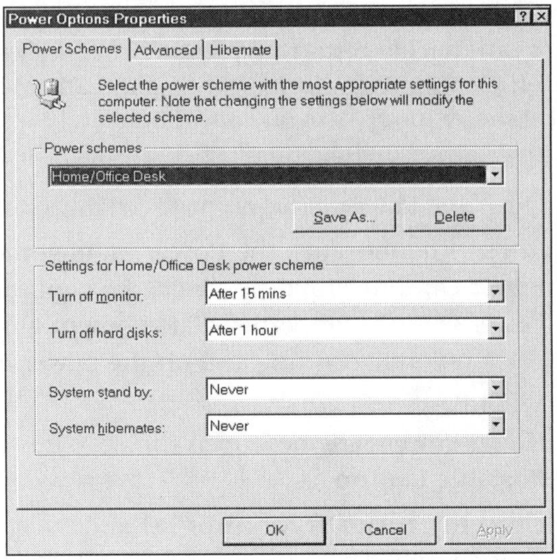

Figure 27.2

The Power Options Properties dialog box provides settings for automatically powering down your computer.

Some computers do not support standby and hibernation modes. Other computers might require you to enter a startup setting to enable the built-in power saving features in which case you must check your system's documentation to learn how to enter the required settings. Even if your system does support standby and hibernation modes, Windows might have disabled these modes if your computer had trouble restarting two or more times. In such cases, you might be able to restore standby and hibernation modes by taking one of the following steps:

➤ To restore standby mode, **Alt+double-click My Computer** and click the **Device Manager** tab. Click the plus sign next to **Floppy Disk Controllers**, click the name of the floppy disk controller, and click **Remove**. Click **OK** to confirm the action and then restart your computer. Windows will reinstall the floppy disk controller, and you now should have a Standby option in the Power dialog box.

➤ To reenable hibernation mode, open the **Start** menu, click **Run**, type **msconfig**, and press **Enter**. Click the **General** tab and then click the **Advanced** button. Next to **Hibernation Feature Is Disabled**, click the **Enable** button. You now should have a **Hibernation** option and tab in the Power dialog box.

➤ If you are still having trouble, use the **Start, Find, Files or Folder** option or the **Start, Search, For Files or Folders** option to locate a file called **PMRES.EXE**. Click the file; if you're lucky, you'll get a screen telling you why Standby mode has been disabled.

➤ If the problem persists, use the **Start, Find, Files or Folder** option or the **Start, Search, For Files or Folders** option to locate a file called **NOHIBER.TXT**. Click the file; if you're still lucky, you'll get a message indicating which device driver on your system caused Windows to disable standby and hibernation modes.

Contact the manufacturer of the device to obtain an updated device driver and install it. (After installing the new driver, you might need to take the steps described in the first two bullets to reenable standby and hibernation modes.)

If you have Internet Explorer on your computer and your Windows desktop is displayed as a Web page, the active desktop components can add a lot of time to the Windows startup. If you don't use the desktop components, turn them off. Right-click a blank area of the desktop, point to **Active Desktop**, and choose **Customize My Desktop**. Remove the check mark next to every desktop component and click **OK**. Also consider turning off **View As Web Page**; right-click the desktop, point to Active Desktop, and if **View As Web Page** or **Show Web Content** is checked, click the option to remove the check mark.

Cleaning Your Hard Disk Without the Maintenance Wizard

Your hard disk probably contains temporary and backup files that your programs create without telling you. These files can quickly clutter your hard disk drive, taking room you need for new programs or new data files that you create. You can easily delete most of these files yourself.

The first candidates for removal are temporary (.TMP) files. These are files that your programs create but often forget to delete. You can safely delete all temporary files from your hard drive. Click the Windows **Start** button, point to **Find** or **Search**, and click **Files or Folders**. Type *.tmp and press **Enter**. Press **Ctrl+A** to select all the files and press **Shift+Delete**. If asked to confirm, click **Yes**. Gone! You now should have an extra megabyte or more of disk space. (Windows might not be able to delete some .TMP files that it is currently using. If Windows refuses to delete a specific file, write down the file's name and then deselect that file by Ctrl+pointing or Ctrl+clicking its name, and then press **Shift+Delete** again.)

Whoa!

As you can guess from all the troubleshooting tips listed here, power management features are not perfect. Many computers have trouble waking up after being placed in standby or hibernation modes. If you experience persistent problems with your computer locking up after you enable standby or hibernation modes, disable these features.

Whoa!

When you save a file that you created, most programs create a backup file that contains the previous version of the file. These files typically have the .BAK extension. If you mess up a file, you can open the backup file instead. Before deleting backup files, make sure you don't want the previous versions of your files.

To remove temporary files that your Web browser saves, clear the disk cache in your browser. To clear the disk cache in Internet Explorer, open the **View** or **Tools** menu and click **Internet Options**. Under **Temporary Internet Files**, click the **Delete Files** button. In Navigator, open the **Edit** menu, click **Preferences**, click the plus sign next to **Advanced**, click **Cache**, and click **the Clear Disk Cache** button.

While you're at it, open your e-mail program and delete any e-mail messages you no longer need. When you delete e-mail messages, some e-mail programs, such as Outlook Express, stick the deleted messages in a separate folder (called Deleted Items in Outlook Express); also be sure to delete the messages from that folder.

Most of the stuff you deleted is sitting in the Recycle Bin, where it is still hogging disk space. First, double-click the **Recycle Bin** icon (on the Windows desktop) and scroll down the list of deleted files to make sure you will never, ever again need anything in the Bin. If you find a file you might need, drag it onto the Windows desktop for safe-keeping. Now open the **File** menu and click **Empty Recycle Bin.**

Refreshing and Repairing Disks with ScanDisk

Windows comes with a utility called ScanDisk that can test a disk (hard or floppy), repair most problems on a disk, and refresh the disk, if needed. What kind of problems? ScanDisk can find defective areas on a disk and block them out to prevent your computer from using defective storage areas in the future. ScanDisk also can find and delete misplaced (usually useless) file fragments that might be causing your computer to crash.

You should run ScanDisk regularly (at least once every month) and whenever your computer seems to be acting up (crashing for no apparent reason). Also, if you have a floppy disk that your computer cannot read, ScanDisk might be able to repair the disk and recover any data from it. To run ScanDisk, take the following steps:

Notable Note

If Windows shuts down improperly (if you press the power button on your system unit before Windows is ready, the power goes out, or Windows locks up), Windows might run ScanDisk automatically when you restart your computer. It reminds you to shut down properly next time even though usually it's not your fault.

1. Choose **Start**, **Programs**, **Accessories**, **System Tools**, and then click **ScanDisk**. The ScanDisk window appears, as shown in Figure 27.3.

2. Click the letter of the drive you want ScanDisk to check.

3. To check for and repair only file and folder errors, click the **Standard** option; to check the disk for defects (in addition to file and folder errors), click **Thorough**. (Thorough can take hours; select it only if you're on your way to bed.)

4. If you want ScanDisk to fix any errors without asking for your confirmation, make sure that **Automatically fix errors** is checked. (I always choose this option and have never encountered problems with ScanDisk doing something it was not supposed to do.)

5. Click the **Start** button.

Figure 27.3

ScanDisk can repair most disk problems.

Defragmenting Files on Your Hard Disk

Whenever you delete a file from your hard disk, you leave a space where another file can be stored. When you save a file, your computer stores as much of the file as possible in that empty space and the rest of the file in other empty spaces. The file then is said to be *fragmented,* because its parts are stored in different locations on the disk. This slows down your disk drive and increases the likelihood that your computer will lose track of a portion of the file or the entire file.

Every month or so, you should run a defragmentation program. If you ran the Maintenance Wizard, as explained earlier in this chapter, Windows Disk Defragmenter automatically performs the operation at the scheduled time. If you did not run the Maintenance Wizard, you can run Disk Defragmenter yourself.

Whoa!

If you have an original version of Windows 95, you might have the DOS version of Defragmenter on your computer. Never use the DOS Defragmenter program. It can't handle the long filenames that Windows 95 and newer versions allow for. It also might destroy some of your files. Run Disk Defragmenter from the Start menu only.

To have Disk Defragmenter put your files back together, take the following steps:

1. Save any documents that are open, close any programs that are running, and disable any power saving features. Running programs commonly interfere with Defragmenter making it restart and causing the defragmentation process to take much longer than it normally would.

2. Click **Start, Programs, Accessories, System Tools,** and click **Disk Defragmenter.** A dialog box appears, as shown in Figure 27.4, asking which disk drive you want to defragment.

3. Open the **Which drive do you want to defragment?** drop-down list, and click the desired disk. You can defragment all your disks by clicking **All Hard Drives.** (You don't need to defragment floppy disks.)

4. Click **OK.** Another dialog box might appear indicating both the percent of file fragmentation on the disk and whether or not you need to defragment the disk. In Windows Me and newer versions, defragmentation starts immediately.

5. If necessary, click the **Start** button. Defragmenter starts to defragment the files on the disk.

6. Wait until the defragmentation is complete. It's best to leave your computer alone during the process because this might change a file and cause Defragmenter to start over.

Inside Tip

The **Advanced** or **Settings** button in the opening Disk Defragmenter dialog box enables you to specify how you want Defragmenter to proceed.

Figure 27.4

Select the disk you want to defragment.

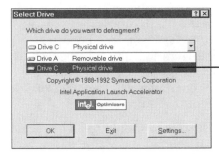

Click the disk you want to defragment.

Doubling Your Disk Space

As computers become more complex, program and document files are becoming larger and larger. Five years ago, a typical program would take up a couple megabytes of disk space. Nowadays, each program can consume 100 megabytes or more. In addition, as you explore the Internet, you commonly encounter graphics and audio and video clips that consume more than 1 megabyte!

As files become larger and as your own thirst for the latest programs and media increases, your hard disk quickly becomes packed. To help, Windows offers a couple of utilities that can make your hard drive use its storage space more efficiently: *Drive Converter* (available only in later versions of Windows) and *DriveSpace*. (Drive Converter might be called FAT32 Converter in your version of Windows.)

To understand Drive Converter, you must understand how older hard disk drives stored data in the past. If you have a hard drive larger than 500 megabytes, older operating systems (using FAT16) would use 32 kilobytes of hard drive space to store every file with 32 kilobytes or less of data. For example, a 2-kilobyte file would still take up 32 kilobytes of disk space. You could *partition* your hard disk drive into units smaller than 500 megabytes to make the operating system store files in 4K chunks instead saving you as much as 40 percent of wasted space. However, partitioning the hard disk drive destroys any data that it contains. Drive Converter can perform the optimization without destroying data.

The only problem with Drive Converter is that it doesn't work on smaller hard disks. If your hard drive is smaller than 512 megabytes, you can use a different utility—DriveSpace. DriveSpace compresses the files on the hard drive, so they take up less space when not in use. When you run a compressed program or open a compressed file, DriveSpace automatically decompresses it. Because DriveSpace must decompress files when you run a program or open a document, it slightly decreases overall system performance; however, if you're strapped for storage space, the trade-off is worth it.

Inside Tip

In My Computer, right-click the icon for your hard drive and click **Properties.** Next to File System, you should see FAT32 or FAT16.

To use Drive Converter (or find out if it can even help), take the following steps (the conversion may take more than one hour):

1. Choose **Start, Programs, Accessories, System Tools,** and click **Drive Converter** or **FAT32 Converter.**

2. Click **Next.** Drive Converter analyzes your hard disk drive to determine which drives are currently using FAT16.

3. Click the drive you want to optimize. Drive Converter displays a warning indicating you will not be able to access the converted drive using a previous version of Windows, MS-DOS, or Windows NT.

4. Click **OK.** Drive Converter checks for any running programs that might interfere with its operation and displays a list of them.

5. Close any of these programs and click **Next**. Drive Converter prompts you to back up the files on your hard disk before continuing.

6. Click **Create Backup** and refer to Chapter 31, "Backing Up for the Inevitable Crash," for details on how to proceed.

7. When you return to Drive Converter, click **Next**. Drive Converter indicates that it must restart your computer in MS-DOS mode.

8. Close any programs that are currently running and click **Next**.

Whoa!

Because Windows Me is designed for newer computers, it is phasing out the FAT32 converter. You must run it from your Windows Startup diskette. (Refer to Chapter 32, "Do-It-Yourself Fixes for Common Ailments," to learn how to create a startup diskette. Insert the diskette, restart your computer, and choose the option for booting your computer without CD-ROM support. At the DOS prompt (which looks something like A:>), type cvt c: and press **Enter**. (To convert a drive other than drive C, type that drive's letter in place of c.)

Whoa!

In Windows Me, you can use DriveSpace only to access compressed drives, reallocate space on compressed drives, and de-compress floppy disks. It does not allow you to compress drives.

If you cannot use Drive Converter on your hard drives, or if you need additional storage space, take the following steps to run DriveSpace (this can take a long time, too):

1. Back up all files on the hard disk drive that you want to compress, as explained in Chapter 31.

2. Click **Start, Programs, Accessories, System Tools,** and click **DriveSpace**.

3. Click the disk drive you want to compress.

4. Open the **Drive** menu and click **Compress**. The Compress a Drive dialog box displays a graph of how much free space the drive currently has and how much it will have after compression, as shown in Figure 27.5.

5. Click the **Start** button. A confirmation dialog box appears prompting you to create or update your Windows Startup disk before proceeding.

6. Click **Yes** and follow the onscreen instructions to create a startup disk if you don't already have one. Another confirmation dialog box appears prompting you to back up your files before proceeding, which you should have done in step 1.

7. Click **Compress Now.** Wait until the compression is complete. This can take from several minutes to several hours depending on the size of the hard disk, the amount of RAM, and the speed of your processor.

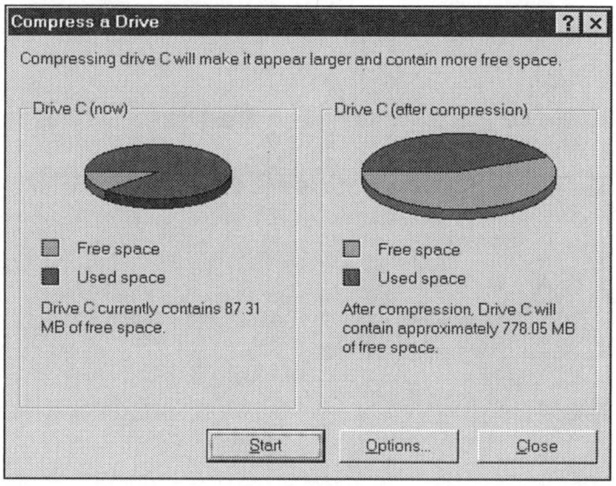

Figure 27.5

DriveSpace displays pie charts to illustrate how much disk space it can save you.

If, after compressing a drive, you have trouble running a particular application, you can uncompress the drive and return your system to normal (open the **Drive** menu and select **Uncompress**). In such a case, you can leave your original drive uncompressed and create a new, compressed drive for storing your data files or any new programs that you install. To create a separate compressed drive, run DriveSpace, open the **Advanced** menu, and click **Create Empty.**

Making the Most of Your Computer's Memory

Your computer can't do anything without memory, and it can't do anything very well or very quickly if it doesn't have enough memory. Windows does a pretty good job of managing memory for you and of using your hard disk for additional memory (called *virtual memory*). Although virtual memory is slower than real memory, it can help you avoid getting Insufficient Memory error messages when you try to load large programs or run several programs at one time.

If you are receiving Insufficient Memory messages on a regular basis or if you have more than one hard disk drive, you should check the virtual memory settings. Open the **Control Panel** and double-click the **System** icon. Click the **Performance** tab, and click the **Virtual Memory** button. Check for the following:

➤ Make sure that **Let Windows Manage My Virtual Memory Settings** is selected, as shown in Figure 27.6.

➤ Make sure you have at least 30MB of free space on the disk drive that Windows is using for virtual memory. (If the space dips below that, clear files from your hard disk, as explained earlier in this chapter.)

➤ If you have more than one hard disk drive installed, click **Let Me Specify My Own Virtual Memory Settings**, and choose your fastest hard disk drive that has the most free space from the **Hard Disk** drop-down list. Click **OK**, and then click the **Virtual Memory** button again. Click **Let Windows Manage My Virtual Memory Settings** and click **OK**. This enables Windows to manage the settings on the disk that you chose.

Make sure that Windows is managing the virtual memory.

Figure 27.6

Windows does a fine job of managing the virtual memory.

Virtual Memory	? X

⚠ These settings can adversely affect system performance and should be adjusted by advanced users and system administrators only.

Virtual memory

⦿ Let Windows manage my virtual memory settings. (Recommended)

○ Let me specify my own virtual memory settings.

Hard disk | C:\ 14417MB Free

Minimum: | 0

Maximum: | No maximum

☐ Disable virtual memory (Not recommended)

OK   Cancel

Techno Talk

Your display card may have its own Control Panel for additional performance settings. Check the **Start, Programs** menu for a program group or icon for running the display card's Control Panel.

Speeding Up the Video

If video clips on the Web or in your multimedia programs seem clunky and choppy, you might be able to trade off some video quality for speed. Try setting the video resolution no higher than 800×600 and the colors to 256. Your display card and Windows must work much harder to render screens at higher resolutions and color depths, and you won't notice much of a dip in quality on most of your video clips and graphics. Take the following steps:

1. Right-click a blank area of the Windows desktop and choose **Properties**.

2. Click the **Settings** tab.

3. Open the **Colors** drop-down list and choose **256**. Don't go any lower, or your graphics will look lousy. (If images do look lousy, try the next higher setting.)

4. Drag the **Screen Area** slider to set the area at 800×600.

5. Click the **Advanced** button to see what's available. You might see a dialog box with hardware acceleration settings and screen refresh rate settings that you can use to increase the display performance even more. Click **OK** when you're done.

6. Click **OK** to save your settings. Windows might prompt you to restart.

The Least You Need to Know

➤ Use the Windows Maintenance Wizard to schedule regular tune-ups.

➤ Take programs you don't use off the StartUp menu.

➤ Delete temporary files, temporary Internet files, and e-mail messages you no longer need.

➤ Defragment files on your hard disk, if needed.

➤ Check your hard drives regularly with ScanDisk to recover any lost file fragments and repair damaged directories.

➤ To increase the storage capacity drives more than 512MB, use Drive Converter to convert the drives to FAT32. For smaller drives, use DriveSpace to compress files on the drives.

Chapter 28

Life on the Run: Notebook Computing

In This Chapter

➤ Take your show on the road with a laptop or notebook PC

➤ Go farther on a single battery

➤ Stick PC cards in the little slots and get them to work

➤ Dock with the mothership (docking stations)

➤ Phone home to connect when you're on the road

➤ Use a computer that fits in the palm of your hand

Going portable introduces several issues you might not have faced with your stationary desktop PC. You need to know how to transfer files from your notebook to your desktop PC, connect to your company's network, insert and remove PC cards, and conserve battery power when you're trying to meet a deadline on the road. Fortunately, Windows provides the tools you need to deal with these and other notebook computing issues.

Taking Your Work on the Road with My Briefcase

If you have both a notebook and desktop computer, you probably need to transfer files from your desktop computer to your notebook computer to take work with you on trips. If you edit the files on your notebook computer, you then must copy them back to the desktop computer to ensure that you have the most recent versions on both computers.

Of course, you can simply copy the files to a floppy disk, but then you run the risk of replacing the new versions of your documents with older ones. Fortunately, Windows offers a convenient tool for safely transferring files between computers: *Briefcase*. Briefcase helps you decide which files should be replaced. To use Briefcase, take the following steps:

1. On your desktop computer, drag files from My Computer or Windows Explorer over the **My Briefcase** icon on the Windows desktop and release the mouse button. (Or, select the files in My Computer, right-click one of the files, point to **Send To**, and click **My Briefcase**.)

2. If the Welcome to Windows Briefcase dialog box appears, click **Finish**.

3. Insert a blank floppy disk, drag the **My Briefcase** icon over the floppy disk icon in My Computer, and wait until the files are transferred to the floppy disk.

4. Take the floppy disk home or on the road and edit the files as you normally would. (Open them from the floppy disk and save them to the floppy disk.)

5. When you return, insert the floppy disk into your desktop computer's floppy disk drive.

6. Run My Computer, double-click the floppy disk drive icon, and double-click **My Briefcase**. A window appears displaying the files. (You can rest the mouse pointer on a file's icon to display a Screen Tip indicating whether the file needs updating.)

7. Click the **Update All** button. Briefcase displays a list of files it will replace, as shown in Figure 28.1.

8. To prevent a file from being updated, right-click its name and click **Skip**.

9. Click the **Update** button.

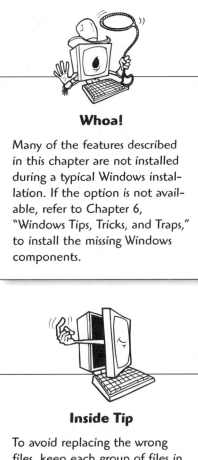

Whoa!

Many of the features described in this chapter are not installed during a typical Windows installation. If the option is not available, refer to Chapter 6, "Windows Tips, Tricks, and Traps," to install the missing Windows components.

Inside Tip

To avoid replacing the wrong files, keep each group of files in its own briefcase. To create a new briefcase, right-click the Windows desktop, point to **New**, and choose **Briefcase**. Give each briefcase a unique name. This also works if you deleted the Briefcase icon from your desktop thinking you would never need it.

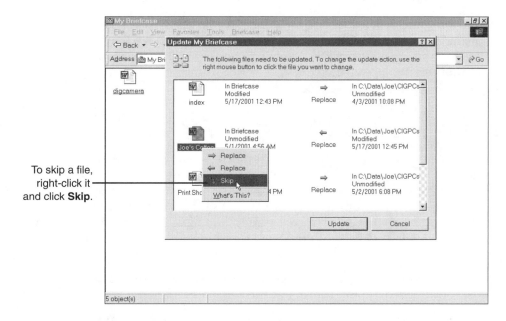

To skip a file, right-click it and click **Skip**.

Figure 28.1

My Briefcase helps you decide which files to update.

Conserving Battery Power

With a fully charged battery, a notebook computer can operate for about three hours; and it can take two to five hours to recharge depending on the notebook, the battery, and whether the notebook computer is in use during the recharge period. Three hours is not much time when you're putting in a full day's work on the road. Fortunately, Windows has some advanced power saving features designed specifically for notebook computers. These features can double the time between charges by powering down your monitor and hard disk drive after a specified period. You can even activate warnings to have Windows notify you when the battery is running down, so you can save your work and shut down Windows before the battery goes dead.

To change any of the power saving settings in Windows, double-click the **Power Management** or **Power Options** icon in the Windows Control Panel. Enter the desired settings and click **OK**.

Notable Note

Many notebook PCs have built-in power saving features that might conflict with those that Windows offers. Check your notebook PC's documentation to determine whether it is okay to use the Windows features.

301

When your notebook is running on battery power, the system tray on the right end of the taskbar displays a battery icon. Point to the icon to see how much battery power remains, or right-click the icon and click **Open Battery Meter.** For more information on the Windows power management features, see "Making Windows Start Faster," in Chapter 27, "Do-It-Yourself Computer Tune-Ups."

Inserting and Ejecting PC Cards

Most newer notebook computers make it much easier to upgrade memory, drives, modems, and so on, by using *PCMCIA cards* (commonly called *PC cards*). (PCMCIA is short for Personal Computer Memory Card International Association.) PC cards are small devices that plug directly into expansion slots on the outside of the computer. These cards are about the size of credit cards, and most notebook PCs enable you to insert them when the power is on (check your notebook's documentation to make sure). It's a little like inserting a disk into a floppy disk drive.

When shopping for a PC card, keep in mind that there are three types of cards. They are all the same length and width, but their thickness varies:

➤ Type I cards (up to 3.3mm thick) are used primarily for adding memory to a computer.

➤ Type II cards (up to 5.5mm thick) typically are used to add a fax modem, network adapter, or CD-ROM drive (the drive is connected to the PC card with a cable).

➤ Type III cards (up to 10.5mm thick) usually are used for adding a hard disk drive.

Whoa!

The PC card slots typically are numbered 0 and 1. Insert your first card in the 0 slot and the second one in the 1 slot; otherwise, the cards might not work properly. Check your computer's documentation to determine which slot is which.

Your notebook computer should have one or more PC card slots. These slots also come in three types:

➤ Type I slots can use only one Type I card.

➤ Type II slots can use one Type I card or two Type II cards.

➤ Type III slots can use one Type III card or one Type I card and a Type II card.

If you insert the card with the power on, Windows automatically detects it, sounds a two-tone beep, and runs the Add New Hardware Wizard, which leads you through the process of installing a driver for the card. (The next time you insert the card, Windows remembers it, so you don't have to reinstall the driver.) To remove the PC card, take the following steps:

1. Click the **PC Card (PCMCIA) Status** icon in the system tray and select the **Stop** option for the card that you want to remove. A dialog box appears indicating that it is safe to remove the card.

2. Click **OK**.

3. Press the **Eject** button next to the PC card slot. The card pops out of the slot and Windows emits a two-toned beep (high tone followed by a medium tone). Pull the card out of the slot.

Going Full Featured with a Docking Station

A docking station or port replicator provides the portability of a notebook PC with the advanced features of a desktop PC. The docking station is a unit that contains ports for a monitor, printer, keyboard, mouse, speakers, and other devices. You turn off your notebook computer, insert it into the docking station, and pretend that it's a big, powerful computer.

The trouble with docking stations is that your notebook is set up to use its own built-in monitor, keyboard, and speakers. It is not set up to use the hardware that's connected to the docking station. If your notebook is plug-and-play compatible, you won't have any problem. Just connect it to the docking station and Windows takes care of the details. (Some notebook computers enable you to dock without turning off the power.)

If your notebook PC is not plug-and-play compatible, connect it to the docking station, make sure all docking station devices are turned on, and then turn on your notebook. Windows detects new nonplug-and-play devices and runs the Add New Hardware Wizard to lead you through the process of installing the drivers. If Windows does not detect a device, open the Control Panel, and run the Add New Hardware Wizard to install the driver.

After you install the necessary drivers, you have a driver for each device on your notebook and each device connected to the docking station. These drivers might conflict, and Windows chooses

Inside Tip

If you don't have a docking station, you still might be able to connect your notebook PC to a standard monitor, keyboard, mouse, and speakers. Check the back and sides of your notebook PC for additional ports.

Whoa!

Before disabling devices, make sure you have a recent Windows Startup disk. If you disable the wrong device, use your Windows Startup disk to start your computer and then reenable the device. (See Chapter 32, "Do-It-Yourself Fixes for Common Ailments," to learn how to create a startup disk.)

which one it wants to use. To solve this problem, create two separate hardware pro-files to deal with the docked and undocked configurations. You then can disable de-vices in each profile.

Take the following steps to create a new hardware profile and disable devices:

1. Right-click **My Computer** and click **Properties.**

2. Click the **Hardware Profiles** tab. If your notebook is plug-and-play compatible, you should see two options—Docked and Undocked. In this case, click **OK** and skip the remaining steps.

3. If you see only one option, **Original Configuration,** click it and click the **Copy** button.

4. Type Docked as the name of your new configuration and click **OK.** The Docked configuration is selected, so you can disable notebook devices when the note-book is docked.

5. Click the **Device Manager** tab.

6. Click the plus sign next to one of the notebook devices that you want to disable when the notebook is docked.

7. Double-click the name of the device that you want to disable.

8. Click **Disable in This Hardware Profile** and click **OK,** as shown in Figure 28.2.

9. Repeat steps 6 and 8 to disable additional devices.

10. Click the **Hardware Profiles** tab and choose **Original Configuration.**

11. Click the **Device Manager** tab and click the plus sign next to one of the dock-ing station devices that you want to disable when the notebook is undocked.

12. Complete steps 6 to 9 to disable all docking station devices and click **OK.**

Figure 28.2

To prevent conflicts, dis-able devices that you do not use.

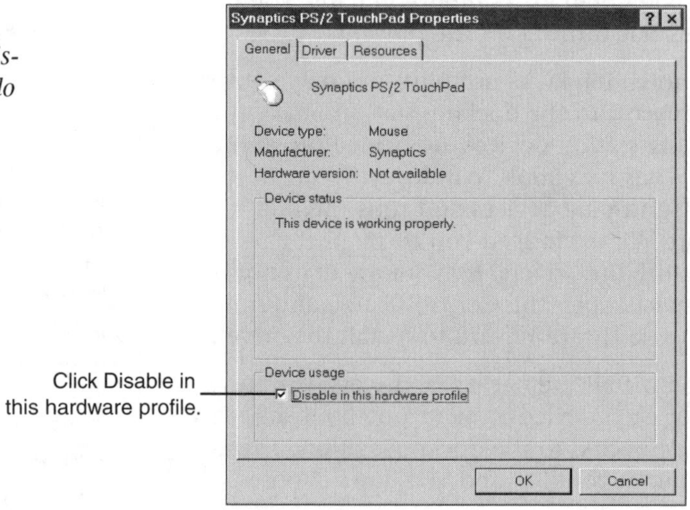

Click Disable in this hardware profile.

Whenever you start your notebook, Windows attempts to determine which configuration to use. If Windows can't make this determination, it displays a list of available configurations: **Original Configuration** and **Docked.** Type the number next to the configuration you want to use.

Linking Your Notebook and Desktop Computers

Windows includes a feature called Direct Cable Connection, which enables you to connect two computers using a serial or parallel cable. After the computers are connected, you can use one computer to link to the other computer and use its files, programs, and printer just as if you were typing at its keyboard. The Direct Cable Connection is especially useful if you need to transfer large amounts of data from one computer to another.

Set Up a Connection

To set up a direct cable connection, you must connect the serial or parallel ports on the two computers using a data or file transfer cable. A standard parallel printer or serial modem cable will not work. Connecting the parallel ports is the preferred method because they transfer data 10–15 times faster than the serial ports.

After you have installed the cable, you must set up one computer as the *host* and the other as the *guest.* The host usually is the more powerful of the two computers—typically the desktop PC. Take the following steps to set up the connection in Windows:

1. Turn off the two computers, connect them with the required cable, and turn them back on.

2. On the host computer, choose **Start**, **Programs**, **Accessories**, **Direct Cable Connection.** (If Direct Cable Connection is not listed, see "Installing and Uninstalling Windows Components" in Chapter 6 to install it.) The Direct Cable Connection Wizard appears.

3. Click **Host** and click **Next**, as shown in Figure 28.3. You are prompted to pick the port in which you plugged the cable.

4. Select the port and click **Next.**

5. (Optional) To prevent unauthorized access to your computer, choose **Use Password Protection.** Click the **Set Password button**, enter the password in the two text boxes, and click **OK.**

6. On the guest computer, choose **Start**, **Programs**, **Accessories**, **Direct Cable Connection.**

7. Click **Guest** and click **Next.** You are prompted to pick the port in which you plugged the cable.

8. Select the port and click **Next**.

9. Go back to the host computer and click **Finish**. The host computer displays a dialog box indicating that it is waiting for the guest computer to connect.

10. On the guest computer click **Finish**. If you set password protection on the host computer, a dialog box appears on the guest computer prompting you to enter the password. Type the password and click **OK**.

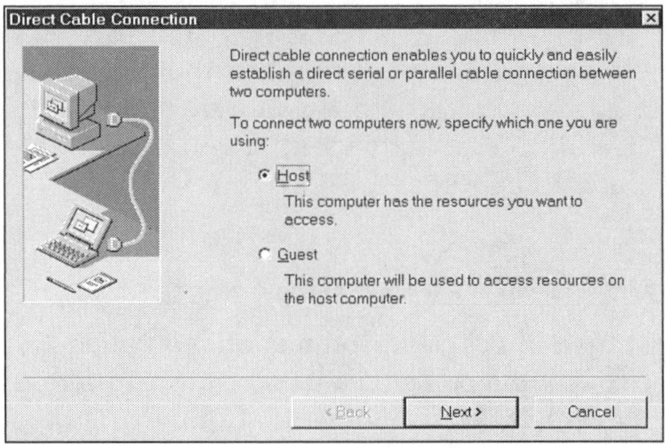

Figure 28.3

Direct Cable Connection leads you through the process of connecting your computers.

Sharing Resources

A direct cable connection works very much like a network connection. Before you can share files and printers over a direct cable connection, you must enter share settings for disk drives, folders, files, and printers on the host computer. For details on how to share disks, files, folders, and printers, see Chapter 18, "Networking (for Those Corporate Types)."

Calling Your Desktop Computer or Network Using Your Modem

If you are on the road and need to use your desktop computer or log on to your network, you can use Dial-Up Networking to place the call. You then can use your notebook computer to copy files and run programs from your desktop computer or network server. Although sharing files and programs over a modem connection provides relatively slow performance, it does give you access to resources that you otherwise would not be able to use.

To use your notebook computer to dial into your desktop computer from a remote location, you must set up your desktop computer as a Dial-Up Networking *server*. This enables the desktop computer to answer incoming calls and establish communications with your notebook computer. Your notebook acts as the Dial-Up Networking client. You must create a new Dial-Up Networking connection, supplying Dial-Up Networking with your desktop computer's phone number.

Although this isn't a complicated task to pull off, it is tedious and consists of more steps than you find in the Washington Monument (898, in case you're wondering). Instead of boring you with the details, here's the boiled-down overview:

1. Double-click the **Network** icon in the Control Panel and use the **Add** button to install the following network components on both computers: **Client for Microsoft Networks, Dial-Up Adapter,** and a network protocol (**TCP/IP, NetBEUI, or IPX/SPX**). Stay in the Network box until step 4.

2. Make sure **Primary Network Logon** is set as **Client for Microsoft Networks.** Do this on both computers.

3. Click **File and Print Sharing** and activate all the options.

4. Still in the Network box? Double-click **File and Printer Sharing for Microsoft Networks,** select **Browse Master,** and make sure its Value is set to **Automatic.** Click **OK.** You're done with the Network box so click **OK.**

5. On the desktop computer, enter share settings for any disks or folders you want to be able to access. See Chapter 18.

6. Set up your desktop computer to answer the phone. Run **Dial-Up Networking** from My Computer or the Control Panel, open the **Connections** menu, and choose **Dial-Up Server.** Enter your preferences making sure to require a password; otherwise, anyone with a PC, modem, and too much free time can break into your computer. A Dial-Up Server icon appears in the system tray.

7. On your notebook computer, run **Dial-Up Networking** from My Computer or the Control Panel, and double-click the **Make New Connection** icon. Follow the instructions to create an icon for dialing your desktop computer. (If your desktop PC is going to be outside your destination's area code, keep that in mind when you're typing the phone number.)

Before you leave on your big trip, turn on your desktop PC, or it won't answer the phone. When you're on the road, simply plug your notebook's modem into a phone jack, double-click the Dial-Up Networking icon you created, and click **Connect** to dial your desktop computer. When your desktop computer answers, double-click the **Network Neighborhood** or **My Network Places** icon on your Windows desktop to access your desktop PC's disks and folders.

Whoa!

Getting your Dial–Up server to work properly can be difficult. If you have problems, check out Microsoft's technical support information on the Web at **www.microsoft.com** (as explained in Chapter 33, "Help! Finding Technical Support").

Subcompact Computing with Palm and Pocket PCs

Back in the '90s, you weren't considered a professional unless you lugged around a Franklin Day Planner packed with all the information you needed to survive your professional and personal life. Subcompact computers (palm, handheld, and pocket computers) are essentially condensed, computerized day planners. Most come complete with their own software, including an address book, calculator, calendar, to do list, e-mail program, and memo pad. Using special stylus that is included with the handheld device, you tap a touch screen to run programs and select menu commands, as shown in Figure 28.4. You also use the stylus to jot down notes or tap the keys of an onscreen typewriter to enter text.

Figure 28.4

Tap and draw on the touch screen to enter commands and "type."

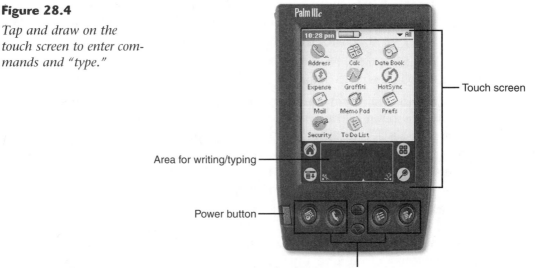

Touch screen

Area for writing/typing

Power button

Buttons for the calendar, phone list, to-do list, and memo pad

If you prefer to type appointments and contact information on your desktop computer, you can enter the information on your desktop computer and then *synchronize* your handheld device with the desktop computer to copy the information. You also can copy information from your handheld device to your desktop computer to use as a backup just in case you ever lose your handheld device. Most handheld devices include a *cradle,* which plugs into a power source and connects to a serial or USB port on a desktop computer. You plug the handheld device into the cradle to recharge its battery, install software, and synchronize data between the handheld and desktop computers.

Handheld computers are much more than overpriced day planners. With additional software and add-on devices, you can use your minicomputer to play games, download stock quotes, check and reply to e-mail messages, browse the Web, scan business cards, read the latest news, navigate roads and highways, and even take photos! Most subcompact computers also have an infrared port that enables you to *beam* files and software from one compact computer to another, making it easy for you and your friends and colleagues to share programs and files.

The Least You Need to Know

➤ Use My Briefcase to safely transfer files between your desktop and notebook PCs.

➤ Conserve your battery, so you can work longer.

➤ Install a fax modem or network PC card without disassembling your computer.

➤ When plugging your notebook PC into a docking station, resolve any hardware conflicts by disabling the hardware you don't use when connected to the docking station.

➤ Connect your notebook and desktop PCs using a data transfer cable for fast file transfers.

➤ Use Dial-Up Networking to connect your notebook PC to your home or office PC when you're on the road.

➤ If you have notes scattered all over your home and office and commonly lose track of dates, miss appointments, and misplace addresses, consider purchasing a palm- or hand-held computer.

Now for the Fun Stuff! Computer Gadgets and Gizmos

In This Chapter

➤ Snapping digital photos to print, e-mail, or place on the Web

➤ Recording and playing your favorite CD tracks on your computer

➤ Editing your home videos and recording them to CDs

➤ Watching TV and DVD videos on your computer

➤ Taking a peek at what the future PC market has in store for you

---

Were you the last one on the block to buy a computer? Do you have shoeboxes full of old, unlabeled photos? Do you still suffer through an entire music CD to hear only one or two of your favorite tunes? Do you have reels of home video footage that you never watch? Do you still have to hunt for your TV's remote control?

If so, the latest technology has passed you by. Fortunately, the sections in this chapter will bring you up to speed. Here, you learn how to digitize your photos and store them on your computer's hard disk and on CDs, copy and play digital music clips from the Internet, edit your camcorder videos and copy them to CDs or tapes, and even watch TV and DVD videos on your computer.

Ordering Your Photos on CD

If you're not ready to trade in your 35mm camera for a new digital camera, consider having your next roll of photos stored on CD. Most photo developers, including your local pharmacy, offer the option of ordering photos on CD. The developer typically creates the standard negatives and prints but also converts the photos to a digital format and saves each photo as a separate file on a CD.

One of the most popular offerings is the Kodak Picture CD, which includes Kodak's digital image manager, a program that enables you to view your pictures onscreen; adjust the brightness, contrast, and colors; sharpen photos; remove the red eye effect (if present); send photos through e-mail; create your own photo albums; and print your photos.

Let's take a look at how this works. You drop off your next roll of film at the developer and order a Kodak Picture CD. When you pick up your prints, you receive a set of prints along with a CD, which includes the Kodak Picture CD software. When you bring your Kodak Picture CD home, take the following steps to install the Kodak Picture CD software and view your pictures on your computer:

1. Pop the Kodak Picture CD into the CD-ROM drive. The Kodak Picture CD installation routine should start. If it doesn't, do the following:

   Double-click **My Computer.**

   Double-click the icon for your **CD-ROM drive.**

   Double-click the **Launch** icon.

2. Follow the onscreen instructions to install the Kodak Picture CD software. When the installation is complete, the Kodak Review magazine appears.

3. Click the arrow in the lower-right corner of the Kodak Review magazine cover to display the table of contents and thumbnail versions of your photos, as shown in Figure 29.1.

4. To view a photo, click its thumbnail version.

From the main menu, you can take a quick tour of the Kodak Picture CD software and learn how to modify and print photos, create greeting cards, e-mail your photos, or even use a photo as your Windows background.

After you install the Kodak Picture CD software for the first time, you can run the program at any time by selecting it from the **Start, Programs, Kodak Picture CD** menu. To view a full-screen slide show of your photos, click View Your Pictures on the Contents Page (the main menu). The Kodak Picture CD flips one by one through the entire roll. After familiarizing yourself with the basic functions, you can move on to using the Kodak Picture CD software to create a photo album, enhance and print photos, and attach digitized photos to outgoing e-mail messages.

Whoa!

The Kodak Picture CD installation routine might indicate that Windows needs to be set up to use small fonts. Right-click the Windows desktop, click **Properties,** click the **Settings** tab, and click the **Advanced** button. On the **General** tab, open the **Font size** list and click **Small Fonts.** You might need to restart Windows.

Thumbnail view of your photos

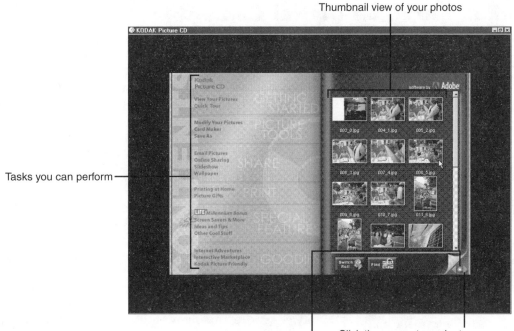

Tasks you can perform

Click the arrows to navigate.

Click the dot between the arrows to display the master menu.

Figure 29.1

Kodak Picture CD displays your photos and lists the tasks you can perform.

Inside Tip

What about those boxes of old photos stashed in the attic? How do you transfer those to your computer? Get a scanner. With a high-quality scanner and the accompanying software, you can pull photos and other images off prints and store them on your hard drive. With a photo management program, such as FlipAlbum, you can create virtual photo albums, index your photos, and flip the pages onscreen. To pick up a free 30-day demonstration copy of PhotoRecall, go to **www.flipalbum.com.**

Smile! You're on Digital Camera

After you have experimented with digital imaging via a photo CD, you might consider trading in your old camera for a new digital camera. With a digital camera you take your photos and then copy them directly from the camera to your PC using a serial or USB cable connection. Most digital cameras come with the software you need to copy the photos to your PC and organize, enhance, and print your photos. Some software packages even offer tools for e-mailing your photos and creating fancy photo albums.

Techno Talk

A digital camera, like a scanner, is built around a *CCD* (charge-coupled device). When you snap a picture, the shutter opens and bombards the CCD with light. The CCD converts the light into electrical impulses, which then are applied to a magnetic storage medium such as a disk or PC card.

Shopping for a digital camera is nearly as complicated as shopping for a computer. Prices range from $100 to more than $1,000 and features vary widely. You need to consider resolution, color depth, memory, flash options, battery life, storage options, zoom features, and the method used to download photos to a computer. Special features, such as voice annotation, an LCD viewfinder, and optical zoom, come at a premium price. As with any big-ticket item, try before you buy, and read current reviews. If you have an Internet connection, try pulling up a buyer's guide. Go to **www.zdnet.com**, click the **Buying Guides** link, and click the link for **Digital Cameras.**

Taking Pictures

Because digital cameras are modeled on standard 35mm cameras, snapping a picture is easy. You just point and shoot. However, before you snap too many pictures, you should check the camera settings. Most digital cameras have two buttons: one for changing modes (such as flash, image quality, timer, and audio); another for changing the mode settings. You change to the desired mode (for instance, Flash) and then press the other button to change the setting (for instance, Auto Flash or Flash On). Check the following settings before taking a picture:

➤ **Resolution**   To fit more pictures in storage, crank down the resolution setting. For higher-quality pictures, choose a higher setting. Lower resolutions generally are acceptable for viewing photos onscreen, e-mailing photos, and placing photos on the Web. If you plan to print the photos, use a higher resolution.

➤ **Flash**   In most cases, leave the flash setting on Auto. If you're taking all your pictures outside, turn off the flash. For backlit scenes, turn on the flash if this option is available on your camera.

➤ **Audio**   If your camera supports audio input, turn on Audio if desired. Keep in mind that audio recordings consume quite a bit of storage space.

Copying Pictures to Your Computer

Digital cameras come with their own software that transfers the image files from the camera to your computer. In addition, the camera should include a cable for connecting to one of the ports on your PC (typically the serial, USB, or FireWire port). Some digital cameras require a PC card reader.

To transfer the images, connect the cable to your camera and to the specified port. Refer to the camera and software's documentation to run the photo transfer utility, and then enter the command to retrieve the images. The program retrieves the images from the camera and displays them onscreen. The program then deletes the images from the PC card or other storage area or gives you the option of having the images deleted.

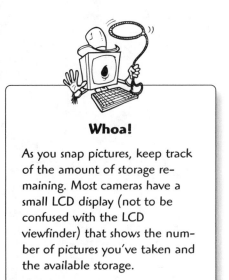

Whoa!

As you snap pictures, keep track of the amount of storage remaining. Most cameras have a small LCD display (not to be confused with the LCD viewfinder) that shows the number of pictures you've taken and the available storage.

Ordering High-Quality Photo Prints Online

Of course you can print your pictures using the software that came with your digital camera or with special photo management software, but what do you do if you want some high-quality 5×7-inch prints? Fortunately, you can drop off your "film" online at any of several online film developers, such as Shutterfly (**www.shutterfly.com**) or Snapfish (**www.snapfish.com**).

The process is pretty simple. You can either e-mail your photo files to the online photo shop or use the online photo shop's software to upload your photo files to the service. For example, at Shutterfly, you simply drag your photos from your digital camera's program into a special Shutterfly window, as shown in Figure 29.2. You then complete an order form, specifying the size and number of prints you want and your billing and delivery information. Shutterfly processes your pictures and then mails them to you.

If you're in a big hurry and need one-hour processing (or faster), take your digital camera to a professional photo shop. Most photo shops have special printers that can transfer your digital photos into high-quality prints in a matter of minutes.

Figure 29.2

At Shutterfly, you drop off your "film" by dragging and dropping the photos you want developed.

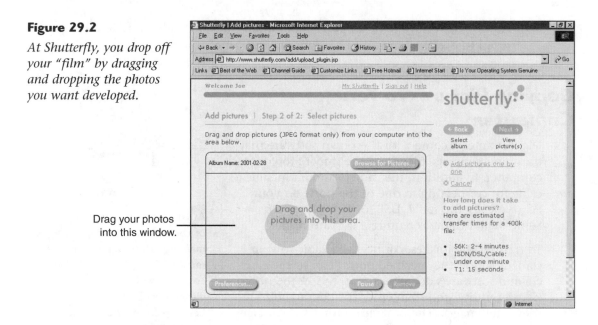

Drag your photos into this window.

I Want My MP3: Digitizing Your Music Collection

In Chapter 4, "Playing Disk Jockey with Hard Disks, Floppy Disks, CDs, and DVDs," you learned how to play audio CDs through your computer's CD-ROM drive, sound card, and speakers. This makes your computer little more than an overpriced audio CD player. To take full advantage of your computer's superior audio capabilities, record your favorite audio clips to your computer's hard drive. This provides you with a virtual jukebox, which you can program to play only the songs you want to hear in the order in which you want to hear them.

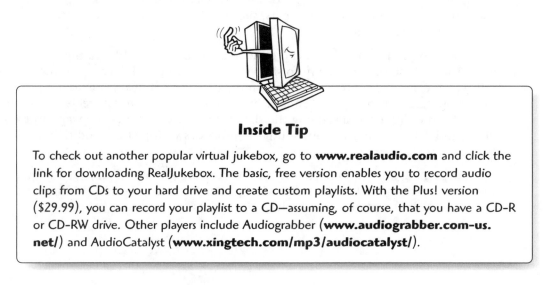

Inside Tip

To check out another popular virtual jukebox, go to **www.realaudio.com** and click the link for downloading RealJukebox. The basic, free version enables you to record audio clips from CDs to your hard drive and create custom playlists. With the Plus! version ($29.99), you can record your playlist to a CD—assuming, of course, that you have a CD-R or CD-RW drive. Other players include Audiograbber (**www.audiograbber.com-us. net/**) and AudioCatalyst (**www.xingtech.com/mp3/audiocatalyst/**).

Included as part of Windows Me, Media Player not only plays audio CDs; it can copy entire CDs or selected tracks to your computer's hard drive to create custom *playlists*. To see whether Media Player is installed on your computer, check the Windows **Start, Programs** menu option or **Start, Programs, Accessories, Entertainment.** If Media Player is not installed, you can install it from the Windows Me CD, or if you have an earlier version of Windows (and you have an Internet connection), pick up a copy of Windows Media Player at **www.microsoft.com/windows/windowsmedia/en/** and install it.

Creating a Custom Playlist with Windows Media Player

Windows Media Player is a type of program called a *CD ripper.* A CD ripper converts audio clips from a CD into the MP3 format or another format that a computer equipped with the required software and audio equipment can play. A CD ripper is commonly called a *jukebox* because it stores all the clips you record and lets you play each clip simply by selecting it from a list.

Using Windows Media Player, take the following steps to record your favorite CD tracks to your computer's hard drive and create a custom playlist:

1. Run the Windows Media Player by selecting Start, Programs, Windows Media Player or Start, Programs, Accessories, Entertainment, Windows Media Player.

2. Insert a CD that has one or more tracks you want to record. (Your computer might have a CD player other than Media Player that runs when you insert an audio CD. At this point, you can either use the player that appears or close the player and proceed with these steps.)

3. In Media Player, click the CD Audio button. After some time, Windows displays a list of the tracks stored on the CD.

Whoa!

If the track names still do not appear, manually label each track. Click the track number to select it, click it again to highlight the track number, and then type the track name. (If the tracks have no names, identifying the tracks later is nearly impossible.) You also can enter artist names for each track. To enter the same artist for every track, click the first track, **Shift+**click the last track, right-click **Unknown Artist,** click **Edit Selection,** type the artist's name, and press **Enter.**

4. If the track names do not appear and you have an Internet connection, click the Get Names button above the track list to obtain the track names and other information from the Web. (Assuming that Media Player finds the information for the right CD, click the Confirm button to copy the information.)

5. Click the check box next to each track you do not want to record to remove the check mark from the box.

6. Click the **Copy Music** button. Media Player displays the progress of the copy operation next to each track as it records the track.

7. Repeat steps 2 through 6 for each CD that has one or more tracks you want to record.

8. Click the **Media Library** button so you can create a custom playlist.

9. Click the **New Playlist** button. The New Playlist dialog box appears prompting you to type a name for the playlist.

10. Type a descriptive name for the playlist, such as **Exercise Warmup**, and click **OK.** A new folder with the name you typed appears below My Playlists, as shown in Figure 29.3.

Click the icon for the CD that contains the recorded track.

Figure 29.3

Drag and drop the audio tracks you recorded to your playlist.

Drag the track and drop it on the icon for your playlist.

11. If a plus sign appears next to **Album**, click the plus sign to display a list of CDs from which you recorded clips.

12. Click the icon for the CD that has the song you want to add to your playlist. The tracks you recorded from the CD appear in the window on the right.

13. Drag the desired track over the icon for the playlist you created and then release the mouse button. The track is added to your playlist.

14. Repeat steps 12 and 13 for the remaining tracks you want to add to your playlist.

15. To display your playlist, click its icon.

16. To move a song up or down on the playlist, click its name and then drag it up or down in the list to the desired location and release the mouse button.

17. To play your clips, click the clip you want to start playing and then click Media Player's **Play** button. Media Player plays the selected song and then the remaining songs in your playlist.

The best way to track down a specific tune on the Web is to use an MP3 search tool. Most MP3 search sites enable you to search for individual tunes by song title or artist. The search typically returns one or more links you can click to download the desired version of the song. Most sites require you to register, and many sites charge a user fee. (You might need to download a special MP3 player to play the clips you download.) Here are some sites to get you started:

➤ AudioGalaxy (www.audiogalaxy.com)

➤ Palavista (www.palavista.com)

➤ Look4MP3 (www.look4mp3.com)

➤ MP3Board (www.mp3board.com)

➤ Audiofind (www.audiofind.com)

➤ MusicMatch (www.musicmatch.com)

➤ MP3Search (www.mp3search.nu)

Copying MP3 Clips to a Portable MP3 Player

Building a huge music library on your computer is cool, but a computer is a bit too bulky to replace your Walkman. How do you take your music collection, or at least a portion of it, on the road? The easiest way is to purchase a portable MP3 player. Portable MP3 players typically come equipped with 32–128 megabytes of RAM, enough to store 4–8 hours of music clips.

Portable MP3 players include a serial, parallel, or USB cable connection that plugs into your computer. Players typically come with their own software for copying files between your computer and the player, but Windows Media Player can handle the job:

1. Connect your portable MP3 player to your computer as instructed in the portable MP3 player's documentation. (If you connect the device using a USB cable, you need not turn off your computer to make the connection; otherwise, you might need to shut down the computer.)

2. Run the Windows Media Player by selecting **Start, Programs, Windows Media Player** or **Start, Programs, Accessories, Entertainment, Windows Media Player.**

3. Click the Media Library button.

4. Click the CD or playlist that contains the clips you want to transfer to your portable MP3 player.

5. Click the **Portable Device** button. Media Player displays two windows. The window on the left displays a list of audio clips in the selected CD or playlist, and the window on the right displays the names of any audio clips already stored on your portable MP3 player.

6. In the window on the left, be sure there is a check mark next to each audio clip you want to copy to your portable MP3 player.

7. Click the **Copy Music** button.

8. Repeat steps 3 through 7 to copy additional audio clips to your portable player.

9. Exit Media Player and disconnect your portable MP3 player as instructed in its documentation.

Inside Tip

If your computer has a CD-R drive, you can transfer your MP3 music clips to a CD using a program called a *CD burner* and play your custom CD in any audio CD player. A CD burner typically provides options for duplicating an audio CD or transferring only selected tracks to a CD. You'll get better results using high-quality CD-R discs rather than CD-RW discs. Check out Roxio's Easy CD Creator at **www.roxio.com** or Ahead Software's Nero at **www.nero.com.**

Editing Your Home Videos

If you're into home video, you know the problems that are inherent in managing your video collection. The tapes are bulky; you have to fast-forward through several minutes of tape to find your favorite clips, and transferring your camcorder tapes to VHS can be an exercise in futility. The new millennium has made the latest video technology, *digital video,* available to the novice filmmaker allowing us to transfer, edit, and catalog our video clips using a computer.

What You Need to Get Started

You can approach digital video from two different directions, depending on how much you have invested in an older camcorder, how many old tapes you have, and how much money you're willing to spend. If you don't have a camcorder or old tapes and you have some cash on hand, purchase a digital camcorder and start filming. Digital camcorders record video in a much higher resolution than analog VHS or 8mm camcorders, and the digital clips won't lose quality when copied to your computer. (The quality of video clips recorded with analog camcorders suffers when they are converted from an analog to a digital format.)

When shopping for a digital camcorder, you need to think about how you will connect the camcorder to your computer. Most digital camcorders have an IEEE-1394 (FireWire) or USB connector. If your computer does not have an IEEE-1394 or USB port, you will need to install an expansion board to add the required port.

If you already have an analog camcorder and plenty of old tapes or if your computer budget is already strained, consider adding a video capture device to your computer. You have several options here. The most convenient way to go is to purchase an external unit that connects to your computer's parallel, USB, or IEEE-1394 port. Figure 29.4 shows the Dazzle Hollywood DV-Bridge. Note that you plug the cables from the camcorder or VCR into the jacks on the front of the unit. For a more permanent addition, purchase a video capture board, which plugs into an expansion slot inside your computer.

Techno Talk

IEEE-1394 is a standard for transferring data between devices very quickly—at a rate of 400Mbps (megabits per second). Compare that to the USB standard of 12Mbps and you can see why IEEE-1394 is the preferred method of transferring video to a computer. IEEE-1394 goes by many names, the most common of which is Apple's *FireWire*. You also might see IEEE-1394 labeled *i.link* or *Lynx*.

Video capture boards and external units have special ports that enable you to connect your camcorder to your computer. They typically capture video at a rate of 15 or more frames per second, and they do a fairly good job of converting your analog clips into a digital format. If you're looking for a way to convert your collection of old camcorder or VHS tapes into a digital format and store them on CDs, this is the way to go.

Figure 29.4

An analog-to-digital converter lets you connect a camcorder or VCR to your computer.

(Photo courtesy of Dazzle, Inc.)

Capturing and Saving Your Clips

Your digital camcorder or video capture device probably came with its own program for recording and editing your video footage. Most of these programs are similar and follow the same overall procedure for recording and editing video. Here's a quick overview of the process:

1. Connect your camcorder or VCR to the video capture device.

2. Run your video recording program and enter the command to start recording.

3. Use your camcorder or VCR controls to play the video you want to record.

4. When you're ready to stop recording, enter the command to stop recording and press the **Stop** button on the camcorder or VCR. The video recording program chops the recording into *clips* to make them more manageable. It displays a thumbnail view of each clip.

5. Trim the clips to retain only the portion of the clip you want to include in your custom video.

6. Arrange the clips in the order in which you want them played. (This typically consists of dragging and dropping the thumbnail version of each clip on a time-line bar.)

7. Add background music, if desired.

8. Add transitions between clips. For example, you can have a clip fade out at the end and fade into the next clip.

9. Save your movie to your hard drive.

10. Record your movie to a CD or tape, or e-mail the movie clip.

Windows Me includes its own video recording and editing software (Windows Movie Maker), so let's use it to run through the basics. If you have Windows Me, open the **Start, Programs, Accessories menu,** and click **Windows Movie Maker.** Windows Movie Maker appears. Figure 29.5 shows Movie Maker in action. Use Movie Maker's Help system to learn how to record and edit your own videos.

Use the commands on the File menu to save your video to disk.

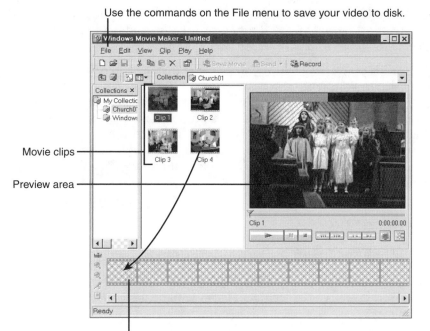

Figure 29.5

Windows Movie Maker makes it easy to record video clips and rearrange them to create a custom video.

Movie clips

Preview area

Drag a clip from this list to the film strip.

Watching TV on Your PC

To take advantage of the latest computer/television technology, you have two choices: The first option is to purchase a WebTV or other computer box for your TV set (commonly called a *set top box*), complete with a wireless keyboard, and use your TV to surf the Web and manage e-mail, in addition to watching TV. Your other option is to add TV capabilities to your computer by installing a TV tuner card. You then can watch TV on your computer or set aside a small portion of your screen to display the news or your favorite daytime TV show as you work. The following sections show you how to add a TV tuner to your computer and use it to flip channels.

Making Your Computer Act Like a TV

Most computers are not cable ready. They have no jack for connecting a TV cable or antenna. To add TV capabilities to a computer, you must install a *TV tuner card,* which is a circuit board that plugs into your computer's motherboard.

When shopping for a TV tuner card, don't buy the first card you see. If you have an older computer, use this purchase as an opportunity to upgrade your display card as well. For instance, with an ATI All-in-Wonder card, you can replace your old display card with a new card that offers faster video, TV tuner capabilities, and video capture support so that you can record and edit your video clips (as explained earlier in this chapter). If you have a newer computer, you don't need to shell out more money for a new display card, but consider buying a TV tuner card that includes a video capture port in case you decide to record and edit videos later.

Installing the video card is pretty easy, but if you've never installed a circuit board, obtain help from a friend or colleague who has experience. Carefully read and follow the installation instructions and safety precautions. The procedure typically consists of opening the system unit case, removing an expansion board cover from the back of the computer (one screw), and plugging the expansion board into an open expansion slot. The card should come with a cable that connects the audio output jack on the TV tuner card to the audio input jack on your sound card. Make the other cable connections as instructed in the installation guide.

Tuning In with Windows

Although your TV tuner probably came with its own program for flipping stations, Windows 98 and Windows Me include WebTV, an excellent program for flipping channels and controlling the TV window. WebTV also enables you to download programming information from the Web, placing a TV guide right on your screen, where you'll never misplace it.

WebTV is not installed during a typical Windows installation. To install WebTV, refer to "Installing and Uninstalling Windows Components" in Chapter 6, "Windows Tips, Tricks, and Traps," and click the check mark next to **WebTV for Windows.**

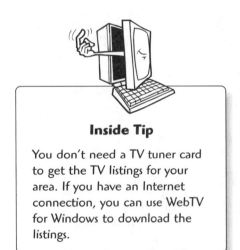

Inside Tip

You don't need a TV tuner card to get the TV listings for your area. If you have an Internet connection, you can use WebTV for Windows to download the listings.

After Web TV is installed, click the **Launch WebTV** icon in the Quick Launch toolbar to run it. WebTV runs through some standard introductory screens to welcome you to WebTV and explain some of its features. At the end of the introduction, WebTV prompts you to scan for channels. Click the **Scan** button. Web TV flips through the available stations and adds the numbers of any stations that provide signals of sufficient strength.

To preview a channel, click its number. WebTV displays the program in a small box in the upper-right corner of the screen. To display the channel in its own window, click **WATCH**, as shown in Figure 29.6. (Because of technical difficulties and legal issues, I can't show you a figure of what a typical TV show looks like on a computer monitor, but take it from me: The picture probably is clearer than the view you get on your TV set, although much smaller.)

Click a channel to preview the program.   The program preview area

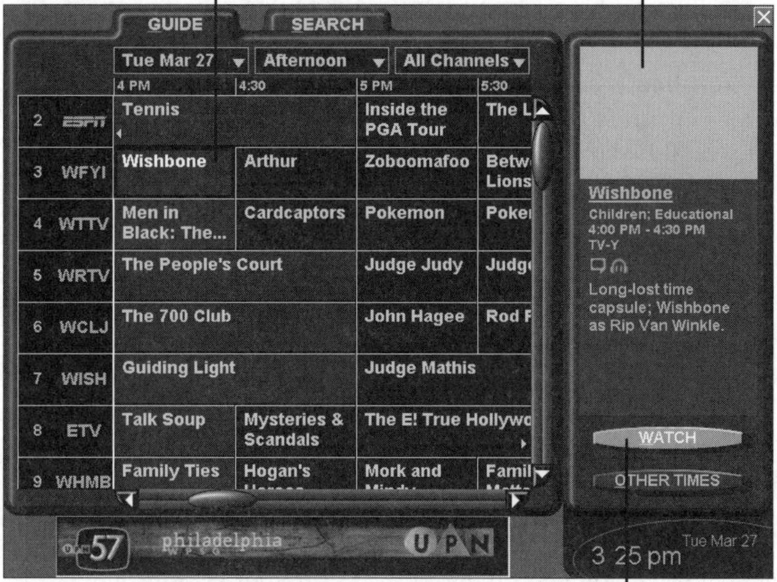

Figure 29.6

Web TV displays an electronic channel changer.

Click **WATCH** to display the program in its own window.

More Cool Stuff in the Works

If you think the gadgets and gizmos covered in this chapter are intriguing, you're really going to be impressed at what the future has in store for you. I'm not talking decades down the road; in fact, by the time this book is published, many of these technical marvels might be on the shelves at your local computer electronics store:

➤ **Windows XP**   The new version of Windows, designed for home and small business users, promises to merge the home-based features of Windows Me with the reliability of Windows 2000. In short, Windows XP won't crash your computer so often. This new Windows likely will be available in late 2001.

➤ **DDR RAM**   Double Data Rate RAM is a super-fast memory module that's currently being used in many video accelerators. DDR RAM will soon be installed in computers to rev up their speed.

➤ **USB 2.0**   This new USB standard will crank up the speed of USB ports from the modest 12 megabits per second all the way up to 480 megabits per second! This will make the new breed of USB ports ideal for video capture and digital imaging.

➤ **Bluetooth**   This short-range (up to 10 meters), high-speed radio technology promises to make it easier to transfer data between computer devices, such as a

325

PC, notebook, digital camera, hand-held computer, cell phone, and even a printer. In short, with Bluetooth you won't have fifty tangled cables at the back of your computer.

➤ **.Net (pronounced "dot-net")**   This new Internet technology, spearheaded by Microsoft, promises to integrate the end user's computer more fully with the Internet. With .Net, you'll be able to rent software on the Internet and pay for only those components you use. In addition, .Net gives users greater flexibility in accessing any data they store on the Internet and provides additional support for voice and handwriting recognition.

The Least You Need to Know

➤ The least expensive way to get started with digital photography is to have your next roll of film processed on a CD.

➤ To save money on film and developing, invest in a good digital camera.

➤ With Windows Media Player, you can rip audio tracks off your favorite music CDs and create custom playlists.

➤ To carry your custom playlists around with you, transfer them to an MP3 player or use a CD burner to write them on CDs.

➤ If you have an analog camcorder, you can use a video capture device to transfer videos to your computer and edit them to create custom videos.

➤ To watch TV on your PC, you must install a TV tuner card; you then can use WebTV for Windows to flip channels.

➤ Keep abreast of the exciting new technologies on the horizon to make your computing experience easier and more satisfying.

Part 6

"Houston, We've Got a Problem"

Even if you're not a computer nerd, using the computer to do your work, explore your interests, or even socialize can be fun—assuming everything goes as planned. However, when things go wrong, your computer can become your bitter enemy offering you no clue to what went wrong or how to fix it.

In this part, you will learn how to keep your computer in peak operating condition, protect the document files you create, and diagnose and cure common computer ailments. And, for those computer problems you cannot fix on your own, this part shows you how to get technical support over the phone and on the Internet.

Chapter 30

Free (or at Least Cheap) Computer Maintenance

In This Chapter

➤ Exterminate dust bunnies

➤ Take a windshield wiper to your monitor

➤ Make your mouse cough up some hairballs

➤ Dry clean your printer

➤ Spin clean your disk drives

When you purchased your computer, the dealer probably didn't mention that in addition to letting you run programs and play games, your computer functions as an excellent clean-air machine. Most system units have two fans—one sucking in and one blowing out to pull all the dust and smoke from your room and deposit it on the sensitive electrical components inside your computer. In addition, the static electricity that builds up in the monitor, printer, and other devices is like a dust magnet gathering all those tiny particles that the system unit misses.

If you don't clean this dust and gunk from your computer regularly, it builds up quickly and can cause problems. Your mouse pointer might skip around on the screen, you might receive disk errors, and the dust buildup eventually can cause your new Pentium CPU to experience a meltdown. Besides, who wants to work or play in a dustbowl? In this chapter, you learn how to keep your computer spic and span.

Tools of the Trade

Before you start cleaning, turn off your computer and any attached devices, and gather the cleaning tools and supplies you need to do the job right. Of course, you can run out and purchase a special toolkit designed specifically for maintaining computers, but you would end up spending more than necessary. The following list helps you assemble your own computer cleaning toolkit using items found in most homes:

➤ **Screwdriver or wrench for taking the cover off of your system unit**   If you don't feel comfortable going inside the system unit, take your computer to a qualified technician for a thorough annual cleaning. It really does get dusty in there.

➤ **Computer vacuum**   Yes, they have vacuum cleaners especially designed for computers.

➤ **Can of compressed air**   You can get this at a computer or electronics store. If you decide to forego the vacuum cleaner, you can use the compressed air to blow dust out of the system unit.

➤ **Soft brush**   A clean paintbrush with soft bristles will do. Use the brush to dislodge any stubborn dust that the vacuum won't pick up.

➤ **Toothpicks**   The only tool you need to clean your mouse.

➤ **Cotton swabs**   Cotton swabs are essential for swabbing dust and gunk out of mice, keyboards, and other tight places.

➤ **Paper towels**   To wipe the smudges off your monitor, nothing works better than a barely damp paper towel.

➤ **Swiffer sheets**   These make a great addition to any computer cleaning kit. These sheets are designed for dusting floors, where they act as dust magnets, making them great for dusting computers. You can find Swiffer sheets in most grocery stores.

➤ **Alcohol**   Not the drinking kind; save that for when you're done.

➤ **Distilled water**   You can get special wipes for your monitor, but paper towels and water do the trick.

➤ **Radio or CD player**   When you're cleaning, you need music.

Don't run out and buy a floppy disk or CD-ROM cleaning kit. If your drive is having trouble reading disks, clean it. If it's running smoothly, let it be.

Vacuum and Dust Your System

Work from the top down and from the outside in. Start with the monitor. (You can use your regular vacuum cleaner for this part; if you have a brush attachment, use it.)

330

Get your vacuum hose, and run it up and down all the slots at the top and sides of the monitor. This is where most of the dust settles. Work down to the tilt-swivel base and vacuum (you might need a narrow hose extension to reach in there). Vacuum your printer, speakers, and any other devices. If the dust is stuck to a device, wipe it off with a damp (not soaking wet) paper towel.

Now for the system unit. When vacuuming, make sure you vacuum all the ventilation holes, including the floppy disk drive, power button, CD-ROM drive, open drive bays, and so on. If you have a CD-ROM drive, open it and gently vacuum the tray.

Now for the tough part—inside the system unit. Before you poke your vacuum hose in there, you should be aware of the following precautions:

➤ Use only a vacuum designed for computers or use a can of compressed air to blow out the dust. Don't use a Dust Buster, your regular vacuum cleaner, or your ShopVac. These can suck components off of your circuit boards and can emit enough static electricity to fry a component. A computer vacuum is gentle and grounded.

➤ Be careful around circuit boards. A strong vacuum can suck components and jumpers right off the boards.

➤ Touch a metal part of the case to discharge any static electricity from your body, and keep your fingers away from the circuit boards, cables, and any other objects inside the case.

Take the cover off the system unit and vacuum any dusty areas. Dust likes to collect around the fan, ventilation holes, and disk drives. Try to vacuum the fan blades, too. If you can't get the tip of the vacuum between the blades, gently wipe them off with a cotton swab. Some fans have a filter where the fan is mounted. If you're really ambitious, remove the fan (careful with the wires) and clean the filter.

Inside Tip

Some PCs have a fan that pulls air from the outside and pushes it through the ventilation holes. If the system unit case has openings near the fan, cut a square of sheer hosiery fabric, stretch it over the openings, and tape it in place with duct tape keeping the tape away from the openings. Check the filter regularly and re-place it whenever dust builds up.

Wiping Gunk off the Monitor

If you can write "WASH ME" on your monitor with your fingertip, the monitor needs cleaning. Check the documentation that came with your computer or monitor to see if using window cleaner on the monitor is okay—the monitor might have an antiglare coating that can be damaged by alcohol—or ammonia-based cleaning solutions. (If it's not okay, use water.) Spray the window cleaner (or water) on a paper towel, just

enough to make it damp, and then wipe the screen. Don't spray window cleaner or any other liquid directly on the monitor; you don't want moisture to seep in. You can purchase special antistatic wipes for your monitor. These not only clean your monitor safely; they discharge the static electricity to prevent future dust buildup.

Brushing Off the Keyboard

Your keyboard is like a big place mat, catching all the cookie crumbs and other debris that fall off your fingers while you're working. The trouble is that, unlike a place mat, the keyboard isn't flat; it's full of nooks and crannies that are impossible to reach. And the suction from a typical vacuum cleaner just isn't strong enough to pull up the dust (although you can try it).

The easiest way I've found to clean a keyboard is to turn it upside down and shake it gently. Repeat two or three times to get any particles that fall behind the backs of the keys when you flip it over. If you don't like that idea, get your handy-dandy can of compressed air and blow between the keys.

For a more thorough cleaning, shut down your computer and disconnect the keyboard. Dampen a cotton swab with rubbing alcohol and gently scrub the keys. Wait for the alcohol to evaporate before reconnecting the keyboard and turning on the power.

> **Inside Tip**
>
> Don't waste your money on antistatic wipes. Wipe your monitor with a used dryer sheet. (Note: A new dryer sheet might smudge the screen with fabric softener.)

> **Inside Tip**
>
> If you spill a drink on your keyboard, try to save your work and shut down the computer fast, but properly. Flip the keyboard over and turn off your computer. If you spill water, just let the keyboard dry out thoroughly. If you spill something sticky, give your keyboard a bath or shower with lukewarm water. Take the back off of the keyboard, but do not flip the keyboard over with the back off or parts will scurry across your desktop. Let it dry for a couple of days (don't use a blow-dryer), and put it back together. If some of the keys are still sticky, clean around them with a cotton swab dipped in rubbing alcohol. If you still have problems, buy a new keyboard; they're relatively inexpensive.

Picking Hairballs out of Your Mouse

If you can't get your mouse pointer to move where you want it to, you can usually fix the problem by cleaning the mouse. Flip the mouse over and look for hair or other debris on the mouse ball or on your desk or mouse pad. Removing the hair and wiping off your mouse pad fixes the problem 90 percent of the time.

If that doesn't work, remove the mouse ball cover (typically, you press down on the cover and turn counterclockwise). Wipe the ball thoroughly with a moistened paper towel. Now for the fun part: Look inside the mouse (where the ball was). You should see three rollers, each with a tiny ring around its middle. The ring is not supposed to be there. The easiest way I've found to remove these rings is to gently scrape them off with a toothpick. You have to spin the rollers to remove the entire ring. You also might try rubbing the rings off with a cotton swab dipped in rubbing alcohol, but these rings are pretty stubborn. When you're done, turn the mouse back over and shake it to remove the loose crumbs. Reassemble the mouse.

Notable Note

If you have an optical mouse, it has no mouse ball. A tiny sensor at the bottom of the mouse controls the movement of the mouse pointer. If the clear cover gets dirty, you should wipe it off, but you don't need to disassemble the mouse to clean it.

Basic Printer Maintenance

Printer maintenance varies widely from one printer to another. If you have a laser printer, you need to vacuum or wipe up toner dust and clean the little print wires with cotton swabs dipped in rubbing alcohol. For an inkjet printer, you might need to remove the print cartridge and wipe the print heads with a damp cotton swab. If you have a combination scanner/printer, you might have to wipe the glass on which you place your original.

You also need to be careful about the cleaning solution you use. Most printer manufacturers tell you to use only water on the inside parts—print rollers, print heads, and so on. In other cases, you can use a mild cleaning solution. Manufacturers also recommend rubbing alcohol on some parts. Even with these variables, there are a few things the average user can do to keep the printer in peak condition and ensure high-quality output:

Inside Tip

Rubbing alcohol is an excellent cleaning solution for most electronic devices because it cleans well and dries quickly. Use it for your keyboard, plastics, and most glass surfaces (except for some monitors). Avoid using it on rubber (for example, your mouse ball) because it tends to dry out the rubber and make it brittle.

333

➤ When turning off the printer, always use the power button on the printer (don't use the power button on your power strip) or press the Online button to take the printer offline. This ensures that the print head is moved to its rest position. On inkjet printers, this prevents the print head from drying out.

➤ Vacuum inside the printer. Open any doors or covers to get inside.

➤ If the ink starts to streak on your printouts (or you have frequent paper jams in a laser printer), get special printer-cleaner paper from an office supply store and follow the instructions to run the sheet through your printer a few times.

➤ Using a damp cotton ball, wipe paper dust and any ink off of the paper feed rollers. Do not use alcohol. Do not use a paper towel; fibers from the paper towel could stick to the wheels.

Cleaning Your Disk Drives

Don't bother cleaning your floppy or CD-ROM or DVD drives unless they're giving you trouble. If your CD-ROM drive is having trouble reading a disc, the disc is usually the cause of the problem. Clean the disc and check the bottom of the disc for scratches. If the drive has problems reading every CD you insert, try cleaning the drive using a special CD-ROM drive cleaning kit. The kit usually consists of a disc with some cleaning solution; you squirt the cleaning solution on the disc, insert it, remove it, and your job is done.

If you have a floppy disk drive that has trouble reading every disk you insert, you can purchase a special cleaning kit that works like the CD-ROM cleaning kit. Although cleaning the disk drive might solve the problem, the problem also can be caused by a poorly aligned read/write head inside the drive, which no cleaning kit can correct.

The Least You Need to Know

➤ Vacuum your system, especially around its ventilation holes.

➤ Wipe the dust off your screen using a paper towel and the cleaning solution recommended by the manufacturer.

➤ Blow the crumbs out your keyboard with compressed air.

➤ Remove those nasty mouse rings with a toothpick.

➤ Vacuum any ink dust that accumulates inside your printer.

➤ Clean your floppy or CD-ROM drive if it is having trouble reading disks.

Chapter 31

Backing Up for the Inevitable Crash

In This Chapter

➤ Stick the entire contents of your hard drive on a backup disk

➤ Back up only the data files that you have created

➤ Pick a backup plan you can live with

➤ Recover files when disaster strikes

Backing up a hard disk poses the same question that airline passengers have faced for a long time: Is safety worth the added time and inconvenience of baggage checks and metal detectors? Yes. Can your hard drive crash? Yes. Can you lose all your files? Yes. Can someone steal your computer? Yes. Are you willing to do what it takes to recover from such a disaster? Probably not.

Backing up regularly seems like nothing more than a hassle until disaster strikes. You delete a file and dump the Recycle Bin, lightning strikes destroying your hard drive, or your computer won't start no matter what you do. In the event of such a mishap, you probably could reinstall your programs, but what about your data? Would you remember all the data that you entered in your personal finance program? Do you have all the e-mail addresses of your friends, relatives, and business contacts written down somewhere? Would you be able to rebuild your spreadsheets and all the other documents that you had painstakingly created? Probably not.

Back up your files regularly. Using a backup program, you can create backup copies of all the files on your hard disk. If you ever destroy a file by mistake, or lose one or more files for any reason, you simply restore the file from your backups.

Backup Strategies for the Real World

Backups are worthless if you don't have a backup strategy—a plan that ensures the backup copies are up to date. If you restore your files from old backups, you get old files losing any changes you've made since the last backup. Like most strategies, backup strategies vary depending on how you work and how you organize your files. The following is a list of common strategies that might help you to develop your own plan:

➤ **The data only, hope nothing happens strategy**   Create a DATA folder and save all the files that you create in folders under the DATA folder. Don't worry about backing up Windows or your programs; you can reinstall them. The trouble with this strategy is that you lose all your Windows and program settings if your hard drive dies, including your Internet connection settings, e-mail messages, address book, network settings, desktop enhancements, and plenty else. (By the way, this is my strategy.)

➤ **The I feel lucky today strategy**   This consists of backing up when you feel like it. People who follow this strategy rarely back up and are at a high risk of losing data.

➤ **The standard strategy**   Back up your entire system monthly and back up only those files that have changed daily. This is the best strategy for making sure that you can recover everything. To do this, you perform a *full* backup monthly. On a daily basis you perform an *incremental* backup, which backs up only those files that have changed since the last backup.

➤ **The I'm special; I have a backup drive strategy**   This is for people who have a special backup drive that can store gobs of data per tape or cartridge. You schedule a full backup every week and an incremental backup at the end of the day. As you're driving home from work, your backup program backs up all your files for you. Most backup programs have a built-in scheduler. Microsoft Backup (covered in this chapter) does not allow for scheduled backups.

Whoa!

The Windows Backup utility is not installed during a typical Windows installation. If Backup is not listed on your menu and you're running Windows 98 or 95, see "Installing and Uninstalling Windows Components" in Chapter 6, "Windows Tips, Tricks, and Traps," for instructions on how to install it. If you're running Windows Me, insert the Windows CD and run Msbexp.exe from the Add-ons\Msbackup folder.

Shopping for Practical Backup Options

Backing up even a modest 5 gigabytes to standard floppy disks would be a nightmare—the procedure would require thousands of disks and take several days to complete. Obviously, floppy disks are not a feasible backup medium. So what are some viable backup options? Here's a list of recommendations:

➤ Iomega's Peerless drive uses 10 or 20GB removable disks and backs up data at a rate of up to 15MB per second. Because backup programs can compress data by a 2-to-1 ratio, you can back up a 40GB drive to a single 20GB disk. The Peerless drive doesn't come cheap—starting at $359 for the 10GB bundle, which includes the drive and one 10GB disk.

➤ Iomega's Zip drive stores only 100 or 250 megabytes per disk, which makes the drive practical for storing data-only backups. If you have a huge hard drive and want to do full backups, you'll find that a Zip drive is limited.

➤ CD-RW drives can store up to 640 megabytes of data on a single disc. You'll still need 8–10 discs to back up a small (5GB) drive, but that's doable.

➤ If you have a DSL, cable modem, or other speedy Internet connection, you can back up your data on the Web. Many of these backup Web sites offer free 10–50 megabytes of space—not enough to back up your entire system, but enough to back up critical data files. Go to **www.idrive.com**, **www.xdrive.com**, or **www.freedrive.com** for details.

Inside Tip

Most external backup drives connect to a parallel, SCSI, Firewire, or USB port. If your computer is equipped with a USB port, choose the USB version of the backup device rather than the parallel port version. Firewire devices support faster transfer rates than both parallel port and USB 1.0 devices, but the USB 2.0 standard will bring USB up to speed with Firewire. SCSI also provides fast data transfer rates, but you're better off going with USB or Firewire, which are much more common.

Backing Up in Windows

Windows comes with its own Backup utility, which can back up files using your floppy disk. It also supports many special backup drives. However, it does not support some of the newer backup drives. If your backup drive came with its own backup program, use that program instead.

If Windows does not support your backup drive and your drive did not come with its own backup utility, you can check out some shareware backup utilities at **download.cnet.com**. Click the **Downloads** link, click **Utilities**, and click **Backup**. If you don't have an Internet connection, visit your local computer store for a backup program.

If you don't have a special backup program, use the Windows Backup utility. To run Backup choose **Start, Programs, Accessories, System Tools, Backup**. In Windows 95, Backup displays a couple introductory dialog boxes, which you can skip with the click of a mouse. (Windows also might search for a tape drive and prompt you to test your drives.) In Windows 98 and Me, the Backup Wizard starts (see the following section for details). Backup then displays a list of the hard disks on your system. After dealing with the preliminaries, take one of the following steps:

Inside Tip

In Windows 95 Backup, to select all the folders and files on a disk, the folder list must not be expanded. If the list is expanded, checking the box selects only the files on the root directory of the disk. Collapse the folder list by clicking the minus sign next to the disk. (Windows 98 Backup does not have this problem.) If the check box is gray with a check mark in it, some files or folders on the disk or in the selected folder are selected; others are not.

➤ To back up all the folders and files on a drive, check the box next to the drive's letter.

➤ To back up some (but not all) of the folders and files on a drive, click the plus sign next to the icon for the drive. You then can check the boxes next to individual folders and files to mark them for backup (see Figure 31.1).

Inside Tip

Whenever a backup program copies a file, it turns the file's *archive attribute* off, indicating that the file has been backed up. (The archive attribute flags files that have been modified since they were last backed up.) If you edit the file, your computer turns the archive attribute on, indicating that the newly edited file has not been backed up. If you then perform an incremental backup, the backup program knows that it must back up this changed file. When you perform a full backup, the backup program copies all the files, no matter what the archive attribute is set to. The backup program then turns off the archive attribute for all those files.

Click the plus sign to expand the folder list.

Check the box to back up all the files on the disk.

Figure 31.1

You can back up entire disks or selected folders and files.

You can choose to back up individual files and folders.

After marking your disks, folders, and files for backup, click the **Next** or **Next Step** button. Backup prompts you to choose the drive that you want to use to store the backup files. Click the icon for the drive you want to use to store the backup files. This can be a floppy drive, CD-R or CD-RW drive, backup drive, network drive, or another hard disk drive. If you're backing up to a floppy drive or a tape backup unit, make sure you have a disk or tape in the drive. Click the **Start** or **Start Backup** button, type a name for this backup, and click **OK.**

Using the Windows Backup Wizard

Backup includes a Backup Wizard, which steps you through the backup process. If Backup is already running, open the Tools menu and select **Backup Wizard** to initiate the operation. If Backup is not running, choose **Start**, **Programs**, **Accessories**,

Inside Tip

To back up only selected disks, folders, and files, choose **Back up selected files**, **folders**, and **drives** in the first Backup Wizard dialog box. You then can mark the items that you want to back up just as in Windows 95 Backup.

System Tools, Backup. Choose **Create a New Backup Job**, click **OK**, and follow the wizard's instructions to complete the operation (see Figure 31.2).

Figure 31.2

The Backup Wizard leads you through the process.

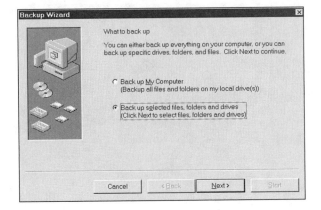

Backing Up Your Entire System

If you do a full system backup using the Windows Backup Wizard, Backup does a complete backup of your system, including the all-important Windows Registry file. This file contains all the settings that make Windows tick. If you choose not to use the wizard, click the **Options** button at the bottom of the Backup Window, click the **Advanced** tab, and make sure **Back Up Windows Registry** is checked.

Whoa!

Before you store your backup files for safekeeping, test them to make sure they are not corrupt. To test your backup files, restore one or two of the files from the backup to a separate folder on your hard drive. The next section explains how to restore files from your backup.

In Windows 95, backing up your entire C drive omits the Windows Registry. If you restore Windows from your backup, Windows won't run. To back up your entire system in Windows 95 Backup, run Backup, open the **File** menu, and choose **Open File Set.** Click **Full System Backup** and click **Open.** Now proceed with the backup as you normally would. (Windows Backup includes the Full System Backup backup set, which prompts Backup to back up everything on your system.)

Restoring Files from Your Backups

Rarely, if ever, do you need to restore your entire system. If you delete a file accidentally, pull it out of the Recycle Bin and make sure you have recovered the latest version of the file. If the Windows Registry becomes corrupted, start your computer with an up-to-date

Windows Startup disk and restore the registry. If an error message appears indicating that a file for running one of your programs is missing, restore that one file from your backup disks or tapes, or reinstall the program.

In short, don't panic and restore everything when you encounter one little mishap. If your backup files are old, even a couple of days old, you could lose much of your work by restoring everything when you need restore only one or two files.

With that warning in mind, you can proceed to restore files from your backups. In Windows 98 or Me, use the Backup Wizard to restore files. Run Backup (**Start, Programs, Accessories, System Tools, Backup**), click **Restore Backed Up Files**, and click **OK**. Follow the onscreen instructions to restore all the files or only selected files, as shown in Figure 31.3.

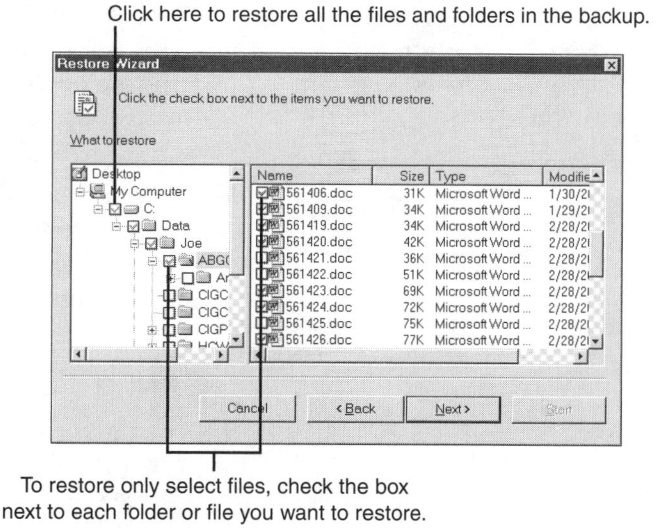

Click here to restore all the files and folders in the backup.

Figure 31.3

In Windows 98 or Me, use the Restore Wizard to restore damaged files.

To restore only select files, check the box next to each folder or file you want to restore.

In Windows 95, the restoration procedure is a little more convoluted. The following steps lead you through the process of restoring selected files from your backups in Windows 95:

1. Choose Start, Programs, Accessories, System Tools, Backup.
2. Click the Restore tab.
3. Insert your backup tape or the last floppy disk of the backup set into the drive.
4. In the Restore from list, click the drive that contains the backup disk or tape.
5. In the Backup Set list, if there is more than one backup set listed, click the name of the backup set you want to restore.
6. Click the Next Step button. A list appears showing all the folders and files on the backup tape or disks.

Inside Tip

Copy two or three files to a separate folder on your hard disk, and practice backing up and restoring the files until you feel comfortable working with Backup. Open the **Settings** menu and choose **Options** to view available options for backing up and restoring files.

7. Under **Select files from the backup set**, take one of the following steps:

   To select all the files in the backup, make sure no folder names are displayed under the drive letter, and check the box next to the drive letter. Skip to step 9.

   To restore one or two files or folders, click the plus signs to display the folder or contents of the folder you want to restore. Go on to the next step.

8. To restore the contents of an entire folder, check its box. To restore selected files in a folder, click the name of the folder that contains the file (not the folder's check box), and then check the box next to each file that you want to restore.

9. Click the **Start Restore** button. If you are restoring from floppy disks a dialog box appears, indicating which disk to insert. Follow the onscreen instructions.

Inside Tip

A *backup set* is a collection of saved backup settings that tells Backup which disks, files, and folders to back up and how to back them up—compressed or uncompressed—which backup drive to use, and so on. To save your backup preferences as a backup set, take the steps to back up your files and choose a drive to back up to. Open the **File** menu, select **Save As,** and name and save the file. To perform the same backup later, open the **File** menu, select Open **File Set,** and choose the backup set you created. (In Windows 98 and more recent versions, Backup refers to backup sets as *backup jobs*. The Wizard enables you to choose a backup job when you start Backup.)

The Least You Need to Know

➤ Pick a backup strategy that works for you and follow it.

➤ Don't forget to run your backup utility regularly.

➤ You can back up selected disks, folders, and files instead of backing up entire hard drives.

➤ If you're running Windows 98 or Me, back up files using the Backup Wizard.

➤ Every month or so, back up your entire system, including the Windows Registry.

➤ After you perform a backup, restore one or more files from the backup files to a separate folder on your hard drive to make sure your backup files are not corrupt.

➤ If you accidentally erase a file permanently or lose a file during a system crash, use your backups to restore selected folders and files.

Do-It-Yourself Fixes for Common Ailments

In This Chapter

➤ Figure out what to do and not do in a crisis

➤ Sniff out the cause of a problem

➤ Recover safely when your computer locks up

➤ Get your speakers to say something

➤ Make your modem dial

With a little patience, you can solve most of your own problems (your computer problems, that is). You just need to know how to go about it—what to do and what not to do. The overall approach is twofold: You need to trace the problem to its cause and avoid making the problem worse than it already is.

In this chapter, you will learn how to react in a crisis and how to solve your computer woes. Although I can't cover every problem, I cover many common ones and give you some strategies for solving problems that aren't covered here.

Troubleshooting Tactics: Pre-Panic Checklist

When you run into a problem that doesn't have an obvious solution, the best course of action is inaction—that is, don't do anything. If you're fidgeting to do something, take a walk or watch *Oprah*. Then come back and walk through this checklist:

➤ **Are there any onscreen messages?** Look at the monitor for any messages that indicate a problem.

➤ **Is everything plugged in and turned on?** Turn everything off and check the connections. Don't assume that just because something looks connected, it is; wiggle the plugs.

➤ **When did the problem start?** Did you install a new program? Did you enter a command? Did you add a new device? When my speakers went mute, I realized that the problem started after I installed a new hard drive. I had knocked a tiny jumper off the sound card during the hard drive installation.

➤ **Is the problem limited to one program?** If you have the same problem in every program, the problem probably is caused by your computer or Windows. If the problem occurs in only one program, focus on that program.

➤ **When did you have the file last?** If you lost a file, it probably did not get sucked into a black hole. It probably is somewhere on your disk, in a separate folder. Open the **Start** menu, choose **Find** or **Search**, and start hunting.

Inside Tip

Most computer problems are not the computer's fault and are rarely caused by viruses. The problem is usually in the software—Windows or one of your programs. Of the problems that people blame on computer viruses or the computer itself, 95 percent actually are bugs in the software or problems with specific *device drivers* (the instructions that tell your computer and Windows how to use the device).

My Computer Won't Start

A computer is a lot like a car; the most frustrating thing that can happen is that you can't even get the engine to turn over. You turn on your computer (or think you turned it on) and you come face-to-face with a dark, clueless screen. Without an error message of any kind to give you direction, where do you start? To solve the problem, consider these questions:

➤ **Is the computer on?** Make sure the power switch on the system unit is turned on. Some computers have a power button you have to press and hold for a couple of seconds.

➤ **Is the surge strip on?** If your PC is plugged into a surge suppressor or UPC, make sure the power is turned on.

➤ **Is the screen completely blank?** If you heard the computer beep and you saw the drive lights go on and off, the computer probably booted fine. Make sure the monitor is turned on and the brightness controls are turned up. Try moving your mouse or pressing the **Shift** key; your computer might be in sleep mode and this wakes it up.

➤ **Is there a disk in drive A?** If you see a message onscreen that says Non-system disk or disk error, you probably left a floppy disk in drive A. Remove the disk and press any key to start from the hard disk.

➤ **Can you start from a floppy disk?** Insert the Windows Startup disk in drive A and press **Ctrl+Alt+Del**. If you can start from a floppy, the problem is on your hard disk. You need some expert help to get out of this mess.

Inside Tip

Windows comes with a utility that can transform a floppy disk into a Startup disk. Open the Windows Control Panel, double-click the **Add/Remove Programs** icon, and click the **Startup Disk** tab. Click the **Create Disk** button, and then follow the onscreen instructions. Of course, you can't create the disk if your computer won't boot, but after you get your computer started, make a Startup disk.

My Computer Locked Up

The computer might be too busy to handle your request, so wait a few minutes. If it's still frozen, press **Ctrl+Alt+Del**. A dialog box should appear, showing you the names of the active programs. Next to the program that's causing the problem, you should see [not responding]. Click the program's name and click **End Task**. Frequently, a second End Task confirmation dialog box appears a few seconds after clicking the End Task button; repeat the command to end the task. (You might lose data when you close a program that is not responding.) You now should be able to continue working.

If you close the errant program and Windows is still locked up, press **Ctrl+Alt+Del** again, and close any other programs that are causing problems. If you still cannot regain control of your computer, you might have to press **Ctrl+Alt+Del** again or use your computer's Reset or Power button. Do this only as a last resort. Shutting down your system without exiting programs properly causes you to lose any unsaved work. (Files saved to your hard disk are safe.)

It Could Be a Program

Many programs, especially Web browsers, games, and antivirus programs, typically are buggy. They have programming code that makes the program conflict with Windows, other programs, one of your hardware devices, or even your computer's memory. One common problem is that the program never frees up the memory it uses after it is done with it.

The only permanent solution is to install a *patch* or *bug fix* from the manufacturer, as-suming a patch is available. (A patch is a set of program instructions designed to fix a programming bug or add capabilities to a program.) Contact the manufacturer's tech support department to determine whether they have a fix for the problem, as ex-plained in Chapter 33, "Help! Finding Technical Support." For a temporary solution, use the program in spurts. Use the program for a while, save your work, exit, and restart before your computer locks up. If your computer seems to be sluggish, try restarting Windows to free up memory.

Check Your Mouse Driver

Windows might be having a problem with the mouse driver (the instructions that tell Windows how to use your mouse). Check to make sure you don't have two conflict-ing mouse drivers installed. **Alt+click My Computer** and click the **Device Manager** tab. Click the plus sign next to **Mouse**. If you have more than one mouse listed, you have more than one mouse driver installed.

Before you remove one of the mouse drivers, make a Windows Startup disk, as ex-plained earlier. If you disable the wrong mouse driver, you're in for some heavy-duty troubleshooting. To disable a mouse driver, double-click the **mouse** icon that doesn't match the type of mouse you have, click **Disable in This Hardware Profile**, and click **OK**. Click **OK** again and restart your computer.

If that doesn't fix the problem, check the mouse manu-facturer's Web site to determine if an updated mouse driver is available. If you can't use your mouse to get on the Internet, use a friend's computer or call the tech support department for the mouse manufacturer and ask if they have an updated driver (they send it to you through e-mail or on a floppy disk). In most cases, the updated driver contains the fix for the problem. (See "Updating the Software for Your Hardware" later in this chapter to learn how to install an updated driver.)

Whoa!

If you pick the wrong mouse driver, you won't have a mouse pointer in Windows, making it tough to navigate. If you pick the wrong driver, start your com-puter with the Windows Startup disk, and then you can navigate Windows and pick a different driver.

If you cannot obtain an updated mouse driver, try using one of the standard drivers that comes with Windows. Open the **Control Panel** and double-click the **Add New Hardware** icon. Click the **Next** button to advance from the Welcome dialog box and click **Next** to have Windows search for new devices. Click **No, the device isn't in the list** and click **Next**. Click **No, I want to select the hardware from a list** and click **Next**. Click **Mouse** and click **Next**. Select one of the standard mouse types, as shown in Figure 32.1, and click **OK**.

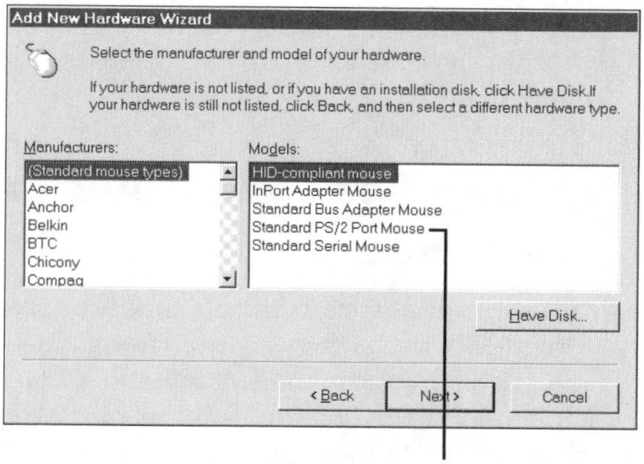

Figure 32.1

Mouse drivers commonly cause problems.

Select a standard mouse type.

Check the Windows Graphics Acceleration Setting

Windows initially is set up to exploit the full potential of your computer. Unfor–tunately, sometimes Windows is too aggressive, especially when it comes to your system's video acceleration. Windows cranks up the video acceleration rate to the maximum, which sometimes can cause your system to crash without displaying an error message. Try slowing it down:

1. Right-click the **My Computer** icon and select **Properties**.
2. Click the **Performance** tab and click the **Graphics** button.
3. Drag the **Hardware Acceleration** slider to the second or third hash mark, and click **OK**.
4. Click **Close**.
5. When asked whether you want to reboot your system, close any programs that might be running and click **Yes**.

Obtain an Updated Video Driver

Hiding behind the scenes of every video card and monitor is a video driver that tells your operating system (Windows) how to use the card and monitor to display pretty pictures. Occasionally, the driver contains a bug that can lock up your system. More

Inside Tip

Some programs have trouble dealing with a large number of colors. Right-click the **Windows desktop,** choose **Properties,** and click the **Settings** tab. Choose **256 Colors** from the **Colors** drop-down list. Don't go lower than 256; some programs do not work with a lower setting.

frequently, the driver becomes outdated causing problems with newer programs. In either case, you should obtain an updated driver from the manufacturer of the video card. You can call the manufacturer's tech support line and have them send the driver to you on a floppy disk or obtain the driver from the company's Web site (see "Updating the Software for Your Hardware" later in this chapter to learn how to install an updated driver).

Dealing with Windows in Safe Mode

Windows typically starts in Safe mode if you install a wrong device driver (especially a wrong video or mouse driver). In Safe mode, "Safe mode" appears at each corner of the desktop. In most cases, you can simply restart Windows to have it load the previous driver. If on restarting, the Windows desktop is not visible or you cannot use the mouse, restart your computer in Safe mode by performing the following steps:

1. If the Windows desktop is visible and Windows responds to your keyboard, shut down Windows using your keyboard. (Press **Ctrl+Esc** or the **Windows** key to open the **Start** menu, and then press the **Up Arrow** key and press **Enter** to select **Shut Down.** Use the arrow keys to select the **Shut Down** option and press **Enter.**)

2. Turn off your computer.

3. Turn on your computer and immediately start performing the next step.

4. Tap the **F8** key every two seconds as the computer boots up. This tells Windows to load a startup menu rather than loading the operating system. (You can try pressing F8 once right when the computer beeps, but you'll have a better chance of bringing up the Startup menu by tapping the F8 key.)

5. Type the number next to the option for starting Windows in Safe mode.

6. Press **Enter.**

Windows loads a standard mouse and video driver in Safe mode, so you can see what you're doing and use the mouse to point and click. This allows you to install a different or updated driver or change settings back to what they were before you encountered problems.

My Screen Is Flickering

If your screen is flashing or turning odd colors, the plug that connects the monitor to the system unit probably has come loose. Turn everything off and then check the connection. If the plug has screws that secure it to the system unit, tighten the screws.

Magnetic fields (from speakers, phones, and other sources) also can cause your screen to freak out just as they can cause problems with a standard TV; subwoofers, which commonly are not shielded, are especially suspect. You may see a band of color along one edge of the screen. Move any electrical appliances away from your monitor. The problem might go away immediately or take a day or two to correct itself.

I Can't Get the Program to Run

If you try to run a program using a shortcut icon, the icon might be pointing to the wrong program. Right-click the shortcut, choose **Properties**, and check the entry in the **Target** text box. This shows the path to the program's folder followed by the name of the program file that launches the program. If the text box is blank or points to the wrong file, click the **Find Target** button and use the resulting dialog box to change to the program's folder and choose the right program file.

If the program starts and immediately closes, you might not have sufficient memory or disk space on your computer. Right-click **My Computer** and select **Properties**. Click the **Performance** tab and click the **Virtual Memory** button. Make sure you have at least 30 megabytes of free space on the disk that Windows is using for virtual memory. If you have any less, you have to clear some files from your hard disk.

If the program still won't run, try reinstalling it. If that doesn't work, contact the program manufacturer's tech support department to determine the problem and the required fix. The program might require special hardware or additional software that is not available on your system.

I Have a Mouse but I Can't Find the Pointer

After you get your mouse working, you probably will never have to mess with it again (except for cleaning it, which we talked about back in Chapter 30. The hard part is getting the mouse to work in the first place. If you connect a mouse to your computer and you don't see the mouse pointer on-screen, there are a few possibilities you should investigate:

Whoa!

Write down changes you make to your system. It takes a little extra time, but it enables you to retrace your steps later.

➤ **Am I in a program that uses a mouse?**   Some old programs don't support a mouse, so you won't see the mouse pointer in these programs. For example, you won't see a mouse pointer at the DOS prompt or in many DOS computer games. Run a program that you know uses a mouse to see whether it works there.

➤ **Is the mouse pointer hidden?**   Mouse pointers like to hide in the corners or edges of your screen. Roll the mouse on your desktop to see whether you can bring the pointer into view. (If you have a notebook computer, the mouse pointer might disappear when you move the mouse quickly.)

➤ **When you connected the mouse, did you install a mouse driver?**   Connecting a mouse to your computer is not enough. You must install a program (called a *mouse driver*) that tells the computer how to use the mouse. Follow the instructions that came with the mouse to figure out how to install the driver.

Inside Tip

If you slide the mouse around on your mousepad, and the mouse pointer doesn't move or skips erratically across the screen, you probably have a dirty mouse. Clean your mouse, as explained in Chapter 30.

Inside Tip

Windows comes with several hardware troubleshooters that can help you track down problems with your mouse, sound card, monitor, network, and other devices. To view a list of troubleshooters, open the **Start** menu, click **Help,** and search for "troubleshooter."

I Can't Hear My Speakers!

Sometimes, for no apparent reason, computers lose their ability to emit sounds. Your computer might be playing audio CDs and other sounds one day and become completely mute the next day. Several things can cause your speakers to go mute. Check the following:

➤ Are your speakers turned on?

➤ Is the speaker volume control turned up?

➤ Are your speakers (or headphones) plugged into the correct jacks on your sound card? Some sound cards have several jacks, and it's easy to plug the speakers into the input jacks instead of the output jacks.

➤ If you're having trouble recording sounds, make sure your microphone is turned on and plugged into the correct jack.

➤ Does your sound card have a volume control? Some sound cards have a volume control dial on the back of the card (near the speaker jacks). If your sound card has a dial on it, crank the dial all the way up.

➤ Right-click the **Speaker** icon on the Windows taskbar and choose **Open Volume Controls.** Open the **Options** menu, choose **Properties**, and make sure that every volume control in the list at the bottom of the dialog box is checked. Click **OK.** Use the sliders to crank up the overall volume, CD volume, and Microphone volume. Make sure the **Mute** options are not checked.

If you still can't get your speakers to talk, right-click **My Computer**, select **Properties**, and click the **Device Manager** tab. Scroll down the list and click the plus sign next to the **Sound** … option. If your sound card is not listed, you need to reinstall the sound card driver. If the sound card is listed but has a yellow circle with an exclamation point on it, the sound card is conflicting with another device on your system. Check your sound card's documentation to determine how to resolve hardware conflicts. This can be pretty complicated and might require you to change settings on your sound card (you might have to go inside the system unit).

I Can't Get My Modem to Work

If your modem can't dial, Windows can help you track down the problem. Double-click the **Modems** icon in the Control Panel, click the **Diagnostics** tab, and click the **Help** button. The Windows Modem Troubleshooter appears. Answer the questions to track down and correct common modem problems, as shown in Figure 32.2.

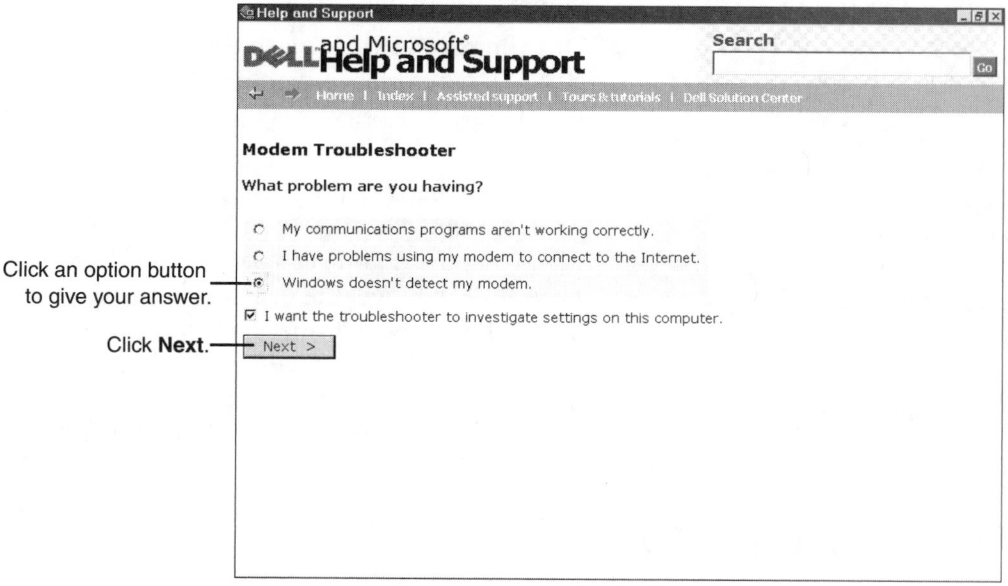

Figure 32.2

Windows comes with a modem troubleshooter.

The Computer Won't Read My Floppy Disk

Don't feel bad; it happens to everyone. You stick a floppy disk in the disk drive, close the drive door, change to the drive, and you get an error message saying basically that the disk is no good. Your computer can't read it, write to it, or even see that it's there. What happened? That depends. Check the following:

➤ **Is the disk inserted properly?** Even the most experienced computer user occasionally fails to push the disk in all the way. Press the disk drive's eject button and reinsert the disk.

Notable Note

If a disk is bad, you might be able to salvage it using the ScanDisk, as explained in Chapter 27, "Do-It-Yourself Computer Tune-Ups." If a drive is bad, you have to take it to a computer mechanic to get it fixed or replace the drive (which might be the cheaper option). Usually the problem is that the drive is not spinning at the right speed or that the arm that reads and writes data to the disk is not aligned properly on the disk.

➤ **Is the disk write-protected?** If the disk is write-protected, you won't be able to save a file to the disk. For a 3^1/$_2$" disk, slide the write-protect tab so you can't see through the little hole.

➤ **Is the disk full?** If you try to save a file to a disk and you get an Insufficient space message, the disk has insufficient free space to hold any more data. Use a different disk.

➤ **Is the disk formatted?** If you buy new, unformatted disks, you must format the disks before you can use them.

➤ **Did you format the disk to the proper density?** If you format a high-density disk as a low-density disk, or vice versa, you probably will run into problems when you try to use the disk.

➤ **Is the disk bad?** Although it's rare, disks do go bad. Some disks even come bad from the manufacturer. If you get a Sector not found or Data error message, the disk might be bad. Then again, the drive might need a tune-up. Try some other disks. If you're having problems with all disks, the problem is in the drive. If you are having trouble with only one disk, it's the disk.

My Printer Won't Print

There's nothing more frustrating than a printer that botches the job. The printer might completely refuse to print a document, or it may print only a portion of the document or print a bunch of strange looking symbols instead of the text or graphic you were expecting. If you run into printer problems, you probably have to do more fiddling than Nero. Look for the following:

➤ **Is your printer plugged in and turned on?** Make sure your printer is plugged in. If it is plugged into a power strip or surge suppressor, make sure the power strip or surge suppressor is turned on. If the printer has a power switch or button, turn it on. (Many printers have no power switch.)

➤ **Does your printer have paper?** Is the paper tray inserted properly?

➤ **Is the printer's online light on (not blinking)?** If the online light is off or blinking, press the On Line button to turn on the light.

➤ **Is your program set to print to a file?** Many Print dialog boxes have a Print to File option, which sends the document to a file on your disk instead of to the printer. Make sure this option is not checked.

➤ **Is the print fading?** If so, your printer might need a new toner or ink cartridge. If your inkjet cartridge has plenty of ink, check your printer manual to determine how to clean the print head. Inkjet cartridges have some sensitive areas that you should never clean, so be careful.

➤ **If you have an inkjet printer, check the print head and the area next to the print head for tape, and remove the tape.** Ink cartridges usually come with two pieces of tape on them. You must remove both pieces before installing the cartridge.

➤ **Is your printer marked as the default printer?** In My Computer, double-click the **Printers** icon. Right-click the icon for your printer and make sure that **Set as Default** is checked. If there is no check mark, select **Set as Default**.

➤ **Is the printer paused?** Double-click the **Printer** icon in the taskbar, open the **Printer** menu and make sure **Pause Printing** is not checked. If there is a check mark, click **Pause Printing**.

➤ **Is the correct printer port selected?** In My Computer, double-click the **Printers** icon and double-click the icon for your printer. Click the **Details** tab and make sure the correct printer port is selected—LPT1 in most cases.

➤ **Did you get only part of a page?** Laser printers are weird; they print an entire page at one time, storing the entire page in memory. If the page has a big, complex graphic image or a lot of fonts, the printer might be able to store only a portion of the page. The best fix is to get more memory for your printer. The quickest fix is to use fewer fonts on the page and try using a less complex graphic image.

➤ **Is it a printer problem?** If you have a standard printer that's connected to your computer's parallel port, try printing a simple file list outside of Windows. Go to the DOS prompt (choose **Start, Programs, MS-DOS prompt** or **Start, Programs, Accessories, MS-DOS prompt**), type dir > lpt1 and press **Enter**. This prints the current directory list. If it prints okay, the problem is in the Windows printer setup. If the directory does not print or prints incorrectly, the problem probably is the printer. (Many printers have a button combination you can press to have the printer perform a self test. Check your printer manual.)

➤ If error messages keeps popping up on your screen, Windows might be sending print instructions to the printer faster than your printer can handle them. In My Computer, double-click the **Printers** icon, right-click your printer's icon, and choose **Properties**. Click the **Details** tab and increase the number of seconds in the **Transmission Retry** text box.

Updating the Software for Your Hardware

Notable Note

Windows 98 and more recent versions can check for updated drivers at Microsoft's Internet site and download the updated driver for you. To run it, open the **Start** menu and click **Windows Update.**

Inside Tip

Some drivers come with their own installation program. Try changing to the disk and folder in which the driver file is stored and running the installation program.

Computer hardware and software is in constant transition. Whenever Microsoft updates Windows, manufacturers have to ensure that the hardware they're coming out with works with the new operating system, and Microsoft does its best to make sure that the new operating system can handle most hardware devices. In this rush to get its products to market, the computer industry often releases products that contain bugs—imperfections that cause problems.

To help make up for these shortcomings, hardware manufacturers commonly release updated drivers for their devices. The driver works along with the operating system to control the device. You can solve many problems with your display, sound card, printer, joystick, modem, and other devices by installing an updated driver.

The best way to get an updated driver is to download it from the Internet, as explained in "Finding Tech Support on the Web," in Chapter 33. If you don't have an Internet connection and you suspect that a device driver is causing problems, call the manufacturer's technical support line and ask whether they have an updated driver. They can send it to you on a floppy disk (see Chapter 33 for details about technical support).

After you have the updated driver, take the following steps to install it:

1. If you have the updated driver on a floppy disk, insert the disk.

2. Right-click **My Computer** and choose **Properties.**

3. Click the **Device Manager** tab.

4. Click the plus sign next to the type of device that requires a new driver.

5. Double-click the name of the device.

6. Click the **Driver** tab and then click the Update Driver button.

7. Choose the option for searching for a better driver and click **Next.** If the driver is on a floppy disk, Windows finds it and prompts you to install it. Follow the onscreen instructions and skip the remaining steps.

8. If you downloaded the driver from the Internet, click the **Other Locations** button, choose the disk and folder where the driver file is stored, and click **OK.**

9. Follow the onscreen instructions to complete the installation.

The Least You Need to Know

➤ Use the **Ctrl+Alt+Del** sequence to thaw your computer when it freezes.

➤ Don't go into shock when Windows starts in Safe mode. Shutting down and restarting your PC usually corrects the problem.

➤ If your mouse pointer moves erratically across the screen, open it and clean the rollers.

➤ If your modem won't dial, check Use Windows to ensure that the correct modem driver is installed to check your modem settings.

➤ If your printer won't print, check the cables and the online indicator. You can avoid most printer problems by making sure your printer has plenty of paper and is online before you start printing.

➤ Check regularly for Windows and device driver updates and install any updated drivers.

Chapter 33

Help! Finding Technical Support

In This Chapter

➤ Prepare for your tech support phone call

➤ Find answers and updates on the Web

You just flipped through the previous chapter and found that none of the problems described there pertained to the problem you're having. At this point, you're probably cursing the arrival of the computer age and thinking of taking a sledgehammer to your system unit. Before you do that, try one other solution: Contact the technical support (tech support) department for the program or device that's giving you problems. In this chapter, you will learn the ins and outs of tech support—what they can and cannot help you with, what to ask, what information you should have ready, and how to find answers to common questions on the Internet.

Phone Support (Feeling Lucky?)

The documentation that came with your program or hardware device usually contains a phone number in the back for contacting technical support. It's usually printed really small to discourage people from calling. Flip through your manuals to find the number you need.

Before you call, be aware that the quality of technical support over the telephone varies widely from one company to another. Most places have a computerized system that asks you to answer a series of questions, usually leading to a dead end. Other places keep you on hold until you eventually give up and call a relative or friend for help. Yet, some tech support departments provide excellent toll-free service enabling you to talk with a qualified technician who can walk you through the steps required to solve your problem.

Even if you get to speak with a great tech support person, you need to be prepared. No tech support person can read minds. You must be able to describe the problem you're having in some detail. Before you call, here's what you need to do:

➤ Write down a detailed description of the problem explaining what went wrong and what you were doing at the time. If possible, write down the steps required to cause the problem again.

➤ Write down the name, version number, and license (or registration) number of the program with which you are having trouble. You can usually get this information by opening the **Help** menu in the problem program and choosing the **About** ... command.

➤ Write down any information about your computer, including the computer brand, chip type (CPU) and speed, monitor type, amount of RAM, and the amount of free disk space. In Windows, go to **Start, Programs, Accessories, System Tools** and click **System Information**. The opening System Information screen gives you most of the details you need.

➤ Make sure your computer is turned on. A good tech support person can talk you through most problems if you're sitting at the keyboard.

➤ Make sure you're calling the right company. If you're having trouble with your printer, don't call Microsoft. If you even get through to a Microsoft Windows tech support person, the person will tell you to call the printer manufacturer.

➤ Don't call when you're mad. If you start screaming at the technical support person, the person is going to be less likely to offer quality help.

Inside Tip

If your system seems a little sluggish or you just want to find out if it's running at peak performance, have your system evaluated online. Several companies on the Web have free utilities that can inspect your computer and recommend tweaks and upgrades to improve its performance. To have your hardware evaluated, go to PC Pitstop at **www.pcpitstop.com.** For a more thorough evaluation and automated driver updates and bug fixes, subscribe to McAfee's Oil Change Online or First Aid Online at **www.mcafee.com.**

Finding Tech Support on the Web

Nearly every computer hardware and software company has its own Web site where you can purchase products directly and find technical support for products you own. If your printer is not feeding paper properly, you're having trouble installing your sound card, you keep receiving cryptic error messages in your favorite program, or you have some other computer-related problem, usually you can find the solution on the Internet.

In addition, computer and software companies often upgrade their software and post both updates and fixes (called *patches*) on their Web sites for downloading. If you are having problems with a device, such as a printer or modem, you should check the manufacturer's Web site for updated drivers. If you run into problems with a program, check the software company's Web site for a patch—a program file that you install to correct the problem.

Table 33.1 provides Web page addresses of popular software and hardware manufacturers to help you in your search. Most of the home pages listed have a link for connecting to the support page. If a page does not have a link to the support page, use its search tool to locate the page. You also might see a link labeled FAQs (frequently asked questions), Common Questions, or Top Issues. This link can take you to a page that lists the most common problems other users are having and answers from the company, as shown in Figure 33.1.

Table 33.1   Computer Hardware and Software Web Sites

Company	Web Page Address
Acer	global.acer.com
ATI Technologies	www.ati.com
Borland	www.borland.com
Brother	www.brother.com
Canon	www.usa.canon.com/consumer
Compaq	www.compaq.com
Corel	www.corel.com
Creative Labs	www.creativelabs.com
Dell	www.dell.com
Epson	www.epson.com
Fujitsu	www.fujitsu.com
Gateway	www.gw2k.com
Hewlett-Packard	www.hp.com
Hitachi	www.hitachipc.com
IBM	www.ibm.com
Intel	www.intel.com
Iomega	www.iomega.com
The Learning Company	support.learningco.com

continues

Table 33.1 Computer Hardware and Software Web Sites (continued)

Company	Web Page Address
Lotus	www.lotus.com
Micron Electronics	www.micronpc.com
Microsoft	www.microsoft.com
Modem Express	www.modemexpress.com
Motorola	www.mot.com
NEC	www.nec.com
Packard Bell	www.packardbell.com
Panasonic	www.panasonic.com
Sony	www.sony.com
Toshiba	www.toshiba.com
3COM (U.S. Robotics)	www.3com.com

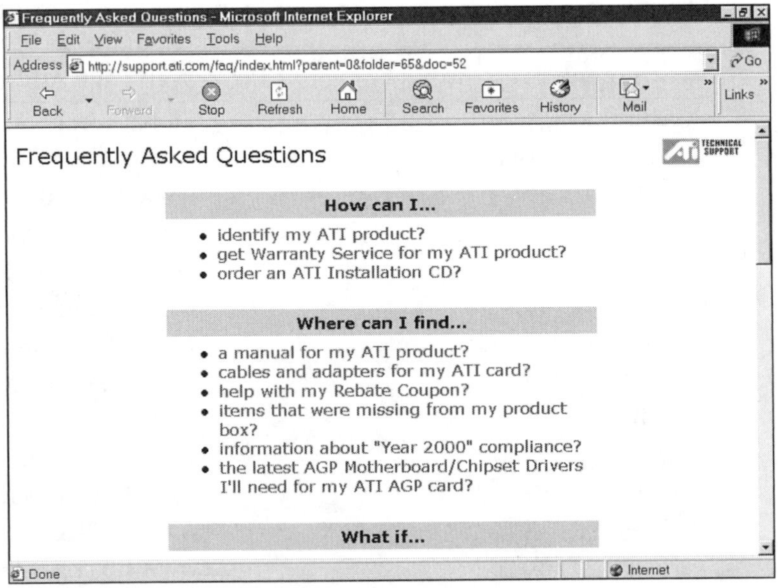

Figure 33.1

Check out the FAQs or Top Issues link for answers to common questions.

If the manufacturer you're looking for is not listed in this table, don't give up. Connect to your favorite Web search page and search for the manufacturer by name or search for the problem you're having. You also should seek help from online computer magazines.

One excellent resource is ZDNet at **www.zdnet.com.** It is packed with articles on general computing, hardware and software reviews, tips, and answers to specific questions. Click the **Help & How To** link to access the troubleshooting collection, as shown in Figure 33.2. Ziff Davis Media is ZDNet's sister site. Here you find links to the wide selection of Ziff Davis magazines, including *FamilyPC, Electronic Gaming Monthly, PC Magazine,* and *Yahoo! Internet Life.*

CNET Help.com at **www.help.com** is a great place if you need technical support for Internet problems. It's also a great place to check out gaming information and obtain shareware programs. Although you don't find as much information about general computing issues as you find at ZDNet, the information you do find is very useful. Additionally, Help2Go.com at **www.help2go.com** features free tutorials, a Q&A area, and live support for your computer problems.

Notable Note

Although manufacturers like to keep the tech support phone number a secret, they want you to know their Web page address so that you can check out their other products. The Web site's technical support areas also cut down on calls to tech support.

Figure 33.2

ZDNet's Help! area might have just the fix you need.

The Least You Need to Know

➤ Prepare for a productive phone conversation with a tech support person by having as much specific information about your PC and the problem before calling.

➤ Check out your computer manufacturer's tech support Web page.

➤ Find technical support using computer magazines and support sites on the Web.

Speak Like a Geek: The Complete Archive

The computer world is like a big exclusive club complete with its own language. If you want to be accepted into the Royal Order of Computer Geeks, you had better learn the lingo. The following mini-glossary helps you start. Keep in mind that you never achieve full geekhood by passively reading the terms and definitions. Try to say the term aloud and then use it in a sentence. When your fellow geeks hear you reciting computer terms to yourself, they will immediately accept you into their group.

active desktop components   Objects on the Windows desktop that obtain their information from the Internet and automatically download up-to-date information from the Internet. Examples of active desktop components include stock tickers, sports scoreboards, and weather maps.

ActiveX   A technology that makes it easy to embed animated objects, data, and computer code in the documents that you create and share those objects with others. For example, with ActiveX, you can open a file created in Microsoft Word in your Web browser (for instance, Internet Explorer), and edit it just as if you had opened it in Word.

AGP (Accelerated Graphics Port)   A display card standard that increases the speed at which display instructions travel from your system unit to the monitor. AGP is about four times faster than the previous display standard.

application   Also known as program, a set of instructions that enable a computer to perform a specific task, such as word processing or data management. An application also can be a collection of programs called a *suite*.

ASCII file   A file containing characters that any program on any computer can use. Sometimes called a text file or an ASCII text file. (ASCII is pronounced "ASK-key.")

ATA drive   Short for AT Attachment, a common standard for IDE and EIDE drives. ATA actually is another name for IDE drives. Fast ATA is the same as EIDE. The Ultra ATA drive is a step up from EIDE drives, offering a 33MBps transfer rate. ATA/66 drives offer transfer rates of 66MBps.

BIOS (basic input/output system)   The BIOS, pronounced "BUY-ose," is the built-in set of instructions that tells the computer how to control the disk drives, keyboard, printer port, and other components that make up your computer.

bit   The basic unit of data in a computer. A computer's alphabet consists of two characters: 1 and 0. 1 stands for on; 0 stands for off. Bits are combined in sets of eight to form real characters such as A, B, C, and D. See also *byte*.

bits per second (bps)   A unit for measuring the speed of data transmission. Remember that it takes eight bits to make a byte (the equivalent of a single character). Modems have common bps ratings of 28,800 to 56,600.

boot   To start a computer and load its operating system software (usually Windows).

bps   See *bits per second*.

bus   A superhighway that carries information electronically from one part of the computer to another. The wider and faster (speed is measured in MHz) the bus, the faster your computer. The old ISA bus could carry 16 bits of data at a time; the newer PCI bus can carry 32 bits or 64 bits.

byte   A group of eight bits that usually represents a character or a digit. For example, the byte 01000001 represents the letter A.

cable modem   A modem that supports high-speed connections to the Internet through a TV cable connection. (To use a cable modem, you must have a cable company that offers Internet service.) See also *modem*.

cache   Pronounced "cash," a temporary storage area in memory or on disk that computer components and various programs use to quickly access data.

CD burner   A device that can write data to a special type of CD. A CD burner typically uses a laser beam to heat the surface of a disc in order to make some areas of the disk refract light, rather than reflect it. A CD-ROM drive or CD player bounces a low-intensity laser beam against the surface of the disk to "read" data from it.

CD-R (Compact Disc Recordable)   A CD drive that can write data to a disc as well as read data from a disk. A CD-R drive can write data to a CD-R disc only one time; it cannot erase a CD-R disc or write over data stored on a disc. See also *CD-RW*.

CD-ROM (Compact Disk Read-Only Memory)   A storage technology that uses the same kind of discs you play in an audio CD player for mass storage of computer data. A single disk can store more than 600MB of information. Pronounced "see-dee-rahm."

CD-RW (CD-ReWritable)   A CD drive that can write data to a CD-RW disc and erase data from the disc. Unlike CD-R discs, which can be recorded to only once, CD-RW discs are reusable making them useful for storing backups.

cell   The box formed by the intersection of a row (1,2,3 …) and column (A,B,C …) in a spreadsheet. Each cell has an address (such as B12) that defines its column and row. A cell can contain text, a numeric value, or a formula.

central processing unit   See *CPU*.

chat   To talk to another person by typing at your computer. What you type appears on the other person's screen, and what the other person types appears on your screen. You can chat on the Internet or an online service such as America Online.

click   To move the mouse pointer over an object or icon and press and release the mouse button once without moving the mouse.

client   Of two computers, the computer that's being served. On the Internet or on a network, your computer is the client and the computer to which you're connected is the server.

Clipboard   A temporary storage area that holds text and graphics. The cut and copy commands put text or graphics on the Clipboard replacing the Clipboard's previous contents. The Paste command copies Clipboard data to a document.

CMOS (Complementary Metal-Oxide Semiconductor)   Pronounced "sea-moss," this is a battery-powered storage unit that helps your computer remember the date, time, and additional settings.

COM port   Short for COMmunications port. A receptacle, usually at the back of the computer, into which you can plug a serial device, such as a modem, mouse, or serial printer.

command   An order that tells the computer what to do. In command-driven programs, you have to press a specific key or type the command to execute it. With menu-driven programs, you select the command from a menu.

computer   Any machine that accepts input (from a user), processes the input, and produces output in some form.

CPU (central processing unit)   The computer's brain. See also *microprocessor.*

crash   Failure of a system or program. Usually, you realize that your system has crashed when you can't move the mouse pointer or type anything. The term *crash* also is used to refer to a disk crash (or head crash). A disk crash occurs when the read/write head in the disk drive falls on the disk, possibly destroying data.

cursor   A horizontal line that appears below characters. A cursor acts like the tip of your pencil; anything you type appears at the cursor. See also *insertion point.*

data   The facts and figures you enter into the computer that are stored and used by the computer.

database   A type of computer program used for storing, organizing, and retrieving information. Popular database programs include Access, Approach, and Paradox.

density   A measure of the amount of data that can be stored per square inch of storage area on a disk.

desktop publishing (DTP)   A program that enables you to combine text and graphics on the same page and manipulate the text and graphics onscreen. Desktop publishing programs are commonly used to create newsletters, brochures, flyers, resumés, and business cards.

dialog box   An onscreen box that enables you to enter your preferences or supply additional information. You use the dialog box to carry on a "conversation" with the program.

directory   A division of a disk or CD, which contains a group of related files. Think of your disk as a filing cabinet and think of each directory as a drawer in the cabinet. Directories are more commonly called *folders.*

disc A round, flat, optical storage medium. CDs and DVDs are both referred to as discs (with a "c") rather than disks (with a "k"). To read data from a disc, a CD-ROM or DVD drive bounces a laser light off the surface of the disc. The surface consists of a reflective coating that is pitted or dyed during the recording process to create nonreflective spots that store the data. An optical device in the drive receives the reflected and refracted light to read data from the disc.

disk A round, flat, magnetic storage medium. A disk works like a cassette tape, storing files permanently so that you can play them back later. See also *floppy disk* and *hard disk*.

disk drive A device that writes data to a magnetic disk and reads data from the disk. Think of a disk drive as a cassette recorder/player for a computer.

docking station A unit that connects a portable computer to peripherals (including a monitor, keyboard, and mouse) making the portable computer act like a desktop computer. Also called a port replicator.

DOS (disk operating system) DOS, which rhymes with "boss," is an old program that is used to provide the necessary instructions for the computer's parts (keyboard, disk drive, central processing unit, display screen, printer, and so on) to function as a unit. Although Windows makes DOS nearly obsolete, you still see its name floating around in Windows.

DOS prompt An onscreen prompt that indicates DOS is ready to accept a command but provides no clue to what command you should type. It looks something like C> or C:\.

download To copy files from another computer to your computer, usually through a modem. See also *upload*.

DSL Short for digital subscriber line, DSL uses standard phone lines to achieve data transfer rates of up to 1.5Mbps (9Mbps if you're within two miles of an ADSL connection center). Phone companies hope that advances in DSL technology and availability will help them compete with cable companies for Internet access and entertainment.

DVD (digital versatile disc or digital video disc) Discs that can store more than seven times as much data as a CD making them useful for storing full-length movies and complete, multimedia encyclopedias. DVD drives are designed to handle the discs of the future but also can play discs of the past (CDs).

e-mail Short for electronic mail, e-mail is a system that enables people to send and receive messages from computer to computer. E-mail is available on networks, online information services, and the Internet.

EDO (Extended Data Output) A type of DRAM (Dynamic RAM) memory that is faster than your average DRAM but not as fast as SDRAM (Synchronous Dynamic RAM).

EIDE (Enhanced Intelligent Drive Electronics) A type of hard drive that is typically fast and relatively inexpensive. EIDE drives have been popular for years but are being phased out by faster (ATA) drives. See also *ATA drive*.

executable file   A program file that can run the program. Executable files end in .BAT, .COM, or .EXE.

expansion slot   An opening on the motherboard (inside the system unit) that enables you to add devices to the system unit, such as an internal modem, sound card, video accelerator, or other enhancement.

extended memory   Any memory above the standard 640 kilobytes that performs the same way as the standard memory. Extended memory is directly available to the processor in your computer, unlike expanded memory, in which data must be swapped into and out of the standard memory. Most of your computer's memory is extended memory.

extension   The portion of a file's name that comes after the period. Every filename consists of two parts—the base name (before the period) and an extension (after the period). The filename can be up to eight characters in DOS and Windows 3.x (up to 255 characters in Windows 95 and later). The extension (which is optional) can be up to three characters.

FAT32   A fairly recent hard disk innovation that divides large hard disk drives into small storage units so that the drive wastes less space. If you think of your hard disk as a parking lot, Fat32 paints the lines closer together so that it can fit more cars. See also *file allocation table.*

field   A blank in a database record into which you can enter a piece of information (for example, a telephone number, ZIP code, or a person's last name).

file   A collection of information stored as a single unit on a floppy or hard disk. Files always have a filename to identify them.

file allocation table (FAT)   A map on every disk that tells the operating system where the files on the disk are stored. It's a little like a classroom seating chart for files.

File Transfer Protocol (FTP)   A set of rules that govern the exchange of files between two computers on the Internet.

fixed disk drive   A disk drive that has a nonremovable disk, as opposed to floppy drives, in which you can insert and remove disks.

floppy disk   A wafer encased in plastic that stores magnetic data (the facts and figures you enter and save). Floppy disks are the disks that you insert into your computer's floppy disk drive (located on the front of the computer).

folder   The Windows name for a directory, a division of a hard disk or CD that stores a group of related files. See also *directory.*

font   Any set of characters of the same typeface (design) and type size (measured in points). For example, Times New Roman 12-point is a font, Times New Roman is the typeface, and 12-point is the size. (There are 72 points in an inch.)

form   A fill-in-the blank dialog box commonly used in database applications for entering records into the database. When you complete and enter a form, the database stores the information as a record. See also *field, database,* and *record.*

format (disk)   To prepare a disk for storing data. Formatting creates a map on the disk that tells the operating system how the disk is structured. The operating system uses this map to keep track of where files are stored.

format (document)   To establish the physical layout of a document including page size, margins, running heads, line spacing, text alignment, graphics placement, and so on.

FTP   See *File Transfer Protocol*.

function keys   The 10 or 12 F keys on the left side of the keyboard or the 12 F keys at the top of the keyboard (some keyboards have both). F keys are numbered F1, F2, F3, and so on, and you can use them to enter specified commands in a program.

geek   1. An overly obsessive computer user who sacrifices food, sleep, and other pleasantries of life to spend more time at the keyboard. 2. A carnival performer whose act usually includes biting off the head of a live snake or chicken.

gigabyte   A thousand megabytes. See *megabyte*.

graphical user interface (GUI, pronounced "GOO-ey")   A type of operating system that uses graphical elements, such as icons to represent commands, files, and (in some cases) other programs. The most famous GUI is Microsoft Windows.

hard disk   A disk drive that comes complete with a nonremovable disk. It acts as a giant floppy disk drive and usually sits inside your computer.

Hayes compatible   Used to describe a modem that uses the Hayes command set for communicating with other modems over the phone lines. A command set is a language that controls the operation of a device. In the case of modems, the command set tells the modem how to dial a phone number, controls the modem's volume, and enables the modem to connect to other modems.

HTML   Short for HyperText Markup Language, the code used to create documents for the World Wide Web. These codes tell the Web browser how to display the text (titles, headings, lists, and so on), insert anchors that link this document to other documents, and control character formatting (by making it bold or italic).

icon   A graphic image onscreen that represents another object, such as a file on a disk.

infrared   A type of port, normally found on notebooks, that enables cable-free connections. You then can set your notebook in front of your printer (if the printer has an infrared port, too) and print or connect your notebook to your desktop PC or network without a cable. Infrared ports work like TV and VCR remote controls, and you have to point one infrared device right at the other one to get it to work.

insertion point   A blinking vertical line used in most Windows word processors to indicate the place where any characters that you type are inserted. An insertion point is the equivalent of a cursor.

integrated program   A program that combines the features of several programs, such as a word processor, spreadsheet, database, and communications program.

interface   A link between two objects, such as a computer and a modem. The link between a computer and a person is called a user interface and refers to the way a person communicates with the computer or a program.

Internet   A group of computers all over the world that are connected to each other. Using your computer and a modem, you can connect to these other computers and tap their resources. You can view pictures, listen to sounds, watch video clips, play games, chat with other people, and even shop.

Internet service provider (ISP)   The company that you pay in order to connect to their computer and get on the Internet.

IRC   Short for Internet Relay Chat, this is the most popular way to chat with others on the Internet. With an IRC client (chat program), you connect to an IRC server, where you are presented with a list of available chat rooms. You can enter a room and exchange messages with others in the room.

ISDN (Integrated Services Digital Network)   ISDN is a system that enables your computer, using a special ISDN modem, to perform digital data transfers over special phone lines. Non-ISDN modems use analog signals, which are designed to carry voices and not data. ISDN connections can transfer data at a rate of up to 128Kbs compared to about 56Kbps for the fastest analog modems.

ISP   See *Internet service provider*.

keyboard   The main input device for most computers. You use the keyboard to type and to enter commands.

kilobyte (K)   A unit for measuring the amount of data. A kilobyte is equivalent to 1,024 bytes (each byte is a character).

laptop   A small computer that's light enough to carry. Notebook computers and sub-notebooks are even lighter.

load   To read data or program instructions from disk and place them in the computer's memory, where the computer can use the data or instructions.

macro   A recorded set of instructions for a complex task or a task you frequently perform.

megabyte   A standard unit used to measure the storage capacity of a disk and the amount of computer memory. A megabyte is 1,048,576 bytes (1,000 kilobytes). This is roughly equivalent to 500 pages of double-spaced text. Megabyte is commonly abbreviated as M, MB, or Mbyte.

memory   An electronic storage area inside the computer, used to temporarily store data or program instructions when the computer is using them. Also referred to as RAM.

menu   A list of commands or instructions displayed onscreen. Menus organize commands and make a program easier to use.

MHz (megahertz)   Pronounced "mega-hurts," MHz is the unit used to measure the speed at which computer parts work. For example, a Pentium II 300MHz processor is faster than a Pentium II 233MHz processor. However, you should compare speeds

371

only between comparable devices. For example, if one device transmits 32 bits of data per clock cycle at 75MHz and another device transmits only 16 bits of data per clock cycle at 150MHz, the second device isn't any faster overall.

microprocessor   Sometimes called the central processing unit (CPU) or processor, this chip is the computer's brain; it does all the calculations for the computer.

MMX   Developed by Intel, MMX is a multimedia technology that enables your computer's CPU (processor) to take on more of the workload for handling multimedia files. This enables your computer to play media files faster and more smoothly. (MMX is not an acronym; it's just a cute label that Intel slapped on its multimedia technology.)

modem   An acronym for MOdulator/DEModulator. A modem is a piece of hardware that converts incoming signals (from a phone line, cable service, or other source) into signals that a PC can understand and converts outgoing signals from the PC into a form that can be transmitted.

monitor   A television-like screen on which the computer displays information.

motherboard   The big printed circuit board inside the system unit in to which everything else plugs.

mouse   A hand-held device that you move across the desktop to move an arrow, called a mouse pointer, across the screen. Used instead of the keyboard to select and move items (such as text or graphics), execute commands, and perform other tasks.

MS-DOS (Microsoft Disk Operating System)   See *DOS.*

multitasking   The process of performing two computer tasks at the same time. For example, you might be printing a document from your word processor while checking your e-mail in Prodigy.

network computer   A network computer (or NC) is a streamlined version of a standard PC that relies on a network server or on Internet servers for most of its computing power. A typical network computer has a monitor, keyboard, mouse, processor, and memory but no hard drive or CD-ROM drive. Programs are stored on a central network computer. Although NCs cannot replace PCs, NCs are excellent for corporations because they require little maintenance and support.

newsgroup   An Internet bulletin board for users who share common interests. There are thousands of newsgroups ranging from body art to pets (to body art with pets). Newsgroups let you post messages and read messages from other users.

notebook   A portable computer that weighs between four and eight pounds.

online   Connected, turned on, and ready to accept information. Used most often in reference to a printer or modem.

operating system   The software that a computer loads on startup. The operating system enables the user and all other programs to communicate with the computer. The most popular operating system is Microsoft Windows.

pane   A portion of a window. Most programs display panes, so you can view two different parts of a document at the same time.

parallel port   A connector used to plug a device, usually a printer, into the computer.

partition   A section of a disk drive that's assigned a letter. A hard disk drive can be divided (or partitioned) into one or more drives, which your computer refers to as drive C, drive D, drive E, and so on. The actual hard disk drive is called the physical drive, and each partition is called a logical drive; however, these terms don't matter much—the drives still look like letters to you.

patch   A set of program instructions designed to fix a programming bug or add capabilities to a program. On the Internet, you often can download patches for programs to update the program.

path   The route that the computer travels from the root directory to any subdirectories when locating a file.

PC card   An expansion card about the size of a credit card, but thicker, that slides into a slot on the side of the notebook computer. PC cards enable you to quickly install RAM or a hard disk drive, modem, CD-ROM drive, network card, or game port without having to open the notebook computer. See also *PCMCIA*.

PCI (Peripheral Component Interconnect)   A bus standard that effectively doubles or quadruples the amount of data that can travel around the highway system inside your computer. See also *bus*.

PCMCIA (Personal Computer Memory Card International Association)   An organization that sets standards for notebook computer expansion cards. See also *PC card*.

Pentium   The most popular CPU for PCs is manufactured by Intel. During the writing of this book, the Pentium 4 was the latest, greatest chip. You also might encounter an older Pentium, called Pentium (the original), Pentium Pro (a step up from the Pentium), Pentium MMX (Pentium with enhanced multimedia features), Pentium II (essentially a Pentium Pro with built-in MMX support), or Pentium III (still used in many laptop computers).

peripheral   A device attached to the computer but not essential for the basic operation of the computer. The system unit is the central part of the computer. Any devices attached to the system unit are considered peripheral, including a printer, modem, or joystick. Some manufacturers consider the monitor and keyboard to be peripheral, too.

pixel   A dot of light that appears on the computer screen. A collection of pixels forms characters and images on the screen.

PnP   Short for plug-and-play, PnP enables you to install expansion cards into your computer without having to set special switches. You plug it in, and it works.

port replicator   A slimmed-down version of a docking station. See also *docking station*.

ports   The receptacles at the back of the computer. They get their name from the ports where ships pick up and deliver cargo. In this case, the ports enable information to enter and leave the system unit.

PPP   Short for Point-to-Point Protocol, a language that computers use to talk to one another. What's important is that when you choose an Internet service provider, you get the right connection—SLIP or PPP.

373

program   A group of instructions that tells the computer what to do. Typical programs are word processors, spreadsheets, databases, and games.

prompt   A computer's way of asking for more information. The computer basically looks at you and says, "Tell me something." In other words, the computer is prompting you or prodding you for information or a command.

protocol   A group of communications settings that control the transfer of data between two computers.

pull-down menu   A menu that appears at the top of the screen listing various options. The menu is not visible until you select it from the menu bar. The menu then drops down, covering a small part of the screen.

random-access memory (RAM)   A collection of chips your computer uses to store data and programs temporarily. RAM is measured in kilobytes and megabytes. In general, more RAM means you can run more powerful programs and more programs at once. Also called *memory*.

record   Used by databases to denote a unit of related information contained in one or more fields, such as an individual's name, address, and phone number.

ROM BIOS   See *BIOS*.

scanner   A device that converts images, such as photographs or printed text, into an electronic format that a computer can use. Many stores use a special type of scanner to read barcode labels into the cash register.

ScreenTip   A small text box that displays the name of a button when you rest the mouse pointer on the button. ScreenTips help you figure out what a button does when you cannot figure it out from the picture. Also called *ToolTip*.

scroll   To move text up and down or right and left on a computer screen.

SCSI (Small Computer System Interface)   Pronounced "scuzzy," SCSI provides speedier data transfer rates than are available through standard serial or parallel ports and enable you to connect several devices to the same port.

SDRAM (Synchronous Dynamic RAM)   A type of RAM (memory) that is twice as fast as EDO DRAM because it synchronizes itself with the CPU. Although fast (operating at speeds of 100MHz), SDRAM has trouble keeping up with newer processors, which run at speeds of 300MHz. Look for even faster memory chips, such as RDRAM and SLDRAM.

server   Of two computers, the computer that's serving the other computer. On the Internet or on a network, your computer is the client, and the computer to which you're connected is the server.

shareware   Computer programs that you can use free, and then pay for if you decide to continue using them. Many programmers start marketing their programs as shareware, relying on the honesty and goodwill of computer users for income. That's why most of these programmers have day jobs.

shortcut   An icon, typically found on the Windows desktop that points to a disk drive, folder, document, or program. Clicking or double-clicking a shortcut opens a window that displays the contents of the selected disk or folder, opens the selected document, or runs the program that the shortcut represents.

software   Any instructions that tell your computer (the hardware) what to do. There are two types of software: operating system software and application software. Operating system software (such as Windows) gets your computer up and running. Application software enables you to do something useful, such as typing a letter or chasing lemmings.

spreadsheet   A program used for keeping schedules and calculating numeric results. Common spreadsheets include Lotus 1-2-3, Microsoft Excel, and Quattro Pro.

status bar   The area at the bottom of a program window that shows you what's going on as you work. A status bar might show the page and line number where the insertion point is positioned and indicate whether you are typing in overstrike or insert mode.

style   A collection of specifications for formatting text. A style might include information for the font, size, style, margins, and spacing. Applying a style to text automatically formats the text according to the style's specifications.

subwoofer   A speaker that increases the low-end bass output, which provides more realistic sounds for games, audio CDs, and DVD videos.

T1   A dedicated phone line connection that provides data transfer rates of more than 1.5 megabits per second. T1 lines are commonly leased by large corporations and organizations for speedy Internet access.

taskbar   A fancy name for the button bar at the bottom of the Windows desktop.

TCP/IP (Transmission Control Protocol/Internet Protocol)   A set of rules that govern the transfer of data over the Internet. See Chapter 21, "Doing the Internet Shuffle," for additional information.

TFT (thin film transistor)   A technology used to improve the resolution on flat-panel displays, such as those used on notebook computers.

toolbar   A strip of buttons typically displayed near the top of a program window, below the menu bar. The toolbar contains buttons that you can click to enter common commands enabling you to bypass the menu system.

ToolTip   See *ScreenTip*.

touchpad   A pointing device commonly found on laptop computers that enables you to move the mouse pointer by running your finger over the pad.

trackball   A device, often used with laptop computers, which works like an upside-down mouse.

transfer rate   A measure of how much information a device (usually a disk drive) can transfer from the disk to your computer's memory in a second. A good transfer rate is in the range of 500 to 600 kilobytes per second. The higher the number, the faster the drive.

uninterruptible power supply (UPS)   A battery-powered device that protects against power spikes and power outages. If the power goes out, the UPS continues supplying power to the computer so that you can continue working or safely turn off your computer without losing data.

upload   To send data to another computer, usually through a modem and a telephone line or over a network connection.

URL (Uniform Resource Locator)   An address for an Internet site.

USB (Universal Serial Bus)   The ultimate in plug-and-play technology, USB enables you to install devices without turning off your computer or using a screwdriver. USB enables you to connect up to 127 devices to a single port.

USENET (User's Network)   A collection of computers responsible for managing the flow of messages posted in newsgroups. See also *newsgroup*.

virtual memory   Disk storage used as RAM (memory).

virus   A program that attaches itself to other files on a floppy or hard disk, duplicates itself without the user's knowledge, and might cause the computer to do strange and sometimes destructive things, such as formatting your hard drive.

warm boot   To restart a computer without turning the power off. You typically reboot a PC by holding down the Ctrl and Alt keys while pressing the Delete key. This key combination, Ctrl+Alt+Del, is commonly referred to as the *three-key salute*.

Web   See *World Wide Web*.

Web browser   A program that enables you to navigate the World Wide Web (the most popular feature of the Internet). See also *World Wide Web*.

wildcard   Any character that takes the place of another character or a group of characters. In DOS, you can use two wildcard characters: a question mark (?) and an asterisk (*). The question mark stands in for a single character. The asterisk stands in for a group of characters. Wildcards are useful for searching for files and filtering file lists.

windows   A way of displaying information in different parts of the screen. Often used as a nickname for Microsoft Windows.

word processor   A program that enables you to enter, edit, format, and print text.

word wrap   A feature that automatically moves a word to the next line if the word won't fit at the end of the current line.

World Wide Web   A part of the Internet that consists of multimedia documents that are interconnected by links. To move from one document to another, you click a link, which might appear as highlighted text or as a small picture or icon. The Web contains text, sound and video clips, pictures, catalogues, and much, much more. See also *Web browser*.

write-protect   To prevent a computer from adding or modifying data stored on a disk.

Index

379

E

385

P

X – Y – Z

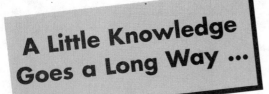
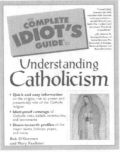

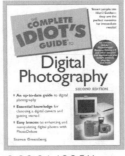
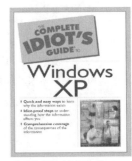